CHARLES I

KING AND COLLECTOR

CHARLES I

KING AND COLLECTOR

ROYAL ACADEMY OF ARTS
IN PARTNERSHIP WITH ROYAL COLLECTION TRUST

First published on the occasion of the exhibition 'Charles I: King and Collector', organised by the Royal Academy of Arts in partnership with Royal Collection Trust

ROYAL COLLECTION TRUST

Royal Academy of Arts, London
27 January – 15 April 2018

Sponsored by

BNY MELLON
RA250 Anniversary Partner

This exhibition has been made possible as a result of the Government Indemnity Scheme. The Royal Academy of Arts would like to thank HM Government for providing Government Indemnity and the Department of Culture, Media and Sport and Arts Council England for arranging the indemnity.

EXHIBITION CURATORS
Per Rumberg
Desmond Shawe-Taylor
assisted by
Lucy Chiswell
Niko Munz

ARTISTIC DIRECTOR
Tim Marlow, Royal Academy of Arts

EXHIBITION ORGANISATION
Stephanie Bush
assisted by
Nancy Cooper

PHOTOGRAPHIC AND COPYRIGHT COORDINATION
Giulia Ariete

EXHIBITION CATALOGUE
Royal Academy Publications
Florence Dassonville
Beatrice Gullström
Alison Hissey
Rosie Hore
Carola Krueger
Peter Sawbridge
Nick Tite

Design: Kathrin Jacobsen
Picture research: Sara Ayad
Indexing: Hilary Bird
Colour origination: DawkinsColour
Printed in Italy by Graphicom, Verona

British Library Cataloguing-in-Publication Data
A catalogue record for this book is available from the British Library
ISBN 978-1-910350-67-6 (hardback)
ISBN 978-1-910350-85-0 (paperback)

Distributed outside the United States and Canada by ACC Distribution, Suffolk, Woodbridge, IP12 4SD

Distributed in the United States and Canada by ARTBOOK / D.A.P., 2nd Floor, 155 6th Avenue, New York, NY 10013

EDITORS' NOTES
Authorship of the catalogue entries on pages 233–54 is indicated by the following initials:

LC	Lucy Chiswell
DE	David Ekserdjian
BF	Barbara Furlotti
EG	Erin Griffey
NM	Niko Munz
GR	Guido Rebecchini
VR	Vanessa Remington
PR	Per Rumberg
KS	Karen Serres
DST	Desmond Shawe-Taylor
LW	Lucy Whitaker
JW	Jeremy Wood
HW	Helen Wyld

Dates are given according to the conventions used at the time (Julian Calendar in England, Gregorian Calendar in Catholic countries), but in the New Style.

Dimensions of all works of art are given in centimetres, height before width.

Front cover:
Anthony van Dyck (1599–1641)
Charles I in the Hunting Field, *c.* 1636 (detail of cat. 76)
Oil on canvas, 266 x 207 cm
Musée du Louvre, Paris, inv. 1236

Pages 2–3: detail of cat. 3
Page 6: detail of cat. 117
Page 9: detail of cat. 25
Page 10: detail of cat. 14
Pages 14–15: detail of cat. 91
Page 16: detail of cat. 140
Page 28: detail of cat. 5
Page 48: detail of cat. 28
Page 80: detail of cat. 38
Page 98: detail of cat. 45
Page 124: detail of cat. 70
Page 148: detail of cat. 78
Page 170: detail of cat. 90
Page 188: detail of cat. 91
Page 204: detail of cat. 122
Page 232: detail of cat. 139

Back cover:
Orazio Gentileschi (1563–1639)
Joseph and Potiphar's Wife, *c.* 1630–32 (detail of cat. 85)
Oil on canvas, 206 x 261.9 cm
The Royal Collection / HM Queen Elizabeth II, RCIN 405477

Foreword by HRH The Prince of Wales 7
Foreword by Christopher Le Brun PRA 8
Sponsor's Preface 11
Acknowledgements and Honorary Committee 12

'The greatest amateur of paintings among the princes of the world' 17
PER RUMBERG AND DESMOND SHAWE-TAYLOR

Chronology 26
LUCY CHISWELL AND NIKO MUNZ

1 ARTISTS AND AGENTS 29
Connoisseurship at the Caroline Court
JEREMY WOOD

2 MADRID AND MANTUA 49
Charles I's Visit to Madrid
GUIDO REBECCHINI

'Rare and unique in this world': Mantegna's *Triumph* and the Gonzaga Collection
BARBARA FURLOTTI AND GUIDO REBECCHINI

3 THE NORTHERN RENAISSANCE 81
Charles I and the Northern Renaissance
DAVID EKSERDJIAN

4 THE ITALIAN RENAISSANCE 99
Charles I and the Italian Renaissance
DAVID EKSERDJIAN

5 THE ROYAL PORTRAIT 125
The 'act and power of a face': Van Dyck's Royal Portraits
DESMOND SHAWE-TAYLOR

6 VAN DYCK AND RUBENS IN ENGLAND 149
Van Dyck, Titian and Charles I
PER RUMBERG

Rubens, Painter and Diplomat
GREGORY MARTIN

7 THE QUEEN'S HOUSE 171
Henrietta Maria, Charles I and the Italian Baroque
KAREN SERRES

8 THE MORTLAKE TAPESTRIES 189
Charles I and Raphael's *Acts of the Apostles*
HELEN WYLD

9 THE WHITEHALL CABINET 205
A 'more solitary place': Charles I and His Cabinet
VANESSA REMINGTON AND LUCY WHITAKER

CATALOGUE 233

Endnotes 255
Bibliography 259
Lenders to the Exhibition and Photographic Acknowledgements 266
Index 267

RAPHEL

CLARENCE HOUSE

The art collections of King Charles I have long been considered the fountainhead of the British Royal Collection. As this catalogue and exhibition demonstrate beyond doubt, one Sovereign's passion for, and discernment in, the visual arts made a fundamental and lasting impact on the cultural life of this country as a whole, opening our eyes to the glories of the Italian Renaissance and to so many masterpieces of Northern and Central European art. It has been suggested, for example, that John Milton's description of Adam and Eve in "Paradise Lost" seems likely to have been formed in his imagination through his memory of Jan Gossaert's painting.

There is evidence that Charles I may have considered the foundation of a royal academy of art some 150 years before this eventually came to pass. In 1771, three years after the Royal Academy of Arts came into being under the patronage of King George III (after a complicated gestation), the great full-length portrait by Van Dyck of Charles I in the hunting field was offered for sale in Paris. For reasons best known to himself, George III decided not to purchase it. The significance of the presence of this – surely the greatest of all royal portraits by Van Dyck – in London for this exhibition, should not be underestimated. This is believed to be the first time that the painting has returned to England since the seventeenth century and, on behalf of the organizers of the exhibition, and also those who come and see it, I should like to express my own special gratitude to the many lenders who have joined in the effort to re-create, at least in part, this spectacular collection.

Ever since 1768, the Royal Family's continuing association with the Royal Academy has taken many forms. Monarchs and their families have regularly visited the annual Summer Exhibition, and many works have been purchased for the Royal Collection in the course of those visits. It is perhaps also worth noting that the present exhibition, to which Her Majesty has graciously contributed more than eighty works from the Royal Collection, is only the latest in a succession of more than 160 exhibitions to which works have been lent. Most spectacular, perhaps, was the loan of more than 500 pictures in 1946 to an exhibition simply entitled "The King's Pictures", staged at Burlington House as a tonic to the nation following the Second World War.

The accounts of the dispersal of the King's possessions in 1649-51, and the inventories taken of the various palaces in his lifetime – long ago published – have enabled scholars to create in their mind's eye a form of 'virtual' re-construction, and to sense the thrill of what it must have felt like to see it all together. Any attempt at bringing even part of the collection back together in physical form has always seemed unattainable, so I hope that as many people as possible will come to the Royal Academy in this most special commemorative year to witness such a glorious reunion. We are fortunate indeed to be able to do so.

Charles

FOREWORD

During his reign, King Charles I assembled one of the most extraordinary art collections in Europe, comprising some of the greatest masterpieces of the fifteenth to the seventeenth centuries. This exhibition reveals not only the richness of the works Charles I acquired, but also their impact on the contemporary artists he commissioned, most notably Anthony van Dyck, who created the enduring image of the King we remember today.

Charles I was executed in 1649. Just months later, commissioners were appointed to put his exceptional group of pictures up for sale. Although a significant number of works were recovered at the Restoration and are now part of the Royal Collection, many hang at the National Gallery in London, the Museo Nacional del Prado in Madrid, the Musée du Louvre in Paris and elsewhere. By enabling us to reunite many of the King's pictures for the first time since the seventeenth century, our lenders have given visitors an unprecedented opportunity to experience the collection that – more than any other – changed the appreciation of art in England.

We are indebted to Her Majesty The Queen for agreeing to lend such a significant and substantial group of paintings, and to HRH The Prince of Wales for his invaluable support. We sincerely thank Jonathan Marsden and Royal Collection Trust for making this partnership such a fruitful one. The exhibition was made possible by BNY Mellon, the Royal Academy's 250th Anniversary Partner in 2018. We are deeply grateful to our lenders for agreeing to take part in this unique event.

The exhibition has been curated by Per Rumberg, Curator at the Royal Academy, and Desmond Shawe-Taylor, Surveyor of the Queen's Pictures. Their close and enthusiastic collaboration is evident in the way the galleries unfold. At the Royal Academy, the project was supported by Tim Marlow, Artistic Director. It would not have been possible without the dedication of Lucy Chiswell, Stephanie Bush and Nancy Cooper, as well as that of the exhibition designers, Cécile Degos and Patrick Morrissey. Last, but not least, I thank our Publications Department for creating a catalogue that so beautifully reflects the splendour of this exhibition.

Christopher Le Brun PRA
President, Royal Academy of Arts

SPONSOR'S PREFACE

During our eleven-year partnership with the Royal Academy of Arts, BNY Mellon has had the privilege to support a number of remarkable exhibitions. 'Charles I: King and Collector' is no exception, reuniting many of the greatest masterpieces from the King's collection for the first time since his death in 1649.

This exhibition, organised in partnership with Royal Collection Trust, boasts important loans from a number of major collections, including the Museo Nacional del Prado, Madrid, and the Musée du Louvre, Paris. Bringing together such historically significant and regal works for 'Charles I: King and Collector' is testament to the importance and value of international collaboration, and a fitting opening to this landmark year for the Royal Academy, as it celebrates the 250th anniversary of its foundation in 1768.

BNY Mellon's commitment to supporting the arts reflects our belief that they play a vital role in building strong, vibrant communities and developing the minds of tomorrow. Public access and education remain central to our international programme of arts sponsorship. The Royal Academy continues to strive to engage with the broadest possible audience through its exhibitions, events, publications and educational activities.

As the Royal Academy's 250th Anniversary Partner, BNY Mellon is delighted to support 'Charles I: King and Collector'. We hope you enjoy this historic exhibition.

Hani Kablawi
Chairman of Europe, Middle East and Africa

BNY Mellon, Anniversary Partner of the Royal Academy of Arts

ACKNOWLEDGEMENTS

In memory of Giles Waterfield (1949–2016)

The Royal Academy of Arts and Royal Collection Trust would like to thank the following individuals for their invaluable assistance during the making of this exhibition and its catalogue:

Sébastien Allard, Stijn Alsteens, Christina Anderson, Nicole Atzbach, Christopher Baker, Maria Balshaw, Hervé Barbaret, Bruce Barker-Benfield, Willa Beckett, Treacy and Darcy Beyer, Thomas Bohl, Kate Brindley, Christopher Brown, Caroline Campbell, Richard Carew Pole, Jeannie Chapel, Hugo Chapman, Jeremy Cheek, Alec Cobbe, Jennifer Coombs, Bart Cornelis, Nicholas Cullinan, Cécile Degos, Vincent Delieuvien, the Earl and Countess of Derby, the Duke of Devonshire, Taco Dibbits, Simon Dickinson, Blaise Ducos, Ann Dumas, Nancy Edwards, David Ekserdjian, Simone Facchinetti, Miguel Falomir, Gabriele Finaldi, Hartwig Fischer, Mark Fisher, Ella Fleming, Susan Foister, Barbara Furlotti, Arturo Galansino, Davide Gasparotto, Helen Ghosh, Emilie Gordenker, Nicola Gray, Erin Griffey, Sergio Guarino, Sabine Haag, Mark Hallett, Karen Hearn, Tristram Hunt, Kathrin Jacobsen, David Jaffé, Ian Jenkins, Paul Joannides, Anna Keay, Roly Keating, Larry Keith, Alastair Laing, Eric M. Lee, John Leighton, Alexandra Libby, Leanda de Lisle, Stephen Lloyd, Catharine MacLeod, Kristina Mandy, Jonathan Marsden, Gregory Martin, Jean-Luc Martinez, John Martin Robinson, Patrick Morrissey, Peta Motture, Felicity Myrone, Scott Nethersole, the Duke of Norfolk, Humphrey Ocean, the Archbishop of Olomouc, Richard Ovenden, Nicholas Penny, Timothy Potts, Earl A. Powell III, the Earl of Radnor, Guido Rebecchini, Vanessa Remington, Orlando Rock, Mark Roglán, Elena Rossoni, Patricia Rubin, Catherine Ruggeri, Sigrid and Bernd Rumberg, Xavier Salomon, Lois Salter, Peter Schade, Karen Serres, Nat Silver, Ben Street, Alexander Sturgis, Luke Syson, David Taylor, Cristina Terzaghi, Jacqueline Thalmann, Simon Thurley, Sue Townsend, Cecilia Treves, Letizia Treves, Jane Turner, Sarah Turner, An Van Camp, Ian Wardropper, Stefan Weppelman, the Duchess of Westminster, the Duke of Westminster, Aidan Weston-Lewis, Arthur Wheelock, Catherine Whistler, Lucy Whitaker, Francesca Whitlum-Cooper, Matthias Wivel, Jeremy Wood, Helen Wyld, and Miguel Zugaza.

HONORARY COMMITTEE

PATRON
Her Majesty The Queen

HONORARY COMMITTEE
His Royal Highness The Prince of Wales
(Chair)

Christopher Baker
Maria Balshaw
Nicholas Cullinan
The Duke of Devonshire
Taco Dibbits
Miguel Falomir
Gabriele Finaldi
Hartwig Fischer
Dame Helen Ghosh
Emilie Gordenker
Tristram Hunt
Roly Keating
Christopher Le Brun
Eric M. Lee
Sir John Leighton
Jean-Luc Martinez
Jonathan Marsden
The Duke of Norfolk
Richard Ovenden
Timothy Potts
Earl A. Powell III
The Earl of Radnor
Mark Roglán
Catherine Ruggeri
Charles Saumarez Smith
Alexander Sturgis
Ian Wardropper
Miguel Zugaza

In ~~the Kings~~ [yor M] longe gallo= rie towards the Orchard are these ~~his Ma[ie]~~ [yor M] pictures at this instant placed as followeth.

		Hight	Breadth within the frames
	1		
done By Sr Anthonie vandike	Inprimis ~~The Kinge~~ [yor M] and Queene, Prince, and the Princes Maria all in one peece Intire figures wherby in a lanskipp Westminster painted and Soe bigg as the life, One of the Queenes litle dogge by. In a Carved Some part guilded frame. upon the right light	9f 8	8f 0
	2		
done by Pollidore Being ye 7 peece done in ffresco.	Item ye picture [painted upon the right light] of the Poeticall gods some 19ten litle intire figures done in ffresco Being the 9th peece of ye nomber of the 23 Itallion collection peeces which ~~the kinge~~ [yor M] bought of ffrezley.	3f 10	5f 3
	3		
done By Georgzon	Item A peece [painted upon the light] being Acteon conteyning in a troupe uppon the first ground Some 12 figurs where Diana & her nimphis are bathing, And in a landskipp Some 14ten litle intire figurs more a farr of in a guilded frame Bought by ~~the Kinge~~ [yor M] of Mr Endimion Porter.	3f 1	6f 0

'THE GREATEST AMATEUR OF PAINTINGS AMONG THE PRINCES OF THE WORLD'

PER RUMBERG AND DESMOND SHAWE-TAYLOR

On 30 January 1649 King Charles I was executed. On his way to the scaffold, erected outside the Banqueting House at Whitehall Palace, he walked past the monumental ceiling paintings (fig. 37) which he had commissioned from Peter Paul Rubens two decades earlier to celebrate the reign of his father, James I, and which epitomised the artistic ambition that had characterised his reign.[1] Rubens had famously described Charles I as 'le prince le plus amateur de la peinture qui soit au monde'.[2] Over the following years, the contents of the royal household were dispersed in the so-called Commonwealth Sale. The crown was dismantled, the gold delivered to the Mint to be coined and its precious stones sold off.[3] In addition to the regalia, the King's legendary collection of works of art, including some of the finest pictures from Italy and Northern Europe, was sold. Rubens's canvases in the Banqueting House were among the few works that remained *in situ*. A great part of the collection was recovered when the monarchy was restored a little over a decade later, but some of the best pictures had been sold abroad and ended up, most notably, at the Spanish and French courts and now form part of the Museo Nacional del Prado in Madrid and the Musée du Louvre in Paris. While the majority of the most valuable paintings in the Sale have been identified, some works are still emerging, many of them bearing Charles's distinctive brand. In reuniting a significant part of the collection, we hope to provide the basis for developing a more nuanced understanding of how it was assembled and what it came to represent.

Charles grew up in a highly cultured and sophisticated environment, and both his father and his elder brother, Henry, Prince of Wales (who died prematurely in 1612) showed a great interest in the arts. In 1623 Charles visited Madrid to arrange his marriage to the Infanta, the sister of Philip IV of Spain (see pp. 50–53). The marriage negotiations failed, but the Habsburg collection made a lasting impression on the future King, who returned to London with works by Titian (cat. 16, fig. 15) and Paolo Veronese (cat. 17), among others. Intent on reflecting his own magnificence by creating a collection that would rival those of other European courts, he acquired the esteemed Gonzaga collection (see pp. 54–59), which had been accumulated by the Dukes of Mantua, and commissioned works from some of the most famous artists of his day, most notably Anthony van Dyck, who was appointed 'principalle Paynter in Ordenarie to their Majesties' in 1632.

Following the failure of the 'Spanish match', Charles I married Henrietta Maria (figs 6–7), the daughter of Henri IV and Marie de' Medici and sister of Louis XIII of France. The Queen's role in shaping the collection has only recently received the attention it deserves.[4] Henrietta Maria kept close relations with the French and other European courts, as well as Rome. Indeed, the most important Italian artist at court, Orazio Gentileschi, eventually worked for her almost exclusively (see pp. 172–79). In collaboration and competition with other collectors close to the Stuart court, namely Thomas Howard, Earl of Arundel (cat. 10), and James I's favourite, George Villiers, Duke of Buckingham (cat. 11), and over a period of only two decades, Charles I and Henrietta Maria amassed a spectacularly rich and varied collection.

It hardly needs pointing out that the Stuarts inherited from the Tudors a strong classical and literary tradition. Important elements of visual culture were also already in place: a superb collection of Flemish tapestries (including a set based on Raphael's cartoons; figs 44–47) and the legacy of Hans Holbein the Younger's English period, in particular the illusionistic mural of Henry VIII and his family at Whitehall Palace (destroyed in the fire of 1698).[5] These and a variety of other sources – prints, medals, books and theatre – had given the English every opportunity to understand visual imagery long before Charles I's paintings arrived.

Charles's unusual cosmopolitanism – his visit to Spain, French wife and Flemish court painter – might have prompted him to observe that many courts outside Italy were in substantially the same position as his. Those in Madrid, Paris and Brussels (to name the three most closely related to London) had all undergone a Renaissance in architecture and letters during the sixteenth century and sought during the seventeenth century to consolidate this modernisation with a more systematic emulation of 'Italian' (meaning by this time 'universal') art and artistic theory.[6]

The seventeenth-century artistic project involved collecting antique sculpture and Italian High Renaissance painting, translating Italian treatises on art and architecture, founding fine-art academies and patronising living artists and architects (preferably home-grown) who would work in this universal language, the inculcation of which was the objective of the entire enterprise. Most courts also saw this as part of a wider commercial enterprise, establishing luxury manufactories, often in royal palaces, to compete with whichever imported goods seemed most exorbitantly priced – which, in the seventeenth century, meant tapestries. Of the courts listed above, the Spanish had the most significant head start through Philip II's collection of paintings by Titian and the building in the universal style of the Escorial in 1563–84. The French proceeded most methodically through the stages, starting with Leonardo da Vinci's work for François I and concluding with state control of the arts, supervised by Jean-Baptiste Colbert on behalf of Louis XIV, a system which was to become the model for any aspiring absolutist monarch.[7] We can assume that Louis's uncle, Charles I, was planning something similar and that the Stuarts would have left a legacy similar to the Bourbons, had their period on the English throne been less fragmented.

Whereas the Elizabethans might have had a Renaissance mindset, the Stuarts sought to join the common currency of seventeenth-century court culture. This enterprise began in the reign of James I with several crucial elements. Original works of antique sculpture were seen for the first time in England in the collection of the Earl of Arundel.[8] Grammatically accurate classical architecture (supported by familiarity with artistic and architectural theory) was introduced by Inigo Jones (cat. 6).[9] Sixteenth-century Italian masterpieces, especially by Titian, were seen by Prince Charles on his visit to Spain in 1623 and the important examples he brought home provided a taste of a new type of evocative painting, the visual equivalent of poetry, which could even be referred to as 'poems' (*poesie*).[10]

Palace workshops also thrived in England though none survived the revolutions of the seventeenth century. The Royal Armoury at Greenwich, established in 1511, produced some of its most distinctive work during the early Stuart period, including the suit of armour made in 1608 for Henry, Prince of Wales (Royal Collection).[11] In 1619 a royal tapestry workshop

Fig. 1 William Dobson (1611–1646), *Abraham van der Doort*, late 1630s. Oil on canvas, 45 x 38 cm. State Hermitage Museum, St Petersburg

was established at Mortlake, with the close involvement of Charles I, then Prince of Wales.[12] The inventiveness of its designs and quality of its craftsmanship are discussed below (pp. 190–97). Once he became King, Charles I maintained his interest in the Mortlake Workshop and other such ventures: he established a foundry at Vauxhall, for the first time allowing life-size bronze sculpture to be cast in England.[13] The accounts provided by George Vertue, a century after the fact, of an 'Academia Musaeum' suggests the existence of something which might have evolved into a Royal Academy of Fine Art, where collectors, artists and theorists could have met to exchange ideas.[14]

Most if not all these ventures depended upon a comprehensive collection of the best examples of every art form. However strong the basis of the Tudor royal collection and the fine works that made their way to Britain during the reign of James I, Charles only really had a chance to undertake serious collecting once he became King in 1625. The range of his collection and the diligence with which it was documented can be assessed from the 1639 inventory of Whitehall Palace, the King's main residence, by Abraham van der Doort (fig. 1), appointed Surveyor of the King's Pictures in May 1625.[15]

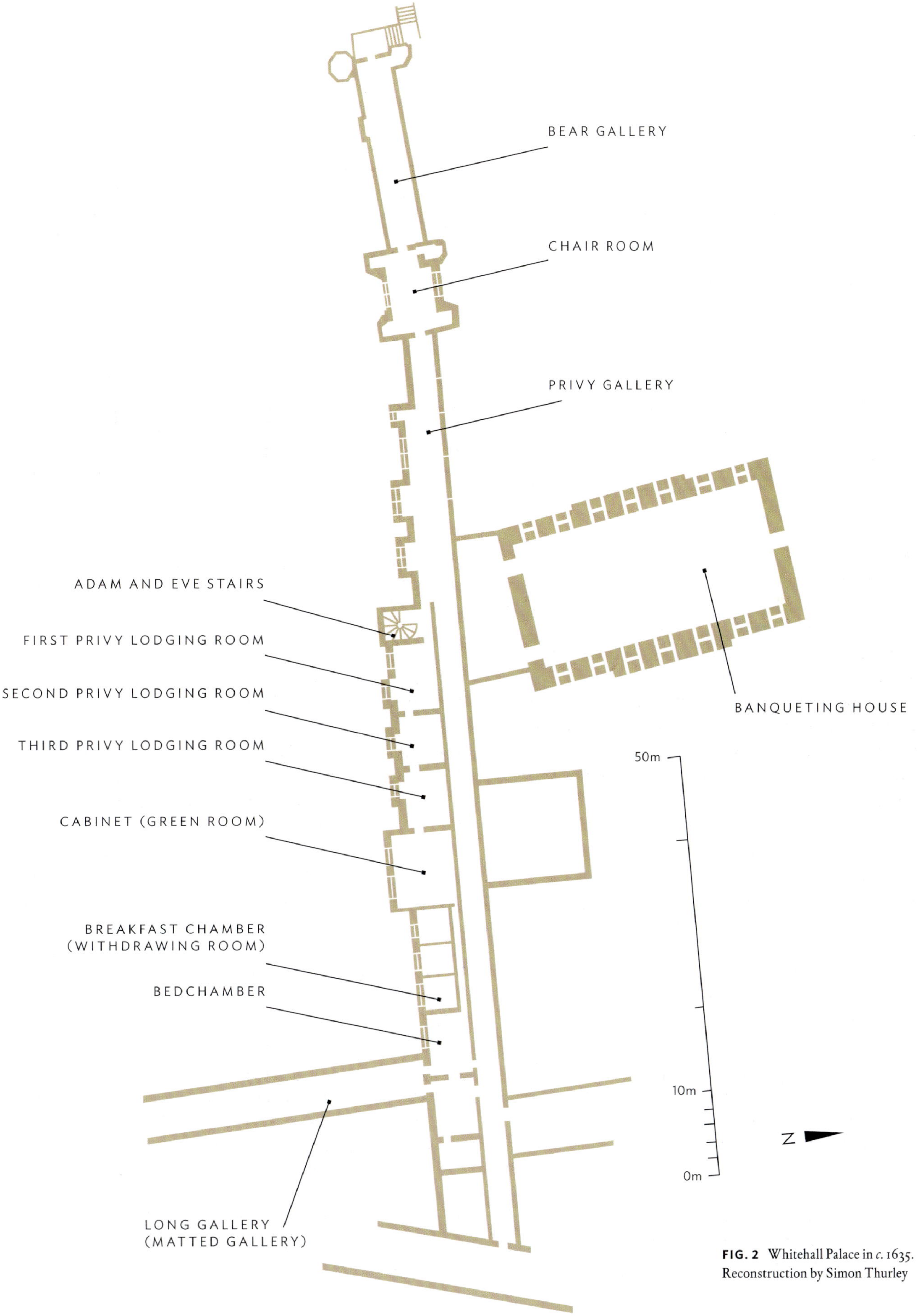

FIG. 2 Whitehall Palace in *c.* 1635. Reconstruction by Simon Thurley

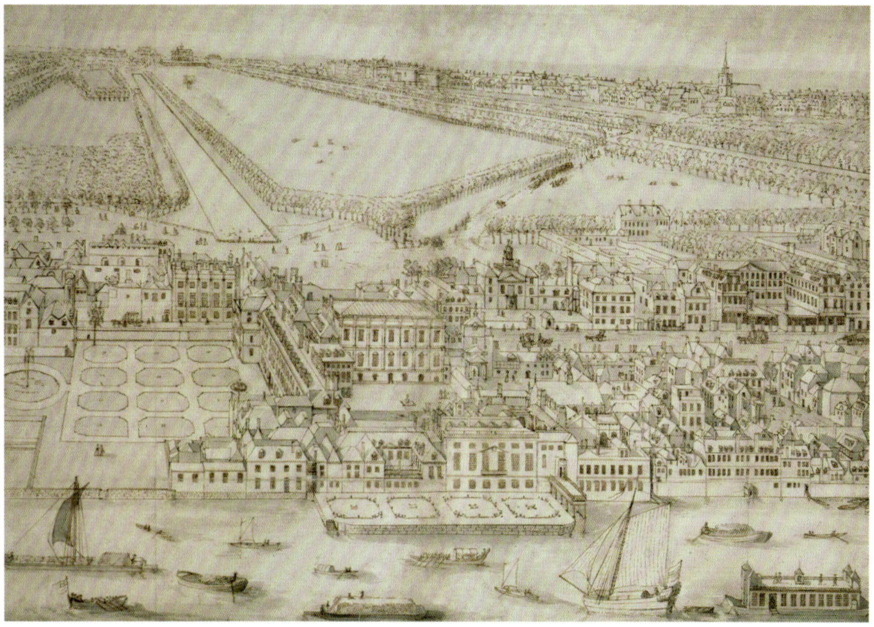

Fig. 3 Leonard Knyff (1650–1722), *Bird's Eye View of Whitehall Palace*, c. 1695. Pen and brown ink and wash on paper, 55.3 x 78.7 cm. City of Westminster Archives, London, inv. E134.1 (024)

Van der Doort's inventory (cat. 140) provides a record of the display of the collection at the time. Located facing the river, Whitehall consisted of a cluster of buildings lacking formal symmetry (fig. 2).[16] Its most imposing structure, the Banqueting House, was commissioned by James I following a fire in 1619 and built to designs by Inigo Jones. The neoclassical structure towering over the other buildings can be seen in the background of Wenceslaus Hollar's view of Whitehall (cat. 1), as well as the later aerial view by Leonard Knyff (fig. 3), recorded just before the palace was destroyed by fire in 1698.

As Van der Doort records, the main royal portrait at Whitehall was Van Dyck's so-called *Greate Peece* (cat. 66), commissioned in 1632 to complement Holbein's *Whitehall Mural*. This monumental family portrait hung on the vista of the Long Gallery overlooking a long row of Italian (cats 48, 54, 56) and Northern (cats 43, 107) paintings, including also Van Dyck's still unframed *Cupid and Psyche* (cat. 78).[17] In contrast to those in the Long Gallery, the 73 paintings in the Privy Gallery were largely dynastic portraits, most of them unattributed. Many were British and usually referred to as 'Whitehall peeces', which often meant they were inherited rather than acquired.[18]

The Privy Gallery must have formed a harsh contrast to the splendour on display in the adjacent Privy Lodging Rooms: from the Adam and Eve Stairs, visitors entered the First Privy Lodging Room, featuring a startling display of works by Titian (cats 45–47, figs 13, 15, 27).[19] Italian Renaissance pictures also dominated the Second and Third Privy Lodging Rooms, which featured Raphael's *La Perla* (fig. 4) and Correggio's *Venus with Mercury and Cupid ('The School of Love')* (cat. 18) and *Venus and Cupid with a Satyr* (fig. 20).[20] The pictures in the Bedchamber (cat. 49) and the Breakfast Chamber (cat. 70) were more personal and would have had special meaning for the King.[21] The 'little room' between the latter and the Privy Gallery was devoted to portraits (cats 12, 50–51), including a series of artists' self-portraits (cats 4, 7).[22]

At the heart of Whitehall Palace, the newly erected Cabinet Room served as a 'study centre' for the entire collection (see pp. 206–11).[23] The 80 paintings on display here are not easily summarised, but they tend to be smaller works with a strong representation of Northern European artists and a mix of masterpiece and curiosity. The Cabinet Room was probably hung around some key Italian masterpieces – Leonardo's *St John the Baptist* (fig. 52) and Raphael's *St George and the Dragon* (fig. 53) – as well as works from the early Renaissance, such as Andrea Mantegna's *Death of the Virgin* (fig. 54). The room was filled with pictures, statuettes and bas-reliefs (fig. 55), while miniatures, books, printing plates, drawings, medals and further precious objects were kept separately and could be studied on a large table in the centre. Another similar room, the Chair Room, included portraits by Albrecht Dürer (cat. 35), Holbein (cat. 38) and Joos van Cleve (cats 40–41).[24] Two modern works provide another clue to the nature of both displays: Van Dyck's oil sketch for his equestrian portrait (cat. 73) is the first painting listed in the Chair Room; Rubens's oil sketch for the Banqueting House was set into the ceiling of the Cabinet Room.[25]

Fig. 4 Raphael (1483–1520), *Virgin and Child with St Anne and the Infant St John the Baptist ('La Perla')*, *c.* 1518. Oil on panel, 147.4 x 116 cm. Museo Nacional del Prado, Madrid, inv. P00301

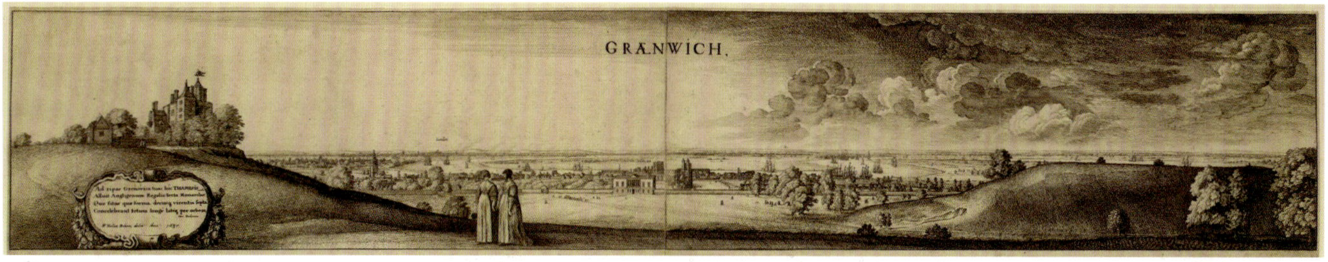

Fig. 5 Wenceslaus Hollar (1607–1677), *Greenwich*, 1637. Etching, 15.2 x 83.2 cm. The British Museum, London, inv. 1850,0223.254

Fig. 6 Anthony van Dyck (1599–1641), *Henrietta Maria*, *c.* 1636. Oil on canvas, 105 x 84.5 cm. Private collection, New York

Beyond the Chair Room, the Bear Gallery's 35 pictures were full-length portraits of monarchs and warriors associated with recent European wars, including *Charles V with a Dog* (cat. 16), one of Charles I's first Titians, a gift from Philip IV during his trip to Madrid. This display was rounded off with Van Dyck's *Hendrik van den Bergh* (cat. 13), acquired before the artist was court painter, and two paintings by Rubens, *Peace and War* (cat. 14) and *Daniel in the Lions' Den* (fig. 38).

As well as Whitehall, many other major Tudor palaces were still in use by the time Charles I ascended the throne, and they too came to house his collection. Of these, St James's Palace was traditionally allocated to the Prince of Wales. Charles's elder brother Henry lived there until his premature death in 1612 and it was then granted to Charles and became his main residence until his father's death in 1625. By the late 1630s the earlier of Van Dyck's two equestrian portraits of Charles I (cat. 72) was placed on the vista of the gallery of St James's, overlooking an array of heroic, mostly biblical scenes (cats 57, 60–61), including Caravaggio's *Death of the Virgin* (fig. 42) and Guido Reni's *Labours of Hercules* (fig. 43). Another important palace used by the King was Hampton Court, in particular for hunting. Pictures on display here included Mantegna's monumental nine canvases, *The Triumph of Caesar* (cats 25–33), as well as Van Dyck's second equestrian portrait of Charles I (cat. 74).

Somerset House, then known as Denmark House, was the main residence of Henrietta Maria. It had been assigned to Charles's mother, Anne of Denmark, by James I. When Anne died in 1619, the palace was granted to Charles, then Prince of Wales, although his principal residence, until 1625, remained St James's. It was given to Henrietta Maria upon her arrival in London. Somerset House housed a considerable collection of paintings, including Van Dyck's *Rinaldo and Armida* (Baltimore Museum of Art), two of his royal portraits (cats 64, 67) and Reni's *Toilet of Venus* (cat. 90). During the Commonwealth Sale, Somerset House was allocated to the Trustees as offices and a number of bedrooms were used to display additional pictures brought here for the Sale.

One of the most notable royal building projects during the reign of Charles I was the Queen's House at Greenwich, which – like the Banqueting House – was designed by Inigo Jones. Hollar's 1637 panorama (fig. 5), dedicated to Henrietta Maria, shows the Queen's House in the centre with a view of London in the far distance. Orazio Gentileschi painted the canvases that decorated the ceiling of its central hall (fig. 40), and a number of his paintings were on display in the same room (cats 84–86). The Queen moved between a number of palaces, and her collection was on display at Greenwich (cats 24, 52), Nonsuch, one of the most ambitious building projects of Henry VIII (it no longer survives), and Wimbledon Manor, which was reacquired for Henrietta Maria in 1639, and pulled down in the early nineteenth century (cat. 58). Another palace, used primarily for hunting, was Oatlands, which had been granted to Prince Henry in 1610 and was given to Queen Anne in the following year. The palace can be glimpsed in the background of a portrait of Queen Anne by Paul van Somer (Royal Collection). Van Dyck's *Charles I in the Hunting Field* (cat. 76) was probably commissioned to replace Van Somer's portrait and it seems likely that Henrietta Maria took it with her when she went into exile in 1644, first to Paris and eventually to the Château de Colombes, near Paris.

In comparison to other monarchs, Charles I undertook few building projects. However, a large number of extant drawings (Worcester College, Oxford) now suggest that he had ambitious plans to redesign Whitehall Palace, perhaps to provide a more appropriate architectural setting for the stunning art collection he had assembled.

All collections are formed by an interaction of opportunity, fashion and personal taste. The first of these elements can be explored in relation to every item in the collection – was it a gift, part of a bulk purchase or something individually sought out? If the last, was it difficult to find? The other two elements are often indistinguishable and more difficult to analyse with any rigour. It is a better reflection of the mindset of the time to think instead of an understanding of art and its traditions, which might be widely shared, at least among an elite.[26] The questions then become: what was the prevailing view of the

F.14
F.14

history of art in the 1620s and 1630s, and to what extent did Charles I's collection reflect, qualify or contradict this view?

It would have been generally accepted at this time that the centre for art was Rome, and that the 'narrative' (as it would now be called) belonged above all to the Carracci (in particular to Annibale), their pupils and apologists.[27] Although it was to take some years to be set down in writing by authors such as Giovanni Battista Agucchi (whose *Treatise on Painting* was written in 1615 but published in 1646), the Carraccian philosophy must have dominated talk in Rome (and elsewhere) and informed the thinking of Charles's advisors, including Jones and Arundel.[28] It taught that the account of Italian painting in Giorgio Vasari's *Lives of the Most Excellent Painters, Sculptors and Architects* (1550/68) should be adjusted and brought up to date in several ways (see pp. 100–05). Raphael should replace Michelangelo as the apogee of art, with a shift away from Florentine mannerism towards a more atmospheric tradition rooted in the work of Leonardo da Vinci.[29] Northern Italian exponents of this tradition, such as Correggio and Parmigianino, were to be brought into the mainstream, as were similarly poetic Venetians, among them Giorgione, Titian and Jacopo Tintoretto.[30] All this represented a return to the depiction of Nature, but with the example of Raphael, which would help artists to temper their enthusiasm for the crude realism of Caravaggio.[31]

It is more difficult to determine how Charles I's contemporaries understood the story of Northern European art, though some of the same elements were in place (see pp. 82–87). Karel van Mander's *Schilder-boeck*, published in 1604, provides Italianate artistic theory and a series of artists' biographies. It was probably little read by the English, but its ideas were perhaps disseminated by the many Dutch-speaking agents and advisors surrounding the Court (not least Van der Doort). Van Mander's view of Northern art 'progressing' from something gothic towards a classical or Italianate ideal would have been reinforced by the examples of Rubens and Van Dyck. Both were Flemings seen to be working in the universal Italian style and considered worthy of joining the canon of Italian art, most obviously by their inclusion in Giovanni Pietro Bellori's *Lives of the Modern Painters, Sculptors and Architects*, published in 1672.

In the prominent position Van Dyck and Rubens enjoyed in so many of Charles I's displays, it is possible to see the idea of a fusion of the Italian and the Northern into a single universal tradition. Of the two, Rubens comes closest to offering a comprehensive view of art, like that of the Carracci, his work respecting the antique and the Italian traditions, but also reflecting the inspiration of key Northern artists, including Dürer, Holbein, Pieter Bruegel the Elder and Adam Elsheimer. Rubens's practice did not give rise to the same theoretical discourse as that of the Carracci, but it is possible to imagine his narrative of European art gaining word-of-mouth currency in the last two decades of his life.

Somewhat ironically, the sale of Charles I's collection provides a unique opportunity to assess contemporary taste in financial terms. The result looks remarkably close to the view of art described above. The most highly valued paintings in the Commonwealth Sale were by Raphael (fig. 4, £2,000) and Correggio (cat. 18, £800; figs 18–20, £1,000 each).[32] Titian comes next with two works sold for £600 (cat. 45, fig. 15), and he is also the artist with the greatest cumulative value (his works and copies after them amounting to over £7,000 in the Sale).[33] Artists with works fetching more than £100 include Leonardo (fig. 52, £140), among others.[34] The Venetian tradition is also strongly represented in this price bracket: Palma Vecchio (fig. 51, £225), Tintoretto (cat. 57, £120) and Palma Giovane (cats 60–61, £100 each).[35] Among contemporary Italian artists the most highly valued is Reni (cat. 90, £200), leading Caravaggio (fig. 42, £150),[36] Orazio Gentileschi (cats 84, 86, £80 each) and Annibale Carracci, whose tiny *Agony in the Garden* (cat. 110) was sold for a respectable £40, while also being selected for reproduction by Lucas Vorsterman (cat. 109).[37] The only paintings dating from the fifteenth century of any significance were by Mantegna, whose nine huge canvases of the *Triumph of Caesar* (cats 25–33) were valued at £1,000.[38]

The only Renaissance artist from the North consistently valued as highly as these Italians was Holbein, his most expensive portrait selling for £120.[39] Otherwise, £40 to £60 is the range for important Northern Renaissance works: Dürer's *Burkhard of Speyer* (cat. 35) sold for £60, a now-lost *St Jerome* by Quinten Massys for £60 and Jan Gossaert's *Adam and Eve* (cat. 34) for £50 10s.[40] Contemporary Northern artists fared no better. The painters at Charles I's court specialising in the minor genres – landscapes, still-lifes, perspectives and small-scale portraits – usually commanded modest prices. The most highly valued exceptions were the miniaturists Isaac and Peter Oliver. The so-called 'limnings' of the latter (cats 111, 113–14, 117) fetched the considerable sums of £50 to £100.[41] Portraits by Dutch immigrants, such as Gerrit van Honthorst and Daniel Mytens, were generally valued at around £20, though Honthorst's monumental *Apollo and Diana* (Royal Collection) sold for £200.[42] Rubens's *Peace and War* (cat. 14) sold for £100;[43] otherwise his prices range from £16 to £60. The most highly valued contemporary artist from the Low Countries was Van Dyck, whose equestrian portraits of the King sold for £200 (cat. 74) and £150 (cat. 72) respectively, and whose works account for a total in excess of £1,700 in the Sale.[44]

The bald impression provided by these numbers is supported by other 'performance indicators', namely how the works were displayed and which were selected for copies. As we

Fig. 7 Inigo Jones (1573–1652), *Costume Study for the Role of Chloris Played by Henrietta Maria*, 1631. Pen and brown ink and wash on paper, 26.5 x 14.9 cm. Collection of the Duke of Devonshire, Chatsworth House, Derbyshire

have seen, the most prestigious hanging spaces in Whitehall Palace, the three Privy Lodging Rooms, were hung with works by the same familiar names.[45] The range of the paintings hanging in the Cabinet Room may be more diverse, but the 'limned' copies kept in the same room in their 'double-shutting cases' bring us back to the core of Charles I's taste, all being copied after the best works by Raphael, Correggio, Titian and Holbein.[46] These miniature replicas were fully coloured and fully detailed, the King appearing to have had no interest in drawings, despite being surrounded by pioneering collectors in the field, such as Nicholas Lanier (figs 9–10) and Arundel.

Although these works were of course highly valued as Raphaels, Titians or Correggios (or copies thereof), this does not imply, as is sometimes suggested, that they were *not* enjoyed as depictions of Venus or the Virgin Mary. Van der Doort was evidently interested enough in subject-matter to describe it accurately; the arrangement of paintings suggests that the King shared his interest. The fact that the rooms were hung with a mixture of sacred and profane indicates not indifference but an ability to synthesise classical and Christian traditions in a way observable in the court masques of the period, many designed by Inigo Jones (fig. 7).

It is here argued that Charles's collection reflects a view of the story of art current in the two most influential circles of the early seventeenth century: the pupils and supporters of the Carracci in Italy and Rubens's studio in the North. It starts to appear idiosyncratic only when viewed in the light of the academic orthodoxy that developed in the later seventeenth century and informed later British writing on art, in particular Sir Joshua Reynolds's concept of the 'grand style'.[47] For example, although Charles collected antique sculpture, there is remarkably little of the classical sculptural ideal (of the kind recommended by Reynolds) in his painting collection. The sort of paintings he liked are strikingly painterly: dominated by pastoral settings, atmospheric light and shade, vivid use of colour and careful exploration of detail. This is not just because the King liked Venetian painting; these things can be seen in his Raphaels and Correggios as well. Even within the area of Venetian painting there is bias towards the down-to-earth realism of early Titian and his more rustic followers, such as Jacopo Bassano. When marking up a posthumous inventory of Rubens's work, Charles showed a particular interest in landscapes.[48]

Of the works that were reserved at the Commonwealth Sale, Raphael's tapestry cartoons (figs 44–47) provide another intriguing insight into Charles I's taste – and how it has come to be misunderstood. It was only during the later seventeenth century that the cartoons came to be displayed and valued in their own right and not, as Charles had intended, as models for tapestries.[49] In them could be found the ideal of generalised simplicity, conception outweighing execution, which for Reynolds defined the 'grand style'. It would be an overstatement to say that nothing approaching a 'grand style' could be found in Charles I's collection, but it would be something much more richly finished, something more poetic and pastoral than anything taught by Reynolds.

CHRONOLOGY

LUCY CHISWELL AND NIKO MUNZ

19 NOVEMBER 1600
Birth of Charles, second son and youngest surviving child of James VI of Scotland and Anne of Denmark, at Dunfermline Palace, Fife.

1603
Death of Elizabeth I; James VI of Scotland succeeds her as James I of Great Britain. Union of Scottish and English Crowns.

1605
Charles becomes Duke of York. Gunpowder Plot to assassinate James I fails.

1611
Charles becomes a Knight of the Garter. Completion of the King James Bible.

1612
Death of Charles's older brother Henry, Prince of Wales, at the age of eighteen; Charles becomes heir apparent.

1613
Elizabeth Stuart, Charles's sister, leaves England to marry Frederick V, Prince Palatine of the Rhine. Thomas Howard, 14th Earl of Arundel, his wife, Aletheia Howard, Countess of Arundel, and Inigo Jones travel to Europe (until 1614).

1615
Inigo Jones is appointed Surveyor of the King's Works.

1616
Charles becomes Prince of Wales. Death of William Shakespeare.

1618
Daniel Mytens arrives in London.

1619
Death of Charles's mother, Anne of Denmark. The Old Banqueting House at Whitehall Palace is destroyed by fire; Inigo Jones is commissioned to design a new Banqueting House. James I establishes a tapestry works at Mortlake.

1620
Anthony van Dyck visits London for the first time; he stays for five months.

1621
Charles attends his first parliament. Death of Philip III of Spain; he is succeeded by Philip IV.

1623
Charles travels to Madrid with George Villiers, 1st Duke of Buckingham, to explore the possibility of marriage to the Infanta Maria Anna of Spain; negotiations eventually break down. Sir Francis Crane purchases seven of Raphael's cartoons of the *Acts of the Apostles* from Genoa for use at Mortlake. Death of Pope Gregory XV; Maffeo Barberini succeeds him as Pope Urban VIII.

1625
Death of James I; he is succeeded by Charles I, who marries fifteen-year-old Henrietta Maria, daughter of Henri IV of France and Marie de' Medici. Abraham van der Doort is appointed Surveyor of the King's Pictures. Hubert Le Sueur arrives in London. War breaks out between the Crowns of England and Spain. Plague in London.

1626
Coronation of Charles I at Westminster Abbey. Orazio Gentileschi arrives in London at the age of 63. Death of Ferdinando I Gonzaga, Duke of Mantua; he is succeeded by Vincenzo II Gonzaga.

1627
Alliance between the Crowns of France and Spain against the Crown of England; English forces, led by the Duke of Buckingham, are defeated by the French at La Rochelle. Daniel Nijs completes the first purchase of pictures from the Gonzaga on behalf of Charles I.

1628
The Duke of Buckingham is assassinated at Portsmouth. The first shipment of the Gonzaga purchase leaves for London. Gerrit van Honthorst visits London.

1629
Charles I dissolves Parliament and begins an eleven-year 'Personal Rule'.

Peter Paul Rubens visits London as a diplomat to the Spanish court; he paints *Peace and War* (cat. 14) and *Landscape with St George and the Dragon* (cat. 83); it is decided he is to decorate the ceiling of the Banqueting House. Peace is agreed between the Crowns of England and France.

1630
Birth of Prince Charles, the future Charles II. The second shipment of the Gonzaga purchase, including Andrea Mantegna's *Triumph of Caesar* (cats 25–33), arrives in London. Rubens is knighted by Charles I at Whitehall Palace before his return to Antwerp. Equestrian statue of Charles I commissioned from Le Sueur. Peace is agreed between the Crowns of England and Spain.

1632
Van Dyck arrives in London; he is appointed Court Painter and knighted by Charles I at St James's Palace; he paints the *Greate Peece* (cat. 66). The third and final shipment of the Gonzaga purchase arrives in London.

1633
Scottish Coronation of Charles I at St Giles' Cathedral, Edinburgh. Birth of Prince James, the future James II and VII.

1634
Van Dyck visits the Southern Netherlands (until 1635). Mytens leaves London. Gregorio Panzani, papal envoy to England, arrives in London.

1636
Rubens's ceiling canvases are reported as safely installed in the Banqueting House. Van Dyck's triple portrait of Charles I (cat. 3) is sent to Gianlorenzo Bernini in Rome. The Queen's Chapel, designed by Jones, opens at Somerset House. Completion of the Queen's House at Greenwich. Cardinal Francesco Barberini, nephew of Pope Urban VIII, sends a gift of paintings to Henrietta Maria from Rome, to give to the King.

1637
Bernini's bust of Charles I arrives at Oatlands Palace, Surrey. Charles I enforces a new prayer book on Scotland; rebellion in Edinburgh.

1639
First Bishops' War between England and Scotland. Van der Doort compiles an inventory of the royal collection (cat. 140). Van Dyck marries Mary Ruthven. Death of Gentileschi.

1640
Second Bishops' War. Charles summons 'Short Parliament' for money to fight the Scots; it is dissolved three weeks later. Charles I summons 'Long Parliament', which lasts until 1650. Death of Van der Doort. Death of Rubens in Antwerp.

1641
Death of Van Dyck; he is buried in Old St Paul's Cathedral. Catholic Rebellion in Ireland. Le Sueur leaves London.

1642
Charles I attempts to arrest five Members of Parliament and fails. Civil War begins in England.

1643
Charles I moves his court and military headquarters to Oxford. Parliamentarians and Scots form an alliance. Henrietta Maria is impeached for high treason.

1644
Parliamentarians, led by Oliver Cromwell, defeat Royalists at the Battle of Marston Moor, Yorkshire. Henrietta Maria flees England for France.

1645
Parliament establishes a 'New Model Army'; the Royalists are defeated at the Battle of Naseby, Northamptonshire.

1646
Charles I surrenders to the Scots.

1647
Charles I is handed over to the Parliamentarians. He escapes imprisonment at Hampton Court and flees to the Isle of Wight, where he is recaptured. Charles I signs a secret treaty with the Scots following the collapse of Scottish–Parliamentarian relations.

1648
Second Civil War; Parliamentarians defeat Scottish–Royalist army.

JANUARY 1649
Charles I is tried by Parliament and found guilty of high treason.

30 JANUARY 1649
Charles I is beheaded in front of the Banqueting House, Whitehall Palace.

1649
Great Britain becomes a republic. The Commonwealth Sale of the royal collection begins at Somerset House.

1660
Charles II returns from exile and is restored to the throne.

1669
Death of Henrietta Maria at the Château de Colombes, near Paris.

1

ARTISTS AND AGENTS

CONNOISSEURSHIP AT THE CAROLINE COURT

JEREMY WOOD

For many people at the court of Charles I, the King must have seemed – and indeed was – inaccessible. He was guarded by his attendants, protected by the ceremony of his court, and remote within its hierarchy. The doors of the Privy Chamber at Whitehall Palace appeared an insuperable obstacle, shielding not only the body of the King but a substantial part of his collection, gathered into the private rooms of the Privy Lodgings.[1] At the same time, a few artists, as well as providers of luxury goods, musicians, writers and sometimes unscrupulous agents,[2] were able to step where others found it difficult to go. Preferment could be gained through reputation, or through introduction by those courtiers who had an interest in art and access to the King and his consort, Henrietta Maria, since the cultural life centred on Charles was the story of two households and several palaces. This essay explores the remarkable network of artists, agents and collectors who fed the royal taste for art.

The artists who shaped the art of the court were, unsurprisingly, of humble birth. Inigo Jones (cat. 6), the son of a clothworker, began his career as a joiner, but ended up as Surveyor of the Office of Works with a huge budget of £8,000 a year.[3] He had the single greatest influence on court culture because he developed a new architectural idiom, devised many court masques, and advised on the purchase of works of art. Anthony van Dyck (cat. 5), whose father, an Antwerp cloth merchant, had suffered financial disgrace,[4] became the leading portrait painter of the age. He first visited London in 1620 and in 1632 was appointed the principal painter to their majesties.[5] Not only did he have access to the King, but, in the summer of 1635, Charles travelled downriver to Van Dyck's house in Blackfriars 'to see his Paintings',[6] an event that reversed the social order. Not least, Ben Jonson, the poet and author of court masques, had been a bricklayer as a young man and was taunted for this during the rest of his life.[7] All three men needed powerful advocates to advance their early careers at court. The world they entered can be glimpsed in a view of Greenwich Palace by Adriaen van Stalbemt and Jan van Belcamp, now in the Royal Collection (fig. 8).[8] A portly man to the left of the party of courtiers surrounding the King and Queen has sometimes been identified as Jones,[9] but he could never have stood as an equal in this group, nor have worn the blue ribbon of the Order of the Garter. More likely this is Thomas Howard, Earl of Arundel (cat. 10), arguably the greatest collector in early Stuart England, shown talking affably to Endymion Porter (cat. 8), one of the most worldly and cosmopolitan of the Gentlemen of the Bedchamber.

Who made it possible for the King and Queen to collect? The direction of command was clear when they commissioned work from the largely foreign-born artists and craftsmen whom they lured to work in London. For example, in 1632 Henrietta Maria ordered Belcamp to make three pictures 'by our direction and for our use'.[10] On the other hand, though the King was said by contemporaries to be remarkably well informed about art, he seldom chose the foreign paintings that were imported for his collection. He relied on the eyes and ears of a number of agents and connoisseurs to spot opportunities on the market and to decide if they were what was claimed. It is true that, in 1636, Arundel advised his agent in Italy that 'you do very well to be careful of getting something of Titian for his Majesty ... but for buying things for the king without order ... I should not advise it, for His Majesty knows best what he hath gusto in'.[11] But that was more true of the mid-1630s, when Arundel was writing, than the 1620s when Charles's tastes were still being formed.

THE CONNOISSEURS

Who were the trusted eyes at court? Jones was certainly a respected connoisseur. Contemporaries recorded his physical excitement when looking at good pictures, and Arundel's son Lord Maltravers reported showing some paintings from Naples to 'Mr Surveyor here, who is mad to see them'.[12] Jones, who had travelled in Italy and knew the language, was one of the few

people in Britain at this time to own a copy of the 1568 edition of Giorgio Vasari's famous lives of Italian artists (it is now at Worcester College, Oxford). He used it as a manual for making attributions, and, as was his habit, annotated it heavily.[13] No less important was Nicholas Lanier, Master of the King's Music, who had been born in London to a family of court musicians, and whose expertise was developed during visits to Italy in the 1610s and 1620s. An unattributed portrait dated 1613 (fig. 9) depicts him as a musician and connoisseur, in striking contrast to Van Dyck's later image of him as a courtier (fig. 10).

Lanier was entrusted with the most ambitious buying expedition undertaken for Charles – setting on one side the very different bulk purchase of the Gonzaga collection (see pp. 54–59) – when, in 1625, he went to Italy to purchase paintings selectively from agents or, in the case of contemporary works, directly from the artists themselves. On 29 January 1626 a licence was issued in Rome to allow the export of a number of his acquisitions.[14] These included a mix of pictures by

Fig. 8 Adriaen van Stalbemt (1580–1662) and Jan van Belcamp (1610–1653), *A View of Greenwich with Charles I and Henrietta Maria among a Group of Courtiers*, c. 1632. Oil on canvas, 83.5 x 107 cm. The Royal Collection, RCIN 405291

sixteenth-century masters, and – perhaps more enterprisingly – examples of the main currents in Roman painting of the 1620s, some of which can be traced in the Whitehall inventories. Charles, of course, had to depend entirely on Lanier to make the selection.

Much more is known about the often fraught importation of works of art – which left a paper trail – than about more transient discussions at court. But what was at stake, and who had the King's ear, emerges from an exceptional exchange of letters between two peripheral figures, Don Gregorio Law, resident in the monastery of San Pietro in Perugia, and David Codner, an English Benedictine.[15] The Italian of these letters is not always clear and even the individuals involved have sometimes been misidentified.[16] Codner was negotiating

Fig. 9 Anglo-Flemish School, *Portrait of a Gentleman, probably Nicholas Lanier*, with Hendrick van Steenwyck the Younger (*c.* 1580–1649), *The Liberation of St Peter* (oval inset), 1613. Oil on panel transferred to canvas, 90.5 x 72 cm. Private collection

Fig. 10 Anthony van Dyck (1599–1641), *Nicholas Lanier*, 1628. Oil on canvas, 111 x 87.6 cm. Kunsthistorisches Museum, Vienna, inv. 501

the purchase of a number of paintings, including a so-called Raphael *Madonna*, from a Perugian merchant. These were to be offered to the King and Queen through the agency of Arundel, his son Lord Maltravers and Arundel's agent in Italy, the Reverend William Petty. Codner reported that he had asked Van Dyck for advice and that the artist had offered to act as intermediary. This is not surprising since Van Dyck had lived in Italy for six years and owned a collection that, though small by aristocratic standards, was high in quality, including no less than nineteen Titians.[17] The letters reveal that Arundel and the King were upset at having sometimes been duped into purchasing works as originals that were only copies, though they had no objection to copies when identified as such. It seems that 'many scandalous tricks had been played here'.[18] Van Dyck repeatedly asked that sketches of the paintings be sent with dimensions, attributions and valuations. He was not only concerned that copies might be substituted but also that the works might be workshop products, since 'the schools of the most excellent artists often produce donkeys'.[19]

Neither Jones nor Lanier was primarily employed to look after the King's collection. This became the job of a less worldly man, Abraham van der Doort (fig. 1), who had specialist knowledge of coins and medals, and had come to England to work for Charles's elder brother, Prince Henry, who had died tragically young. Before his accession Charles appointed Van der Doort as Keeper of the Cabinet Room, and in May 1625 he became Surveyor of the King's Pictures.[20] Other experts were soon to arrive. The Flemish merchant Daniel Nijs, then resident in Venice and architect of the Gonzaga purchase, came to London in 1634, bankrupt and desperate for money owed him by the King. He became what was known in the period as a Projector, in this case promoting a scheme for making London 'more salubrious, and the city cleaner and more convenient for its inhabitants',[21] but his expertise in Italian art remained one of his few assets. One year later, Diego Duarte II was appointed 'jeweller in ordinary' to Charles I.[22] He was a Portuguese merchant, picture dealer and *liefhebber* or art lover with a finger in many pies. Nijs and Duarte were both experienced in doing business across Europe and among their many skills was a knowledge of art. They clustered round the king like bees to a honeypot, but in Nijs's case this led to financial ruin.

Fig. 11 Anthony van Dyck (1599–1641), *Self-portrait with Endymion Porter*, c. 1633. Oil on canvas, 119 x 144 cm. Museo Nacional del Prado, Madrid, inv. P01489

THE INNER CIRCLE

At Whitehall Palace, only the Gentlemen of the Bedchamber and the princes of the blood had unhindered access to the King's most private rooms, the Privy Lodgings.[23] But among the King's closest attendants were several who were knowledgeable about art. One was Endymion Porter, mentioned above, a man from a minor gentry family who rose to preferment after years of service in Madrid to the powerful Don Gaspar de Guzmán, later Count-Duke of Olivares. Porter's usefulness to the King lay in his cosmopolitanism, mastery of languages, and friendship with artists and writers. It was Porter who made friends with Van Dyck, had his portrait painted by the artist while in Antwerp (cat. 8) and was depicted alongside him in a double portrait now in the Prado, Madrid (fig. 11).

But perhaps no less important was Charles's closeness to another – often overlooked – Gentleman of the Bedchamber, Sir James Palmer, who included the painting of portraits in miniature among his accomplishments. He arranged gifts and exchanges of works of art with the King, acted as intermediary as well as selling directly, and painted copies in miniature for him. Palmer's interests in art were very different from Porter's and less Italianate: for example, he was responsible for the purchase of a group of early sixteenth-century Netherlandish works by Aertgen van Leyden, still in the Royal Collection,[24] some court portraits, and, not least, the fourteenth-century masterpiece, the *Wilton Diptych*, now in the National Gallery, London (fig. 21).[25]

At the same time, collecting extended beyond the King and the Gentlemen of the Bedchamber. The court was an arena for national and international politics, where an elite from both inside and outside London could make contact with people from overseas, glimpse international culture, and, not least, indulge in luxury consumption at the New Exchange.[26] Two leading courtiers became pre-eminent and provide a striking contrast: Lord Arundel, the proud and rapacious collector already mentioned, and George Villiers, Marquess (later Duke) of Buckingham (cat. 11). Arundel had returned to favour under James I, after his grandfather, the 4th Duke of Norfolk, forfeited his lands in 1572, a disaster that accounted for his grandson's obsession with the history and honour of his family. Buckingham, however, owed his advancement to personal charm as much as to distinguished lineage.

The taste that Arundel and his wife, Aletheia Talbot, had for Italian art was part of a wider immersion in all things Italian that included learning the language and sympathising with the Church of Rome. For example, Lady Arundel returned from

Italy in 1623 with not only many fine paintings, but a black servant and a gondola that a contemporary said 'will not so well brook our river [Thames]'.[27] Buckingham, on the other hand, never travelled to Italy, bought fast and expediently, and employed an agent, Balthasar Gerbier – a jack of all trades and master of art dealing – to go shopping for him in the Southern Netherlands and in Italy.[28] Not least, Buckingham used a meeting with Peter Paul Rubens in Paris in 1625 to snap up the artist's collection of pictures and antiquities.[29] This trip abroad was also highly significant since the Duke recruited two artists for the English court: Hubert Le Sueur, a sculptor, and Orazio Gentileschi (fig. 12), an irascible and by then elderly Italian artist who had known Caravaggio in Rome and had worked at a number of European courts, including most recently that of Henrietta Maria's mother, Marie de' Medici. In short, both Buckingham and Arundel enlisted artists to work in London, and both had been busy as collectors before Charles came to the throne, but Buckingham was by far the closer to the King.

OBTAINING ART FROM ABROAD

In the first half of the seventeenth century there were many artists' studios in Blackfriars, but London had no dealers with stocks of foreign pictures like those to be found in Venice, Rome, Amsterdam and Antwerp. As a result, the role of agents who could buy abroad became crucial. Lord and Lady Arundel were exceptionally well travelled,[30] but, more generally, great men and women had relatively few opportunities to go abroad and so – as with Buckingham – relied on proxies to obtain luxury items and works of art. These agents bought works on commission but also speculatively, sometimes acquiring pictures individually but also in large consignments if the opportunity arose.

Useful conduits were provided by those English ambassadors who, following the end of war with Spain in 1604, became established in Brussels, Madrid and Venice, all centres of the European art trade. Foremost among them was Sir Dudley Carleton, later Viscount Dorchester, Ambassador to the Venetian Republic between 1610 and 1615. For example, Carleton bought a consignment of paintings and antiquities for Robert Carr, Earl of Somerset, in 1615. Delivered before Carr's fall from favour but never paid for, some were sold on to Arundel.[31] The protracted deal contained the seeds of much future Stuart trading in art: Carleton had bought from the Flemish merchant Daniel Nijs, already mentioned, who a few years later was to facilitate the purchase of the Gonzaga collection for Charles I. Carleton exchanged the antiquities left on his hands with Rubens for paintings. But, in turn, many of these sculptures were to come back to London as part of the deal made between Rubens and Buckingham in the mid-1620s, already mentioned. In 1617 Carleton had found 'some of my own heads wanting' in transit to The Hague,[32] but at least a few of the items that passed from Carleton to Rubens and then to Buckingham can be traced.[33] Rubens was first approached to paint the ceiling of the Banqueting House at Whitehall Palace as early as 1621, and Charles was remarkably keen to obtain a self-portrait by the artist in 1623 (cat. 4), eventually displaying it at Whitehall alongside self-portraits by Daniel Mytens (cat. 7) and Van Dyck. In short, the deals with Carleton and Buckingham helped secure Rubens's place at the forefront of court patronage and smoothed his path to the Banqueting House commission.

The activities of Carleton in Venice and in The Hague between 1616 and 1625 provided a prototype for the more ambitious deals negotiated during the reign of Charles I. A pattern was established in which a well-placed individual might spot an opportunity. Then, a formal approach would be made. An artist or art agent would draw up a list of what was on offer and obtain estimates of value. Final negotiations could then proceed until a price was agreed.[34] One of the most important examples came towards the end of Charles's reign when Basil Feilding, later 2nd Earl of Denbigh, Ambassador in Venice, bought the collection of the merchant Bartolomeo della Nave for the foremost Scottish lord at court, James, 3rd Marquess and later 1st Duke of Hamilton.[35] This collection was reputedly the finest in Venice and the 230 paintings and 40 antique sculptures that Hamilton obtained – which arrived in London in 1638 – bear comparison with the King's earlier purchase of the Gonzaga collection. Feilding's transaction was beset with familiar anxieties about whether the works were all that was claimed, whether copies would be substituted at the last minute, and whether some promised works might mysteriously never arrive in London.

A different strategy had to be used with works that, paradoxically, were not available on the market. Replicas of the most famous classical statues in Rome – works that would never be sold and exported – had become indispensable in princely and aristocratic collections. To this end, Charles followed the example of the King of France, François I, who had sent his court artist, Francesco Primaticcio, to Italy in 1540 to obtain moulds of antique sculptures for casting in bronze for the royal palace at Fontainebleau. Charles dispatched a sculptor to Rome to perform the same task in 1631. This was Hubert Le Sueur, who not only made grand bronze statues of the King (see cat. 137 for a miniature version), but, in 1628, a suit of armour for Henrietta Maria's dwarf, Jeffrey Hudson.[36] He even sold paintings to the King, including a landscape by Paul Bril (cat. 106). In Rome, he obtained moulds of famous antiquities such as the *Antinous*, then in the Vatican Belvedere, which he cast in bronze;[37] the same prototype is reproduced in a small version placed on the table in the 1613 portrait of Nicholas Lanier (fig. 9). This was how the greatest treasures of ancient Rome travelled to the English court.

Not least, works arrived at Whitehall from the continent as diplomatic and political gifts. Most famously, seven pictures sent by Cardinal Francesco Barberini, nephew of the reigning pope, Urban VIII, were presented to Henrietta Maria in January 1636.[38] Pictures were also presented individually. For example, that August the papal agent in England, George Conn, brought the Queen a small devotional image of St Catherine, even though it was unframed. Declaring she would attend to this herself, 'she took away the tin case and the packthread with which it was tied, and gave orders that the picture should be fastened to the curtains of her bed'.[39] This act of appropriation recalls the way the leading noblewoman and diarist Lady Anne Clifford – an omnivorous reader – pinned pieces of paper with texts inscribed on them to her bed curtains and furniture for similarly close scrutiny.[40]

ATTRACTING ARTISTS TO LONDON

The difference between Charles I's expenditure on art in the 1620s and the 1630s is essentially a shift from importing foreign pictures to attracting artists to London who would work to direction, while at the same time continuing to make use of some key figures he had inherited from his father's court. Among these was Daniel Mytens (cat. 7), a portrait painter from the northern Netherlands, who had come to London in the mid-1610s as the protégé of Sir Dudley Carleton. In 1623 Mytens was followed by Francis Cleyn, who had worked at the Danish court of Christian IV, and whose skills as a decorative artist and designer became crucial for Charles's investment in the costly tapestry factory at Mortlake (see pp. 190–97), which, together with his expenditure on Le Sueur's bronze foundry, was among his largest outlays on art.[41]

From this it emerges that the key artists who were enticed to cross the North Sea were employed in very clearly defined ways: Cleyn at the Mortlake tapestry factory, Le Sueur as a bronze sculptor, Rubens as painter of the Banqueting House ceiling, and Van Dyck as court portraitist. At one point, the King seems even to have toyed with replacing Jones as his architect and Surveyor. In 1630 Giovanni Battista Crescenzi, Superintendent of Royal Works to the Spanish monarch, Philip IV,[42] offered Charles a number of good Italian pictures,[43] and the King invited him to London. He declined but offered 'his dearest painting', Rosso Fiorentino's *Challenge of the Peirides* (Musée du Louvre, Paris),[44] a work that was sent to Whitehall and liked so much by the King that he displayed it in his Bedchamber.[45] If Crescenzi had moved to London, Mr Surveyor's nose would have been put seriously out of joint.

A number of other artists were attracted to London, but often not for specific court appointments, and generally for shorter periods of residence than Mytens, Cleyn, Le Sueur and Van Dyck. The exception was Orazio Gentileschi, mentioned above, who seems to have found himself stranded after the assassination in 1628 of Buckingham (the patron who had persuaded him to leave Paris), since Charles tired of both him and his work – understandably enough since Gentileschi was both combative and lazy.[46] But Henrietta Maria did commission a number of large biblical subjects for Somerset House and Greenwich Palace (cats 84–86), and it is not the only paradox of the King's cultural patronage that so much effort should have been made to bring Gentileschi to London and so little use made of him by the King after his arrival. In this respect, Henrietta Maria appears a more independent-minded patron than her husband.

Fig. 12 Anthony van Dyck (1599–1641), *Orazio Gentileschi*, *c.* 1627–35. Black chalk and wash, 23.6 x 17.8 cm. The British Museum, London, inv. Gg,2.238

At court, works of art were often made for specific locations, or, alternatively, their acquisition meant that the places for their display had to be changed to accommodate them. This is part of a larger story that embraces architecture and the skills of woodcarvers, sculptors, plasterers, cabinet makers, tapestry weavers, silversmiths and embroiderers. If, as argued here, the art of the 1620s and 1630s was shaped through a series of interactions between artists, agents and aristocratic collectors in which the King – though influential – did not always dominate, then Henrietta Maria emerges as a crucial figure, and the network of patronage spreads beyond the confines of Whitehall Palace.

1
Wenceslaus Hollar
Whitehall Palace, 1637–43
Pen and grey ink and watercolour
on paper, 9.8 x 29.3 cm
The British Museum, London,
inv. 1859,0806.390

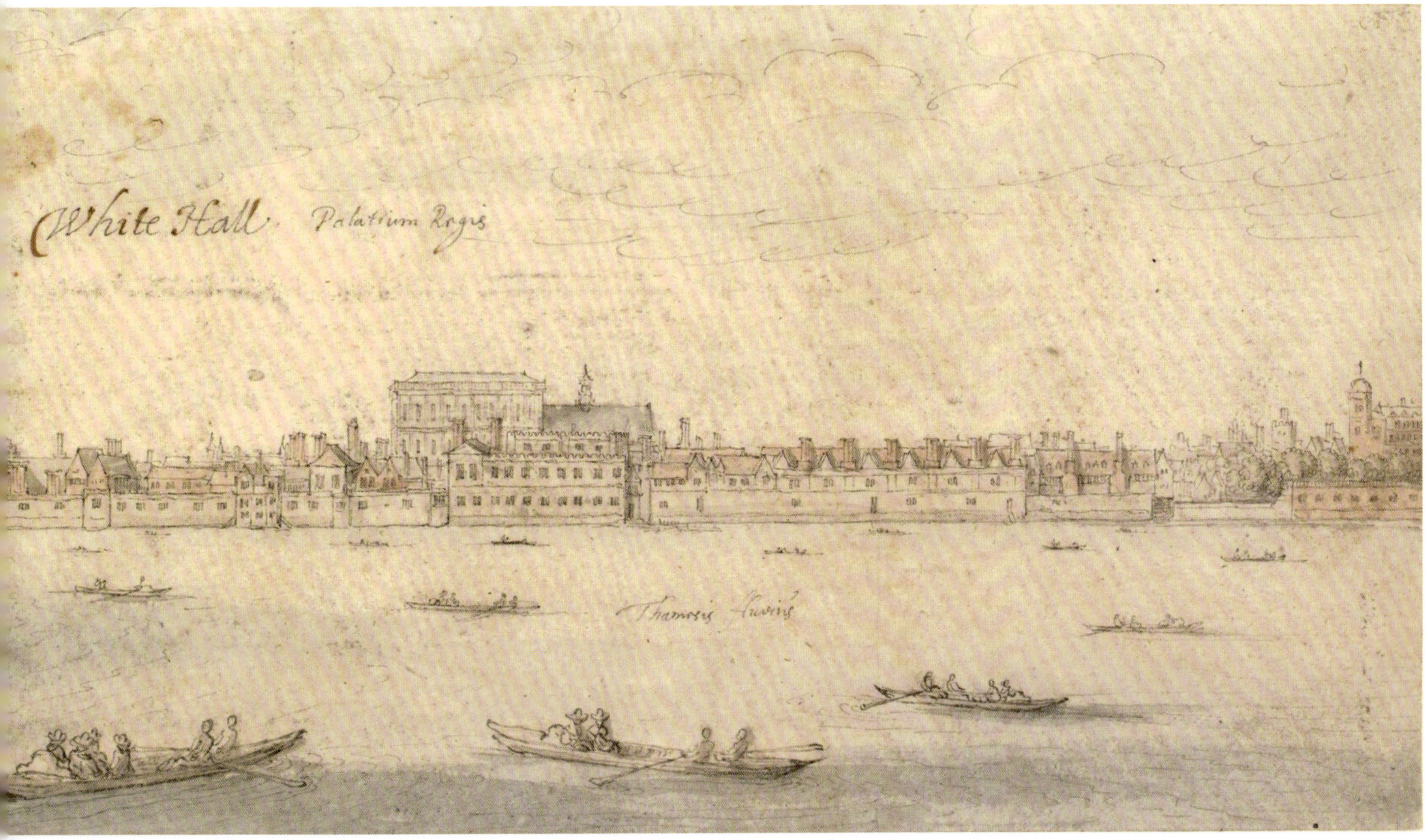
White Hall
Palatium Regis

2
François Dieussart
Charles I, 1636
Marble, height 86.5 cm
The Duke of Norfolk,
Arundel Castle

3
Anthony van Dyck
Charles I in Three Positions, 1635–36
Oil on canvas, 84.4 x 99.4 cm
The Royal Collection / HM Queen
Elizabeth II, RCIN 404420

4
Peter Paul Rubens
Self-portrait, 1623
Oil on panel, 85.7 x 62.2 cm
The Royal Collection / HM Queen Elizabeth II, RCIN 400156

5
Anthony van Dyck
Self-portrait with a Sunflower, *c.* 1633
Oil on canvas, 61.5 x 75.2 cm
Private collection

6
Anthony van Dyck
Inigo Jones, 1632–36
Black chalk and pen and brown ink on paper, 24.4 x 20.1 cm
The Trustees of the Chatsworth Settlement, inv. 1002a

7
Daniel Mytens
Self-portrait, *c.* 1630
Oil on panel, 68.3 x 58.9 cm
The Royal Collection / HM Queen
Elizabeth II, RCIN 404431

8
Anthony van Dyck
Endymion Porter, 1628
Oil on canvas, 114.5 x 94 cm
Private collection

9
Anthony van Dyck
Henrietta Maria, 1638
Oil on canvas, 71.7 x 56.3 cm
The Royal Collection / HM Queen
Elizabeth II, RCIN 400159

10
Anthony van Dyck
Thomas Howard, 14th Earl of Arundel, c. 1620–21
Oil on canvas, 102.6 x 79.7 cm
The J. Paul Getty Museum, Los Angeles, inv. 86.PA.532

11
Peter Paul Rubens
George Villiers, 1st Duke of Buckingham, on Horseback, 1625
Oil on panel, 46.6 x 51.7 cm
Kimbell Art Museum, Fort Worth, Texas, inv. AP 1976.08

SPQR DIVO IVLIO CÆSARI D·P·P·P·
SPQR IVLIVS CAESA

2

MADRID AND MANTUA

CHARLES I'S VISIT TO MADRID

GUIDO REBECCHINI

Prince Charles was 22 years old when, in March 1623, his proposed marriage to the Infanta Maria Anna, sister of Philip IV of Spain, took him to Madrid. A lavish reception was staged and Charles must have been struck by the grandeur of the Spanish court: great efforts were made to impress him with its glory and might. At that stage expecting to become part of the Habsburg family, Charles was eager to explore its treasures. Before this, his experience of collecting had been limited to some artworks he had inherited following the premature death of his brother Henry in 1612. In the 1610s, however, it was becoming increasingly fashionable among Jacobean aristocrats to possess works by sixteenth-century Italian artists. Thomas Howard, Earl of Arundel, a passionate collector of paintings and ancient sculptures, had set the pattern at an early stage, travelling extensively in Italy and throughout Europe, and others, such as George Villiers, Duke of Buckingham, followed in his footsteps. Buckingham, who accompanied Prince Charles to Madrid in 1623, had by that time gained extensive experience of collecting, having since the late 1610s been engaged in intense competition with other aristocrats for works by Italian sixteenth-century masters. In this endeavour he focused his attention on pictures by such Venetian painters as Jacopo Bassano, Tintoretto and Titian, including the latter's spectacular *Ecce Homo* (Kunsthistorisches Museum, Vienna).

Charles's eight-month mission to Spain was to prove a monumental failure from a political and diplomatic point of view, since the wedding did not come to pass, but the visit proved fruitful in the development of the Prince's artistic taste. During his sojourn, Charles was shown the palaces of the Spanish Crown and must have been dazzled by the richness of the artistic collections they held. The Escorial alone housed around a thousand paintings, and Philip had as many again in his other residences. Works by Titian were particularly numerous in these collections, since the Venetian painter had served the austere Holy Roman Emperor Charles V for decades, painting religious pictures and portraits for him. Among these was the portrait depicting Charles on horseback at the Battle of Mühlberg (fig. 32), which was eventually to serve as a model for Van Dyck's depiction of the English monarch in around 1637–38 (cat. 74).[1] Titian's association with the Habsburg family did not end with the abdication of Charles V in 1556, but continued under the reign of his heir Philip II, who, like his father, acted as a patron to the Venetian painter. The celebrated series of Titian's mythological *poesie* was among the range of extraordinary paintings Philip received from Venice. Although Titian hardly ever left Venice, his association with the Habsburg family was instrumental in establishing his reputation as the leading painter for the most important European courts. Accordingly, his works were associated with notions of power and authority, and, as the example of Buckingham confirms, were sought after by collectors all over Europe at the beginning of the seventeenth century.

Responding both to the awe he must have felt on first seeing the Habsburg collection, and to the expert guidance of Buckingham, Charles started to buy paintings on the open market at public sales in Madrid; at one, he managed to acquire Titian's *Woman with a Fur Coat* (fig. 13) and the so-called *'Allegory of Alfonso d'Avalos'* (cat. 47).[2] In addition, Philip IV gave him Titian's full-length portrait of Charles V (cat. 16) and the so-called *Pardo Venus* (fig. 15), two impressive pictures that exemplified their creator's twofold ability to represent authority and to conjure up delightful sensual scenes. As the prospect of a positive conclusion to the wedding negotiations grew slimmer, Charles narrowly failed to obtain the series of Titian's *poesie*

Fig. 13 Titian (*c.* 1488/90–1576), *Woman with a Fur Coat*, 1535. Oil on canvas, 95.5 x 63.7 cm. Kunsthistorisches Museum, Vienna, inv. GG_89

Fig. 14 Giambologna (1529–1608), *Samson Slaying a Philistine*, 1560–62. Marble, height 210 cm. Victoria and Albert Museum, London, inv. A.7-1954

as a gift. On his way back to England, however, he obtained from the Duke of Lerma, presumably on Philip's orders, Paolo Veronese's *Mars, Venus and Cupid* (cat. 17), an erotic painting probably intended as a substitute for Titian's masterpieces.[3] Along with the Veronese, Charles also received from the Duke Giambologna's *Samson Slaying a Philistine* (fig. 14), which he gave to Buckingham the following year to decorate the fountain at the Duke's residence on the Strand.[4] The taste for Titian's erotic paintings and, more generally, Venetian painters' works seems to have dominated the early collecting interests of Charles, who came back to London with a highly select group of pictures, and a new understanding of the importance of possessing a large and prestigious art collection to convey his own dynasty's power and authority.

Not only did the fame, prestige and exemplary nature of Titian's paintings have a deep impact on Charles's and other British collectors' preferences, but it also affected early seventeenth-century painters all over Europe, who were impressed by the Venetian's exciting handling of colour (not to mention his spectacular international success) and, by emulating his style, sought to draw on his prestige to establish themselves. Diego Velázquez, for instance, who had just been appointed court painter to the young Philip IV (cat. 15) and who also painted a now-lost portrait of Charles during the young prince's visit, was deeply impressed, upon his arrival in Madrid in 1622, by Titian's rich and free application of colour. He adopted this himself with enormous success in his portraits of the royal family, eventually becoming the

'official' portrait painter of the Spanish monarchy. Titian was an equally formative influence for Peter Paul Rubens, who was able to study works by the master in Venice in 1600 and later in Mantua, where he served as painter and agent for Duke Vincenzo I Gonzaga until 1608. During these years Rubens not only saw a remarkable group of paintings by Titian that had been collected by previous generations of Gonzaga dukes at Mantua, but was also exposed to further works by the master when, in 1603, he was sent by Duke Vincenzo I to deliver a number of paintings to the Spanish court in Madrid. Throughout his career, Rubens continued to gain further experience of Titian's paintings, which he often freely copied. While in London in 1629 to negotiate the peace between England and Spain (see pp. 156–61), Rubens produced as a gift for Charles *Peace and War* (cat. 14), a work that, in its erotic allure, animation and deep contrasts, is highly reminiscent of the Venetian colouristic tradition and, in details such as the lit torch, echoes some of the most daring flickering luminous effects produced by the late Titian.

No less affected by Titian's art was Anthony van Dyck (see pp. 150–55), who played a fundamental role in shaping Charles's collecting preferences and taste. Having absorbed and developed the instructive example of Titian as a portrait painter during his formative years, after he settled in London in 1632

Fig. 15 Titian (*c.* 1488/90–1576), *Jupiter and Antiope ('Pardo Venus')*, 1552. Oil on canvas, 196 x 385 cm. Musée du Louvre, Paris, inv. 752

Van Dyck was rapidly raised to the status of court painter to Charles I, receiving exclusive authorisation to portray the King and his family. In this way he acquired the same prerogatives that Titian had enjoyed with Charles V and Philip II, and Velázquez had at the same time obtained for himself in Madrid.

Despite the failure of its official purpose, Charles's trip to Madrid in 1623 seems to have deeply shaped his appreciation of art, and the aesthetic sense that was to characterise his acquisitions. There, he could fully understand the importance of the role that an artist like Titian had played in the establishment of the mighty Habsburg dynasty's image and thereafter not only continued to be an eager collector of his paintings, but also required that his most gifted court painter, Van Dyck, conform to the model of the Venetian master. More broadly, this momentous trip seems to have triggered in Charles an acute awareness of the social and political importance of forming a collection that could stand comparison with those of other European dynasties. This is especially pertinent considering that the Stuart family had been established on the English throne only recently, and that his father and predecessor James had shown comparatively little interest in the visual arts.

‘RARE AND UNIQUE IN THIS WORLD’: MANTEGNA’S ‘TRIUMPH’ AND THE GONZAGA COLLECTION

BARBARA FURLOTTI AND GUIDO REBECCHINI

MANTEGNA AND RUBENS

In 1630 or thereabouts, most likely in Antwerp, Peter Paul Rubens painted a pastiche using elements drawn from Andrea Mantegna’s *Triumph of Caesar* – a scene the northern Italian artist had depicted over nine monumental canvases (cats 25–33). Rubens’s painting (fig. 16) is unusual: it is a reassembly and reworking of three canvases by an anonymous (and rather unskilled) artist who had made a copy of Mantegna’s series. Rubens cut these, stitched them together and painted over them freely.[1] The three canvases that served as support for this intervention formed part of a series of copies, once possibly complete, after Mantegna’s *Triumph*, which Rubens had acquired at an unknown point. Three additional canvases from the same series have been identified in the Národní Galerie, Prague, this time reworked by Rubens’s close collaborator Erasmus Quellinus II (presumably after the master’s death, to make them more marketable).

Rubens had seen Mantegna’s original work in Mantua at the beginning of the seventeenth century, while he was in the service of Duke Vincenzo I Gonzaga as an artistic advisor, diplomatic envoy and painter.[2] Rubens had clearly studied Mantegna’s century-old series carefully, as a beautiful drawing now at the Isabella Stewart Gardner Museum in Boston testifies.[3] The curious painting now in the National Gallery in London, executed long after Rubens had seen the original work, attests to the enduring appeal of Mantegna’s paintings for him, and shows how he used them as a stimulus for engaging creatively with the representation of classical antiquity that they evoked. While looking back at his models, Rubens revitalised their compositions, enlivening the elephants, which now seem to move more freely, and adding new figures, such as the lively young women on the left.[4] In this way, Rubens transformed Mantegna’s antiquarian depiction of Caesar’s triumph into a scene full of life and dynamism.

At around the time Rubens first saw Mantegna’s works in Mantua, the series was transferred, perhaps on the advice of Rubens himself, from its previous location in the Palazzo di San Sebastiano to the most prestigious space for displaying art within the Palazzo Ducale: the so-called Galleria della Mostra. There, artists and connoisseurs could admire them alongside some of the most prized paintings of the Gonzaga collection, including works by Giulio Romano or his workshop (cat. 55), Titian and Dosso Dossi (cat. 54), and more modern pictures such as the *Death of the Virgin* by Caravaggio (fig. 42), which Rubens himself had been instrumental in buying for the Gonzaga in Rome in 1607. Together, this impressive display significantly contributed to spread the fame and prestige of the Mantuan ruling dynasty.[5]

The move from a peripheral palace to the centre of Gonzaga power was the result of a concerted re-evaluation of the *Triumph* in the 1590s, as several sets of copies dating from that period testify. As well as the anonymous series acquired by Rubens, another set of copies was painted in the early 1590s by the Mantuan artist Bernardino Malpizzi: it can perhaps be identified with a set painted in tempera, now in the Kunsthistorisches Museum, Vienna. These copies, or perhaps a similar set, were in turn the basis for the celebrated chiaroscuro woodcuts by Andrea Andreani, dating from between 1595 and 1599 (fig. 17). Moreover, in 1602, the Sienese Ludovico Dondi painted a set of copies in oil on copper.[6] The reputation of Mantegna’s series was secured by a myriad of literary texts written after its completion, in which they were praised fulsomely.[7] Perhaps the most influential among these was Giorgio Vasari’s *Lives of the Artists*. In his otherwise rather

Fig. 16 Peter Paul Rubens (1577–1640), *A Roman Triumph*, *c.* 1630. Oil on canvas, 86.8 x 163.9 cm. The National Gallery, London, inv. NG278

misinformed biographical account of Mantegna, Vasari praised the *Triumph*, which he could have seen in Mantua during his visit in 1541, as 'the best thing that he ever executed'.[8] Vasari indulged himself in describing the plentiful details in the paintings:

> *the perfumes, the incense, the sacrifices, the priests, the bulls crowned for the sacrifice, the prisoners, the booty won by the soldiers, the ranks of the squadrons, the elephants, the spoils, the victories, the cities and fortresses counterfeited in various cars, with an infinity of trophies borne on spears and a variety of helmets and body-armour, head-dresses, and ornaments and vases innumerable.*[9]

For him, Mantegna's works were a precious encyclopaedia of ancient motifs, and he marvelled at the variety and subtlety of their depictions in carefully conceived receding planes. Constantly cited by travellers and frequently mentioned in humanist exchanges and literary texts, the *Triumph* epitomised the riches of the Gonzaga collection. Given that documentation of its execution spans the period from 1485 to perhaps as late as 1506,[10] its intended patron and setting cannot be known for certain. The installation of the series in 1506 in the Palazzo di San Sebastiano, built by Marchese Francesco II Gonzaga, seems to suggest that it was meant to be displayed there from its initial conception, but the possibility exists that it was initiated for Francesco's father, Marchese Federico, for his grand palace, known as Domus Nova.[11] A humanist advisor undoubtedly contributed to the conception of the canvases, for they combine humanist sources that describe ancient triumphs – including Flavio Biondo's *De Roma triumphante* (1479) – and historical texts by Appian, Plutarch, Suetonius and Livy.[12] Yet in the absence of any direct reference either to any member of the Gonzaga family, or to any specific historical event, the paintings' patron and purpose remain difficult to determine. Such indeterminacy has led some to suggest that they were in effect primarily, if not exclusively, intended to represent Mantegna's own artistic triumph – a credible proposal considering that Mantegna used a head of Caesar to seal his personal letters.[13]

DANIEL NIJS AND THE ENGLISH ACQUISITION

With this background in mind, one can imagine the sensational interest the *Triumph* would have attracted when, in 1629, news spread that the nine canvases were among the impressive number of paintings, ancient sculptures (cats 19–24), cameos, engraved crystals and tapestries that had been sold to Charles I.[14] In fact, Mantegna's works were among the very last pieces to be included in the negotiations, which took place over two years, between 1626 and 1628. By the mid-1620s, Charles I was undoubtedly aware of the importance of the Gonzaga collection, which had established itself as one of the richest and most refined European art collections of the time and within which the *Triumph* was the jewel in the crown. First-hand information must have reached him following Lord and Lady Arundel's visit to Mantua in 1613 or 1614, and Lady Arundel's second visit in 1623. However, when Charles I sent his court musician, Nicholas Lanier (figs 9–10), to Italy in 1625 to procure paintings for him, he did not instruct him to look for specific artworks in Mantua, nor to contact the Gonzaga court. It was in fact Daniel Nijs, a Flemish merchant and art broker based in Venice and acquainted with Sir Isaac Wake, ambassador in the Veneto both for the Gonzaga and for England, who directed Lanier to Mantua and wrote him a letter of recommendation. Lanier returned from the visit 'all captured and in ecstasy' and Nijs was sure that his praise of the Gonzaga collection would soon be heard at the English court.[15] Lanier's report might have roused Charles I's interest in the Gonzaga collection, but it was on Nijs's initiative that the sale was negotiated with the Duke of Mantua, and there is no evidence that either Nijs or Lanier ever consulted the King about a single piece in the collection. It seems that Charles I gave his agents carte blanche in the selection of which artworks to buy and in the matter of where to procure them.

Preliminary talks between Duke Ferdinando Gonzaga and the Flemish merchant began in 1626, a few months after Lanier's visit to Mantua. A demanding patron and a collector of highly discriminating taste, Ferdinando devoted considerable energy and money to rearranging the display of his art collection in accordance with contemporary criteria. He may have intended to sell only those few of his paintings that did not meet his taste, or that could not be displayed appropriately.[16] The Duke's sudden death in October 1626, and the subsequent succession of his brother, Vincenzo II, whose temperament was utterly different, drastically changed the terms of the negotiations. Vincenzo II, concerned about the mounting debts of the duchy, agreed to sell a considerable number of his masterpieces to Nijs. Once reassured that the sale would be negotiated in secret and that the paintings would be taken out of Italy to avoid the embarrassing possibility of their being seen hanging in other Italian palaces, he left his officials free to settle the deal. Only Mantegna's *Triumph*, to which the Gonzaga family felt a particularly close attachment, was to be excluded from the sale. According to Nijs, the Duke had just prepared the new space in the Palazzo Ducale for the *Triumph*'s display, and in any case the price attached to it was exorbitant enough to make its acquisition impossible. However, other highly praised paintings were part of this first deal, among them Titian's so-called *Eleven Caesars*, a series of now-lost paintings of Roman emperors,[17] and Correggio's *Venus and Cupid with a Satyr* (fig. 20), *Venus with Mercury and Cupid* (cat. 18) and *Allegories of Vices and Virtue* (figs 18–19), as well as Guido Reni's *Toilet of Venus* (cat. 90). In September 1627, after almost an entire year of intense talks and complex negotiations, a first tranche of the Gonzaga collection arrived in Murano, an island near Venice where Nijs had his warehouse. The following April, the artworks were shipped on from there to England.[18] Some of the finest paintings, among them the two allegories by Correggio, travelled by land with Lanier – a decision that was to prove providential, as many of the pieces sent by sea were damaged during the journey by the leakage of a load of mercury.[19]

Although the *Triumph* was not included in this first purchase, foundations for its acquisition were laid soon afterwards. In September 1627, as the first pictures arrived in Murano, talks began between Nijs and the Mantuan officials regarding the sale of the ancient sculptures accumulated by the Gonzaga over almost two centuries of zealous collecting. The negotiations stalled for several months until once again an unforeseen death (of Vincenzo II on 25 December 1627) sped up the process. The new Duke, Carlo I Gonzaga-Nevers, belonged to a French branch of the family, and his subservience to the King of France made him particularly ill-suited to take over the imperial fiefdom of Mantua. Both the Holy Roman Emperor and the King of Spain opposed his succession, and it became clear that he would have to assert his position through military action. Confronted with the prospect of war and the urgent need for extra cash, Duke Carlo had no choice but to

Fig. 17 Andrea Andreani (1558/59–1629) after Andrea Mantegna (1430–1506), *The Triumph of Caesar*, 1595–99. Woodcut, 37.3 x 37.5 cm. The British Museum, London, inv. 1895,0122.1250

Figs 18–19 Correggio (1489–1534), *Allegory of Virtue* and *Allegory of Vice*, 1528–30. Tempera on canvas, both 148 x 88 cm. Musée du Louvre, Paris, inv. 5926, 5927

agree to sell Nijs the Gonzaga antiquities. The deal was finally closed in August 1628, after several months of negotiations. In such turbulent conditions, it was child's play for the cunning Flemish broker to persuade the Mantuan court to include the *Triumph* in this second consignment. Mantegna's paintings, which had been valued in the Gonzaga inventory of 1626–27 at the hefty price of 8,100 lire (roughly £325) – the highest valuation for any work of art in the collection – left Mantua for Murano in 1629.

Although Nijs had been buying on behalf of Charles I, the final destination of the works was to remain uncertain for a few more months. The total cost of this second sale, including the *Triumph* and the making of a series of copies to replace it, an uncertain number of other paintings and the large collection of antiquities apparently amounted to between 50,000 and 72,000 ducats (£12,500–£18,000).[20] In order to beat any possible competitors to the punch, Nijs had to pay this sum out of his own pocket rather than waiting for Charles I's authorisation (as would have been prudent). The Flemish merchant only wrote to England to convince the King to consent to the acquisition in February 1629, a few months after the deal had been closed. He made his case by exalting the exceptional quality of the pieces, which he described as 'rare and unique in this world', and avowed that all the other paintings in the King's collection were

nothing compared to the *Triumph*. In his letter, he promised to send a set of drawings of the Gonzaga antiquities, usually identified with those gathered in the so-called *Whitehall Album* (cat. 139), and engravings of the *Triumph* – undoubtedly the set by Andreani mentioned above (fig. 17) – so that Charles could personally evaluate the quality of the works. The King promptly backed the purchase, but delayed the settlement of his debts with Nijs, who, understandably anxious given his economically vulnerable position, secretly offered the *Triumph* and the ancient sculptures to the Queen of France, Marie de' Medici, and the powerful Cardinal Richelieu. But these French negotiations came to nothing, and Nijs had no choice but to ship the *Triumph* and the sculptures to England, even though he had not yet been paid. In a final attempt to protect his interests, he kept a handful of works in Murano, possibly as a form of guarantee in the event of a further delay in payment. Among these items were some of the most valuable antiquities, including the so-called *Crouching Venus* (cat. 24) and the two *Sleeping Cupids* attributed to Michelangelo and Praxiteles. Charles did eventually sign the payment order for Nijs, and these last pieces were accordingly sent to England in 1632.[21]

THE 'TRIUMPH' IN ENGLAND

Mantegna's paintings were probably moved to Hampton Court soon after their arrival in England late in 1630.[22] In the Commonwealth Sale inventory of October 1649, they were recorded as having the exceptional value of £1,000.[23] However, they escaped the dispersal that awaited most of the King's possessions because, along with other outstanding works, such as Raphael's tapestry cartoons now displayed at the Victoria and Albert Museum (figs 44–47), they were among the items reserved for the use of the State. Even so, the *Triumph* had very little impact on artists active in England at the time. Mantegna's canvases were products of a very specific court culture, and it seems that once they reached England, they appealed more to rulers as representational and decorative objects than to painters as inspirational models (their poor state of conservation would not have helped in this regard).[24] In this context, Rubens's *Triumph* (fig. 16) is an interesting exception, although, as mentioned above, his work was most likely painted in Antwerp, where Rubens had cultivated his antiquarian interests within a learned circle of fellow artists and humanists, and so was not a direct response to the arrival of the original pictures in England. *The Triumph* was so deeply linked to Mantua and its ruling dynasty that, once removed from the Palazzo Ducale, its original *raison d'être* was largely lost. In the eyes of patrons and artists who enthused – in an entirely different cultural and artistic context – about the sensual brush strokes of Titian and the startling contemporary paintings by the likes of Rubens and Van Dyck, the *Triumph* must have seemed an exotic masterpiece, cold and distant, and difficult to assimilate and appropriate.

Notwithstanding the fact that it did not win the same degree of appreciation in England as it had in Mantua, the *Triumph*'s sale to Charles I may well have saved its nine canvases from destruction. On 18 July 1630, at the peak of the war for the succession to the Duchy of Mantua, imperial troops marched into the city and looted it for fourteen months.[25] The Palazzo Ducale and other Gonzaga residences were raided and their remaining contents – paintings, sculptures, precious hangings and textiles, engraved crystals and inlaid furniture – were either burned or taken away and sold by Imperial troops and their officials. While Mantua was going through one of the darkest pages of its history, the *Triumph* was at least safe in Murano, in Nijs's hands, waiting to be shipped to England.

Fig. 20 Correggio (1489–1534), *Venus and Cupid with a Satyr*, 1524–27. Oil on canvas, 188 x 125 cm. Musée du Louvre, Paris, inv. 42

12
Peter Paul Rubens
Vincenzo II Gonzaga, *c.* 1604–05
Oil on canvas laid down on panel,
67.3 x 57.2 cm
Saltram, The Morley Collection,
inv. NT 872186

13
Anthony van Dyck
Hendrik van den Bergh, 1627–32
Oil on canvas, 114 x 100 cm
Museo Nacional del Prado,
Madrid, inv. P01486

14
Peter Paul Rubens
Minerva Protects Pax from Mars
('Peace and War'), 1629–30
Oil on canvas, 203.5 x 298 cm
The National Gallery, London,
inv. NG46

15
Diego Velázquez
Philip IV, *c.* 1623–24
Oil on canvas, 61.9 x 48.9 cm
Meadows Museum, SMU, Dallas,
Algur H. Meadows Collection,
inv. MM.67.23

16
Titian
Charles V with a Dog, 1533
Oil on canvas, 194 x 112.7 cm
Museo Nacional del Prado,
Madrid, inv. P00409

17
Paolo Veronese
Mars, Venus and Cupid, *c.* 1580–85
Oil on canvas, 165.2 x 126.5 cm
National Galleries of Scotland,
inv. NG 339

18
Correggio
Venus with Mercury and Cupid
('The School of Love'), *c.* 1525
Oil on canvas, 155.6 x 91.4 cm
The National Gallery, London,
inv. NG10

19
Roman
Marcus Aurelius, mid-second century AD
Marble, height 66 cm
The Royal Collection / HM Queen Elizabeth II, RCIN 1296

20
Roman
Faustina the Younger, after AD 161
Marble, height 63 cm
The Royal Collection / HM Queen Elizabeth II, RCIN 1299

21
Roman
Livia Drusilla, mid-second century AD
Marble, height 57.5 cm
The Royal Collection / HM Queen Elizabeth II, RCIN 1300

22
Roman
Antinous, first century AD
Marble, height 87.5 cm
The Royal Collection / HM Queen Elizabeth II, RCIN 1298

23
Roman
Bust of a Young Man, mid-second century AD
Marble, height 68.5 cm
The Royal Collection / HM Queen Elizabeth II, RCIN 1297

24
Roman
Aphrodite ('The Crouching Venus'), second century AD
Marble, height 119 cm
The Royal Collection / HM Queen Elizabeth II, RCIN 69746

25
Andrea Mantegna
The Triumph of Caesar: The Trumpeters, *c.* 1485–1506
Tempera on canvas, 270.3 x 280.7 cm
The Royal Collection / HM Queen Elizabeth II, RCIN 403958

26 *(page 72)*
Andrea Mantegna
The Triumph of Caesar: The Triumphal Carts, *c.* 1485–1506
Tempera on canvas, 270.3 x 281.1 cm
The Royal Collection / HM Queen Elizabeth II, RCIN 403959

27 *(page 73)*
Andrea Mantegna
The Triumph of Caesar: The Trophy Bearers, *c.* 1485–1506
Tempera on canvas, 270.3 x 280.5 cm
The Royal Collection / HM Queen Elizabeth II, RCIN 403960

28 *(page 74)*
Andrea Mantegna
The Triumph of Caesar: The Vase Bearers, *c.* 1485–1506
Tempera on canvas, 269.5 x 280 cm
The Royal Collection / HM Queen Elizabeth II, RCIN 403961

29 *(page 75)*
Andrea Mantegna
The Triumph of Caesar: The Elephants, *c.* 1485–1506
Tempera on canvas, 270 x 280.7 cm
The Royal Collection / HM Queen Elizabeth II, RCIN 403962

30 *(page 76)*
Andrea Mantegna
The Triumph of Caesar: The Corselet Bearers, *c.* 1485–1506
Tempera on canvas, 270.8 x 280.4 cm
The Royal Collection / HM Queen Elizabeth II, RCIN 403963

31 *(page 77)*
Andrea Mantegna
The Triumph of Caesar: The Captives, *c.* 1485–1506
Tempera on canvas, 270 x 280.2 cm
The Royal Collection / HM Queen Elizabeth II, RCIN 403964

32 *(page 78)*
Andrea Mantegna
The Triumph of Caesar: The Musicians, *c.* 1485–1506
Tempera on canvas, 270.2 x 280.5 cm
The Royal Collection / HM Queen Elizabeth II, RCIN 403965

33 *(page 79)*
Andrea Mantegna
The Triumph of Caesar: Julius Caesar on His Chariot, *c.* 1485–1506
Tempera on canvas, 270.4 x 280.7 cm
The Royal Collection / HM Queen Elizabeth II, RCIN 403966

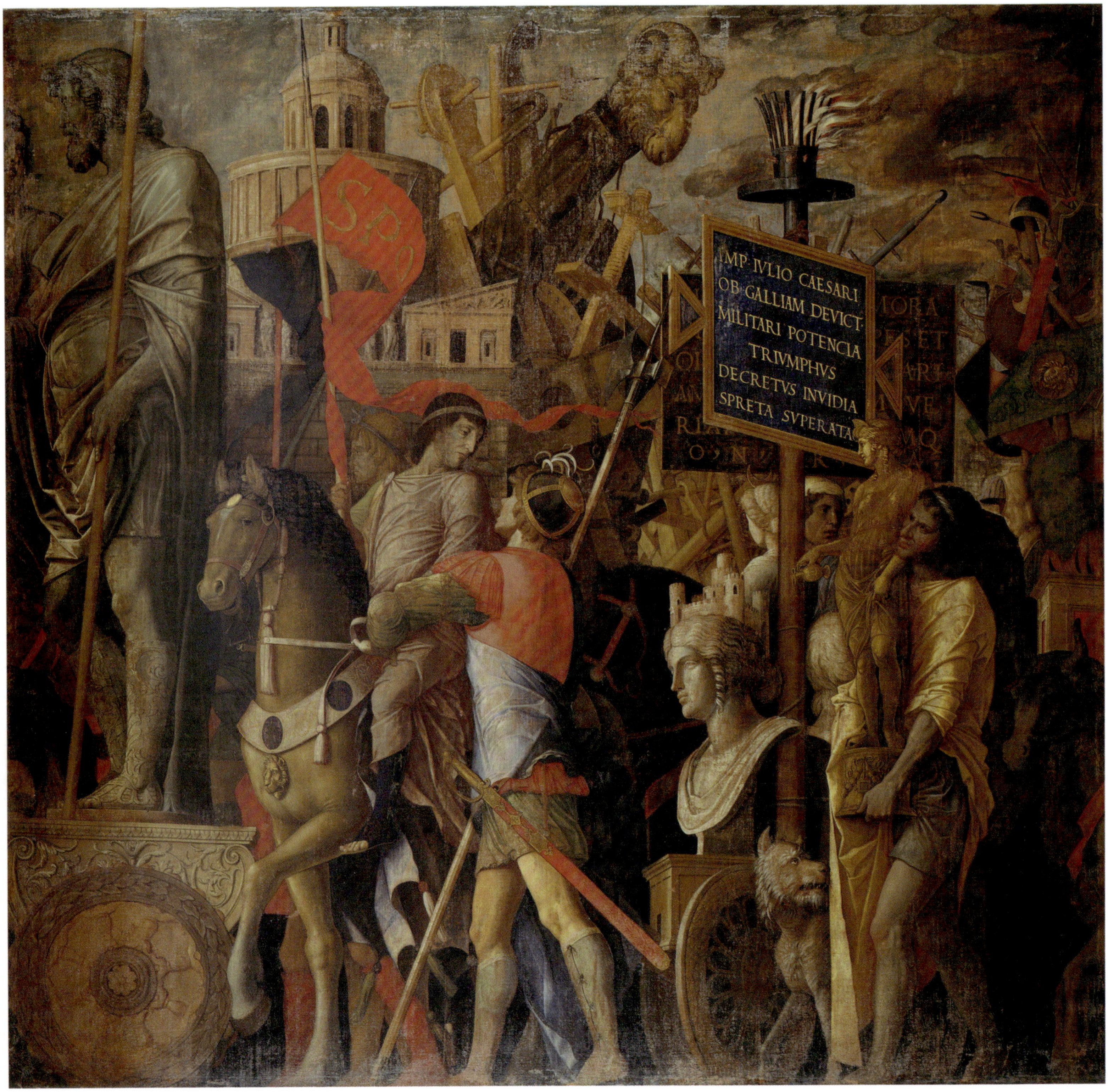
IMP IVLIO CAESARI
OB GALLIAM DEVICT
MILITARI POTENCIA
TRIVMPHVS
DECRETVS INVIDIA
SPRETA SVPERATA

SPQR DIVO IVLIO CÆSARI D·P·P·P·
SPQR IVLIVS CAESAR P·M·

S P Q R
LIBERATORI VRBIS

3

THE NORTHERN RENAISSANCE

CHARLES I AND THE NORTHERN RENAISSANCE

DAVID EKSERDJIAN

Charles I possessed an eye-wateringly illustrious array of Northern Renaissance paintings, of which a distinguished selection features here, but it is far from certain that he loved and appreciated them as much as we may. In consequence, in addition to discussing the nature of his collection, above all concentrating on its highlights, it seems important to try to explain whether it is true that he was surprisingly indifferent to his Northern paintings, and – if so – why.

One major argument in favour of the case for the prosecution, so to speak, is that the pattern of his collecting – and there is no more direct kind of evidence – indicates that as he grew older his enthusiasm for Northern art waned. In his youth Charles I may have taken some interest in early Netherlandish painting and particularly in mid-sixteenth-century portraits, but as his love for Italian – and especially Venetian – painting developed, his taste for painting north of the Alps declined.[1]

A second argument is that it is wrong to suppose that Charles followed the example either of his royal predecessor Henry VIII – who had after all employed Hans Holbein the Younger as his court painter – or indeed of his somewhat older contemporary Thomas Howard, Earl of Arundel. Arundel's diplomatic missions to Germany and Austria had made him very conscious of the art of the greatest of all German Renaissance painters, Albrecht Dürer, and of the cult which surrounded it in Central Europe. Such attention to Northern art must have appeared distinctly old-fashioned to many collectors (including, one suspects, the King).[2] Moreover, whereas Arundel had a deep passion for Holbein, in Charles's case it was above all ancestral piety that motivated his in any event singularly lukewarm enthusiasm for his work.[3]

It is important to recognise, however, that a case for the defence can also be mounted. It has been contended that a duality of taste for Italian and Northern Renaissance art was not only characteristic of the English court under Henry VIII, but also that it survived in the persons of Charles I and the Earl of Arundel, and was not diminished by their taste for the Italian Baroque (see pp. 172–79). Indeed, it has been argued that their admiration for Italian Renaissance art was by no means exclusive, but was matched – or even surpassed by – their enthusiasm for the art of the Northern Renaissance.[4]

Regardless of what one thinks more generally about Charles's taste for Northern Renaissance art – or lack of it – it is to all intents and purposes inevitable that, like any collector at any period, he was a child of his time. One uncomplicated result is that he can have had almost no taste for paintings dating from before around 1500. As has previously been discussed (pp. 54–59), in the Italian context a kind of exception was made for Andrea Mantegna, whose obsessive study and worship of the art of antiquity made him seem ahead of his age, not least in his *Triumph of Caesar* (cats 25–33). More generally, however, the extraordinary achievements of the holy trinity of the early sixteenth century – Leonardo da Vinci, Michelangelo and Raphael – had inadvertently made virtually all that came before seem unacceptably inferior.

Conversely, Charles can only have looked with favour upon such extraordinary masterpieces as the *Wilton Diptych* (fig. 21) and Hugo van der Goes's *Trinity Altarpiece* panels (Royal Collection) by seeing them through the benignly distorting lens of family affection. The former, which includes a portrait of Richard II and on the basis of heraldry may be dated between 1395 and 1399, has a gold leaf background, and – both for that reason and on account of its figure style – must have seemed unforgivably naive.[5] Moreover, the latter, which includes donor portraits of James III, King of Scots, with his son James, and Margaret of Denmark, Queen of Scots, and must have been commissioned in the 1470s and completed before the artist's death in 1482, would have looked resolutely

Fig. 21 English or French, *Richard II Presented to the Virgin and Child by His Patron Saint St John the Baptist and St Edward and St Edmund ('The Wilton Diptych')*, *c.* 1395–99. Tempera and gold on panel, 53 x 37 cm. The National Gallery, London, inv. NG4451

old-fashioned even by comparison with the likes of Dürer and Holbein.[6]

It is not only because they respectively date from the fourteenth and fifteenth centuries that these two pictures differ from almost all Charles's other Northern Renaissance pictures, but also by virtue of their subject-matter. The overwhelming majority of these works were portraits, with the result that the handful of religious, mythological, genre or landscape paintings inevitably stand out.[7] Interestingly, a number of them were in the Gonzaga collection, including two still in the Royal Collection: a fine triptych by Jan Provoost listed by Abraham van der Doort in his 1639 inventory without attribution, and an entirely unremarkable *Massacre of the Innocents* after Pieter Brueghel the Younger, listed by Van der Doort with appropriate caution as 'Said to be of the old Brugill'.[8] The best by far of the Northern haul from Mantua was a small but exquisite triptych of the *Virgin and Child with St Michael, St Catherine and a Donor* by Jan van Eyck (fig. 22), now in the Staatliche Kunstsammlungen in Dresden. Heartbreakingly, neither its tranquil perfection nor its spatial assurance are likely to have attracted Charles's notice, but since it bears the 'CR' brand as well as the date 1437 on its original frame, there can be no doubt concerning its provenance.[9] In terms of Charles's apparent lack of enthusiasm for Northern Renaissance religious pictures, it is very possibly revealing that Holbein's magnificent *'Noli me tangere'* (cat. 44) cannot be traced back to him, but is instead first recorded in the collection of his widow, Henrietta Maria, and then passed to Charles II on her death in 1669.[10] Be that as it may, its arresting power is immediately apparent, above all in the intensity of the central encounter between the risen Christ and Mary Magdalene, but also in the romantic drama of the cloud-flecked sky beyond, and the highly unusual vignette of the two angels glimpsed within the light-filled sepulchre at bottom right.

For all the qualities of these works by Van Eyck and Holbein, by far the most sheerly impressive of all the religious paintings, not least for its monumental scale, is the panel of *Adam and Eve* of around 1520 by Jan Gossaert (cat. 34), better known as Mabuse after his place of birth, the town now called Maubeuge in Northern France.[11] *Adam and Eve* was a favourite subject of Mabuse's, and in fact there is also a fractionally larger variation on the theme by him in the Gemäldegalerie in Berlin, but – in spite of its almost balletic energy – it cannot compete with the overwhelming sense of looming tragedy that dominates Charles's picture, as our first parents gaze deep into one another's eyes and Adam meditatively sucks the index finger of his right hand.[12] To a modern eye, it may look strikingly Italianate for a Netherlandish picture – and Mabuse had indeed lived in Rome in 1508–09 – but it is less clear that it would have seemed so to seventeenth-century viewers. In any event, it was not Charles's only work by Mabuse; it was complemented by a group portrait of the children of Christian II of Denmark (Royal Collection), by the *Man Holding a Glove* (cat. 97), which were respectively in the Privy Gallery and the Cabinet Room at Whitehall Palace, and by an untraced painting listed as 'An old man: don by Mabuse' at Hampton Court.[13] By an odd coincidence, the other great Netherlandish Renaissance portraits were two pairs: Joos van Cleve's *Self-portrait* with his wife, Katlijne (bought by Charles from 'a Dutch Merchant Called David Kint' and since the Restoration back in the Royal Collection; cats 40–41), and Quinten Massys's portraits of Desiderius Erasmus (cat. 95) and Pieter Gillis (cat. 96).[14] In neither case is the artist exactly a household name, but these affectionate and probing likenesses are without question among their supreme achievements, and underline quite how accomplished such masters could be.

Mabuse's *Adam and Eve* was part of the so-called 'Dutch Gift' to the King, one of four paintings presented to him in March 1636 by the States of Holland, along with various other items, including seven white carriage horses, a clock, a mother-of-pearl casket and a mass of ambergris.[15] Two of the other paintings were a pair of panels by Geertgen tot Sint Jans representing the *Lamentation* and the extremely rare subject of the *Burning of the Bones of St John the Baptist* (both now in the Kunsthistorisches Museum, Vienna).[16] Geertgen was an

Fig. 22 Jan van Eyck (active 1422, d. 1441), *Virgin and Child with St Michael, St Catherine and a Donor*, 1437. Oil on panel, 33 x 27.5 cm (central panel) and 33 x 13.5 cm (side panels). Staatliche Kunstsammlungen, Dresden, inv. 799

Figs 23–24 Lucas Cranach the Elder (1472–1553), *Johannes Cuspinian* and *Anna Cuspinian*, 1502. Oil on panel, both 60.3 x 45.5 cm. Oskar Reinhart Collection 'Am Römerholz', Winterthur, inv. 1925-1b, 1925-1a

immensely gifted late fifteenth-century artist, from Haarlem in what is now Holland, who died young, and these works, which formed the right wing of his celebrated high altarpiece for the Chapel of the Knights of St John in his native city, are virtually the only ones indisputably by him. Memorably described by Lorne Campbell as 'among the most beautiful [pictures] executed in the Low Countries in the fifteenth century', they reveal Geertgen to have been a compelling portraitist and at the same time a painter of quirkily idiosyncratic religious narratives.[17] The last element of the 'Dutch Gift' was a *St Jerome* said to be by Lucas van Leyden, but in all probability to be identified with a picture of the same subject attributed to Aertgen van Leyden in the Rijksmuseum, Amsterdam, which perfectly matches the extremely detailed description given by Van der Doort.[18] Charles almost at once gave the two panels by Geertgen to the Marquess of Hamilton, who was one of the most notable collectors in his circle, but held on to the *Adam and Eve* and the *St Jerome*.[19]

Reference has been made above to the fact that works left Charles's collection through both gifts and exchanges. In the case of the Geertgen panels, he received in return two paintings – an *Adam and Eve* and a *Portrait of Martin Luther* – by Lucas Cranach the Elder, the only works by the artist he ever owned (apart from a pair of portraits of the historian Dr Johannes Cuspinian and his wife Anna; figs 23–24).[20] Neither the *Adam and Eve* nor the *Luther* appears to have survived, but numerous versions of both subjects by the artist are known, and give a good impression of how they must have looked.[21] In much the same spirit, he parted with Holbein's *Portrait of Erasmus* (Musée du Louvre, Paris), and an untraced Titian *Madonna*, formerly owned by the poet John Donne, in order to obtain Leonardo's *St John the Baptist*, now also in the Louvre (fig. 52), from the Duc de Liancourt, which for once looks to have been a smart move.[22] Arguably the most shocking quid pro quo of all saw Charles hand over an entire volume of portrait drawings by Holbein (including cats 98, 100–02) to Philip Herbert, 4th Earl of Pembroke, admittedly in exchange for a painting by Raphael of *St George and the Dragon* (fig. 53).[23] By an odd trick of fate, the drawings made their way back into the Royal Collection, while

Fig. 25 Albrecht Dürer (1471–1528), *Self-portrait*, 1498. Oil on panel, 52 x 41 cm. Museo Nacional del Prado, Madrid, inv. P02179

the Raphael – after travelling as far afield as St Petersburg – has ended up in the National Gallery of Art in Washington, D.C.[24]

The Earl of Pembroke swiftly passed the Holbein drawings on to Arundel, his brother-in-law, whose passion for the artist's works knew no bounds.[25] In fact, Arundel also obtained other works by Holbein directly from Charles, of which the most notable were the *Triumph of Riches* and the *Triumph of Poverty*, two large-scale decorative paintings executed on fine linen, and now known only in the form of preliminary studies and later copies.[26] All told, the inventory of Arundel's collection runs to a mind-boggling 44 paintings by Holbein, including further masterpieces such as the now-lost group portrait of the *Family of Sir Thomas More* and the portrait of *Christina of Denmark*, now in the National Gallery in London, and very possibly the portrait of *Derich Born* (cat. 37).[27]

By comparison to the wealth of them in Arundel's collection, if not by any other standard, the few Holbeins that were still in Charles's possession at the time of his death may seem relatively modest. Nevertheless, the three now in the Royal Collection and included here are all immensely powerful living presences. The first in terms of its date of execution is the portrait of *Johannes Froben* (cat. 36), which was executed in around 1522–23.[28] Froben, also known as Johannes Frobenius, was one of the most celebrated of all Renaissance printers. Like Holbein, whom he employed to provide woodcuts for a number of his books, he was based in Basel, and was an extremely close friend of Erasmus, many of whose works he printed. Next comes the portrait of *'Hans of Antwerp'* (cat. 38), which is dated 1532 on the letter in front of the mysterious sitter, and last but by no means least there is *William Reskimer* (cat. 99) of much the same date.[29] In this final instance, the existence of a preparatory drawing of the subject (cat. 98) demonstrates how unerringly faithfully Holbein translated his likeness into paint.

All in all, and most unusually, Charles's German Renaissance pictures were unarguably even better than his Netherlandish ones, not just because of his Cranachs and Holbeins, but perhaps above all because of his Dürers. These too came his way in 1636, a golden year for Charles in terms of acquisitions, and were gifts from the City of Nuremberg, delivered by Arundel, for whom their collection in November 1635 and subsequent surrender on 18 March of the following year must have bordered on torture, given how much more he cared for them than did his sovereign.[30] They represent another intimate pairing: a self-portrait of Albrecht Dürer himself on the left (fig. 25), together with a portrait of his father, Albrecht Dürer senior. Both originally had rhyming inscriptions identifying the sitters and giving their respective ages (26 and 70). Both the portraits given to Charles survive, but – like the Massys diptych discussed above – are no longer together. The former, which is dated 1498, is now in the Prado in Madrid, while the latter, which is considerably less well preserved and whose autograph status is currently doubted, is dated 1497 and is in the National Gallery in London.[31] If the panel in London is not by Dürer, then evidently the now-lost original of which it must be a copy and the self-portrait had gone their separate ways by 1627, when they are first recorded, if not before. In any event, they must always have made a somewhat ill-matched pair, since the ledge on which Dürer rests his arms, not to mention the corner of the room and the sliver of landscape glimpsed through the window, strike a jarring note against the uniform backdrop behind his father. On the other hand, the contrast between the fearless confidence and peacock swagger of youth and the unflinchingly dogged seriousness of old age must have been entirely deliberate. As if this were not enough, Charles also owned Dürer's splendid portrait of *Burkhard of Speyer* (cat. 35).

For all that Charles actually acquired works either by or attributed to such later figures as Antonis Mor, Adriaen Thomasz. Key and Willem Key, the lion's share of his Northern Renaissance collection dated from the first half of the sixteenth century.[32] An enchanting exception with which to conclude this survey is Pieter Bruegel the Elder's *Three Soldiers* (cat. 42), curiously given by Van der Doort to 'Pieter Bruegel the Younger', which is signed and dated 1568. Virtually square, it measures a mere eight inches by seven, and is painted in grisaille on an oak panel.[33] It is hard to imagine anyone not succumbing to its charm, but then again – as we know only too well – Charles I was not anyone.

580

34
Jan Gossaert
Adam and Eve, *c.* 1520
Oil on panel, 169.2 x 112 cm
The Royal Collection / HM Queen Elizabeth II, RCIN 407615

35
Albrecht Dürer
Burkhard of Speyer, 1506
Oil on panel, 31.7 x 26 cm
The Royal Collection / HM Queen Elizabeth II, RCIN 404418

36
Hans Holbein the Younger
Johannes Froben, *c.* 1522–23
Oil on panel, 48.8 x 32.4 cm
The Royal Collection / HM Queen Elizabeth II, RCIN 403035

37
Hans Holbein the Younger
Derich Born, 1533
Oil on panel, 60.3 x 44.9 cm
The Royal Collection / HM Queen Elizabeth II, RCIN 405681

38
Hans Holbein the Younger
'Hans of Antwerp', 1532
Oil on panel augmented with canvas, 63 x 48.4 cm
The Royal Collection / HM Queen Elizabeth II, RCIN 404443

39
Hans Holbein the Younger
Robert Cheseman, 1533
Oil on panel, 58.8 x 62.8 cm
Mauritshuis, The Hague, inv. 276

40
Joos van Cleve
Self-portrait, *c*. 1535–40
Oil on panel, 64.7 x 50.8 cm
The Royal Collection / HM Queen
Elizabeth II, RCIN 405780

41
Joos van Cleve
Katlijne van Mispelteeren
(The Artist's Wife), *c*. 1535–40
Oil on panel, 64.7 x 50.3 cm
The Royal Collection / HM Queen
Elizabeth II, RCIN 405779

42
Pieter Bruegel the Elder
Three Soldiers, 1568
Oil on panel, 20.3 x 17.8 cm
The Frick Collection, New York,
inv. 1965.1.163

43
Hans Vredeman de Vries
Christ in the House of Martha and Mary, 1566
Oil on panel, 79.4 x 109.2 cm
The Royal Collection / HM Queen Elizabeth II, RCIN 405475

44
Hans Holbein the Younger
'Noli me tangere', 1526–28
Oil on panel, 76.7 x 95.8 cm
The Royal Collection / HM Queen
Elizabeth II, RCIN 400001

4

THE ITALIAN RENAISSANCE

CHARLES I AND THE ITALIAN RENAISSANCE

DAVID EKSERDJIAN

It is not hard to see why Charles I has been described as the owner of 'the finest collection of pictures ever assembled in this country'.[1] What is more – in spite of the merits of the collection's countless other riches – in the end it is arguably its holdings of Italian Renaissance art that set it above all possible rivals, and these works do also seem to have been the King's true passion.

As is discussed elsewhere in this volume, Charles shared this taste with a number of prominent and slightly older collectors, such as Thomas Howard, Earl of Arundel, and George Villiers, Duke of Buckingham.[2] He was also profoundly influenced both by the enthusiasms of his short-lived older brother, Henry,[3] and by his visit to Madrid in 1623, which had the effect of ensuring that – as far as he was concerned – no painter could hope to rival Titian in his affections.[4]

The King's virtual addiction to the works of Titian has to be seen in the context of his more general admiration of Venetian painting after 1500, which will be returned to in due course, but what needs to be made clear at the outset is that as a rule his conception of the pecking order among Italian artists of the sixteenth century was entirely in conformity with the attitudes of his age. In truth, this is wholly to be expected, but what may seem distinctly surprising is the degree to which – with only occasional and invariably slight ups and downs – the goalposts have pretty much failed to shift ever since.

This is above all because the roll of honour established in Giorgio Vasari's *Lives of the Artists*, first published in 1550 and then again in a considerably enlarged edition in 1568, has stood the test of time so remarkably well.[5] It has to be admitted that the *Lives* betray a definite bias in favour of Tuscan art, and central Italian art more generally, but its extent is often exaggerated, and it did not blind their author to the merits of the best painters active elsewhere in Italy. In the main, therefore, Vasari's judgements concerning which artists were the greatest of their various ages still seem entirely sound, but the same can no longer be said for his relative disdain for the art of previous centuries. In Vasari's account, art is seen in evolutionary terms and reaches a kind of perfection in the person of Michelangelo, with the result that even the greatest geniuses of the fourteenth and fifteenth centuries cannot begin to compare with their sixteenth-century successors. Inevitably, we feel compelled to part company with him on this point, but for Charles I and his contemporaries it seemed only natural to follow his lead unquestioningly.

In consequence, as far as Charles was concerned, the Italian Renaissance really began around 1500. The main exception to this unwritten rule in terms of his collection were the works of Andrea Mantegna. Even so, had it not been for his acquisition *en bloc* of the Gonzaga collection (see pp. 54–59), Mantegna would no doubt scarcely have featured on the King's radar. As it was, however, it was in essence the *Triumph of Caesar* (cats 25–33) that made all the difference, since – for all its undoubted beauty – a work such as his significantly earlier *Death of the Virgin* (fig. 54) was representative of an earlier age. Conversely, the *Triumph* canvases, though begun in the 1480s, were probably not finished until the early 1500s, and – better yet, from the King's point of view – possessed the additional merit of looking forward to the art of the next generation.[6]

As far as Vasari was concerned, the transformation of art was accomplished at the outset of the sixteenth century by a

Fig. 26 Gianfrancesco Penni (*c.* 1496–after 1528), *Holy Family with St John the Baptist and St Catherine*, 1510s. Oil on panel, 115.5 x 95 cm. National Museum in Warsaw, from the collection of the Potocki family in Krzeszowice and Krakow, inv. M.Ob.601

triumvirate of unrivalled distinction: Leonardo da Vinci, Michelangelo, and Raphael. For Charles, obtaining works by them was formidably difficult, because they had long been accorded semi-divine status by the time he came on the scene as a collector. It should come as no great surprise, therefore, if – at least in terms of sheer numbers – the outcomes were distinctly uneven.

In the case of Leonardo, there were two all but insurmountable problems. The first was that Leonardo was notoriously unproductive, which meant that his *oeuvre* was painfully small, and the second was that the lion's share of it was in the French royal collection. It is true that the Duke of Buckingham had had the nerve to attempt to purchase none other than the *Mona Lisa* from that very source, but of course he had got nowhere.[7] The King made no such overtures to his fellow monarch, but did incomparably better, because he actually managed to acquire an autograph painting by the master, his darkly mysterious late *St John the Baptist* (fig. 52).[8] It cost him a Titian and a Holbein portrait, but there can be no doubt that he felt he got the better end of the bargain.[9]

There was absolutely no possibility of obtaining a picture by Michelangelo: as a consequence of his notorious reluctance to paint, the only entirely secure work by his hand not in fresco was the *Doni Tondo*, now in the Uffizi in Florence, with which the Medici would never have parted. On the other hand, almost miraculously Charles did own a sculpture in marble by Michelangelo. This was his early *Sleeping Cupid*, which belonged to Cardinal Raffaele Riario in Rome as early as 1496, at which point – as a result of a suggestion made by the artist's Florentine patron, Lorenzo di Pierfrancesco de' Medici, to the effect that the subterfuge would increase its commercial value – it was masquerading as an antiquity. That very year, letters between Isabella d'Este and an agent prove that she was interested in acquiring it, but in the end did not do so, perhaps because it had been outed as a modern counterfeit. Then, in 1502 it was given to her by Cesare Borgia, the son of the reigning pope, Alexander VI. Isabella was evidently enchanted with it, and commented that 'for a modern piece it has no equals'.[10] Tragically, when it reached London from Mantua, its importance appears to have been forgotten, and its ultimate fate is unknown.[11] There is no evidence of its having been destroyed: in theory, therefore, it may still be waiting to be rediscovered.

An impressive number of the star items in the King's collection came from the Gonzaga collection, but by no means everything derived from that source. The most striking case in point are Raphael's tapestry cartoons (figs 44–47), which Charles was pursuing even before his life-changing visit to Spain in 1623. A letter he wrote home from Madrid on 28 March of that year asking for money referred to 'certaine patterns to be brought out of Italy, and sent to us into England for the making thereby a Suite of Tapestry'.[12] It seems clear that in this instance the cartoons were intended from the outset to serve a practical function, and it was in all probability this that led to their retention by the Council of State after Charles's fall and execution.[13]

Another non-Gonzaga Raphael was the *St George and the Dragon* (fig. 53), which the King acquired from the Earl of Pembroke, who received a number of drawings by Holbein in exchange (including cats 98, 100–02).[14] This is one of the most commanding works of the artist's Florentine period, but is on an intimate scale, and was subsequently to be complemented by a significantly larger late panel representing the *Virgin and Child with St Anne and the Infant St John the Baptist* (fig. 4), which did indeed come from the Gonzaga. This work subsequently came to be known as *La Perla*, reputedly because its next owner, Philip IV of Spain, declared it to be the 'pearl' of his collection.[15] Be that as it may, it was already immensely highly esteemed when it was in Charles's collection, and was initially valued at £2,000 at the time of the Commonwealth Sale, although ultimately the crafty Spanish diplomat, Alonso de Cárdenas, bought it for a mere half of the asking price.[16]

In the intervening centuries, as is so often the way with old masters, *La Perla* has not always been accepted as an autograph production by Raphael, but at least for the time being it is wholly back in favour.[17] Considering such fluctuations in any given work's status, the crucial thing to bear in mind when seeking to understand its value – both emotional and financial – within a particular collection is what it was believed to be at the time, regardless of what it is now deemed to be. This point is no less relevant when it comes to the *Virgin and Child with the Infant St John the Baptist* (cat. 49). It, too, was purchased by Cárdenas, who would surely not have entertained the slightest suspicion of its not being by Raphael. From today's perspective, it seems clear enough that all previous ages erred on the side of over-optimism when it came to attributing works to great masters, but no less importantly the fact that the picture in question is currently thought to be the work of Raphael's pupil, Gianfrancesco Penni, must not be allowed to mean we go to the opposite extreme and fail to appreciate its undoubted merits.[18] The quality of Penni's work is clear in his *Holy Family* (fig. 26), purchased by Charles I as part of the Gonzaga acquisition.

In terms of the art-historical hit parade, although Correggio is still immensely highly esteemed, he no longer shares the top spot with Raphael, as he did in earlier centuries.[19] In the early seventeenth century, however, he was absolutely revered, and Charles's collection was thought to boast no fewer than nine paintings by him. Of these, the *Allegory of Virtue* and the *Allegory of Vice* (figs 18–19) had been added to the *studiolo* of Isabella d'Este by Correggio in around 1528–30. Most

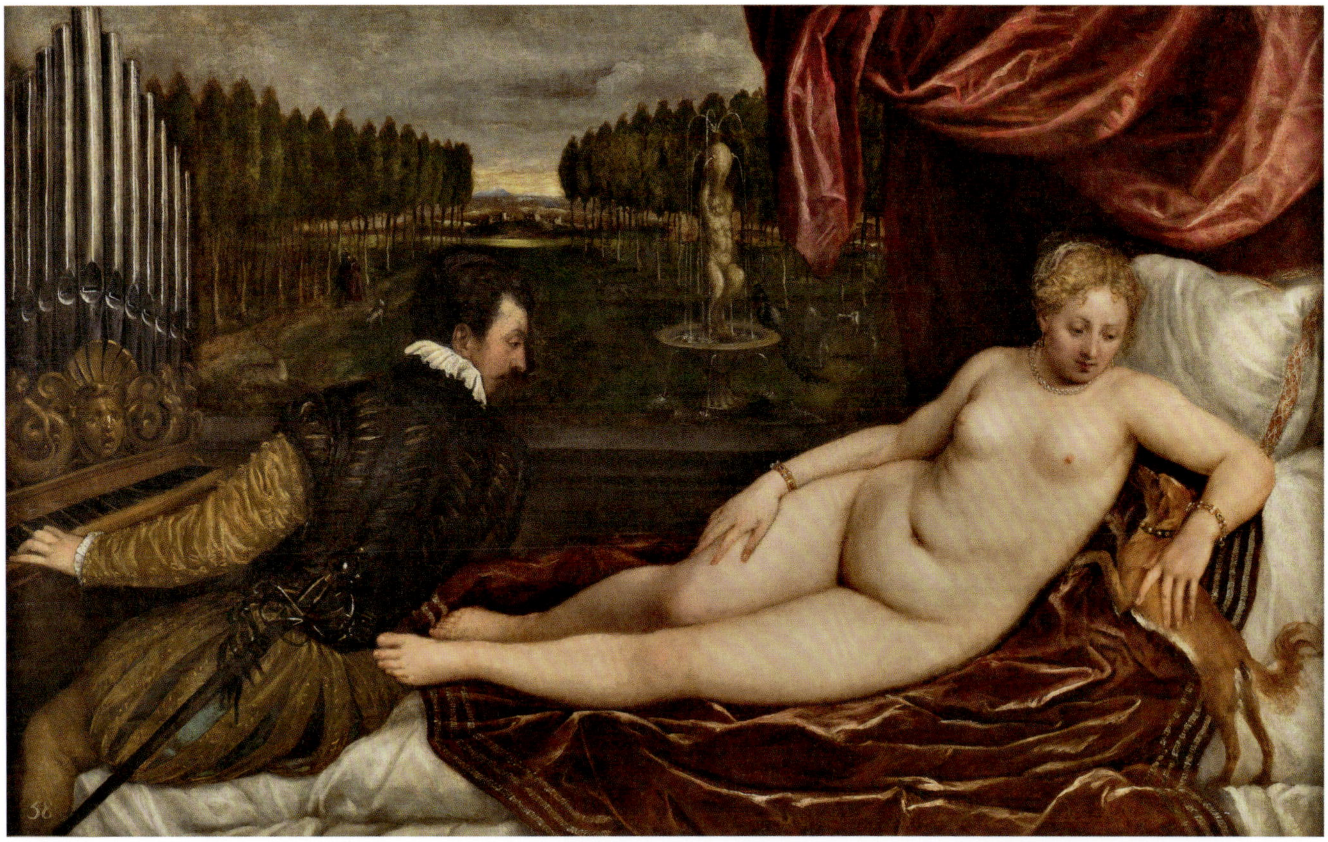

Fig. 27 Titian (*c.* 1488/90–1576), *Venus and Music*, *c.* 1550. Oil on canvas, 138 x 222.4 cm. Museo Nacional del Prado, Madrid, inv. P00420

unusually for this slightly later period, the artist executed them in tempera as opposed to oil in an attempt to harmonise them with the earlier group of works in the *studiolo* dating from around 1500, although they must still have created a jarring impression on account of their relative opulence of form and boldness of touch.[20]

The *Allegories* were not the only non-religious pictures by Correggio owned by the King, but were joined by another, somewhat earlier pair of canvases, which must date from the mid-1520s. Although they do not have the same dimensions, and never can have, they are first recorded in Mantua, in the collection of Count Nicola Maffei, who was a close associate of Marchese Federico Gonzaga, and were then owned by Maffei's grandson in 1589 before eventually reaching the Gonzaga collection in time to be part of its purchase by Charles. In spite of the discrepancies of scale, their subject-matter, not to mention their history, both support the idea that they were conceived as a pair. In the one that has come to be known as the *School of Love* (cat. 18), Venus is shown – in the company of her son, Cupid, and his father, Mercury – with wings, which allude to her celestial status. Conversely, its counterpart in the Louvre, the *Venus and Cupid with a Satyr* (fig. 20), portrays the sleeping goddess being unveiled for our delectation and reclining in a pose of blatantly earthly sexual abandon.[21]

At least one other work by Correggio, his *Holy Family with the Infant St John the Baptist* (Musée des Beaux-Arts, Orléans), datable to around 1518–19, must have been in Charles's collection, since it has the 'CR' brand on its reverse.[22] In all probability, it was accompanied by the compositionally and stylistically very similar *Holy Family with St Jerome* (cat. 52), which seems to date from the beginning of the 1520s, but is not absolutely securely identifiable within the inventories compiled prior to the Civil War.[23] The same goes for Correggio's half-length of *St Catherine Reading* (cat. 53), first recorded in the collection of James II, a canvas that must date from after 1530.[24]

Before concluding with some observations concerning Charles's love of sixteenth-century Venetian paintings, it is worth underlining the fact that some of the finest pictures in his collection were by Florentine artists. In the case of a memorable trio of portraits, respectively by Franciabigio (cat. 50), Puligo (Royal Collection) and Bronzino (cat. 51), it would appear that at the time all three were believed to be by the then more admired Andrea del Sarto, who even today is a bigger name than the first two, if not perhaps than Bronzino.[25] Only the first depicts a male sitter, and represents an identifiable individual; it is monogrammed and dated 1523, and must be a work recorded by Vasari, who explains that the subject was the '*fattore*' (steward) of Pierfrancesco di Lorenzo de' Medici (1487–1525).[26] In contrast, we have not a clue whom either of the two female portraits represents, but they both give the impression of being actual likenesses, and not simply idealised beauties of a type by no means uncommon at the time.

Titian was the Venetian painter the King adored above all others. Precisely what he admired is not easy to evaluate, but we may suspect it was both the sheer quality of his works and the range of his accomplishments. Here Titian emerges as a superlatively versatile genius. In the *Supper at Emmaus* (cat. 45), he displays his mastery as a religious artist, bringing to life the grand drama of revelation in a manner that directly foreshadows Caravaggio, but at the same time delighting in the playful skirmish between a cat and a dog under the table. In both the *Allocution of Alfonso d'Avalos to His Troops* and the *Conjugal Allegory* (cats 46–47), he combines acutely penetrating individual portraiture with a sense of the bigger picture, whether historical or allegorical. Last but not least, in the *Venus and Music* in the Prado (fig. 27) he creates an intensely erotic mythology, in which the intimate bedroom scene is set against an expansive pastoral backdrop, and there can be no doubt about the direction of the amorous musician's enraptured gaze. Amusingly enough, it would appear that one of Charles I's many Titians was actually a signed canvas by the Brescian painter Girolamo Savoldo representing the *Virgin Adoring the Christ*

Fig. 28 Paolo Veronese (1528–1588), *The Finding of Moses*, *c.* 1580. Oil on canvas, 57 x 43 cm. Museo Nacional del Prado, Madrid, inv. P00502

Child with Two Donors (Royal Collection), which seems to correspond to a work in Charles's collection 'done by Tytsian'.[27] It kept company with a considerable number of paintings by members of the Bassano family on themes both sacred and secular, of which the most impressive – and not just on account of its scale – is Jacopo's *Adoration of the Shepherds* (cat. 58), whose composition is in part inspired by an invention of Titian's made popular by a woodcut after it by Giovanni Britto.[28]

In conclusion, we should note that the King also owned works of real distinction by Titian's closest rivals of the younger generation, namely Tintoretto and Veronese. Fate has decreed that in the finest of their pictures still in the Royal Collection, Tintoretto operates on a monumental scale, both in his *Esther before Ahasuerus* (cat. 57) and in his *Muses*, whereas – at least by comparison – Veronese comes across as a virtual miniaturist in his *David* and *Judith*. Between them, all these works – and others such as Veronese's *Finding of Moses* (fig. 28) and Tintoretto's *Abduction of Helen* (fig. 29) and – demonstrate the continuing vitality of Venetian painting and the thrilling bravura of its brushwork right up to the end of the sixteenth century, and give no sense of the artistic decline that was so soon to ensue. Moreover, the last gasp of the Venetian Renaissance was represented by a pair of exceptionally fine canvases depicting the *Triumph of David* (cat. 60) and the

Fig. 29 Jacopo Tintoretto (1518–1594), *The Abduction of Helen*, 1578–79. Oil on canvas, 186 x 307 cm. Museo Nacional del Prado, Madrid, inv. P00399

Conversion of St Paul (cat. 61) by Palma Giovane, who had been entrusted with the daunting task of completing Titian's final *Pietà* (Gallerie dell'Accademia, Venice). Charles I was also a passionate collector of the works of the leading Italian painters of his own century, but when it came to what – for him – was modern art, it was above all to Bologna and Rome that he looked for masterpieces.

45
Titian
The Supper at Emmaus, *c.* 1534
Oil on canvas, 169 x 244 cm
Musée du Louvre, Paris, inv. 746

46
Titian
The Allocution of Alfonso d'Avalos to His Troops, 1540–41
Oil on canvas, 223 x 165 cm
Museo Nacional del Prado, Madrid, inv. P00417

47
Titian
Conjugal Allegory ('The Allegory of Alfonso d'Avalos'), *c.* 1530–35
Oil on canvas, 121 x 107 cm
Musée du Louvre, Paris, inv. 754

48
Lorenzo Costa
Virgin and Child, *c.* 1520–30
Oil on panel, 53.2 x 37.8 cm
Private collection

49
Circle of Raphael
Virgin and Child with the Infant St John the Baptist ('The Bankes Madonna'), 1516–17
Oil on panel, 76 x 53.3 cm
Kingston Lacy, The Bankes Collection, inv. NT 1257083

50
Franciabigio
Jacopo Cennini
('Il Fattore'), 1523
Oil on panel, 65.4 x 49.6 cm
The Royal Collection / HM Queen
Elizabeth II, RCIN 405766

51
Agnolo Bronzino
Portrait of a Woman in Green,
c. 1530–32
Oil on panel, 76.6 x 66.2 cm
The Royal Collection / HM Queen
Elizabeth II, RCIN 405754

52
Correggio
The Holy Family with St Jerome, *c.* 1519
Oil on panel, 68.9 x 56.6 cm
The Royal Collection / HM Queen
Elizabeth II, RCIN 400029

53
Correggio
St Catherine Reading, *c.* 1530–32
Oil on canvas, 64.5 x 52.2 cm
The Royal Collection / HM Queen
Elizabeth II, RCIN 405768

54
Dosso Dossi
Virgin and Child with Saints, *c.* 1527–28
Oil on canvas, 169.7 x 172.7 cm
The Royal Collection / HM Queen
Elizabeth II, RCIN 402853

55
Workshop of Giulio Romano
Sacrifice of a Goat to Jupiter, *c.* 1536–39
Oil on panel, 123 x 66.2 cm
The Royal Collection / HM Queen Elizabeth II, RCIN 406166

56
Polidoro da Caravaggio
Psyche Abandoned, *c.* 1527–28
Oil on panel, 87.5 x 161.5 cm
The Royal Collection / HM Queen
Elizabeth II, RCIN 402919

57
Jacopo Tintoretto
Esther before Ahasuerus, *c.* 1546–47
Oil on canvas, 207.7 x 275.5 cm
The Royal Collection /
HM Queen Elizabeth II,
RCIN 407247

58
Jacopo Bassano
The Adoration of the Shepherds, c. 1546
Oil on canvas, 139.1 x 218.5 cm
The Royal Collection / HM Queen Elizabeth II, RCIN 405772

59
Jacopo Bassano
The Journey of Jacob, *c.* 1561
Oil on canvas, 129.4 x 184.2 cm
The Royal Collection / HM Queen
Elizabeth II, RCIN 402928

60
Palma Giovane
The Triumph of David, *c.* 1590–95
Oil on canvas, 207 x 337 cm
Museo Nacional del Prado,
Madrid, inv. P00271

61
Palma Giovane
The Conversion of St Paul, *c.* 1590–95
Oil on canvas, 207 x 337 cm
Museo Nacional del Prado,
Madrid, inv. P00272

5

THE ROYAL PORTRAIT

THE 'ACT AND POWER OF A FACE': VAN DYCK'S ROYAL PORTRAITS

DESMOND SHAWE-TAYLOR

Strange! That thy hand should not inspire
The beauty only, but the fire:
Not the form alone, and grace,
But act and power of a face.

Edmund Waller, *To Van Dyck*, ll. 19–22[1]

Court portrait painting in Britain during the reign of James I was of much the same standard as that in most continental courts, largely because that standard was not very high. The prevailing style could be appreciated at the Cross Gallery at Somerset House, the residence of Queen Henrietta Maria, which was hung with full-length portraits of British and continental monarchs, past and present.[2] The artists representing 'British' portraiture were in fact both Dutch – Paul van Somer and Daniel Mytens – and were at least a match for their continental rivals: Ferdinand Elle from France, Frans Pourbus II from the Spanish Netherlands and Juan Pantoja della Cruz from Spain.[3] None of these artists would have seemed hugely advanced in comparison with works of the previous century, such as the anonymous portraits of Henry VIII and Elizabeth I.[4] In the courts of Europe the need to show every detail of fine costume, coupled with a veneration for the fashions of the previous century, seems to have reduced portrait painting to a stiff and mechanical activity.

The best early Stuart portrait painter of this generation was Mytens, whose portrait of Charles I (cat. 63) achieves a brightness and sharpness of detail, doing full justice to the King's splendid costume, while at the same time giving at least some ease to the posture and mobility to the features. Mytens contributed eleven full-length portraits to another important historical picture hang, the Bear Gallery at Whitehall Palace, most of which subsequently sold for a respectable £20 each in the Commonwealth Sale.[5] In the Bear Gallery, Mytens joined more examples of this journeyman generation: Jacob Bunel from France and fellow Dutchmen Van Somer, Michiel Jansz. van Miereveld and Gerrit van Honthorst (cat. 62).[6] These two displays – the Cross Gallery and the Bear Gallery – also permitted a comparison with two artists of a different order: Titian, whose legacy overshadowed this generation, and Anthony van Dyck, whose arrival eclipsed it.[7]

Van Dyck was one of a select group of artists who transformed portraiture during the first half of the seventeenth century, joining Rubens, Frans Hals, Bernini, Velázquez and Rembrandt. All were inspired to some degree by Titian; all produced mature work during the reign of Charles I; all but one (Hals) contributed to his collection. The rebirth of portraiture was a European phenomenon, and Charles I appreciated it and made a distinct contribution to it. The destruction or disappearance of portraits of the King by Bernini and Velázquez and the apparent undervaluing of self-portraits by Rubens (cat. 4) and Rembrandt (Walker Art Gallery, Liverpool) means that it is mainly through Van Dyck's royal portraiture that we can appreciate this contribution today.[8] To understand Van Dyck's importance for painting in England we need to imagine visiting the Cross Gallery at Somerset House and comparing the pearl-counting portraits of Pourbus, Pantoja, Van Somer et al. with Van Dyck's magnificently painterly portrait of the King (cat. 67). Defining this difference is more difficult. Many in the seventeenth century and subsequently have tried to convey the 'extra something' of Van Dyck's portraits: a member of Marie de' Medici's entourage in 1638 felt that the King was brought 'to life with his brush'; Roger de Piles thought that Van Dyck imitated nature accurately but 'heightened her as far as

he could', his performances having 'a great character of spirit, nobleness, grace and truth'; while for David Piper, Van Dyck's arrival opened the window onto the airless 'display boxes' of previous portraiture – 'a breeze moves through the room, draperies move in it and the light itself seems to stream with it'.[9]

Fig. 30 Anthony van Dyck (1599–1641), *The Three Eldest Children of Charles I*, 1635. Oil on canvas, 151 x 154 cm. Galleria Sabauda, Turin, inv. 285, cat. 264

For many the difference could be explained by reference to poetry. The parallel between the arts of poetry and painting was made in antiquity and often repeated at the Stuart court, as when Ben Jonson noted:

> *Poetry and picture are arts of a like nature, and both are about imitation. It was excellently said of Plutarch, poetry was a speaking picture, and picture a mute poesy. For they both invent, feign and devise many things, and accommodate all they invent to the use and service of Nature.*[10]

According to Sir Philip Sidney, it was precisely this appealing 'pictorial' side that distinguished poetry from prose: 'For the question is, whether the fashioned Image of Poetrie, or the regular instruction of Philosophy, hath the more force in teaching?'[11] What painters have to gain from the comparison is access to what is still known as 'poetic licence', which Sidney more extravagantly described as 'that high flying libertie of conceit proper to the Poet'.[12] Sidney imagines the poet 'as he goeth hand in hand with nature, not enclosed within the narrow warrant of her gifts, but freely raunging within the Zodiack of his owne wit'.[13] It is this 'liberty of conceit' that Edmund Waller admired in Van Dyck, when he writes of his ability to convey 'fire' as well as 'form' in the quotation that heads this essay. William Sanderson remarked that Van Dyck was the first painter 'that e're put Ladies dresse into a careless Romance' (Romance here meaning a poem in the manner of Torquato Tasso or Edmund Spenser). The implication is that Van Dyck's painting in general is like poetry after prose in comparison to the mechanics of the previous generation.[14] This analogy helps us to be more specific about what 'poetic licence' might mean in relation to Van Dyck's work, because what is so vaguely implied in discussions of paint is precisely defined when it comes to words: what elements – metre, rhyme, alliteration, assonance – belong with the sounds of words rather than their sense; which rhetorical device may be invoked to justify what strictly understood would be nonsense.[15] Van Dyck's most direct source for these ideas would have been Franciscus Junius, whose image appears in his *Iconographie* and whose *De pictura veterum* of 1637 explores the painting of antiquity entirely on the basis of literary sources, making many analogies between the two arts.[16]

We can appreciate Van Dyck's skills as a 'paint-smith' with the licence of a poet in the technique of this same royal portrait (cat. 67). His Titian-like handling of the brush has an independence from his subject, giving a rough texture and energy and allowing him to omit irksome details (such as the full quota of black ermine tails or the join between the floor and wall) in the interests of a more general evocation of the play of light. A part suggests the whole: like the vivid high-lit cloth of gold in the top left, which implies that this hanging is all of equally rich stuff, however summarily painted. Van Dyck's work doesn't look unfinished, it seems rather to convey a complete thing coming into being; this we can imagine the King appreciating when he visited the artist to watch him paint.[17]

The most obvious type of 'poetic portrait' for Van Dyck's contemporaries was one with a mythological personification, a type favoured by many in Charles I's court, including the Duke of Buckingham and Sir Kenelm Digby.[18] The surprisingly informal portrait of Charles I by Honthorst (cat. 62) is closely linked to the depiction of the King in just such a poetic painted masque, *Apollo and Diana*, commissioned by the Duke of Buckingham (Royal Collection).[19] Charles I admired Van Dyck's poetic narratives – he had already acquired Van Dyck's *Rinaldo and Armida* (Baltimore Museum of Art) in 1629 before the artist came to England – but when it came to portraiture he seems to have favoured an element of 'romance' that is implied rather than stated.[20] This is seen in his involvement of four artists in the development of a much-reworked poetic portrait idea. Around 1630 Charles I commissioned from Daniel Mytens a double portrait in which the King hands a wreath to his Queen, to be used as an overmantel at Somerset House. Mytens's first composition is recorded in a copy at Welbeck Abbey, Nottinghamshire;[21] in about 1632 he was required to alter this idea, superimposing a new design of the Queen (based on a portrait painted by the recently arrived Van Dyck) on top of the old (Royal Collection). This reworked composition remained in the collection, but lost its place as the Somerset House overmantel, for in the same year Van Dyck was commissioned to create a fresh version of the composition (cat. 64). This in turn gave rise to two copies, a print by Robert van Voerst (cat. 134) dated 1634 and a miniature by John Hoskins dated 1636 (Alnwick Castle, Northumberland).[22] Most of these works are described in inventories, all of which agree that the wreath (given by the King to the Queen) is of laurel while one specifies that the sprig (given by the Queen to the King in most versions of the composition) is olive.[23] In this case the symbolism is clear: the King seeks honour and glory only in order that he may invest his Queen with its laurels, while she in return offers an emblem of peace.[24] The message is reinforced by the addition of the crown and orb behind the King in Van Dyck's version, presumably to suggest that a simple laurel crown, earned by virtue, is a more valuable gift than a real crown. Van Dyck improves on Mytens in other ways: he makes the draperies glossier and more flowing and refines the play of hands, giving and receiving. Henrietta Maria has taken the laurel from above with her right hand; Charles has released it and reaches gracefully for the olive in her left.

The rubric of Van Voerst's print asks what shoot will issue from this union of James I's son and Henri IV's daughter. The answer to the question is provided in a series of similarly intimate Van Dyck portraits of the royal children: a group of the three eldest (fig. 30), painted in 1635, was sent to Henrietta Maria's sister, Christine, Duchess of Savoy; another of the same three painted in the same year was recorded at Somerset House in the Commonwealth Sale (Royal Collection).[25] The last group of royal children of 1637 (cat. 70) is recorded in the Breakfast Chamber, one of the most private rooms of Whitehall Palace, hanging 'above the table' (which may mean as an overmantel).[26] In the King's Bedchamber next door, Honthorst's portrait of Buckingham and his family (Royal Collection) of 1628 hung in the comparable position over the mantel and offers some

Fig. 31 Robert Peake (*c.* 1551–1619), *Henry, Prince of Wales, with Sir John Harington in the Hunting Field*, 1603. Oil on canvas, 201.9 x 147.3 cm. The Metropolitan Museum of Art, New York, inv. 44.27

obvious echoes in the relationship between tender sibling and unruly baby.[27] What these overmantels have in common is the idea that the hearth is the realm of wife and children: the King yields his wreath to the Queen; Buckingham yields centre stage to his Duchess; a group portrait is dominated by a seven-year-old boy. In the *Five Eldest Children*, Prince Charles looks out with princely confidence and pride, but the rest of the image is as much about the boy as the prince: we are reminded how small and young he is by the huge Lyme Mastiff which might at any moment get up and shake itself, while the eager and noisy baby prompts us to observe that he presides over a childish court, ruled by affection rather than by authority.

Van Dyck's most important public images of the King were his equestrian portraits, which he produced throughout his English career. The centrality of horsemanship as an image of control hardly needs to be insisted upon; the Royal Seal showed the King seated on a throne on one side and on a horse on the reverse. Charles I was familiar with a range of equestrian portraits: of his brother, Henry, Prince of Wales, by Robert Peake (fig. 31); of his friend the Duke of Buckingham (cat. 11); of his father-in-law, Henri IV of France; and of the Emperor Charles V (fig. 32).[28] As well as the paintings, Charles I also appeared on horseback on medals, in prints and in bronze: Hubert Le Sueur's famous equestrian monument was created in 1633 for Richard, Lord Weston, and now stands in Trafalgar Square. The earliest painted portrait of this type was created in the same year (cat. 72); it is first recorded hanging in the Gallery at St James's Palace, presumably at one end as it is the first picture listed there by Van der Doort.[29] No records exist of the dimensions or design of the Gallery, which was destroyed in the fire of 1809, but it is likely that the portrait was designed to fit precisely between the dado and the cornice in the manner of a tapestry. Notably its dimensions are those of a tapestry: with a typical frame of the period it would have measured some four by three metres.[30] In such a position the painted architecture would have completed the Gallery with a triumphal arch, seeming to open onto the landscape beyond, and have introduced Cyclopean scale, out of all proportion to that of the actual room. Assuming that the giant column has the slender proportions of the Corinthian or Composite order, it would require a canvas of double the present height to include it and its entablature.[31]

Van Dyck seeks to match this statement of heroic classical grandeur by employing the qualities described by Giovanni Pietro Bellori in his *Lives of the Artists* (1672), who tells us that he had

> *justly acquired the greatest name any painter had ever merited since Titian; and indeed, apart from the likeness he gave a certain nobility to the heads and grace to the poses, qualities for which Apelles became supremely famous after painting Alexander and Antigonus.*[32]

In this passage Bellori makes clear that this quality depends upon invoking the great artists of the past: Apelles and Titian. As no works survive by Apelles, Van Dyck settles for Titian. In the Mantuan sale Charles I acquired the moveable contents of the Gabinetto dei Cesari, including the *Eleven Caesars* by Titian. Van Dyck had been asked to repair one of these Titians and replace another even before he arrived in England.[33] Seven of the Titian emperors were hanging in the Gallery at St James's Palace, along with the same number of mounted warriors (then believed to depict the emperors themselves) by Giulio Romano.[34] Van Dyck paints Charles I as another emperor with a swaggering posture and dramatic flashing of light on his armour, learned at first hand from Titian's canvases.[35]

The care in the conception and execution of the architecture in the portrait at St James's is quite unlike Van Dyck's work in general, where architecture tends to be casually conceived and painted with a soft, scrubbing technique. It is highly likely that these passages were painted by another

Fig. 32 Titian (*c.* 1488/90–1576), *Charles V on Horseback*, 1548. Oil on canvas, 335 x 283 cm. Museo Nacional del Prado, Madrid, inv. P00410

artist, probably a specialist within Van Dyck's studio. Such collaborations were common within Charles I's collection, but apparently not to Van Dyck's taste; on 22 November 1639 Van der Doort lists large perspective pieces for portraits of the King and Queen delivered to the Banqueting House Room, but adds 'Sir Antony Van Dyck had no mind thereto'.[36] Van Dyck's next equestrian portrait, painted around 1637–38 (cat. 74), rejects the slightly formulaic apparatus of the previous. A reduced version of the composition (cat. 73) was displayed in the King's Chair Room at Whitehall Palace. Though more complete than a conventional oil sketch, this served as a preparatory *modello*, according to Van der Doort, who also reveals that the finished work then hung in the 'Prince's Gallery, Hampton Court'.[37] This Hampton Court equestrian portrait is exactly the same height as the one in St James's Palace and could therefore similarly have filled the space between dado and cornice.[38]

As Bellori points out, this painting was created 'in imitation of Charles V as represented by Titian' (fig. 32), which Charles I would have seen during his 1623 visit and Van Dyck (and Bellori for that matter) would have known through copies.[39] Van Dyck repeats Titian's composition and adopts its fundamentally poetical idea that there is an elision between the forms of the figure and the landscape and a metaphorical relationship between them. Both horses sink into the landscape; both royal heads shine against the sky like a celestial body; in both, every part of the figure and landscape is saturated in the colours of the evening sky. Van Dyck goes further than Titian in a kind of alliteration of the patterns of light on the horse's coat compared with those in the sky, or between the horse's mane and the foliage. Van Dyck also reverses the mood: Charles V is a man of war, blood-red and stormy; Charles I is a man of peace, like a chaste moon within a cool, silvery and serene summer sky.

It is common to liken a monarch to the sun: in 1633 Nicolas Briot produced a medal celebrating Charles I's return to London after being crowned in Scotland (cat. 133); the obverse shows the King in profile mounted, in armour and with truncheon of command (not unlike cat. 74); the reverse shows London with the sun breaking through clouds, with the motto 'Sol orbem rediens sic rex illuminat urbem' ('as the sun returning to the world, so the King illuminates the city').[40] Charles I could have commissioned Van Dyck to paint this allegory, much as Buckingham commissioned Rubens to depict himself crowned by Victory and blown by auspicious winds (cat. 11), but chose rather to have these things suggested.

The final image of Charles I (cat. 76) is presumed to be a royal commission, although there is no evidence as to its intended recipient or location. It is usually identified as *Charles I in the Hunting Field* or *'Le Roi à la chasse'*, following its listing in Van Dyck's pidgin French ('Le roi à la ciasse'), in a memorandum written by the artist in 1638.[41] Whereas it might be said that the St James's portrait (cat. 72) shows a Roman Emperor and the Hampton Court portrait (cat. 74) an Arthurian Knight, this portrait depicts a modern cavalier. Its over-size full-length format is identical to and presumably derived from Paul van Somer's 1617 depiction of Anne of Denmark hunting (Royal Collection), which stood out in the line of full-lengths at the Bear Gallery by its size and by the Salviati angels that hung above it to provide a heavenly source for the rays of light and banderole across the top of the painting.[42] *Charles I in the Hunting Field* would presumably have hung in the same way at the centre of a group of standard-format full-lengths. Hunting portraits at this time were rare and delightfully idiosyncratic: in around 1605 Robert Peake depicted Charles's elder brother Prince Henry with a companion in a stag hunt immediately after the kill (fig. 31);[43] in around 1630 Daniel Mytens showed the King and Queen setting off for the chase, hand in hand and showered with roses by a Cupid in the sky (Royal Collection).[44] Van Dyck's image would seem to depict a moment of relaxation during a hunt, most likely the kill, perhaps performed by huntsmen 'off-stage' to the left, while the page carries a cloak to wrap up the corpse and Charles I strolls over to 'try the meat' (a ceremony whereby the lord of the hunt makes the first cut into the carcass to sample its quality).[45] This would mean that the furious energy and excitement of the horse – bowing its head, neighing with a wide and foaming mouth and pawing the ground – was a sort of warming-down after the chase.

We have seen in many examples of Van Dyck's portraiture a mixture of icon and anecdote where a principal figure expresses timeless dignity while a subsidiary figure provides a bustling and inconsequential piece of local colour: Jeffrey Hudson beside the Queen (cat. 68), Monsieur de St Antoine beside the King (cat. 72) and the infant Princess Anne beside the Prince (cat. 70) to name three. In this case the two are complementary as well as contrasting: Charles borrows for himself the aura of power from his barely controllable steed – he has after all just ridden it to this pitch of excitement – but he himself remains calm, fresh, easy and nonchalant.

This contrast is supported by the same kind of allusive or metaphorical painting seen in the Hampton Court picture (cat. 74). The horse, equerry and page join the trees, stump and vegetation to make a clump of dark, shaggy matter; Charles is silvery and shimmery against the evening sky, his breeches and flesh tones picking out the red of the setting sun. This might be intended symbolically: his head is certainly suggestive of the sun (a common image of royalty, as we have seen). It is more likely that this is a sort of alliteration – something paint can do in its own way just as much as words, conveying not so much that the King is the sun but that, like Shakespeare's Cleopatra, he is 'fire and air', his other elements given to 'baser life'.[46]

62
Gerrit van Honthorst
Charles I, 1628
Oil on canvas, 76.2 x 64.1 cm
National Portrait Gallery, London, inv. NPG 4444

63
Daniel Mytens
Charles I, 1628
Oil on canvas, 219.4 x 139.1 cm
The Royal Collection / HM Queen Elizabeth II, RCIN 404448

64 *(overleaf)*
Anthony van Dyck
Charles I and Henrietta Maria Holding a Laurel Wreath, 1632
Oil on canvas, 104 x 176 cm
Archbishopric of Olomouc, inv. KE 2372, O 406

65
Anthony van Dyck
Charles I and Henrietta Maria with Prince Charles and Princess Mary, 1632
Oil on panel, 19.7 x 23.5 cm
The Royal Collection / HM Queen Elizabeth II, RCIN 408584

66
Anthony van Dyck
Charles I and Henrietta Maria with Prince Charles and Princess Mary ('The Greate Peece'), 1632
Oil on canvas, 303.8 x 256.5 cm
The Royal Collection / HM Queen Elizabeth II, RCIN 405353

67
Anthony van Dyck
Charles I in Robes of State, 1636
Oil on canvas, 248 x 153.6 cm
The Royal Collection / HM Queen Elizabeth II, RCIN 404398

68
Anthony van Dyck
Henrietta Maria with Sir Jeffrey Hudson, 1633
Oil on canvas, 219.1 x 134.8 cm
National Gallery of Art, Washington, Samuel H. Kress Collection, inv. 1952.5.39

69
Anthony van Dyck
George Villiers, 2nd Duke of Buckingham, and Francis Villiers, 1635
Oil on canvas, 137.2 x 127.7 cm
The Royal Collection / HM Queen Elizabeth II, RCIN 404401

70
Anthony van Dyck
The Five Eldest Children of Charles I, 1637
Oil on canvas, 163.2 x 198.8 cm
The Royal Collection / HM Queen Elizabeth II, RCIN 404405

71
William Dobson
Charles II, when Prince of Wales, with a Page, c. 1642
Oil on canvas, 153.6 x 129.8 cm
National Galleries of Scotland, inv. PG 1244

72
Anthony van Dyck
Charles I on Horseback with M. de St Antoine, 1633
Oil on canvas, 370 x 270 cm
The Royal Collection / HM Queen Elizabeth II, RCIN 405322

73
Anthony van Dyck
Charles I on Horseback, *c.* 1635–36
Oil on canvas, 96 x 86.3 cm
The Royal Collection / HM Queen Elizabeth II, RCIN 400571

74
Anthony van Dyck
Charles I on Horseback, *c.* 1637–38
Oil on canvas, 367 x 292.1 cm
The National Gallery, London, inv. NG1172

CAROLVS

75
Anthony van Dyck
Charles I, *c.* 1632–36
Black chalk on paper, 47.9 x 36.5 cm
Rijksmuseum, Amsterdam,
inv. RP-T-1887-A-1162

76
Anthony van Dyck
Charles I in the Hunting Field, *c.* 1636
Oil on canvas, 266 x 207 cm
Musée du Louvre, Paris, inv. 1236

CAROLVS I REX

6

VAN DYCK AND RUBENS IN ENGLAND

VAN DYCK, TITIAN AND CHARLES I

PER RUMBERG

On 17 March 1636 Charles I wrote to Gianlorenzo Bernini in Rome, asking him to make a marble portrait bust 'after the painted portrait which we shall send to you immediately'.[1] The painting in question was Anthony van Dyck's famous portrait of the King in three positions (cat. 3). Bernini's bust was destroyed in the fire at Whitehall Palace in 1698, but a bust made by François Dieussart at the same time and probably from the same portrait survives at Arundel Castle (cat. 2).[2] The idea of depicting Charles in this way was derived from a picture in the King's collection, then attributed to Titian and on display in the Second Privy Lodging Room at Whitehall Palace (fig. 33).[3] Charles I greatly admired Titian, a passion he shared with his court artist. The process of transformation implied here is as intriguing as it is complex: the Renaissance portrait acts as a model for Van Dyck, whose adaptation is to serve as a model for Bernini. Although the *Portrait of a Goldsmith in Three Positions* is now given to Lorenzo Lotto, its attribution to Titian at the time acts as a reminder that even connoisseurs as well informed as Charles I, and Van Dyck no less, could confuse the work of major sixteenth-century Venetian artists. Nevertheless, it was to Titian that Van Dyck turned on more than one occasion for his development of the compositions of his royal portraits,[4] even if the link is not always as obvious as in the triple portrait.

During Van Dyck's first visit to London in 1620, he was introduced to Thomas Howard, Earl of Arundel (cat. 10), the great art collector and connoisseur, whose extraordinary collection, including many works by Titian, greatly impressed the young artist from Antwerp.[5] The following year, Van Dyck moved to Italy. Based largely in Genoa, he visited, among other places, both Rome and Venice, where he joined the entourage of the Countess of Arundel.[6] In order to remember the pictures he encountered on his travels, he recorded many of them in his *Italian Sketchbook* (cat. 77). More than a quarter of the drawings in the sketchbook, around 60, are devoted to works by Titian.[7] Van Dyck seems to have been chiefly interested in the formal aspects of the compositions, the arrangement of the figures and their relationship to one another, as well as to Titian's mastery of pictorial space. He absorbed the expressive decorum of Titian's compositions as he developed his own artistic language, not least in his attempts to liberate himself from the mould of Rubens, for whom he had worked in Antwerp.[8]

In 1632 Van Dyck returned to London, where Charles I appointed him 'principalle Paynter in Ordenarie to their Majesties'. The artist would have been deeply impressed by the collection assembled by the King, which included at least two pictures he had seen in Venice and recorded in his sketchbook a few years earlier: Titian's *Jacopo Pesaro Being Presented by Pope Alexander VI to St Peter* (fig. 34) and his *Venus and Music* (fig. 27). Both were on display in the First Privy Lodging Room at Whitehall Palace.[9]

Van Dyck's first major commission upon his arrival in London was the so-called *Greate Peece* (cat. 66), a monumental family portrait for the vista of the Long Gallery at Whitehall Palace.[10] It shows Charles I with Henrietta Maria and their two children, Prince Charles, then about two years old, and the infant Princess Mary. The royal insignia – crown, orb and sceptre – are placed prominently on the table to the left. The monumental column in the background establishes Charles as the centre of the composition. His role as *pater patriae* is further underlined by the distant view of Westminster Hall and the Houses of Parliament that can be glimpsed over his shoulder. A preparatory oil sketch (cat. 65) suggests that Van Dyck constructed the composition in stages. In this initial and still rather intimate sketch he focused largely on the figure group

Fig. 33 Lorenzo Lotto (1480–1556), *Portrait of a Goldsmith in Three Positions*, *c.* 1525–35. Oil on canvas, 52 x 79 cm. Kunsthistorisches Museum, Vienna, Gemäldegalerie, inv. 92

itself; it was not until later that he added the elaborate setting, which plays such a dominant role in the final composition.

An obvious point of reference for Van Dyck was the now-lost mural of Henry VIII with Jane Seymour and his parents, Henry VII and Elizabeth of York, painted by Hans Holbein the Younger in 1537. Like Bernini's bust, it was destroyed in the fire at Whitehall Palace, but its composition is recorded in a seventeenth-century copy by Remigius van Leemput (Royal Collection).[11] The imposing scale of Holbein's original can be appreciated from his surviving cartoon of Henry VIII (National Portrait Gallery, London). Similar in scale and ambition to Holbein's mural, Van Dyck's *Greate Peece* shows the King and Queen seated, as did another unattributed portrait dating from around 1545 (Royal Collection), showing Henry VIII with Jane Seymour and Prince Edward, later Edward VI, at either side.

Although Van Dyck's *Greate Peece* clearly echoes these earlier English prototypes, it also draws on models from further afield. Various details in the painting reveal Van Dyck's obsession with Titian during his Italian sojourn. In Rome, for example, he visited Palazzo Farnese, where he would have seen Titian's famous portrait of Pope Paul III (Museo Nazionale di Capodimonte, Naples).[12] In fact, Charles's pose in Van Dyck's sketch for the *Greate Peece* seems to echo that of the Pope in Titian's painting (although it changes in the final composition). In the same palace, Van Dyck also encountered another portrait of Pope Paul III: Titian's haunting depiction of him with his scheming grandsons, Alessandro and Ottavio Farnese (fig. 35).[13] Despite the fact that the painting was unfinished, Van Dyck seems to have been intrigued by its complex composition and recorded it in his sketchbook.[14] The work's main compositional elements, including the opulent curtain, the throne and the table, all feature in Van Dyck's portrait of the royal family. *The Greate Peece*, however, is considerably larger than either of Titian's portraits of Paul III, and although both pictures may have served as models for certain aspects of his composition, Van Dyck seems to have turned not only to portraits as inspiration but, more unexpectedly, also to altarpieces. One such altarpiece made a particularly lasting impression on the artist and deserves more attention in this context.

On his sojourn in Venice in 1623, Van Dyck visited the Basilica di Santa Maria Gloriosa dei Frari, where he seems to have been less interested in the spectacular *Assumption of the Virgin* on the High Altar than in another work by Titian, displayed in an adjacent family chapel: the so-called *Pesaro Madonna* (fig. 36), which shows the donor, Jacopo Pesaro,

Fig. 34 Titian (*c.* 1488/90–1576), *Jacopo Pesaro Being Presented by Pope Alexander VI to St Peter*, *c.* 1510–12. Oil on canvas, 147.5 x 189 cm. Koninklijk Museum voor Schone Kunsten, Antwerp, inv. 357

kneeling to the left as he is presented to the Virgin by St Peter.[15] Van Dyck seems to have been exceptionally intrigued by this work, for he made not one but two drawings of it.[16] His first sketch, which has been largely overlooked, can be found towards the beginning of the sketchbook.[17] Drawn quickly in black chalk, it is somewhat difficult to read, especially as a study of the Virgin and Child shows through from the other side of the sheet. Nevertheless, it contains all the main figures of the composition: Jacopo Pesaro kneeling in the left foreground, his father Benedetto to the right, St Peter, the Virgin and Child, the man with a turban, the standard-bearer next to him and the faint outline of St Francis to the right.

Van Dyck's second sketch concentrates on the upper half of the composition.[18] Most evident are the putti at the top of the sheet; the other figures are more difficult to make out. Drawn in faint red chalk, gone over in pen and brown ink, the figures are partly obscured by two sketches of the Virgin and Child that were added at a later stage. In both sketches, Van Dyck recorded the outlines of the two monumental columns, which dominate the architectural setting, suggesting his particular interest in Titian's powerful construction of pictorial space.[19]

The prominence of the donor and his family in the *Pesaro Madonna* recalls Titian's earlier *Jacopo Pesaro Being Presented by Pope Alexander VI to St Peter* (fig. 34). Van Dyck must have been particularly impressed with the way Titian embedded these portraits within a more complex narrative and spatial setting. Although the *Greate Peece* must be seen in the tradition of the earlier Tudor portraits, it also bears an uncanny likeness not only to Titian's portraits of Pope Paul III but also to the artist's religious works, most notably his *Pesaro Madonna*.

Fig. 35 Titian (*c.* 1488/90–1576), *Pope Paul III with Alessandro and Ottavio Farnese*, 1545–46. Oil on canvas, 210 x 176 cm. Museo Nazionale di Capodimonte, Naples, inv. Q 129

The monumental column behind Charles I, which dominates the upper half of the composition, may be seen as a tribute to the spatial grandeur of Titian's altarpiece. Van Dyck stopped short only of including the putti. A few years later Philip Herbert, Earl of Pembroke, with whom Charles I had exchanged his Holbein drawings (cats 98, 100–02) for Raphael's *St George and the Dragon* (fig. 53), commissioned Van Dyck to paint a portrait of his own family (Wilton House, Wiltshire). Yet again, the artist returned to the model of the *Pesaro Madonna*, and this time included not only the two columns but also the clouds and even the putti.[20]

Another example of Van Dyck drawing inspiration from a religious work by Titian is his portrait of Charles I in the hunting field (cat. 76). Like the *Greate Peece*, this portrait must be seen in the context of others in Charles's collection, in this case a portrait of the King's mother, Anne of Denmark, by Paul van Somer (Royal Collection) and a portrait of his elder brother, Prince Henry, by Robert Peake the Elder (fig. 31). However, Van Dyck also included a detail from a painting he had seen and copied in Italy:[21] Titian's *Adoration of the Magi*.[22] The pose of the horse, which Van Dyck adopted from Titian, shows it pawing and neighing with its head lowered, adding a sense of realism to the scene, and this may be one reason why the King appears so much less formal here than in Van Dyck's other royal portraits (see pp. 126–31).[23]

Unsurprisingly, Van Dyck's *Cupid and Psyche* (cat. 78), one of his last paintings and the only mythological painting to survive from his time in England, is similarly indebted to Titian. The reclining figure of Psyche, particularly, must be seen in relation to at least a couple of works by Titian in the collection of Charles I: the *Pardo Venus* (fig. 15), which was presented to Charles by Philip IV in 1623, and *Venus and Music* (fig. 27), one of Charles's pictures Van Dyck had first seen in Venice. Another obvious point of reference would have been Titian's lost *St Peter Martyr*, formerly at the Basilica di Santi Giovanni e Paolo in Venice.[24] That altarpiece, which was destroyed by fire in 1867, is known through prints and copies, and served as a model for the symbolic tree in the background of Van Dyck's composition. Although Van Dyck did not record the composition in his sketchbook, he is known to have visited that great Venetian church.[25] *Cupid and Psyche* may also be seen in relation to Titian's *Bacchus and Ariadne* (National Gallery, London).[26] Painted in 1520–23 for Alfonso d'Este, Duke of Ferrara, for the so-called Camerini d'Alabastro conjoining the Castello Estense and the Palazzo Ducale in Ferrara, Titian's canvas was hanging at Palazzo Aldobrandini by the time Van Dyck visited Rome. Although the composition is not recorded in his sketchbook, Van Dyck did note his visit to the palace.[27] Not only the overall dimensions of Van Dyck's canvas but also the figure of Cupid and the animated, swirling drapery recall Titian's example.

Van Dyck's admiration for Titian is well documented; he also owned a significant group of works by the Renaissance master. When Marie de' Medici, Henrietta Maria's mother, visited Van Dyck in Antwerp, shortly before his arrival in London, her secretary referred to the artist's collection as a 'Cabinet de Titien'.[28] Among Van Dyck's Titians were the *Vendramin Family* (National Gallery, London) and *Perseus and Andromeda* (Wallace Collection, London).[29] Van Dyck not only collected Titian but, as we have seen, repeatedly returned to his compositions – and not only portraits but also altarpieces – as an inspiration for his own work.

Van Dyck died on 9 December 1641, aged 42, and was buried at Old St Paul's Cathedral. Arguably the most important portraitist of his day, he had absorbed Titian's mastery of visual narrative. This Venetian influence had brought to his portraiture a psychological and spatial depth, giving it a distinct grandeur and gravitas that were clearly of great appeal to his royal patron.

Fig. 36 Titian (*c.* 1488/90–1576), *Pesaro Madonna*, *c.* 1519–26. Oil on canvas, 478 x 266 cm. Santa Maria Gloriosa dei Frari, Venice

RUBENS, PAINTER AND DIPLOMAT

GREGORY MARTIN

When Peter Paul Rubens arrived in London early in June 1629, he did so in his capacities as diplomat in the service of the King of Spain and as artist with a magnificent commission in prospect. His task as envoy was to obtain a further step in the hitherto secret peace *pourparlers* between the Crowns of Spain and Great Britain, which had been officially at war for the last four years.[1] But of long-term consequence was the second, artistic aspect of his role. That he should have found himself at the centre of talks conducted at the highest level of the British court is remarkable enough, but that he should prepare for one of his greatest artistic projects and also paint two masterpieces about the outcome of his diplomacy and in tribute to his sojourn adds a distinctive, aesthetic dimension to this the most significant mission of his public career.

RUBENS THE PUBLIC SERVANT

Rubens's whole life was spent under the cloud of the Eighty Years' War for Dutch independence (1568–1648), which brought suffering and impoverishment particularly to Antwerp – his base for much of his career, and to which he had moved as a youngster following his family's exile. He was not drawn into service at the Brussels court of the Governor of the Spanish Netherlands, the Archduchess Isabella Clara Eugenia, until his mid-forties, by which time he was already a highly successful artist; indeed in 1621 he had been approached by both the British and French Crowns to execute ambitious projects in celebration of their respective royal eminences.[2] But the same year also saw the end of the Twelve Years' Truce and renewed hostilities between the Spanish Crown and the Estates General of the seven United Provinces in the north. A desire to serve, inspired by the ethical altruism extolled by Cicero, among other influential classical authors, and to contribute to the public welfare, would have been the motivation that led the artist partially to lay aside his brushes. He first entered the muddy world of secret, low-level parley and then, some years later, the splendid stage of top-level discussions with statesmen.

Rubens's reputation as an artist undoubtedly outweighed his 'menial' occupation and his lack of noble birth – both long considered an obstruction to public service to his Spanish monarch[3] – but it also came to endear him to the two chief protagonists with whom he was to deal: the Habsburg, Philip IV of Spain, and the Stuart, Charles I of Great Britain. Both were young men and would have welcomed the mature painter, whose works they so greatly admired.

The sequence of events that brought Rubens face to face with Charles in 1629 did not take place in the Netherlands and stretched back to the beginning of the decade. Then the Battle of the White Mountain, near Prague, had deprived Charles's Protestant brother-in-law, the Prince Palatine, of his territorial possessions and seen the first battle of the Thirty Years' War, during which the Habsburg Holy Roman Emperor sought to re-establish Catholicism in the German lands. This conflict, and that in the Netherlands, became linked in British eyes after Spanish troops were permitted to occupy key towns in the Palatinate, the restitution of which became an avowed objective of British foreign policy.[4] War with both Spain – to avenge the failure of Charles's 'Spanish match' – and then with France – to support the Huguenots – resulted to a degree from the populist policies of the royal favourite, George Villiers, Duke of Buckingham. British military operations were ignominious

Fig. 37 The Banqueting Hall, Whitehall, London, with ceiling paintings by Peter Paul Rubens

failures and Buckingham's murder in 1628 greatly increased the desire to bring an end to Britain's bellicose policy.

Rubens had met Buckingham in Paris, three years previously, when the Duke had sat for his portrait; also present at the sitting was Balthasar Gerbier, the Duke's artistic agent and advisor.[5] This contact was subsequently exploited as one of several channels through which peace with Spain was sporadically and secretly explored. In August/September 1628 the epistolary documentation was taken by Rubens to Madrid to provide yet further evidence of Britain's pacific intentions. But it was probably only the fear in Madrid of being outflanked by a Franco–British peace settlement that galvanised action, and Rubens was sent hurrying to London via Paris, Brussels and Antwerp.

The artist was travelling incognito, not as a private individual but now as a public officer of the Spanish Crown – he had just been sworn in as secretary of the royal Privy Council in Brussels[6] – and he was carrying highly sensitive state documents. Arrangements for his crossing from Dunkirk had still to be made, and a letter from the British agent there is a unique record of Rubens – self-confessedly not given to outward displays of emotion – showing fear: he required as transport a British navy ship as 'hie is mychtelie afrrayit of the hollanderis',[7] whose warships were ominously stationed offshore.

Six days later the *Adventure* – captained by the capable John Mennes, later a friend and (irritating) colleague of Samuel Pepys on the Navy Board – put the party ashore at Dover. On 5 June Rubens was taken downstream by royal barge from Westminster to Greenwich for his first meeting with the King. Such was the urgency of getting the peace talks under way before the arrival of the French ambassador to celebrate the treaty that Gerbier had commandeered the barge without official permission.[8] The pressure came from the very top, as is clear from Rubens's account of that first meeting. To his dismay, the King would have none of the cautious, step-by-step approach central to Rubens's instructions. The diplomat had to hold his nerve and be careful not to exceed his brief. Such was his resolve that he was able to arrange a second meeting with Charles later the same day to obtain confirmation of the royal wishes, a move which caught the King's closest ministers unawares.[9]

From the end of June to mid-December Rubens wrote at length to the Spanish chief minister, the Count-Duke of Olivares: twenty-three dispatches are extant amounting roughly to some fifty thousand words or more. The dispatches are a record of Rubens's hard-won success in limiting the scope of the treaty with the French, in countering their ambassador's obstruction and in fulfilling the royal desire for an exchange of ambassadors without committing the Spanish Crown to a great deal more than an expression of good intentions about the Palatinate. This required persuasive agility towards his – at times suspicious – British counterparts and robust self-defence against Olivares's complaints that he had exceeded his terms of reference.

As winter drew in, Rubens had to face down increasing criticism at court about the delayed arrival of the Spanish ambassador Don Carlos Coloma following the departure of his English counterpart, Sir Francis Cottington, to Madrid. Rubens wrote urgently to the Archduchess on 4 December that Lord Treasurer Weston – the most powerful of the King's ministers with whom he was in regular and never easy contact – had displayed the 'greatest agitation and emotion' on the matter. Now Rubens once more betrayed his feelings and expostulated that the delay 'was so unfortunate that I curse the hour when I came to this kingdom'.[10] In the event Coloma was not to arrive in London until 10 January. His official reception took place at the Banqueting Hall. This lavishly staged occasion, in which Rubens was duly prominent, saw the accomplishment of the diplomatic task assumed by the artist – or the 'public minister of the Archduchess' as he was on occasion described – almost six months earlier to the day.

RUBENS THE ARTIST

The public minister's round of meetings the previous summer must have been time-consuming, but Rubens must also – we think – have been required especially by the King to focus on the commission for the ceiling of the Banqueting Hall. The first approach for a decorative cycle, made in 1621 when James I's new Banqueting House was nearing completion, had elicited Rubens's proud credo: 'I confess that I am, by natural instinct, better fitted to execute very large works than small curiosities.'[11] Rubens must have felt that this claim would indeed be put to the test when he visited the hall eight years later and viewed the ceiling's nine openings – the majority very large – which Inigo Jones had devised and which he was required to fill (fig. 37).

When he arrived in England, Rubens already had some idea of the desired subject-matter as it is likely that two programmes for the cycle, earlier contrived in London, had been forwarded to him. His response was the inspired, large-scale *bozzetto* (cat. 82), in which he set out proposals for seven of the openings. He would have relished the challenge of celebrating the late King's reign, because of his likely admiration of James's dedication to the pursuit of international peace.[12]

We can imagine discussions in 1629, using as a basis the programmes and the *bozzetto*, between Rubens and, among others, Inigo Jones and perhaps two connoisseurs whom he had earlier known when they were exiled in Antwerp, the Catholics Tobie Matthew[13] and George Gage,[14] now both settled in London. Little doubt that then the idea of his modification of the apotheosis theme sketched in the *bozzetto* would have

Fig. 38 Peter Paul Rubens (1577–1640), *Daniel in the Lions' Den*, *c.* 1614–16. Oil on canvas, 224.2 x 330.5 cm. National Gallery of Art, Washington, D.C., inv. 1965.13.1

been explained, the new subject of King James as *rex pacificus* introduced to the scheme and motifs developed concerning the union of the Crowns of Scotland and England, which the King had achieved by inheritance. Also requiring study in London would have been portraits of James at different ages, his costume, the uniforms of the sergeants-at-arms and the royal regalia. To be settled too would have been a contract.

On the basis of such discussions and study, individual *modelli* were executed once Rubens had returned to Antwerp. Although evidently much had been settled already, Charles had still to approve the artist's proposal for the ceiling decoration as a whole; the overall *modello* (lost in the Whitehall Palace fire of 1698) was thus also executed and sent back to London. In fact, work did not begin on the canvases until 1632–33, and further delays outside Rubens's control meant that their shipment did not take place until the autumn of 1636. They have remained in place ever since, apart from their removal during the last world war and subsequent cleaning and restoration, which add up to an absence of eleven years from the Banqueting House.[15] Their presentation and now – after a long time – the appearance of Inigo Jones's magnificent carved ceiling itself are under active consideration by Historic Royal Palaces.

These matters may have occupied Rubens intermittently in the autumn and winter of 1629; but already by the middle of August he had been able to do some sightseeing, most probably conducted by Gerbier, under whose roof in the north frontage of York House, near Charing Cross on the Strand, he and his party were staying. Two letters show that he had visited some of the nearby town palaces. In one, he stated:

> *This island ... seems to me to be a spectacle worthy of the interest of every gentleman ... not only for the splendour of the outward culture ... but also for the incredible quantity of excellent pictures, statues, and ancient inscriptions which are to be found in this Court ...*[16]

He specified the deceased Duke of Buckingham's collection at York House itself, the royal collection (presumably that part housed at Whitehall and St James's Palaces) and, further east along the Strand, the antique statues and inscriptions belonging

Fig. 39 Peter Paul Rubens (1577–1640) and Frans Snyders (1579–1657), *Diana and Her Nymphs Spied upon by Satyrs*, *c.* 1616. Oil on canvas, 203 x 309.6 cm. The Royal Collection, RCIN 405553

to the Earl of Arundel. On view, too, would have been the King's recent acquisitions from the Gonzaga collection in Mantua, which Rubens had known some 25 years previously. But one masterpiece – Titian's *Ecce Homo* (Kunsthistorisches Museum, Vienna), which Gerbier had famously acquired for Buckingham in 1621 – may well have come as a surprise: as we would come to expect from his earlier copying activity in Madrid, Rubens made two (drawn) copies of it.[17]

Rubens would have been struck and perhaps gratified by the number of his own works on display, not only those recently acquired by Buckingham, whose equestrian portrait (cat. 11) was at York House. In early June Rubens had been entertained by the Secretary of State, Viscount Dorchester, at whose house he might have seen his *Daniel in the Lions' Den* (fig. 38),[18] which his host had obtained over a decade previously, or upon enquiry he may have learnt that this large work had already been given to the King. A further surprise would have been his portrait of the Gonzaga Duke, Vincenzo II (cat. 12), which he had painted about a quarter of a century ago, and which had been acquired by Charles when Prince of Wales, at about the time that, out of admiration for the artist, he had requested a self-portrait (cat. 4). These would have been on view in Whitehall Palace; at Oatlands Palace, which Rubens visited in August, he may well have seen his magnificent *Diana and Her Nymphs Spied upon by Satyrs* (fig. 39).[19]

Rubens had written from Madrid, 'Here I keep to painting, as I do everywhere ...';[20] in London because of his other commitments his artistic output was much reduced. But we know of two painted copies after portraits by Titian of which only one is extant,[21] while Arundel and a noted physician, Sir Theodore Turquet de Mayerne, an expert on the technology of oil painting who lived not far off the Strand, sat for their portraits.[22] His most ambitious work of portraiture was his group of Gerbier's wife and four children (National Gallery of Art, Washington, D.C.). This he may have well begun in London, but his intention to complete it back in Antwerp was never realised.[23]

The support for the family portrait was made up of several pieces of canvas stitched together and in this respect is to a degree comparable to those of the two masterpieces that

Rubens planned and in one case certainly completed while he was in London. The great *Peace and War* (cat. 14) was given by Rubens to the King.[24] A few years after it was painted, Van der Doort described it:

> *In the Beare Gallorie* [in Whitehall Palace] … *A Picture,* … *of an Emblin wherein the differencs and ensuencees betweene peace and warrs is Shewed which Sr Peet^er Paule Rubins when he was here in England did paint and Was presented by him to ju* [your] *M.* [Majesty] …[25]

In the centre is Minerva, the goddess of wisdom, who pushes away Mars, the god of war, who is accompanied by his followers: a harridan, representing famine (as it now seems), and a harpy denoting pestilence. Below, a group of contented children collect grapes from a cornucopia, as the eldest girl is crowned by the young Hymen, god of marriage, and offered a grape by Cupid, god of love. The children are gathered at a bower beneath which sits the figure of Peace – Pax – who gives her milk to her baby, Plutus, god of wealth. A satyr, with the proffered cornucopia, and a playful leopard are at her feet. These denizens of the wild, by nature habitually either lustful or ferocious, are now benign, transformed by the influence of peace and love. They have approached Pax's arbour leading two maidens, representing perhaps craft and dance, for which only the circumstance of peace can engender.[26]

Van der Doort's 'emblin' – a pictorial parable – had been conjured by Rubens into a composition, both restful and dynamic, to show how wisdom can dispel the horrors of war to create the joys of peace. To do this he drew on his encyclopaedic store of visual and literary sources; what saved the allegory from academic dryness is the startling image of the satyr's playful generosity to the enchanting children. Rubens contrasts the timeless personifications of the ancients with the charm of the everyday, for the children are those in the Gerbier group portrait. He had prepared for this gift to the King by making sketches of his host's children posing in his lodging.[27] The gift would have gratified and complimented the King for it focused on the ongoing, efficacious deployment of his royal wisdom.

Somewhat smaller, but still on an impressive scale, is the second masterpiece Rubens painted on a similarly made-up support, both probably typical of the artist's practice when working on his own account. In contrast to the sophisticated, learned sources that inspired *Peace and War*, which was intended for display in a gallery, the story of St George and the dragon (cat. 83)[28] was a popular legend; the work is more poignant in atmosphere and lyrical in its landscape setting. Joseph Mead, a well informed scholar and purveyor of news, referred to it in a letter of 16 March 1630, thus before the artist had left the country:

> [Rubens] *in honour of England & of our Nation, from whom he hath received many courtesies, hath drawen with his pensill the History of St George; wherein, if it be possible, he hath exceeded himselfe: but the picture he hath sent home to Flanders; To remain there as a monument of his abode & employment here.*[29]

In the centre, St George, having subdued the dragon, returns to the princess her girdle so that she can lead it back to the town, whose inhabitants convert to Christianity as the saint slays the dragon. The scene is witnessed by an audience, some fearful, others admiring or respectful. Understandably the heroic couple has traditionally been identified as Charles and his consort, although the princess's hair is light brown whereas in Henrietta Maria's formal portraits it is dark. The demon dragon should be taken both as a symbol of the Puritan faction in the kingdom, known to Rubens as a threat to stability,[30] and of the King's violent, parliamentary opponents who had recently been imprisoned.[31] Rubens's association of Charles with England's patron saint would have been stimulated by the Order of the Garter's badge of St George, always worn by the King, not least at their interviews. The artist's earlier expressed admiration for the English countryside is evident in the tranquil landscape view,[32] probably inspired by the stretch of the River Thames he would have seen looking west from York House.

OFFICIAL FINALE

On 3 or 4 March 1630, the public minister had his farewell audience with the King, who dubbed him a knight and gave him jewellery;[33] such awards were normally reserved for departing ambassadors. This 'undewness from precedent' most likely stemmed from the King's gratitude for and admiration of both Rubens's diplomatic skills and his art, although the diploma dated 15 December 1630 refers only to the former.[34]

77
Anthony van Dyck
Italian Sketchbook, 1621–27
19.9 x 15.2 cm
The British Museum, London, inv. 1957,1214.207

78
Anthony van Dyck
Cupid and Psyche, 1639–40
Oil on canvas, 200.2 x 192.6 cm
The Royal Collection / HM Queen Elizabeth II, RCIN 405571

79
Anthony van Dyck
Margaret Lemon, *c.* 1638
Oil on canvas, 93.3 x 77.8 cm
The Royal Collection / HM Queen
Elizabeth II, RCIN 402531

80
Anthony van Dyck
Self-portrait, *c.* 1640
Oil on canvas, 56 x 46 cm
National Portrait Gallery, London,
inv. NPG 6987

81
Anthony van Dyck
Charles I and the Knights of the Garter in Procession, *c.* 1639–40
Oil on panel, 29.2 x 130.8 cm
Ashmolean Museum, Oxford, inv. A1247

82
Peter Paul Rubens
The Apotheosis of James I and Other Studies, *c.* 1628–30
Oil on panel, 94.7 x 63 cm
Tate, London, inv. T12919

83
Peter Paul Rubens
Landscape with St George and the Dragon, 1630–35
Oil on canvas, 152.5 x 226.9 cm
The Royal Collection / HM Queen Elizabeth II, RCIN 405356

7

THE QUEEN'S HOUSE

HENRIETTA MARIA, CHARLES I AND THE ITALIAN BAROQUE

KAREN SERRES

'The King prefers old paintings' was the guidance given in 1635 by the Pope's envoy to England, Gregorio Panzani, to his superior, Cardinal Francesco Barberini.[1] The Cardinal had correctly sensed that the gift of works of art was an effective way of getting the King's attention and, having at his disposal the riches and painters of Rome – then the foremost artistic centre in Europe – he had sought Panzani's advice on Charles I's taste in contemporary Italian art. However, despite Barberini's diplomatic efforts, the Italian Baroque was met with a somewhat mixed appreciation among English collectors, including the King himself. This ambivalent attitude is somewhat surprising, given that the two artists who today visually define Charles I's reign, Peter Paul Rubens and Anthony van Dyck, both spent long periods of time in Italy and adopted a Baroque aesthetic. However, the emergence of an unprecendent market for Renaissance art at the Caroline court – with 'old' Cinquecento Venetian and Roman paintings at its pinnacle – must have partly sated any further appetite for Italian art.[2]

Despite its limited scope, Stuart patronage and collecting of Italian Baroque art remains a remarkable episode, even more so if one considers the religious and geographical obstacles faced by English collectors, as well as the absence of any recent trend or substantive tradition of collecting foreign art in a nation that had been cut off from the Continent for half a century. Charles I's engagement with the Baroque was certainly of a somewhat haphazard and opportunist nature. He nevertheless set the tone as well as the ambition: just a quarter of a century after he started collecting, Whitehall and other palaces boasted Baroque masterpieces that were the envy of Europe's most fervent collectors.

The two most prominent Italian Baroque works of art in the Stuart royal collection were a marble bust of Charles I by the Roman sculptor Gianlorenzo Bernini, and a monumental painting of Bacchus and Ariadne by the Bolognese painter Guido Reni. Both required sensitive diplomatic relations to reach British shores. Although their significance is sometimes underestimated due to the fact that both works are lost, these commissions were highly influential in the seventeenth century and stemmed from Queen Henrietta Maria's relationship with the papal court: she was Urban VIII's goddaughter and the advocate for Catholics in England.

The daughter of Henri IV of France and the Florentine Marie de' Medici, Henrietta Maria married Charles in 1625 in a union that required a special papal dispensation to authorise such an alliance between a Catholic princess and an Anglican king. Their first years of marriage were marked by religious tensions and personal alienation. This was to change after the assassination in 1628 of the Duke of Buckingham – her rival for the King's ear – and the birth of a male heir in 1630, which enhanced the Queen's position at court and brought about a relative easing of religious sanctions against Catholics throughout the 1630s. The enterprising Cardinal Barberini saw an opportunity for a *rapprochement* with the English Crown and dispatched Panzani as papal emissary in late 1634. Although both men were careful not to correspond directly with the King, it was to him that their largesse was directed, in an effort to promote the Catholic cause. The King appears to have been receptive: the Queen playfully lamented that any significant painting sent to her from Rome would rapidly be appropriated by her husband.[3] The lawyer and Puritan pamphleteer William Prynne denounced these machinations to 'seduce the King

Fig. 40 The Queen's House, Greenwich, Great Hall, with reproductions of the ceiling paintings by Orazio Gentileschi

Fig. 41 Giovanni Battista Bolognini (1611–1688), after Guido Reni (1575–1642), *Bacchus and His Companions Finding Ariadne Abandoned on the Island of Naxos*, *c.* 1650–80. Etching, 49.2 x 106 cm. The British Museum, London, inv. 1874,0808.704

himself with Pictures, Antiquities, Images & other vanities brought from Rome'.[4] This condemnation was directly related to a marked distrust then current in some English circles of the grandeur and sensuality of contemporary Italian art, as well as a perceived link between connoisseurship and idolatry. However it must be said that, among these 'vanities', neither the Bernini bust nor Reni's ambitious canvas were, strictly speaking, gifts. The Barberini had authorised and steered the commissions, but the works were paid for by Charles I and Henrietta Maria respectively.

Bernini's bust of Charles I was an exceptional commission, the sculptor's first portrait of a foreign monarch, carved with the guidance of Van Dyck's triple portrait of the King (cat. 3).[5] Bernini reportedly had qualms at having to work from an image rather than from life, but this did nothing to lessen the quality of his work. The arrival of the bust in England in July 1637 was a momentous event. Few Englishmen had ever seen anything like it, despite the presence in London of several foreign sculptors, including the French Hubert Le Sueur (cat. 137) and the Flemish François Dieussart (cat. 2), who had both trained in Italy, and the Florentine Francesco Fanelli (cats 115–16).[6] The Queen wrote to Bernini that the work did 'great honour to all Italy in this kingdom' and soon requested a bust of herself, a commission that was never executed.[7] Though the bust was destroyed in the fire that devastated Whitehall Palace in 1698, two plaster casts as well as a contemporary engraving provide an idea of its original appearance.[8]

The second Baroque masterpiece commissioned by the royal couple had an international reputation even before its broad diffusion through at least four full or partial painted copies and two reproductive engravings (including fig. 41). In March 1637, a few months before the arrival of the Bernini bust in England, the Queen asked the Barberini to act as facilitators for another commission, this time to Guido Reni for the ceiling of her bedroom in the newly completed Queen's House at Greenwich. She also asked Francesco Barberini to choose the subject-matter, which presented a challenge for the Cardinal.[9] He settled first on 'Cephalus and Aurora', a traditional theme for a bedchamber, but later asked Reni to alter the composition to 'Ariadne found by Bacchus', possibly as an allusion to Henrietta Maria's plight as a Catholic on an apostate island. That Barberini was particularly attuned to the diplomatic issues surrounding such commissions from Rome can be garnered from his worry that the painting might appear too lascivious, 'especially in these Parliamentary times'.[10] He was eager not to alienate the English by playing up to the cliché that Italian art only represented, in Balthasar Gerbier's melodramatic summation, 'robustrous boistrous druncken-headed imaginary gods'.[11] The King and Queen however had no such qualms and the commission went ahead.

The monumental canvas left Bologna in April 1641 but it remains uncertain whether it ever reached an increasingly war-torn England. It is recorded in the Queen's possession in 1648 during her exile in France, when she tried to sell it for less than half its initial cost.[12] It later entered the collection of the French financier Michel Particelli d'Émery, whose widow, shocked by the lustful nature of the subject-matter that had so worried Cardinal Barberini, is said to have destroyed it.[13] It is more likely that she cut the huge canvas into pieces to make it easier to sell.[14]

Its 'lascivious' subject-matter was in fact very much in keeping with other large-scale history paintings in the Queen's House, including Orazio Gentileschi's *Lot and His Daughters* (cat. 84) and *Joseph and Potiphar's Wife* (cat. 85), as well as one of Van Dyck's rare narrative paintings, *Cupid and Psyche* (cat. 78), possibly also commissioned for Greenwich – not to mention the numerous reclining nude figures by Titian in the royal collection. The prevalence of works by Gentileschi in Greenwich is one of the most intriguing aspects of Stuart patronage of Italian artists. It represents in many ways its final episode as it played out after the first fury of collecting in the late 1620s and early 1630s and was sustained by the Queen rather than the King.

Charles had, early on, tried to attract foreign – and especially Italian – artists to the English court, understanding that they would enhance its prestige. The Bolognese painter Guercino reportedly declined the offer, put off by the weather and the company of heretics. Charles is also said to have written a personal letter to Francesco Albani, only to be turned down again.[15] Other European courts fared no better in their pursuit.[16] The artists' reluctance is easily understandable, given the absence of any religious commission and the few opportunities for history paintings or grand decorative cycles these invitations could have offered.

The English sojourn of the Tuscan painter Orazio Gentileschi (fig. 12) was prompted not by the royal couple but by the Duke of Buckingham, during the latter's visit to France in May 1625 to finalise the marriage of Charles and Henrietta Maria. England was to be the last stop in Gentileschi's peripatetic career in search of patronage, which took him to Rome, Ancona, Fabriano, Genoa and Paris, where he worked for Marie de' Medici, Henrietta Maria's mother. He moved to London in late September 1626 and remained there until his death in 1639. Only a dozen easel paintings and nine ceiling canvases are known from this artistic period and his stay in England should be perceived less as a coup in attracting a major Italian artist to the British Isles than as a mutually convenient arrangement: Gentileschi was already 63 years old when he arrived, and was accompanied by three dependent sons. Nevertheless, during his stay, he created some mesmerising works. His first commission was a ceiling painting, *Apollo and the Muses*, for Buckingham's residence, York House, just as Rubens was finishing his own contribution to that house, the *Apotheosis of the Duke of Buckingham* (both now destroyed; see cat. 11 for Rubens's preparatory sketch). The perceived competence of Italian artists in ambitious allegorical decorative schemes as well as large-scale history and religious painting meant that, with the notable exception of Rubens, the category was reserved for them. One can understand the frustration of Van Dyck, whose aspiration to paint history cycles was repeatedly thwarted, and of the Painter-Stainers' Company, whose members complained that foreign-born artists were taking away their livelihoods. Such projects however were rare, and Van Dyck certainly found portraiture a more profitable pursuit.

Buckingham's assassination in 1628 brought his architectural and decorative plans to a halt, but in the 1630s the Queen took up the mantle. Henrietta Maria was responsible for two of the most significant Baroque schemes of the period: the addition of a lavish new chapel at Somerset House (then called Denmark House) between 1632 and 1635, and the completion of the Queen's House in 1636 (with most of the interiors being finished by 1639). Both buildings were designed by Inigo Jones (cat. 6).[17] The Queen's House, begun in 1616 under Anne of Denmark, was given by Charles to Henrietta Maria in 1629 in an unfinished state. The Queen supervised its completion and decoration, including the commission to Reni and others to the Flemish painter Jacob Jordaens. The Great Hall (fig. 40) was adorned exclusively with Gentileschi's work, including the vast ceiling composed of nine canvases representing an allegory of Peace surrounded by the Arts. The series, now at Marlborough House, London, is much altered and damaged. The role played in the work's execution by Gentileschi's daughter, Artemisia, remains an open question.[18] The royal collection included seven of her paintings (see cat. 88), a few of which must have reached England before her.[19] Although expected to join her father and brothers for several years, she seems only to have arrived in London in 1638, a few months before her father's death and perhaps too late to play an important role in the ceiling commission. Despite its ambition, the composition of *Peace and the Arts* must have seemed quite tame and stilted compared with the Baroque whirlwind of Rubens's ceiling for the Banqueting Hall (fig. 37), unveiled a few years earlier in 1636. Similarly, Gentileschi's seductive and languid Old Testament scenes on the adjoining walls appear almost frozen and focused more on the lush drapery and Venetian blondness so admired by courtly collectors than on sweeping narratives.

Although she clearly had a strong interest in the arts, Henrietta Maria's taste in painting is not easy to assess. In 1635 the papal envoy Panzani commented on the Queen's disappointment when none of the paintings sent by Cardinal Barberini to the court appeared to be devotional. He also records her greater enthusiasm for reliquaries and novelties such as silk flowers.[20] Attachment to her paintings is, however, evident in her determination to reclaim her collection after the Restoration. The 1669 estate inventory of her last residence, the Château de Colombes on the outskirts of Paris (now destroyed), reveals that in her 'privy chamber' hung Gentileschi's large *Finding of Moses* (cat. 86) and *Joseph and Potiphar's Wife* (cat. 85), mementos of the glory of her British palaces.[21] Both paintings had been sold during the Commonwealth Sale but were returned to Charles II in 1660. Seicento art featured prominently at Colombes: the two Gentileschi works were accompanied by, among others, a *Madonna and Child* attributed to Giovanni Baglione (Royal Collection, now given to Anastasio Fontebuoni), as well as paintings by Reni and Domenico Fetti.

Henrietta Maria's impetus and engagement with the Italian artistic milieu are even more significant given that, as the global centre of Catholicism, Rome, for one, was a city largely off limits. If attracting Italian artists to the British Isles proved difficult, it was equally complex for English travellers to visit Italy and discover contemporary art for themselves. Rome also had some of the strictest export laws in Italy. The grant of a licence in 1626 to Nicholas Lanier (figs 9–10) was a rare occurrence. Travelling on behalf of the King, Lanier returned from Rome with a number of Italian Baroque works, including a *Landscape* and a *Prophet* by Guercino and pictures by Albani, Battistello Caracciolo and Antiveduto Grammatica (all unidentified).[22] One can imagine him doing the rounds of the Roman dealers and the artists' studios, trying to outbid other envoys. During an earlier tour of Italy, in 1621, the Duke of Buckingham's dynamic agent, Balthasar Gerbier, acquired two paintings by the Caravaggesque painter Bartolomeo Manfredi (a *David* and a *Biblical Scene*, unidentified) and the *Four Seasons* by Reni (Kunsthistorisches Museum, Vienna) – probably from the artists themselves – alongside works by the more familiar Venetian Cinquecento masters Titian, Tintoretto and Bassano.[23] Gerbier paid £70 for the Reni, a relative bargain compared to the impressive sum of £275 spent that same year on Titian's *Ecce Homo* (Kunsthistorisches Museum, Vienna).

Stemming from a family of devout Catholics, Thomas Howard, Earl of Arundel, was the only high-ranking member of the royal household to travel to Italy.[24] David Howarth has suggested that, on one of his several trips to Rome, Arundel was able to purchase works directly from artists' studios, including – from his heirs, as this was a few years after the artist's death – the large number of drawings by Annibale Carracci for the ceiling of the Galleria at Palazzo Farnese that were later recorded in the Earl's collection.[25] In his pursuits, Arundel would have been assisted by Marchese Vincenzo Giustiniani, one of the leading patrons of contemporary art in Rome, with whom he stayed around 1613. Arundel lived in the palazzo where Giustiniani had welcomed Caravaggio and others at the beginning of their careers, and must have admired the Marchese's extensive collection of paintings and antiquities. Arundel was obviously keen to keep abreast of artistic developments in Italy. A few years later, he described a painting by Gerrit van Honthorst, who had spent his early career in the Eternal City, as possessing something of 'Caravagioes colouringe, w[hi]ch is nowe soe much esteemed in Rome'.[26]

In contrast, the King and other collectors had to rely on reports from ambassadors and advice from artists. However, Charles's two closest advisors in the 1620s and 1630s, Inigo Jones and Orazio Gentileschi, had not travelled to Rome in decades. Attempting to define the King's taste for Cardinal Barberini, Panzani called on Gentileschi, whom he described as a 'Florentine painter who is here and quite good', for guidance.[27] Gentileschi's recommendations were quite out of date: from the list of possible artists submitted by Barberini,[28] he singled out Giovanni Lanfranco, Jusepe de Ribera and the Carracci – all of whom he knew from his time in Rome – because, he argued, they were not yet represented in the royal collection. He overlooked Domenichino, Pietro da Cortona and Nicolas Poussin, all equally absent, but from a younger generation.

In fact, contemporary Italian painting came into English hands less through direct patronage than as second-hand purchases from established collections on the peninsula and throughout Europe – much as older paintings were acquired. Baroque paintings, however, came in drips (often as part of bulk purchases) rather than through the systematic pursuit that characterised the collecting of Cinquecento paintings.

More than Rome, Venice was an important commercial hub, thanks to its more relaxed export laws, greater religious tolerance and thriving art market, especially as the city's own economic and artistic decline led to an outpouring of works for sale.[29] Gerbier, resourceful as ever, also undertook a prolific shopping trip to Paris in 1624, where he acquired – always for Buckingham – a *St Francis* by Giovanni Baglione, whom he deemed 'as good as Michael Angelo Carajoago [Caravaggio]'.[30] The reputation of 'Caravagioes colouringe' had reached London, and copies of his work as well as paintings by contemporary Caravaggesque painters appear in royal and aristocratic inventories from an early date. In addition to the work by Baglione, Buckingham's collection included a number of works by Manfredi, Honthorst and Orazio Borgianni, as well as three copies after Caravaggio.[31] The Marquess of Hamilton is said to have owned before 1625 a work attributed to Caravaggio, which remains unidentified.[32] Fittingly, the first English collector to own an identifiable work by the master was the King himself, who received the *Death of the Virgin* (fig. 42) in 1627 as part of the Gonzaga collection. The altarpiece, commissioned by Laerzio Cherubini for his family chapel in the church of Santa Maria della Scala in Rome but rejected by the religious authorities, had been purchased twenty years earlier by Duke

Fig. 42 Michelangelo Merisi da Caravaggio (1571–1610), *The Death of the Virgin*, 1601–05/06. Oil on canvas, 369 x 245 cm. Musée du Louvre, Paris, inv. 54

Fig. 43 Guido Reni (1575–1642), *Nessus Abducting Deianeira*, from the series *The Labours of Hercules*, 1617–21. Oil on canvas, 239 x 193 cm. Musée du Louvre, Paris, inv. 537

Vincenzo I Gonzaga on Rubens's advice and admired ever since. In England, it was singled out by Jean Puget de la Serre, one of the few contemporary sources to describe the King's collection *in situ*.[33] It is described hanging in the long gallery at St James's Palace alongside a copy of Caravaggio's *Madonna of Loreto*, masterpieces by Titian, Tintoretto and Jacopo Bassano, and Van Dyck's monumental equestrian portrait of the King (cat. 72) – a fitting cross-section of the highlights of the royal collection.[34]

Despite this apparent progressiveness and avant-garde taste, a certain ambivalence prevailed. Following his gift to Buckingham at their first meeting in 1625 of a work by Manfredi, the Savoyard diplomat Cesare Alessandro Scaglia wondered if the painting would suffice and whether 'it might be appropriate to give him another [picture] by an old master'.[35] Similarly, the Marquess of Hamilton warned his brother-in-law, Basil, Viscount Feilding, acting as his agent in Venice, to avoid confusing Michelangelo Merisi da Caravaggio with Polidoro da Caravaggio when seeking paintings for the King, who favoured the latter.[36]

The King's reported favourite Seicento painter was in fact the one most closely aligned with the classical tradition: Guido Reni, hailed at the time as the heir to Raphael.[37] Although paintings by Reni were in English courtly collections throughout the 1620s (in addition to the *Four Seasons* mentioned above, Buckingham owned at least two others and a copy of Reni's *St Sebastian*; Arundel and Hamilton possessed at least one original work each), the arrival of works from the Gonzaga collection in 1627 made the greatest impact in furthering the Bolognese painter's reputation; included were the *Labours of Hercules*, three of which also hung in the gallery at St James's Palace (including fig. 43).

How did contemporary Italian art fare in the Commonwealth Sale? One might have expected it to share the fate of the Queen's Chapel at Somerset House, ransacked by Puritans, and to have been ostracised for its ostentatious Catholic imagery on the one hand and its flaunting of Baroque sensuality on the other. In fact, the Commissioners followed the King's taste by placing high prices on works by Reni. For example, his 'Venus sitteing to be dressed by ye 3 Graces' (cat. 90) was valued at £200, twice the sum assigned to Titian's *St Margaret Triumphing over the Devil* hanging nearby and of a similar format, while his four *Labours of Hercules* were assigned a total estimate of £400. Gentileschi was also valued highly and his prices probably reflect first-hand knowledge of the payments he had received from his royal patron. *The Finding of Moses* and *Lot and His Daughters* were both valued at £80, on a par with prices fetched by Cinquecento masters. One of the most valuable pieces in the royal collection – and indeed the most expensive work of sculpture (including the antique statues) – was Bernini's bust, at £800.

The presence of this masterpiece in England was the result of one of the singular characteristics of Italian Baroque art at the court of Charles I: the key role played by his Queen. Her ties with the papacy were instrumental in facilitating commissions from artists south of the Alps. In addition, her decade-long patronage of Orazio Gentileschi in London (which may have emulated that of her mother) shaped the interior of the Queen's House into a stunning Baroque ensemble.

It has been argued that the English court had no systematic scheme for the patronage of artists,[38] and indeed the King approached the collecting of paintings less in a programmatic way than as the accumulation of the supreme luxury item. Nevertheless, the dispersal of the royal goods during the Commonwealth Sale and the destruction of significant works of art make it all too easy to forget that, in the second quarter of the seventeenth century, England was home to some of the finest masterpieces by contemporary Italian artists.

84
Orazio Gentileschi
Lot and His Daughters, 1628
Oil on canvas, 226 x 282 cm
Museo de Bellas Artes de Bilbao,
inv. 69/101

85
Orazio Gentileschi
Joseph and Potiphar's Wife, *c.* 1630–32
Oil on canvas, 206 x 261.9 cm
The Royal Collection / HM Queen Elizabeth II, RCIN 405477

86
Orazio Gentileschi
The Finding of Moses, *c.* 1630–33
Oil on canvas, 257 x 301 cm
Private collection. Courtesy
of Pyms Gallery, London

87
Orazio Gentileschi
Head of a Woman,
c. 1630–35
Oil on panel, 42 x 37 cm
Private collection

88
Artemisia Gentileschi
Allegory of Painting, *c.* 1638–39
Oil on canvas, 98.6 x 75.2 cm
The Royal Collection / HM Queen
Elizabeth II, RCIN 405551

89
Cristofano Allori
Judith with the Head of Holofernes, 1613
Oil on canvas, 120.4 x 100.3 cm
The Royal Collection / HM Queen Elizabeth II, RCIN 404989

90
Guido Reni and workshop
The Toilet of Venus, *c.* 1620–25
Oil on canvas, 281.9 x 205.7 cm
The National Gallery, London, inv. NG90

8

THE MORTLAKE TAPESTRIES

CHARLES I AND RAPHAEL'S 'ACTS OF THE APOSTLES'

HELEN WYLD

Charles I's purchase of seven of Raphael's cartoons of the *Acts of the Apostles* (including figs 44–47) is usually seen in the context of his collecting of Italian painting. However the cartoons were not displayed as works of art during Charles's lifetime; they were intended for use at the new tapestry workshop at Mortlake. While connoisseurship of paintings was a new phenomenon in early Stuart Britain, the use of tapestries and rich textiles was part of an established mode of display. Aristotle's concept of 'magnificence', revived in the Renaissance, sanctioned expenditure on buildings, ceremonies and furnishings as a virtuous activity demonstrating fitness to rule.[1] With a rich heritage from his grandfather, James V of Scotland, and Henry VIII of England,[2] Charles understood the importance of such display, and the power of the tapestry medium. At Mortlake these concerns were united with a new appreciation of the visual arts. The use of cartoons by Raphael demonstrated Charles's status as collector and connoisseur, while the vast scale and physical richness of the *Acts of the Apostles* tapestries embodied the magnificence of the King. Many times more expensive than any of the paintings Charles acquired, the Mortlake *Acts* are a reminder of the continued importance of splendour, materiality and ceremony at the Caroline court.[3]

In 1623, Charles instructed Sir Francis Crane, head of the newly founded Mortlake tapestry works, to 'send to Genna [Genoa] for certayne drawings of Raphaell of Urbin, which were desseignes for tapestries made for Pope Leo the X. and for which there is £300 to be payed, besides their charge of bringing home'.[4] Intended solely for use in making tapestries, the cartoons were kept in a chest cut into strips during Charles's lifetime, and only assembled and displayed as works of art some 80 years later. The *editio princeps* of the *Acts*, from which the four tapestries included here (cats 91–94) are drawn, was begun in around 1630 and not completed until 1640–41. At £8 per Flemish ell (a unit of length equivalent to 68.6 centimetres), the tapestries outpriced all others in production at Mortlake, due to the large number of figures and the quantity of gold thread; the set of seven would have cost around £4,500.[5] The *Acts* were greeted with wonder by contemporaries: 'A new tapestry all in silk, which has just come from the workshop, representing the twelve apostles ... we cannot but congratulate the vanity of the artisan, who thus challenges all others in his craft.'[6]

Commissioned by the Medici Pope Leo X in 1515 and woven in Brussels shortly afterwards, the original *Acts* were intended for use in the very specific context of the Sistine Chapel. Raphael's ten designs were comprised of two cycles on the lives of St Peter and St Paul, the dual founders of the Church. Emphasising their mission from Christ to preach to the Jews and the Gentiles as God's representatives on earth, the series underlines the pre-eminence of the Catholic Church as well as the authority of the Papacy. In more immediate terms the commission marked Leo's major contribution to the decoration of the papal chapel: Raphael's tapestries, intended for the lower walls, were to hang below Michelangelo's ceiling and a mural cycle with scenes from the story of Moses and the life of Christ.[7]

When the first of Leo X's tapestries were seen in 1517 they were judged 'the finest in Christendom' and 'the most beautiful thing of this sort that has been made in our age', reactions that respond as much to the opulence of the set as to the strength of the designs.[8] New editions were woven for François I of France in the early 1530s and for Henry VIII in around 1540–42; further weavings went to the Spanish Crown and to Cardinal Ercole Gonzaga. Borders with scenes from the life of Leo X

Fig. 44 Raphael (1483–1520), *The Miraculous Draught of Fishes*, *c.* 1515–16. Bodycolour over charcoal on paper mounted on canvas, 319 x 399 cm. The Royal Collection, RCIN 912944

were replaced in these re-editions with a new scheme, probably designed for François I, on the effects of Good Government – the first of many appropriations of the *Acts* for new purposes.

The fame of the *Acts* was quickly established. Aside from their reproduction in tapestry, the designs were engraved, some before they left Raphael's workshop. The cartoons themselves, on their arrival in Brussels, had an immediate impact. Although artistic cross-currents between north and south were nothing new, Raphael's designs, with their monumental figures, spatial clarity and narrative force, represented a departure from the prevailing style of Netherlandish tapestry design, which was often characterised by crowded compositions and a wealth of surface detail. Raphael's painterly style and expanses of unadorned water, sky and drapery also posed a significant practical and artistic challenge to the weavers. Leo's tapestries and subsequent sixteenth-century weavings (fig. 49), show numerous departures from the cartoons, and it seems probable that they were woven from copies.[9] When the Mortlake workshop came to create their own versions 100 years later, copies were once again used on the looms, but with far more concern for accuracy.

The decision in 1619 to found a native tapestry workshop, the first of its kind in the British Isles, coincided with a broadening of ambition in arts patronage at the Stuart court. Inigo Jones's Banqueting House had been started that year, and it has been convincingly suggested that the Mortlake workshop was initiated partly in order to furnish the new building with tapestries. The protracted negotiations for a 'Spanish match' at this time were also a key motivating factor. On some level at least, the Mortlake enterprise, like the Banqueting House, was part of a new artistic programme designed to enshrine the political and religious harmony that would, it was hoped, ensue from the union of a Protestant prince and a Catholic princess.[10]

By the late sixteenth century small workshops manned by émigré Flemish weavers had been established at many European courts.[11] A committee established by James I to found the workshop noted that:

> *His majesty knowing in his great wisdom that arts and manufactures do add both ornament and wealth to those countries and commonwealths, where they most flourish … Amongst the rest he hath been pleased of late to cast his princely cogitation upon that excellent art of making tapestry, and finding that our neighbouring countries have attained already so great a perfection therein, is not without hopes that the same may be established also in this kingdom.*[12]

The immediate inspiration for the Mortlake works was a new Parisian enterprise set up by Henri IV in 1607, which was the subject of a report submitted to Parliament in 1618. Premises were purchased at Mortlake, on the Thames to the west of the capital, and some 50 weavers came from Brussels, others from Paris.[13] Although King James officially founded the new workshop, Charles, Prince of Wales, who was seventeen years old when the idea was first mooted, clearly played an active role from the start. Not only was the workshop established under the ownership of Sir Francis Crane, then the young prince's secretary, but its first tapestries were woven for Charles rather than for the King.[14]

At first, Mortlake produced versions of sixteenth-century designs, in some cases copied from tapestries already in the royal collection. *The Story of Venus and Vulcan* was the first, with weavings made for Charles and the Duke of Buckingham by 1623, and sets of the *Months* and the *Queen of Sheba* soon followed.[15] These historic subjects were updated with modern border designs, often closely based on recent Parisian examples that must have been brought to London by Philip de Maecht, head of the workshop at Mortlake and formerly a chief weaver in Paris. The early series quickly established the quality and character of Mortlake production, but they did not adequately reflect the taste and ideals of the young prince and collector. It is therefore no surprise that when the opportunity arose in 1623 to acquire seven of the cartoons for Raphael's *Acts*, Charles acted fast. In the same year, efforts were also underway to secure the services of Francis Cleyn, a German artist trained at the Danish court, as designer. Cleyn's input was to be a vital component in realising the *Acts*, and indeed the entire Mortlake enterprise. Isaac Fuller notes that the artist had become known to Sir Henry Wotton, English Ambassador in Venice, while studying in Italy and had been recommended to Charles; Cleyn travelled to England in 1623 and presented himself at court, only to find the Prince away in Madrid. King James nonetheless welcomed him, and in 1624 he returned with his family, and settled in the new Limner's House at Mortlake.

Among Cleyn's first tasks was to create new tapestry designs for production at Mortlake – as Fuller put it, 'his designing being the *soul*, as the working is the *body*, of that mystery [tapestry]'.[16] A bill he submitted to Charles in March 1625 lists a wide variety of work, including five drawings for tapestries of *Love and Folly* (no weavings survive).[17] In the late 1620s Cleyn produced two further series, the *Story of Hero and Leander* and the *Five Senses*.[18] Cleyn's distinctive style in the *Love and Folly* and *Hero and Leander* series shows a clear awareness of the Venetian paintings so beloved of his patron, while the *Senses*, with their grotesque decoration, recall more recent French models. The themes chosen also reflect the preoccupations of the court. *Hero and Leander*, a tragic love story based on Christopher Marlowe's erotic poem of 1598, contains echoes of Charles's failed voyage of courtship to Spain, his affection for the Duke of Buckingham, and recent naval exploits, while the *Senses* can be read as an expression of the neo-Platonic philosophy often explored in court masques.[19] Cleyn's final original series for Mortlake, the *Horses*, with stories from Ovid, was designed in the early 1630s.[20] He also created copies of paintings for reproduction in tapestry, including Titian's *Diana and Callisto* and *Supper at Emmaus* (cat. 45),[21] and designed at least one single piece, *St George and the Dragon*, whose relationship with Van Dyck's possible project for a mural or tapestry series of the Procession of Garter Knights (see cat. 81) is intriguing.[22] Cleyn may have been involved in translating sixteenth-century designs of *Playing Boys* into cartoons for use at Mortlake.

The Acts of the Apostles was undoubtedly the most ambitious tapestry series produced at Mortlake. Far more than a simple reweaving of old designs, the series demonstrates a complex engagement with the central artistic and religious preoccupations of Charles's reign. Indeed, through additions, complex new borders and the astonishing faithfulness with which Raphael's cartoons are reproduced, the series actively recruits the Renaissance master into the service of the Stuart king.

Cleyn's 1625 bill shows that by this date he had already produced for use at Mortlake copies of two of Raphael's original cartoons, the *Death of Ananias* (fig. 45) and the *Blinding of Elymas* (fig. 46), and one design for a 'great border about it with his Majesty's arms'. The large sums charged – £70 and £60 respectively – show that Cleyn worked on the

copy cartoons alone, and indicate the extreme care taken to ensure that Raphael's designs were faithfully reproduced.[23] This becomes evident through comparison of the original cartoons and the Mortlake tapestries, which 'correct' a number of deviations found in the sixteenth-century weavings – deviations that must have arisen in the copy cartoons used in Brussels (it is interesting to note that Cleyn seems to have referred to Henry VIII's sixteenth-century weavings as well).[24] In the *Sacrifice at Lystra* (fig. 47), for example, details such as the crutches at the lower edge, which had been rearranged in the sixteenth-century weavings (fig. 49), revert to their original form at Mortlake, and instances where the colours of drapery were altered are corrected.[25] More tellingly, the Mortlake weaving demonstrates a far greater understanding of the qualities of perspective and chiaroscuro found in Raphael's cartoons. Spatial depth is more convincing, and the shadows cast by Raphael's figures on the paving and buildings, which have disappeared or been misunderstood in the earlier tapestry, reappear in the Mortlake version. Recent analysis of Raphael's cartoons has shown that under Charles I they were mounted so that, although still in strips, they could be hung and viewed as complete pieces. This may have been to facilitate Cleyn's copies but was perhaps also to inform the weaving process directly;

Fig. 45 Raphael (1483–1520), *The Death of Ananias*, *c.* 1515–16. Bodycolour over charcoal on paper mounted on canvas, 342 x 532 cm. The Royal Collection, RCIN 912947

in 1639, by which time Cleyn's copies were complete, some of the cartoons had been sent 'to Mr ffranciscus Cleane at Moore clap to make hangings by'.[26]

Of Raphael's original ten cartoons, only seven were acquired in Genoa in 1623. Leaving aside *Paul in Prison*, the fate of which is unknown,[27] the remaining two, the *Stoning of Stephen* and the *Conversion of Saul*, seem to have been in the collection of the Medici family by the early seventeenth century. In 1627 an attempt was made via Amerigo Salvetti, the Florentine resident in London, to secure copies of these for use at Mortlake (his plea noting that 'these things are central to the genius and delight of the King').[28] It may have been following the failure of this attempt that Cleyn designed a new scene for the *Acts*: *The Death of Sapphira*.[29] Sapphira was the wife of Ananias, and both were struck down for keeping back a portion of money they had promised to the church. Both tales underline the duty of the faithful to their spiritual government, with interesting implications in the years around 1630. It has been suggested that *Sapphira* can be seen as a response to

Fig. 46 Raphael (1483–1520), *The Blinding of Elymas (The Conversion of the Proconsul)*, c. 1515–16. Bodycolour over charcoal on paper mounted on canvas, 342 x 446 cm. The Royal Collection, RCIN 912948

public protests against royal taxes raised for an expansion of the fleet and, fittingly, the edification of Old St Paul's. The only known weaving of the *Death of Sapphira* survives as part of the set of *Acts* made in 1636–37 for the Earl of Pembroke, now at Boughton House, Northamptonshire (fig. 50); it seems probable, though, that the scene was also included in Charles's first weaving, but is now lost.[30] Cleyn's design clearly makes references to the *Death of Ananias*, and draws on figures from elsewhere in the *Acts* as well, setting them within a Bramantean portico reminiscent of one of Inigo Jones's stage sets. Numerous drawings for the composition survive (including fig. 48), charting Cleyn's struggle to imitate Raphael's style.[31]

The Death of Sapphira points to a key question raised by the Mortlake *Acts*: what did a series designed to enshrine the authority of the Catholic Church mean to a Protestant monarch? It is very likely that Henry VIII's acquisition of *Acts* tapestries a century earlier had a calculated significance, it coming shortly after the break with Rome. Henry's propagandists asserted that all bishops and priests of the church are equal inheritors of the apostolic mission, directly challenging the authority of the Pope; the acquisition of the *Acts of the Apostles* was intended to bolster Henry's claim as the new St Paul.[32] For the Stuarts in the early seventeenth century, the apostolic tradition was again the basis of the King's authority as Supreme Governor of the Church of England, and once again the *Acts* were repurposed to support this alternative ecclesiastical lineage.

Charles's reign was dogged by religious controversy. The Catholic match, pursued by his father from 1618 as a route to religious harmony in Europe, led to division at home, alienating many devoted Protestants, who were branded Puritans, and setting them against supporters of the King. These divisions were compounded under Charles, whose love of church decoration and liturgical ceremony, combined with the presence of a Catholic faction surrounding his wife at court, spurred outrage at his perceived closeness to Rome. The policies of Archbishop Laud, which included the reform of church practice on the one hand, and the banning of debate on contentious issues such as predestination on the other, added fuel to the fire during the 1630s. Nonetheless, far from being closet Catholics, both Charles and Laud were committed to ecumenical unity. Laud stressed that the Anglican faith was just one of the

Fig. 47 Raphael (1483–1520), *The Sacrifice at Lystra*, c. 1515–16. Bodycolour over charcoal on paper mounted on canvas, 347 x 542 cm. The Royal Collection, RCIN 912949

Fig. 48 Francis Cleyn (1582–1658), *Study of a Boy Leading a Blind Man*, c. 1626–35. Black and white chalks on blue paper, 17.4 x 13.5 cm. Southampton University, Special Collections, inv. MS 292, fol. 16

Churches of Christ; Charles, married to a Catholic, would have 'given one of his hands' in return for reconciliation with Rome – a subject of open discussion at court in the late 1630s.[33]

Traces of these concerns may be found in the Mortlake *Acts*. The spectacular new borders created by Cleyn – 'perhaps the most sumptuous in the history of tapestry' according to Jean Vittet – have been compared to Jones's proscenium-arch designs for the masques; both provide a framework for interpreting the main action.[34] A central royal coat of arms and *trompe-l'œil* framing devices are augmented by narrative panels and figures that expand on the moral lesson of the main scenes, and, as Isabelle Denis has shown, certain larger themes emerge across the series, often via emblems derived from Andrea Alciato (commonly known as Alciati) and Cesare Ripa. On the *Death of Ananias*, for example, we find putti with

Fig. 49 Jan Van Tieghem (fl. 1540–73) and other workshops after Raphael (1483–1520), *The Sacrifice at Lystra*, 1528–57. Tapestry, wool and silk thread, 495 x 610 cm. Palazzo Ducale, Mantua

the attributes of the cardinal and theological virtues; however, alongside Faith and Hope, Charity is conspicuously absent. Denis suggests that this is a pointed rejection of the Catholic doctrine of salvation through good works, insisting rather on justification by faith alone, a central tenet of the Anglican 'middle way' between the Catholic position and the Calvinist insistence on predestination. Elsewhere, depictions of Faith are repeatedly accompanied by closed books, modifying traditional representations. In the *Death of Ananias* a female figure is accompanied by an infant with three closed books and a shining sun, representing Divine Truth, which transcends the scriptures. Falsehood on the other hand is accompanied by an infant holding a mask, for dissimulation, with an open book with a sword resting on it, recalling but subverting Ripa's allegory of Doctrine (symbolised by a sun over a sceptre and an open book). The sword and open book can be read as a warning against demanding a strict adherence to the scriptures by forceful means, and a call for tolerance; the sun with closed books as a renewed insistence on the importance of faith over knowledge. It is tempting to read these allegories in light of Laud's suppression of debate (intended to avoid conflict, whatever its actual effects), but also of Charles's commitment to ecclesiastical unity, an interpretation that chimes with the larger theme of the *Acts* in their English context: parity, and a shared lineage, between the Anglican and the Roman church.

No record of the intended location of the *Acts* has survived, though the theory that they were displayed at the Banqueting House is appealing for a number of reasons. The use of rich textiles to dramatise royal power has its origins in liturgical practice, a fitting appropriation in the context of Divine Right monarchy under the early Stuarts.[35] The Banqueting House was the location for the enactment of a cult of royal divinity in the 1630s: the site of diplomatic receptions, touching for the 'king's evil', and the ceremonies of the Order of the Garter, whose foundations of loyalty and faith were reinforced by Charles, its aim redefined as the pursuit of peace, not war.[36] Although their subjects were not specified, 'rich hangings' were in evidence on all these occasions; what better subject than the *Acts*, with their message of religious harmony and faith in the King as Governor of the Church, to hang beneath Rubens's ceiling glorifying

Fig. 50 Mortlake Workshop, *The Death of Sapphira*, *c.* 1650–60. Border design by Francis Cleyn (1582–1658), with the arms of the Earl of Pembroke. Tapestry, wool and silk thread, 432 x 648 cm. Buccleuch Collection, Boughton House, Northamptonshire

James as peacemaker and unifier of nations? After the outbreak of Civil War, Charles's *Acts*, which so powerfully embody the most ambitious, and contentious, aspects of his reign, were the first of the royal tapestries to be sold, disappearing before the Commonwealth inventories were drawn up.[37]

91
Mortlake Workshop after Raphael,
borders designed by Francis Cleyn
The Miraculous Draught of Fishes, c. 1636–37
Wool, silk and gilt-metal-wrapped thread, 530 x 580 cm
Mobilier national, Paris, inv. GMTT 16/4

QVID LABOR IN
PONTVM SVDAT.
LABOR OMNIS INANIS,
SE NISI DIVINA DIRIGAT
ARTE LABOR.
RETIA QVID FVGITIS PISCES.
EN CHRISTVS IN ALTV
DESCENDENS QVI VOS CONDIDIT,
IPSE CAPIT.

92
Mortlake Workshop after Raphael, borders designed by Francis Cleyn
The Death of Ananias, *c.* 1630–31
Wool, silk and gilt-metal-wrapped thread, 530 x 700 cm
Mobilier national, Paris, inv. GMTT 16/6

93
Mortlake Workshop after Raphael, borders designed by Francis Cleyn
The Blinding of Elymas, *c.* 1631–36
Wool, silk and gilt-metal-wrapped thread, 538 x 713 cm
Mobilier national, Paris, inv. GMTT 16/3

94
Mortlake Workshop after Raphael,
borders designed by Francis Cleyn
The Sacrifice at Lystra, *c.* 1639–40
Wool, silk and gilt-metal-wrapped
thread, 535 x 720 cm
Mobilier national, Paris,
inv. GMTT 16/5

9

THE WHITEHALL CABINET

A 'MORE SOLITARY PLACE': CHARLES I AND HIS CABINET

VANESSA REMINGTON AND LUCY WHITAKER

Charles I's Cabinet Room was a locked, private enclave at the heart of the King's private apartments in Whitehall Palace. It was here that he and his closest associates could retreat from the busy public rooms and thoroughfares of the rambling palace to enjoy his most treasured small-scale paintings and works of art 'in the secresie of a retired and more solitary place'.[1] The 'new erected Cabbonett' was located close to the King's Bedchamber, at the culmination of a sequence of three Privy Lodging Rooms where the King's most important paintings hung.[2] No plan of the room survives, but it was large enough to accommodate 73 paintings, 36 statues, 35 bas-reliefs, 77 limnings and miniatures, 54 books, 4 pieces of gold, 4 agates, about 33 coins and medals, 28 'small objects', 4 'crystals' (polished lenses used to study small objects), 4 framed engravings, 14 silver pieces of plate, about 4 ivories, 17 drawings, some wax sculptures and a number of miscellaneous objects (including silver compasses, mathematical instruments, a telescope and an unspecified musical instrument).[3] In 1630–31 the Cabinet Room was fitted out with cupboards to house the smaller works of art; wainscoting and window shutters were added later in 1632–33.[4] All the sculptures were arranged on platforms in the window embrasures apart from two busts which were placed on a table in the centre of the room. Above the table and fitted into the ceiling was Rubens's sketch for the ceiling of the Banqueting House.[5] The nearby Chair Room served as a smaller cabinet room with 40 paintings and 12 statues, similarly arranged and with fitted cupboards.[6]

The core of the contents of the new Cabinet and the Chair Room was inherited by Charles I from his older brother, Henry, Prince of Wales. Henry's important collection of coins, medals, seals, gems and bronze statuettes had previously been kept at St James's Palace, in the Cabinet designed for him by Inigo Jones.[7] Jones was in charge of Charles I's building works between 1625 and 1642 and had designed a Cabinet for Henrietta Maria at Somerset House. It is likely that he was responsible for the new Cabinet at Whitehall Palace, although there is no contemporary documentary evidence for this.[8] As an inveterate traveller in Italy, however, Jones had more direct experience of the Italian *studiolo*, the model for this sort of display space, than anyone else in England at the time. Charles I's experience of a connoisseur's cabinet of this type may have been limited to his brother's Cabinet at St James's Palace; there is no evidence that he saw anything similar during his visit to Spain in 1623. Charles may therefore have been inspired by accounts from Jones and other close associates of princely and noble cabinet collections in Europe. The Habsburg Emperor Rudolf II's cabinet at Prague Castle, perhaps the finest example of the northern European *kunstkammer* at the time, would have been familiar to Charles from descriptions provided by Abraham van der Doort, who had been in the Emperor's service until about 1609.

Van der Doort had come to the attention of Prince Henry as a wax modeller and engraver of coins and medals and served as Keeper of the Cabinet Room to the Prince until the latter's death in 1612. He was reappointed as 'Keeper of the Cabbonett Room', then still in St James's Palace, soon after Charles I's accession in 1625.[9] His custodial duties included the collection, receipt, sorting and commissioning of copies of the works of art and rarities in his care. In the same year Van der Doort was also appointed Overseer or Surveyor of 'all our pictures of Us, our Heires and Successors'.[10] After the contents of the Cabinet Room were transferred to Whitehall Palace (probably in the early 1630s), Van der Doort took up the challenge of recording all the King's collections. His inventory provides a

full description of the contents of Whitehall and was completed by 1639. For Van der Doort the Cabinet Room and Chair Room were the heart of the King's collection, and the problems he encountered caring for these rooms are likely to have contributed to his eventual suicide in 1640.[11] As the contents of the Cabinet were dispersed in the Commonwealth Sale after Charles I's death, and the room itself probably demolished, Van der Doort's painstaking record is now the only means by which we may analyse the room and its contents.[12] His inventory survives in four manuscript versions; the primary version (cat. 140) was written by a scribe, but contains many annotations in Van der Doort's hand and was his working copy.[13] Charles I is believed to have owned and used a fair copy of the section relating to the Cabinet that survives in the Royal Library at Windsor Castle, perhaps annotated in his hand.[14] Although rendered in Van der Doort's idiosyncratic and phonetic spelling, the entries are detailed and systematic, giving an attribution and provenance for each item and dimensions for paintings, so that the reader can also glean some sense of the appearance of the room. The numbering in the inventory can in several instances be matched to surviving inscriptions on paper labels that were affixed to the reverse of paintings and miniatures. Many of the King's paintings were also identified by the distinctive brand with the crown and the King's initials 'CR' on the reverse.

Fig. 51 Palma Vecchio (*c.* 1480–1528), *Virgin and Child with St Catherine of Alexandria and St John the Baptist*, *c.* 1527–28. Oil on panel, 60 x 81.5 cm. The Royal Collection, RCIN 405723

Van der Doort's description of the contents of the Cabinet Room begins by listing the paintings that were 'placed round about' the walls.[15] Among the largest paintings were Francesco Vecellio's *Lucretia*,[16] then attributed to Titian, and El Labrador's 'Picture of severall sort of fruites in a white earthen vessel, grapes, Aples Chestnutts – and the like'.[17] Also on the large side was Palma Vecchio's *Virgin and Child with St Catherine of Alexandria and St John the Baptist* (fig. 51), yet the majority of the paintings in the Cabinet were far smaller: either the height or the width of almost 50 of the 81 framed pictures measured less than 12 inches (30.5 cm), including Jan Gossaert's 'indifferent

auncient Gentleman' (cat. 97).[18] The smallest painting was Adam Elsheimer's *Witch Riding Backwards on a Goat* (cat. 105) for which Van der Doort gave dimensions of '0 ft 5½ in x 0 ft 4 in'.[19] The number and diminutive scale of the paintings that hung in the Cabinet suggest that this display must have been densely arranged, in accordance with the norm for cabinets at the time. William Sanderson, writing in *Graphice* in 1658, advised 'not to Clutter the Room with too many Pieces, unless in Galleries and *Repositories*, as rarities of severall Artizans intermingled…'.[20] Outstanding among the paintings are Andrea Mantegna's *Death of the Virgin* (fig. 54), Leonardo da Vinci's *St John the Baptist* (fig. 52) and Raphael's *St George and the Dragon* (fig. 53). The King had received the latter in exchange for his volume of Holbein portrait drawings (cats 98, 100–02).[21] Van der Doort was careful to specify the type of frame for each painting: 37 were in black ebony frames, 14 were in plain wooden frames, and the remainder were in gilded frames.

Fig. 52 Leonardo da Vinci (1452–1519), *St John the Baptist*, 1513–16. Oil on panel, 69 x 57 cm. Musée du Louvre, Paris, inv. 775

Fig. 53 Raphael (1483–1520), *St George and the Dragon*, c. 1506. Oil on panel, 28.5 x 21.5 cm. National Gallery of Art, Washington, D.C., inv. 1937.1.26

A notable feature of the Cabinet Room was how few framed drawings hung on the walls.[22] Finished, framed drawings were to be seen in other areas of Whitehall Palace, but almost all the drawings in the Cabinet were kept in portfolios or volumes with the books. One of these was a volume 'in dry Cullors of the Cheifest Nobility and famous men at the tyme in Ffraunce', but

Fig. 54 Andrea Mantegna (1430–1506), *The Death of the Virgin*, c. 1642. Tempera on panel, 54.5 x 42 cm. Museo Nacional del Prado, Madrid, inv. P00248

others seem to have been of a different nature, and constituted practical, working drawings.[23] There was, for example, a large white vellum folio of eight drawings by Orazio Gentileschi, which appear to have been designs for Mortlake tapestries.[24]

The books, listed together with the volumes of drawings, give a flavour of Charles I's interests. Prominent among them was a book of the Statutes of the Order of the Garter given to the King by Anne of Denmark, and there were also emblem books, books concerning antique medals, and a book detailing the usage of mathematical instruments.[25] The statues, half of which were inherited from Henry, Prince of Wales, illustrate the King's interest in the antique. The majority of the statuary was classical in subject-matter with no fewer than three statuettes of Hercules. There were small bronzes by or after Giambologna and contemporary sculptures by François Duquesnoy and Francesco Fanelli (cats 115–16). Most of the bas-reliefs were by the greatly admired Van Vianen family, for example Paul van Vianen's *Jupiter and Io* (fig. 55).[26] A bronze bust of the King by Hubert Le Sueur and a bust of a woman representing Piety were placed on the table in the centre of the room.[27]

A unique aspect of Charles I's Cabinet Room in terms of number and quality was its group of ten miniature copies of oil paintings (including cats 111, 113–14, 117).[28] These limnings, painted in watercolour and bodycolour on vellum, were framed in 'dowble shutting Cases with Locks and keys and glasses over them'.[29] The herald Edward Norgate recounts in his

Fig. 55 Paul van Vianen (1570–1614), *Jupiter and Io*, after 1603. Gilt bronze, diameter 20.3 cm. Museum für Angewandte Kunst, Cologne, inv. H 1019

treatise *Miniatura or the Arte of Limning* (1620) how this new art form was devised by the miniature-painter Peter Oliver at the instigation of Charles I. Peter Oliver had in fact learnt the technique from his father, Isaac Oliver. The earliest dated example of his work for Charles I dates from 1628 (cat. 117). It is possible that these portable copies of the King's favourite paintings were initially intended to travel with this peripatetic monarch to allow him to enjoy his paintings at one remove. When the Cabinet Room was installed at Whitehall Palace, however, the limnings were brought together with Charles's collection of portrait miniatures. Van der Doort was put in charge of commissioning copies, which was extended to other artists such as John Hoskins and Richard Gibson. The status accorded to these limned copies seems to have been high, as attested by the value (typically £50) assigned to them in the valuation of the King's goods for sale. Balthasar Gerbier, who was himself a practising miniaturist, commended 'Isac, Peter Olivier and Haskins for limning' in the same context as citing Raphael, Dürer, Parmigianino, Correggio, Titian, Leonardo and others for their respective painting skills.[30] Peter Oliver inscribed two of his works 'Imitatus Est. Petrus Olivarus', stressing his role as copyist. This may have been in recognition of the art of limning as a gentlemanly if not princely skill, one that was fit for members of the King's immediate circle, including Sir James Palmer as well as Gerbier. It is noteworthy that in 1622 Henry Peacham cited Emmanuel Philibert, Duke of Savoy, as 'a great prince who could draw and limne excellently' and that Horace Walpole later recorded that Charles I himself had been known for his 'singular skill in limning'.[31]

The fulfilment of Charles I's Cabinet Room project at Whitehall was mirrored by the establishment in the 1630s of the Green Closet at Ham House by Sir William Murray, a member of the Whitehall group of connoisseurs who had accompanied Charles to Spain in 1623.[32] Doubtless other members of the King's circle also displayed their artwork in cabinets, although no evidence survives for this in the cases of Buckingham, Arundel or Hamilton. Certainly, by the time of Charles I's death, the fashion for cabinet-room displays had become so entrenched that the regicide Colonel John Hutchinson, having purchased a number of the King's paintings at the Commonwealth Sale, immediately created 'a neat cabinett' for their display at his country home in Nottinghamshire.[33]

95
Quinten Massys
Desiderius Erasmus, 1517
Oil on panel, 50.5 x 45.2 cm
The Royal Collection / HM Queen Elizabeth II, RCIN 405759

96
Quinten Massys
Pieter Gillis, 1517
Oil on panel, 74.5 x 53.4 cm
Longford Castle Collection

97
Jan Gossaert
Portrait of a Man Holding a Glove, *c.* 1530–32
Oil on panel, 24.3 x 16.8 cm
The National Gallery, London, inv. NG946

98
Hans Holbein the Younger
William Reskimer, *c.* 1532–34
Black and coloured chalks, pen and brown ink and metalpoint on pale pink prepared paper, 29 x 21 cm
The Royal Collection / HM Queen Elizabeth II, RCIN 912237

99
Hans Holbein the Younger
William Reskimer, *c.* 1532–34
Oil on panel, 46 x 33.5 cm
The Royal Collection / HM Queen Elizabeth II, RCIN 404422

Iudge More Sr Tho: Mores Father.

101
Hans Holbein the Younger
Anne Cresacre, *c.* 1526–27
Black and coloured chalks on paper, 37.2 x 26.6 cm
The Royal Collection / HM Queen Elizabeth II, RCIN 912270

102
Hans Holbein the Younger
John More, *c.* 1526–27
Black and coloured chalks on paper, 38.1 x 28.1 cm
The Royal Collection / HM Queen Elizabeth II, RCIN 912226

100
Hans Holbein the Younger
Sir John More, *c.* 1526–27
Black and coloured chalks on paper, 35.1 x 27.3 cm
The Royal Collection / HM Queen Elizabeth II, RCIN 912224

103
Hans Holbein the Younger
Charles Brandon, 1541
Watercolour on vellum laid on card, diameter 5.5 cm
The Royal Collection / HM Queen Elizabeth II, RCIN 422295

104
Hans Holbein the Younger
Henry Brandon, *c.* 1541
Watercolour on vellum laid on card, diameter 5.6 cm
The Royal Collection / HM Queen Elizabeth II, RCIN 422294

105
Adam Elsheimer after Albrecht Dürer
Witch Riding Backwards on a Goat,
c. 1596–98
Oil on copper, 13.6 x 9.9 cm
The Royal Collection / HM Queen
Elizabeth II, RCIN 404717

106
Paul Bril
Landscape with Goatherds, *c.* 1620
Oil on copper, 11.3 x 14.3 cm
The Royal Collection / HM Queen
Elizabeth II, RCIN 403033

107
Rembrandt van Rijn
Portrait of a Old Woman
('The Artist's Mother'), *c.* 1627–29
Oil on panel, 61.3 x 47.4 cm
The Royal Collection / HM Queen
Elizabeth II, RCIN 405000

108
Orazio Samacchini
The Risen Christ, after 1564
Oil on panel, 38.1 x 24.8 cm
Cobbe Collection, Hatchlands Park, inv. CC548

109
Lucas Vorsterman
after Annibale Carracci
The Agony in the Garden, 1627
Engraving, 39.5 x 30 cm
The British Museum, London,
inv. U,1.120

110
Annibale Carracci
The Agony in the Garden, *c.* 1596–97
Oil on panel, 39.1 x 30.3 cm
The Royal Collection / HM Queen
Elizabeth II, RCIN 402990

111
Peter Oliver after Titian
Conjugal Allegory ('The Allegory of Alfonso d'Avalos'), 1629
Watercolour and bodycolour with gold paint on vellum, 12.2 x 12.5 cm
The Royal Collection / HM Queen Elizabeth II, RCIN 452459

112
Attributed to Isaac Oliver
after Hans Holbein the Younger
The Dance of Death: The Prince, *c.* 1610–15
Watercolour with gold paint on paper, 6.3 x 5.3 cm
The Royal Collection / HM Queen Elizabeth II, RCIN 452454

113
Peter Oliver after Correggio
Venus and Cupid with a Satyr, 1633
Watercolour and bodycolour on vellum, 20.6 x 14.1 cm
The Royal Collection / HM Queen Elizabeth II, RCIN 452457

114
Peter Oliver after Correggio
Venus with Mercury and Cupid ('The School of Love'), 1634
Watercolour and bodycolour on vellum, 19.1 x 12.2 cm
The Royal Collection / HM Queen Elizabeth II, RCIN 452458

115
Francesco Fanelli
St George and the Dragon, *c.* 1635–40
Bronze, height 19.2 cm
Victoria and Albert Museum,
London, inv. A.5-1953

116
Francesco Fanelli
Cupid on Horseback, *c.* 1635–40
Bronze, height 14.9 cm
Victoria and Albert Museum,
London, inv. A.37-1952

117
Peter Oliver after Raphael
St George and the Dragon, 1628
Bodycolour and gold paint on vellum,
22 x 16.5 cm
The Royal Collection / HM Queen
Elizabeth II, RCIN 452455

118
Nicholas Hilliard
after Hans Holbein the Younger
Henry VII, *c.* 1600
Watercolour and bodycolour on vellum
laid on card, diameter 3.4 cm
The Royal Collection / HM Queen
Elizabeth II, RCIN 420012

119
Nicholas Hilliard
after Hans Holbein the Younger
Henry VIII, *c.* 1600
Watercolour and bodycolour on vellum
laid on card, diameter 3.2 cm
The Royal Collection / HM Queen
Elizabeth II, RCIN 420013

120
Nicholas Hilliard
after Hans Holbein the Younger
Jane Seymour, *c.* 1600
Watercolour and bodycolour on vellum
laid on card, diameter 3.2 cm
The Royal Collection / HM Queen
Elizabeth II, RCIN 420014

121
Nicholas Hilliard
after Hans Holbein the Younger
Edward VI, *c.* 1600
Watercolour and bodycolour on vellum
laid on card, diameter 3.3 cm
The Royal Collection / HM Queen
Elizabeth II, RCIN 420015

122
Isaac Oliver
Henry, Prince of Wales, *c.* 1610
Watercolour on vellum
laid on card, 13.2 x 10 cm
The Royal Collection / HM Queen
Elizabeth II, RCIN 420058

123
Nicholas Hilliard
Henry, Prince of Wales, 1607
Watercolour and bodycolour on vellum laid on card, 6.1 x 5.1 cm
The Royal Collection / HM Queen Elizabeth II, RCIN 420642

124
Nicholas Hilliard
James I, *c.* 1609–15
Watercolour on vellum laid on card, 4.6 x 3.8 cm
The Royal Collection / HM Queen Elizabeth II, RCIN 420039

125
Isaac Oliver
Anne of Denmark, *c.* 1611–12
Watercolour on vellum laid on card, 5.3 x 4.2 cm
The Royal Collection / HM Queen Elizabeth II, RCIN 420041

126
Isaac Oliver
Princess Elizabeth, *c.* 1610
Watercolour on vellum laid on card, 4.9 x 4.1 cm
The Royal Collection / HM Queen Elizabeth II, RCIN 420031

127
Isaac Oliver
Charles I, when Duke of York, *c.* 1611–16
Watercolour on vellum laid on card, 5.4 x 4.1 cm
The Royal Collection / HM Queen Elizabeth II, RCIN 420048

128
Peter Oliver
Charles I, when Prince of Wales, *c.* 1620
Watercolour on vellum laid on card, 5.1 x 3.9 cm
The Royal Collection / HM Queen Elizabeth II, RCIN 420049

129
John Hoskins
Henrietta Maria, *c.* 1632
Watercolour on vellum, 9.2 x 7.9 cm
The Royal Collection / HM Queen Elizabeth II, RCIN 420891

130
Pierre Regnier
Medal Commemorating the Marriage of Charles I and Henrietta Maria, c. 1625 (obverse and reverse)
Silver, cast and chased, diameter 2.3 cm
The Royal Collection / HM Queen Elizabeth II, RCIN 443087

131
Nicolas Briot
Medal Commemorating the Coronation of Charles I, 1626 (obverse and reverse)
Gold, struck, diameter 3 cm
The Royal Collection / HM Queen Elizabeth II, RCIN 443108

132
Nicolas Briot
Medal Commemorating the Scottish Coronation of Charles I, 1633 (obverse and reverse)
Gold, struck, diameter 2.8 cm
The Royal Collection / HM Queen Elizabeth II, RCIN 443093

133
Nicolas Briot
Medal Commemorating the Return of Charles I to London after His Coronation in Scotland, 1633 (obverse and reverse)
Gold, struck, diameter 4.3 cm
The Royal Collection / HM Queen Elizabeth II, RCIN 443109

134
Robert van Voerst
after Anthony van Dyck
Charles I and Henrietta Maria Holding a Laurel Wreath, 1634
Engraving, 42.2 x 57.1 cm
The Royal Collection / HM Queen Elizabeth II, RCIN 601870

135
Roman
Claudius, AD 43–45
Sardonyx, 20.5 x 16 cm
The Royal Collection / HM Queen
Elizabeth II, RCIN 65238

136
Pietro Tacca
Pacing Horse, 1600
Bronze, height 27.3 cm
The Royal Collection / HM Queen Elizabeth II, RCIN 35467

137
Hubert Le Sueur
Charles I on Horseback, *c.* 1630–33
Bronze, height 33 cm
Ickworth, The Bristol Collection,
inv. NT 850841

CATALOGUE

1
Wenceslaus Hollar (1607–1677)
Whitehall Palace, 1637–43
Pen and grey ink and watercolour on paper, 9.8 x 29.3 cm
The British Museum, London, inv. 1859,0806.390
PROVENANCE: acquired in 1859
SELECTED BIBLIOGRAPHY: Binyon 1898–1907, vol. 2, no. 10; Sprinzels 1938, no. 312; Croft-Murray and Hulton 1960, no. 7; New Haven 1994, no. 30; London 2000, no. 11; Pennington 2002, no. 1039

In December 1636 the celebrated draughtsman and printmaker Wenceslaus Hollar came to London in the service of Thomas Howard, Earl of Arundel. His numerous depictions of London provide a valuable record of the city (see fig. 5). The present work dates from his first London period (1636–44) and shows the entire Whitehall Palace complex viewed from the Thames. Lightly sketched wherries ferrying passengers show that the river was the major transport route through the city. The dominant building in the centre, set back from the river, is Inigo Jones's Banqueting House. In a later etching, for which this drawing is likely to be preparatory, Hollar chose to depict only the central section of the palace, including the Banqueting House and the Whitehall jetty. LC/PR

2
François Dieussart (*c.* 1600–1661)
Charles I, 1636
Marble, height 86.5 cm
The Duke of Norfolk, Arundel Castle
PROVENANCE: probably Thomas Howard, 14th Earl of Arundel; thereafter by descent
SELECTED BIBLIOGRAPHY: Whinney 1966, pp. 91–92; London 1972, no. 236; Vickers 1978; Avery 1981, p. 207; Howarth 1989, p. 98; Avery 2006

Van Dyck's triple portrait of Charles I (cat. 3) was sent to Rome in 1636 as a model for Gianlorenzo Bernini to make a bust of the King. Bernini's marble, which arrived in England the following year, was destroyed by the fire at Whitehall Palace in 1698. The Flemish sculptor François Dieussart, who was greatly inspired by the work of Bernini, would have seen Van Dyck's triple portrait in Rome, and probably sent his own marble bust of the King to Thomas Howard, Earl of Arundel, as part of a bid to work for him. LC/PR

3
Anthony van Dyck (1599–1641)
Charles I in Three Positions, 1635–36
Oil on canvas, 84.4 x 99.4 cm
The Royal Collection / HM Queen Elizabeth II, RCIN 404420
PROVENANCE: Charles I; Gianlorenzo Bernini, 1636; thereafter by descent; James Irvine, 1802; Walsh Porter; William Wells; acquired by George IV in 1822
SELECTED BIBLIOGRAPHY: Millar 1963, vol. 1, no. 146; Brown 1982, pp. 174–76; London 1999B, no. 5; Barnes et al. 2004, no. IV.48; Los Angeles 2008, no. 6.2; London 2013, pp. 87, 90, 110–11; Griffey 2015, p. 118

In 1635 Henrietta Maria commissioned a marble bust of her husband from the sculptor Gianlorenzo Bernini. The official purpose of this triple portrait, therefore, was to allow Bernini to create a likeness of the King. Its unofficial purpose was to warn Bernini not to underestimate the artistic culture of the English court. This artistic gauntlet was thrown down with an awareness of similar professional contests described in Pliny's *Natural History*. The three portraits are more finished and varied than they need to be, and their arrangement contains an erudite reference to Lorenzo Lotto's *Portrait of a Goldsmith in Three Positions* (fig. 33), then thought to be by Titian and hanging in the Second Privy Lodging Room at Whitehall. Van Dyck flaunts his powers with paint – melting, mobile features, brilliant highlights in the eyes, and soft, cloudy hair – perhaps knowing that these were reasons that Bernini himself gave for preferring painted to sculpted portraiture.

Henrietta Maria paid for the completed bust in 1638 with a diamond ring valued at 4,000 scudi (about £800). The bust was destroyed in the 1698 fire at Whitehall Palace; before that it had been displayed there for sixty years. Van Dyck's painting fared better: it was kept by Bernini in Rome and exhibited at the Pantheon, where it was apparently much admired by Roman painters of the second half of the century. DST

4
Peter Paul Rubens (1577–1640)
Self-portrait, 1623
Oil on panel, 85.7 x 62.2 cm
The Royal Collection / HM Queen Elizabeth II, RCIN 400156
PROVENANCE: Henry Danvers, later 1st Earl of Danby; given to Charles I, when Prince of Wales, *c.* 1624; Edward Bass and Dividend, Commonwealth Sale, 19 December 1651 (£16); recovered at the Restoration
SELECTED BIBLIOGRAPHY: Millar 1960, p. 37, no. 2 (Whitehall Palace, Little Room between the Breakfast Chamber and the Privy Gallery); Millar 1972, p. 272, no. 250; Filipczak 1987, pp. 98–104; Vlieghe 1987, no. 135; White 2007, no. 61; Auwers 2013, p. 424

Rubens almost certainly began this work for his own pleasure, but it soon turned into a royal commission when, in 1622, Henry Danvers, future 1st Earl of Danby, requested a self-portrait from the artist to be presented to Prince Charles. Rubens, however, did not depict himself as a painter but as a gentleman, seen out of doors against a louring evening sky and a rock that may symbolise fortitude. There is a glimpse of a gold chain at his neck, and the wide-brimmed hat disguises his impending baldness. This was his preferred self-image, as engraved in 1630 by Paulus Pontius. JW

5
Anthony van Dyck (1599–1641)
Self-portrait with a Sunflower, *c.* 1633
Oil on canvas, 61.5 x 75.2 cm
Private collection
PROVENANCE: possibly Robert Grosvenor, 1st Marquess of Westminster; Hugh Grosvenor, 1st Duke of Westminster, by 1885
SELECTED BIBLIOGRAPHY: Filipczak 1987, pp. 104–08; Antwerp 1999, no. 66; Madrid 1999, no. 2; Büttner 2002; Barnes et al. 2004, no. IV.4; Peacock 2006B

Van Dyck was knighted by the King in 1632, and, the following year, received a gold chain, which he self-consciously presents here. As in some other works he painted in England, this self-portrait has symbolic meaning and can be read in various ways. Perhaps the sunflower follows the light of the sun as the artist-courtier follows the monarch, or loves God, or it can be interpreted as an image of painting and the act of looking. The fame of this painting spread through an etching by Wenceslaus Hollar made three years after Van Dyck's death. JW

6
Anthony van Dyck (1599–1641)
Inigo Jones, 1632–36
Black chalk and pen and brown ink on paper, 24.4 x 20.1 cm
The Trustees of the Chatsworth Settlement, inv. 1002a
PROVENANCE: possibly Govert Flinck; Nicolaes Anthoni Flinck; William Cavendish, 2nd Duke of Devonshire; William Cavendish, 3rd Duke of Devonshire; Richard Boyle, 3rd Earl of Burlington; Charlotte Cavendish, *née* Boyle, 6th Baroness Clifford and Marchioness of Hartington; William Cavendish, 4th Duke of Devonshire; thereafter by descent

SELECTED BIBLIOGRAPHY: Vey 1962, vol. 1, no. 271; London 1982, no. 79; New York 1991, no. 72; Jaffé 2002, no. 955; Vicenza 2008, no. 191; New York 2016, no. 48

Van Dyck planned a series of engraved portraits of famous men and women, known as the *Iconographie*. This drawing of Inigo Jones, Surveyor of the King's Works and designer of court masques, was engraved for the series by Robert van Voerst. However, the portrait contains nothing to suggest that Jones was an architect. Van Dyck did not draw Jones from life, but used the head in one of his portraits as a model, basing the idea for the pose on a portrait by Titian of the early sixteenth-century architect and painter Giulio Romano (Palazzo del Te, Mantua), then at Whitehall Palace and familiar to Jones. JW

7
Daniel Mytens (*c.* 1590–1647)
Self-portrait, *c.* 1630
Oil on panel, 68.3 x 58.9 cm
The Royal Collection / HM Queen Elizabeth II, RCIN 404431
PROVENANCE: Charles I; John Hunt and Edward Bass, Commonwealth Sale, 1 March 1653 (£6); recovered at the Restoration
SELECTED BIBLIOGRAPHY: Millar 1960, p. 38, no. 5 (Whitehall Palace, Little Room between the Breakfast Chamber and the Privy Gallery); Millar 1963, vol. 1, no. 114; ter Kuile 1969, no. 70; Millar 1972, p. 264, no. 129; London 2016B, no. 13

Charles I liked artists well enough to keep portraits of them on his walls. Daniel Mytens was born in Delft and worked in London from the mid-1610s until 1634, first for James I and then for his son Charles. This work, almost certainly a direct commission from the King, was displayed at Whitehall next to a famous self-portrait by Rubens (cat. 4) and another by Van Dyck. Mytens's inclusion in this triumvirate suggests he was not as easily cast aside by the King after Van Dyck's arrival in 1632 as is often assumed. JW

8
Anthony van Dyck (1599–1641)
Endymion Porter, 1628
Oil on canvas, 114.5 x 94 cm
Private collection
PROVENANCE: Philip Yorke, 3rd Earl of Hardwicke; Wimpole Hall, Cambridgeshire, by 1798; thereafter by descent
SELECTED BIBLIOGRAPHY: Barnes et al. 2004, no. III.119; London 2009, no. 15

Despite his great access to the King, Endymion Porter was a courtier with limited political influence. However, he was very useful to Charles because of his cosmopolitanism (he had spent seven years at the Spanish court and spoke the language) and his knowledge of art and literature. Porter was travelling on diplomatic business through the Southern Netherlands in 1628 when he met Van Dyck, obtained a major work from the artist, *Rinaldo and Armida* (Baltimore Museum of Art), for the King, and commissioned this portrait. Porter and Van Dyck remained close friends after the artist moved to London in 1632, and Van Dyck recorded the two of them in a double portrait (fig. 11). JW

9
Anthony van Dyck (1599–1641)
Henrietta Maria, 1638
Oil on canvas, 71.7 x 56.3 cm
The Royal Collection / HM Queen Elizabeth II, RCIN 400159
PROVENANCE: first recorded in the collection of James II, 1688
SELECTED BIBLIOGRAPHY: Millar 1963, vol. 1, no. 149; Barnes et al. 2004, no. IV.126; Griffey 2008, pp. 188–91; Griffey 2015, pp. 118, 147

Henrietta Maria had refined tastes and played an active role in cultivating the arts at the Stuart court. After successfully mediating with Pope Urban VIII for Gianlorenzo Bernini to make a bust of her husband, she sought a comparable one of herself. Van Dyck painted the preparatory works required, and two such works for 'Barnino' were recorded in the artist's *c.* 1638 bill (National Archives, Kew), for which the King agreed to pay £15 each. Three works are associated with the studies: two in profile (the other is in the Memphis Brooks Museum of Art) and one frontal view (Royal Collection). This version is a ravishing example of Van Dyck's mastery. The profile is clearly defined and the head carefully modelled. As well as such sharp definition, which would have been invaluable for the translation into sculpture, Van Dyck creates a palpable sense of texture and movement through the delicate rendering of different details of her dress – the intricate lace collar, the heavy folds of her satin gown, the soft sky-blue ribbons and the lighter fabric of her scarf. EG

10
Anthony van Dyck (1599–1641)
Thomas Howard, 14th Earl of Arundel, *c.* 1620–21
Oil on canvas, 102.6 x 79.7 cm
The J. Paul Getty Museum, Los Angeles, inv. 86.PA.532
PROVENANCE: George Villiers, 1st Duke of Buckingham; Philippe II, Duke of Orléans; Louis Philippe, Duke of Orléans; Citoyen Robit; his sale, 1801; Francis Egerton, 3rd Duke of Bridgewater; acquired in 1986
SELECTED BIBLIOGRAPHY: London 1982, no. 2; White 1995; Antwerp 1999, no. 25; Madrid 2002, pp. 196–98; Barnes et al. 2004, no. I.161

Van Dyck first visited London for a few months between October 1620 and March 1621. During this period, he painted the Earl of Arundel, a grandee of the Jacobean court and one of its most knowledgeable and ruthless art collectors. Arundel is shown seated, dressed in what a contemporary called his 'plain Stuff', and toying with the Lesser George, the badge of the Order of the Garter. The rough use of paint, with much of the ground left exposed, shows Van Dyck's development of a way of painting that he had established in Antwerp, when working independently from Rubens during the 1610s. JW

11
Peter Paul Rubens (1577–1640)
George Villiers, 1st Duke of Buckingham, on Horseback, 1625
Oil on panel, 46.6 x 51.7 cm
Kimbell Art Museum, Fort Worth, Texas, inv. AP 1976.08
PROVENANCE: Claude-Maurice-Henri Roxard de la Salle; Louis Stern, 1881; by descent to Sylvie de Langlade; private collection, London, 1974; acquired in 1976
SELECTED BIBLIOGRAPHY: Held 1976; Held 1980, vol. 1, no. 292; Vlieghe 1987, no. 81a; Greenwich 2004, no. 15

Rubens met George Villiers in Paris in May 1625, and agreed to paint two large works for the Duke's London mansion, York House on the Strand. As was his usual working method, Rubens made this small oil sketch in preparation for one of these much larger commissions, probably delivered in 1627, but destroyed by fire in 1949. As recorded here, it showed the Duke on horseback as Lord Admiral of the Fleet, watched admiringly by Neptune and a sea nymph, and showered with flowers by a figure representing Fame, who holds a trumpet. JW

12
Peter Paul Rubens (1577–1640)
Vincenzo II Gonzaga, *c.* 1604–05
Oil on canvas laid down on panel, 67.3 x 57.2 cm
Saltram, The Morley Collection. Accepted in lieu of tax by HM Treasury and transferred to the National Trust in 1957, inv. NT 872186
PROVENANCE: Charles I, when Prince of Wales; Edward Bass and Dividend, Commonwealth Sale, 19 December 1951 (£30); Edmund Harrison; Ralph Bankes, by 1659; Charles II, after 1660; John Parker, 1st Earl of Morley, by 1819; thereafter by descent; transferred to the National Trust in 1957
SELECTED BIBLIOGRAPHY: Millar 1960, p. 39, no. 11 (Whitehall Palace, Little Room between the Breakfast Chamber and the Privy Gallery); Millar 1972, p. 264, no. 127; Huemer 1977, no. 15; London 1981, no. 257

Rubens painted this portrait while he was in the service of Duke Vincenzo I Gonzaga in Mantua between 1600 and 1609. The sitter can be identified as the young Vincenzo II Gonzaga, due to similarities with a portrait fragment (Kunsthistorisches Museum, Vienna) for Rubens's dismantled *Adoration of the Trinity*, which featured various members of the Gonzaga family. Charles supposedly acquired the portrait when he was still Prince of Wales. A few years later, his acquisition of the Gonzaga collection would have given the portrait new relevance at Whitehall Palace. PR

13
Anthony van Dyck (1599–1641)
Hendrik van den Bergh, 1627–32
Oil on canvas, 114 x 100 cm
Museo Nacional del Prado, Madrid, inv. P01486
PROVENANCE: Charles I; Jan Baptist Gaspars, Commonwealth Sale, 2 April 1650 (£29); Philip IV; transferred to the Prado in 1819
SELECTED BIBLIOGRAPHY: Millar 1960, p. 2, no. 3 (Whitehall Palace, Bear Gallery); Millar 1972, p. 269, no. 207; Barnes et al. 2004, no. III.69; Díaz Padrón 2012, vol. 2, no. 78

Hendrik van den Bergh was of Dutch origin but spent most of his career in the service of the Spanish forces. During the Thirty Years' War (1618–48), he led the Spanish cavalry in Flanders, before being suspected of treason in 1629. He eventually joined the Dutch rebels in 1632 in their attempt to free the Netherlands from Spanish rule. This portrait, completed just before Van Dyck's arrival in England, celebrates Van den Bergh's military success, depicting him in full armour with a commander's baton and a sword. The sumptuousness of the fabric of his armband shows the impact of Van Dyck's recent visit to Italy (1621–27); indeed, the landscape background and warm skin tones pay particular homage to Venetian painting of the sixteenth century. The picture served as a model for Paulus Pontius's engraving in Van Dyck's *Iconographie*, a celebrated series of prints illustrating portraits of eminent contemporary figures. LC/PR

14
Peter Paul Rubens (1577–1640)
Minerva Protects Pax from Mars ('Peace and War'), 1629–30
Oil on canvas, 203.5 x 298 cm
The National Gallery, London. Presented by the Duke of Sutherland, 1828, inv. NG46
PROVENANCE: Charles I; Edmund Harrison and Dividend, Commonwealth Sale, 8 September 1649 (£100); Luis Méndez de Haro y Guzmán, 6th Marqués of Carpio; Ambrogio di Giorgio Doria, Marchese of Montaldeo, by 1788; Arthur Champernowne and William Buchanan, 1802; George Leveson-Gower, later 1st Duke of Sutherland, 1803; acquired in 1828
SELECTED BIBLIOGRAPHY: Millar 1960, p. 4, no. 13 (Whitehall Palace, Bear Gallery); Burchard and d'Hulst 1963, vol. 1, nos 146, 172; Millar 1972, p. 70, no. 25; Martin 1970, no. 46; Roy 1999; Meij 2001, no. 23; Heinen 2011; Büttner forthcoming; McGrath forthcoming

Painted in London and presented to Charles as a gift, this picture marks Rubens's successful peace negotiations in England on behalf of Philip IV of Spain. Pax (Peace) is protected by Minerva (Wisdom) who pushes away Mars (War). Inspired by Tintoretto and Veronese, Rubens elaborated the composition with motifs from his own repertoire, such as the female nude (reminiscent of Albrecht Dürer), the cornucopia, the satyr and the leopard. The figure of Hymen, holding the torch, and the two young girls to the right have been identified as the children of Balthasar Gerbier, who was Rubens's host in London and in the service of Charles I at the time. PR

15
Diego Velázquez (1599–1660)
Philip IV, *c.* 1623–24
Oil on canvas, 61.9 x 48.9 cm
Meadows Museum, SMU, Dallas, Algur H. Meadows Collection, inv. MM.67.23
PROVENANCE: Philip IV; Cardinal Andrea Carlo Ferrari; Cardinal Pietro Gasparri; Therese Kuhn Straus; Wildenstein & Co.; private collection, France; acquired in 1967
SELECTED BIBLIOGRAPHY: Aznar 1964, vol. 1, pp. 288–92; Harris 1968; Harris 1982, pp. 57–74; Brown 1986, p. 45; Orso 1993, pp. 42–43; López-Rey 1996, vol. 2, no. 28; Madrid 2005, no. 24; Checa 2008, no. 20; Gallagher 2010; Dallas 2012, no. 2

Diego Velázquez was appointed Court Painter to Philip IV of Spain in 1623. The present portrait, thought to be his earliest of the King, was painted shortly after the young artist had arrived in Madrid and probably served as the model for two early full-length portraits of Philip (Museo Nacional del Prado, Madrid; The Metropolitan Museum of Art, New York). Velázquez here highlights the King's youthful complexion, but makes no attempt to flatter his distinctive features. When Charles visited Madrid in 1623, he commissioned Velázquez to paint his own portrait, which is now lost. LC/PR

16
Titian (*c.* 1488/90–1576)
Charles V with a Dog, 1533
Oil on canvas, 194 x 112.7 cm
Museo Nacional del Prado, Madrid, inv. P00409
PROVENANCE: Charles V; Philip II; Philip IV; given to Charles I, when Prince of Wales, 1623; Balthasar Gerbier, Commonwealth Sale, 21 June 1650 (£150); Philip IV, 1651; transferred to the Prado in 1819
SELECTED BIBLIOGRAPHY: Millar 1960, p. 4, no. 12 (Whitehall Palace, Bear Gallery); Wethey 1969–75, vol. 2, no. 20; Millar 1972, p. 269, no. 203; Bodart 1998, pp. 107–13; Madrid 2002, no. 22; Madrid 2003, no. 18; Ferino-Pagden and Beyer 2005; Hope 2005; Madrid 2008, no. 112; Bodart 2011, p. 131

This full-length portrait of the Holy Roman Emperor Charles V is thought to have been painted in Bologna in early 1533 after a work by Jakob Seisenegger, dated 1532 (Kunsthistorisches Museum, Vienna). The earlier picture was presumably commissioned by Ferdinand of Habsburg but Charles V may have requested Titian's version for himself. Though Titian followed Seisenegger's model, he transformed the painting in certain respects, omitting several details, making the subject more slender and alert, and lowering the horizon. Charles V was so pleased with the portrait that, in March 1533, he gave Titian 500 ducats, bestowed on him the title of Count Palatine, and appointed him as his official portrait painter. According to Giorgio Vasari, he thus invoked the role Apelles had played for Alexander the Great, establishing a key precedent for the court painters of the seventeenth century. Charles I received the portrait from Philip IV, great-grandson of Charles V, as a gift during his visit to Madrid in 1623. GR

17
Paolo Veronese (1528–1588)
Mars, Venus and Cupid, *c.* 1580–85
Oil on canvas, 165.2 x 126.5 cm
National Galleries of Scotland. Purchased by the Royal Institution, 1859; transferred to the National Gallery of Scotland, 1867, inv. NG 339
PROVENANCE: Francisco Gómez de Sandoval y Rojas, 1st Duke of Lerma; Philip III, 1606; Philip IV; given to Charles I, when Prince of Wales, 1623; Jan Baptist Gaspars, Commonwealth Sale, 28 January 1650 (£11); Sampson Gideon, by 1761; Sampson Eardley, 1st Baron Eardley; thereafter by descent; acquired in 1859
SELECTED BIBLIOGRAPHY: Millar 1972, p. 205, no. 323; Washington 1988, pp. 136–37; London 2014, no. 43; Verona 2014, no. 4.3

From the late 1570s to the 1580s Veronese produced a series of large mythological paintings inspired by Ovid. The series, which includes a *Rape of Europa* (Palazzo Ducale, Venice), a *Venus and Adonis* (Museo Nacional del Prado, Madrid), a *Hermes with Herse and Aglauros* (Fitzwilliam Museum, Cambridge) and a *Perseus and Andromeda* (Musée des Beaux-Arts, Rennes), constitutes a direct response to Titian's *poesie*, which were painted for Philip II of Spain in the 1550s. *Mars, Venus and Cupid* belongs to this group. The figure of Mars, awkwardly fitted in behind Venus, seems to have been a later addition to the composition, as a drawing in the British Museum reveals, probably painted by a member of the workshop. The splendid softness of the goddess's flesh, the humorous detail of Cupid struggling to contain the excitement of the little dog, and the dramatic sunset in the background would have made this painting highly desirable to any collectors and art lovers aware of the prestige of Titian's *poesie*. GR

18
Correggio (1489–1534)
Venus with Mercury and Cupid ('The School of Love'), *c.* 1525
Oil on canvas, 155.6 x 91.4 cm
The National Gallery, London.
Bought 1834, inv. NG10
PROVENANCE: Count Nicola Maffei; by descent to his grandson, Count Nicola Maffei; Dukes of Mantua; Charles I; George Greene and Dividend, Commonwealth Sale, 23 October 1651 (£800), or Thomas Baggley; Enrique Felipe de Guzmán, 2nd Count-Duke of Olivares, 1653–54; Duke of Alba, 1688; Emanuel Godoy, 1802; Joachim Murat, 1808; Charles Vane, 3rd Marquess of Londonderry, 1815; acquired in 1834
SELECTED BIBLIOGRAPHY: Millar 1960, p. 22, no. 13 (Whitehall Palace, Third Privy Lodging Room); Millar 1972, p. 323, no. 20; Gould 1976, pp. 124–27, 213–16; Ekserdjian 1997, pp. 268–72; Parma 2008, no. III.27; Rome 2008, no. 19; Rome 2016B, no. 16

Like Correggio's *Venus and Cupid with a Satyr* (fig. 20), *Venus with Mercury and Cupid* was painted for Count Nicola Maffei before passing to the Gonzaga. It depicts a winged and thus in some sense celestial Venus, goddess of love, with Mercury, god of wisdom, and their son Cupid. The seated Mercury is teaching Cupid his letters, and on more than one copy of the painting the sheet of paper was inscribed and not blank, as it now is in the original. X-rays reveal that originally the artist intended Venus to be looking tenderly down, and Mercury to be represented more frontally. DE

19
Roman
Marcus Aurelius, mid-second century AD
Marble, height 66 cm
The Royal Collection / HM Queen Elizabeth II, RCIN 1296
PROVENANCE: Dukes of Mantua; Charles I
SELECTED BIBLIOGRAPHY: London 1981, no. 247; Angelicoussis 2003, pp. 68–72

This bust of the young Marcus Aurelius is a version of an official portrait-type devised between AD 147 and 151, when the emperor-to-be was still in his youth. The light beard and smooth skin, which shows no sign of wrinkles, indicate his young age, while his military attire, which includes a cuirass adorned with Medusa's head, points to his bravery as a man of arms. Marcus Aurelius married Faustina the Younger (cat. 20) in AD 145. Portraits of the imperial couple were often displayed together in early modern collections as an example of a successful political and marital union. This bust, once part of the Gonzaga collection and acquired by Daniel Nijs in 1628–29, is correctly identified as 'Marcus Aurelius young' in the *Whitehall Album* (cat. 139). It shows signs of restoration in both the lower part of the bust and in the face, particularly the nose and the middle part of the lips. BF

20
Roman
Faustina the Younger, after AD 161
Marble, height 63 cm
The Royal Collection / HM Queen Elizabeth II, RCIN 1299
PROVENANCE: Dukes of Mantua; Charles I
SELECTED BIBLIOGRAPHY: London 1981, no. 248; Fittschen 1982, p. 65; Angelicoussis 2003, pp. 72–76

This bust, recorded in the *Whitehall Album* (cat. 139), is particularly noteworthy for the delicate modelling of the subject's face, and the naturalistic rendering of her hair. The distinctive coiffure, with a neat middle parting and waves of hair on both sides coiled into a large bun, identifies the sitter as Faustina the Younger, daughter of the Emperor Antoninus Pius and wife of Marcus Aurelius (cat. 19). This official portrait type was created in AD 161, the year in which she gave birth to twin boys, and her husband became emperor. At least three busts of Faustina (either Faustina the Younger or her mother, Faustina the Elder) entered the Gonzaga collection during the sixteenth century, among them Andrea Mantegna's 'dear Faustina in marble, ancient', acquired in 1506 by Isabella d'Este. BF

21
Roman
Livia Drusilla, mid-second century AD
Marble, height 57.5 cm
The Royal Collection / HM Queen Elizabeth II, RCIN 1300
PROVENANCE: Dukes of Mantua; Charles I
SELECTED BIBLIOGRAPHY: Angelicoussis 2003, pp. 82–83

Formerly considered to be an idealised portrait of a generic woman with a diadem, this bust in fact represents Livia Drusilla, wife of the Emperor Augustus. It was one of the many portraits of Roman emperors and empresses which were once displayed in the Gonzaga residences in Mantua. Furnishing ancient heads with modern busts was common practice among sixteenth- and seventeenth-century sculptors and collectors. In this case, the head, which can be dated to the mid-second century on stylistic grounds, has been furnished with a more modern body. The fact that the body can already be seen in the drawing of the sculpture in the *Whitehall Album* (cat. 139), dated *c.* 1628–29, suggests that its addition may date back to the turn of the seventeenth century. The ancient head shows evidence of wear and possibly also of intentional damage, particularly to the upper lip and the eyebrows. BF

22
Roman
Antinous, first century AD
Marble, height 87.5 cm
The Royal Collection / HM Queen Elizabeth II, RCIN 1298
PROVENANCE: Dukes of Mantua; possibly Charles I
SELECTED BIBLIOGRAPHY: Angelicoussis 2003, pp. 65–68

Due to his regular facial features and short curls, this handsome young man has been identified as Antinous, favourite of the Emperor Hadrian. The sphinx that originally topped the Attic helmet, now only partially visible, may refer to his deification; this was promoted by Hadrian after Antinous' untimely death in Egypt. It is also possible that the portrait represents a private individual portrayed as Antinous. Only the head is ancient; the body, with a sculpted leather tunic and cuirass to complement the original helmet, was added at a later stage, possibly around the turn of the seventeenth century. Although its provenance is undocumented, and it does not appear in the *Whitehall Album* (cat. 139), it has been suggested that it too came into Charles I's possession from the Gonzaga collection. BF

23
Roman
Bust of a Young Man, mid-second century AD
Marble, height 68.5 cm
The Royal Collection / HM Queen Elizabeth II, RCIN 1297
PROVENANCE: Dukes of Mantua; Charles I; Edmund Harrison and Dividend, Commonwealth Sale, 23 October 1651, (£40)
SELECTED BIBLIOGRAPHY: Millar 1972, p. 144, no. 96; Angelicoussis 2003, pp. 76–78

The curly hair of this young, meditative boy is adorned with a laurel wreath with berries and a central cluster of fruit, which, perhaps as the result of a prolonged display outdoors, has been severely abraded. Laurel wreaths were often associated with children and youths in Roman funerary sculpture, and this might have been an idealised posthumous portrait of a beloved boy. The bust, which came into Charles I's possession from the Gonzaga collection, is identified as a generic god ('deità') both in the *Whitehall Album* (cat. 139) and the Commonwealth Sale. This sculpture is the result of an early modern restoration. The ancient head, which can be dated to the late Hadrianic or early Antonine period due to its hairstyle, is adjoined to a body which was certainly completed by 1628–29, as the sculpture already appears in its current form in the *Whitehall Album*. The head itself has been extensively restored; the nose and the left portion of the face and hair are later additions. BF

24
Roman
Aphrodite ('The Crouching Venus'),
second century AD
Marble, height 119 cm
The Royal Collection / HM Queen Elizabeth II, RCIN 69746
PROVENANCE: possibly Cardinal Alessandro Peretti; Vincenzo I Gonzaga, Duke of Mantua, 1598; Charles I; Robert Houghton and Dividend, Commonwealth Sale, 23 October 1651 (£600); Peter Lely, after 1651; Charles II, 1682; on loan to the British Museum since 1963
SELECTED BIBLIOGRAPHY: Scott-Elliot 1959, pp. 220, 226; Millar 1972, p. 140, no. 10; Haskell and Penny 1981, p. 321; London 1981, no. 249; Furlotti and Morselli 2003, pp. 60–63; Bober and Rubinstein 2010, pp. 67–68, London 2015, p. 68

One of a large number of Roman copies after a lost Hellenistic archetype, this statue shows Venus, goddess of beauty and love, bathing. Surprised by the arrival of an unexpected audience, she turns her head to the right and tries in vain to hide her nudity, but in doing so just makes herself seem all the more voluptuous. Sometimes erroneously identified as a small Venus acquired by Isabella d'Este from Cesare Borgia in 1502, the piece can be more convincingly associated with a 'marble Venus emerging from the bath', considered to be 'of great value' and to display 'exquisite workmanship', that Cardinal Alessandro Peretti gave to Vincenzo I Gonzaga in 1598. In 1627–28 the statue was listed in the Gonzaga inventory as 'a naked woman sitting on her heels'. Daniel Nijs described it in 1631 as 'the most beautiful of all [the Gonzaga antiquities]' and it appears as 'Helen of Troy' in the *Whitehall Album* (cat. 139). The sculpture, which is exceptional insofar as it retains its original head, particularly appealed to seventeenth-century painters: Rubens, who saw it in Mantua, adopted its crouching pose for some of his paintings, while Peter Lely acquired it for his collection following the Commonwealth Sale. BF

25
Andrea Mantegna (1430–1506)
The Triumph of Caesar:
The Trumpeters, *c.* 1485–1506
Tempera on canvas, 270.3 x 280.7 cm
The Royal Collection / HM Queen Elizabeth II, RCIN 403958

26
Andrea Mantegna (1430–1506)
The Triumph of Caesar:
The Triumphal Carts, *c.* 1485–1506
Tempera on canvas, 270.3 x 281.1 cm
The Royal Collection / HM Queen Elizabeth II, RCIN 403959

27
Andrea Mantegna (1430–1506)
The Triumph of Caesar:
The Trophy Bearers, *c.* 1485–1506
Tempera on canvas, 270.3 x 280.5 cm
The Royal Collection / HM Queen Elizabeth II, RCIN 403960

28
Andrea Mantegna (1430–1506)
The Triumph of Caesar:
The Vase Bearers, *c.* 1485–1506
Tempera on canvas, 269.5 x 280 cm
The Royal Collection / HM Queen Elizabeth II, RCIN 403961

29
Andrea Mantegna (1430–1506)
The Triumph of Caesar:
The Elephants, *c.* 1485–1506
Tempera on canvas, 270 x 280.7 cm
The Royal Collection / HM Queen Elizabeth II, RCIN 403962

30
Andrea Mantegna (1430–1506)
The Triumph of Caesar:
The Corselet Bearers, *c.* 1485–1506
Tempera on canvas, 270.8 x 280.4 cm
The Royal Collection / HM Queen Elizabeth II, RCIN 403963

31
Andrea Mantegna (1430–1506)
The Triumph of Caesar:
The Captives, *c.* 1485–1506
Tempera on canvas, 270 x 280.2 cm
The Royal Collection / HM Queen Elizabeth II, RCIN 403964

32
Andrea Mantegna (1430–1506)
The Triumph of Caesar:
The Musicians, *c.* 1485–1506
Tempera on canvas, 270.2 x 280.5 cm
The Royal Collection / HM Queen Elizabeth II, RCIN 403965

33
Andrea Mantegna (1430–1506)
The Triumph of Caesar:
Julius Caesar on His Chariot, *c.* 1485–1506
Tempera on canvas, 270.4 x 280.7 cm
The Royal Collection / HM Queen Elizabeth II, RCIN 403966

PROVENANCE: Dukes of Mantua; Charles I; Commonwealth Sale (£1,000, reserved); recovered at the Restoration
SELECTED BIBLIOGRAPHY: Kristeller 1901, pp. 281–316, 544, 546, 568; Millar 1972, p. 186; Martindale 1979; Lightbown 1986, pp. 140–53, 424–33; Hope 1992; London 1992, nos 108–15; Agosti 2005, pp. 48–49, 228–30, 278–80, 435–40; Elam 2008; Paris 2008A, no. 160; Tosetti Grandi 2008

Already underway by *c.* 1485, Mantegna's *Triumph of Caesar* comprises nine paintings. We have only scarce documentary evidence regarding the commission, but the series was presumably completed shortly before the artist's death in 1506. Its large canvases display an imaginative and creative combination of literary and visual sources. Ancient descriptions of triumphal entries (such as those in the works of Appian, Suetonius, Josephus, Pliny, Livy and Plutarch), along with more recent reconstructions of ancient processions (for instance, those in Flavio Biondo's *De Roma triumphante* and Roberto Valturio's *De re militari*), are used to compose a unique repertoire of *all'antica* imagery. Mantegna was exposed to further source material during his sojourn in Rome between 1488 and 1490, when he was able to expand his first-hand knowledge of Roman antiquities. However, it seems he did not precisely reproduce any specific artefacts in the *Triumph*, instead giving free rein to his powers of invention. The individual canvases represent distinct groups of figures, yet they only work in a particular sequence that culminates, to the right, in the chariot of the victorious Julius Caesar, who is draped in gold. He holds a sceptre and a palm branch, and is being crowned with a garland of bay leaves by a winged Victory.

It is not clear for whom Mantegna's series was first intended, but whoever the original patron may have been, the *Triumph* was mostly executed during the reign of Marchese Francesco II Gonzaga, who fashioned himself as a brave and victorious commander in the mould of Julius Caesar. The series was undoubtedly conceived with the assistance of a humanist advisor. In this regard, it may be useful to recall that in the 1440s the humanist Guarino da Verona had been insistent in his recommendation that the Marquess of Ferrara, Leonello d'Este, should follow the example of just and prudent government set by Julius Caesar, who had resolved the chaos of the late Roman Republic by opening the path to leadership for the first emperor, Augustus. Guarino's teaching gave rise to a harsh and widely known quarrel with other humanists, including the Florentine Poggio Bracciolini, who condemned Caesar as responsible for the decline of the Roman Republic. Given the close relationship between Ferrara and Mantua throughout the fifteenth century – Leonello was the uncle of Isabella d'Este, whom Francesco married in 1490 – this longstanding debate must have been in the minds of the humanists, artists and patrons at the Gonzaga court, who would have wanted to side with their Ferrarese relatives by promoting such a positive representation of Julius Caesar. As a celebration of monarchical authority, this series remained politically significant for later Gonzaga dukes, and as such was presumably appreciated by Charles I as well. GR

34
Jan Gossaert (Jean Gossart) (*c.* 1478–1532)
Adam and Eve, *c.* 1520
Oil on panel, 169.2 x 112 cm
The Royal Collection / HM Queen Elizabeth II, RCIN 407615
PROVENANCE: Dutch States General; Charles I, 1636; Richard Marriott, Commonwealth Sale, 17 May 1650 (£50 10s); recovered at the Restoration
SELECTED BIBLIOGRAPHY: Bruyn and Millar 1962; Millar 1972, p. 204, no. 304; Campbell 1985, no. 33; New York 2010, no. 2; Edinburgh 2011, no. 8

Adam and Eve were favourite subjects for Gossaert, as at least nine paintings and drawings attest. A northern translation of classical nudes, the present work is saturated by the influence of Dürer's prints, notably the *Temptation of the Idler* (*c.* 1498)and *Adam and Eve* (1504). Indeed, Charles I would have been familiar with Dürer's anatomical drawings from the artist's *Four Books of Human Proportion* (1532–34), a gift that Charles received when Prince of Wales from Van der Doort, his future Surveyor. It has been suggested that this work inspired John Milton's description of Adam and Eve in the fourth book of *Paradise Lost* (1667). NM/DST

35
Albrecht Dürer (1471–1528)
Burkhard of Speyer, 1506
Oil on panel, 31.7 x 26 cm
The Royal Collection / HM Queen Elizabeth II, RCIN 404418
PROVENANCE: Charles I; Ralph Grynder and Dividend, Commonwealth Sale, 23 October 1651 (£60); recovered at the Restoration
SELECTED BIBLIOGRAPHY: Millar 1960, p. 68, no. 29 (Whitehall Palace, Chair Room); Zampa and Ottino della Chiesa 1968, no. 118; Millar 1972, p. 259, no. 51; London 1988, no. 40; Anzelewsky 1991, vol. 1, no. 97; Venice 1999, no. 57; Crawford Luber 2005, pp. 40–43; Rome 2007, no. 1.11; Edinburgh 2011, no. 23; Frankfurt 2013, no. 6.10; London 2016A, no. 6

Dürer painted this portrait when he visited Venice in 1505–07. The sitter, Burkhard of Speyer, who can be identified from an inscribed miniature (Schlossmuseum, Weimar), also appears in Dürer's *Feast of the Rose Garlands* (Národní Galerie, Prague), which he painted for San Bartolomeo, the German church in Venice, in the same year. Although depicted here in secular dress, Burkhard's presence among ecclesiastical figures in the San Bartolomeo altarpiece suggests he may have had a connection to the church. Dürer's skill and meticulous attention to detail were much admired by contemporary Venetian artists, most notably Giovanni Bellini. This small panel hung in the Chair Room at Whitehall Palace, with Dürer's *Self-portrait* (fig. 25) and a portrait of the artist's father (National Gallery, London). LC

36
Hans Holbein the Younger (*c.* 1497–1543)
Johannes Froben, *c.* 1522–23
Oil on panel, 48.8 x 32.4 cm
The Royal Collection / HM Queen Elizabeth II, RCIN 403035
PROVENANCE: Michel Le Blond, by 1625; George Villiers, 1st Duke of Buckingham; Charles I; John Hutchinson, Commonwealth Sale, 24 May 1650 (£100); recovered at the Restoration
SELECTED BIBLIOGRAPHY: Millar 1960, p. 84, no. 43 (Whitehall Palace, Cabinet); Salvini and Grohn 1971, no. 33; Millar 1972, p. 260, no. 66; Rowlands 1985, no. 14 ; Edinburgh 2011, no. 66

Johannes Froben, the celebrated printer of the works of Erasmus (from 1514 onwards), came from Hammelburg in Franconia, but was already a citizen of Holbein's native Basel as early as 1490, and also worked closely with Holbein, who painted this portrit there. The present panel appears to have formed the left half of a diptych together with a portrait of Erasmus of which there is an example also in the Royal Collection. This explains the fact that the sitter, who is shown behind a stone ledge against a blue backdrop and with a corner of green curtain at top right, fails to meet our gaze and instead looks intently away to the right. DE

37
Hans Holbein the Younger (*c.* 1497–1543)
Derich Born, 1533
Oil on panel, 60.3 x 44.9 cm
The Royal Collection / HM Queen Elizabeth II, RCIN 405681
PROVENANCE: Charles I; possibly Thomas Howard, 14th Earl of Arundel; Charles II, by *c.* 1666–67
SELECTED BIBLIOGRAPHY: Rowlands 1985, no. 44; The Hague 2003A, no. 17; Foister 2004, pp. 206–07; London 2006, no. 158 ; Edinburgh 2011, no. 72

Derich Born (1509/10–after 1549), who came from Cologne, was a member of the trading alliance, the Hanseatic League, and was one of a number of merchants connected with the Steelyard in London whom Holbein painted after his return to England from Basel in the summer of 1532. The inclusion of an elaborate text on the stone parapet, whiere identifies the sitter and records both his age and the work's date of execution, and also adds a eulogy to the uncanny realism of the likeness, as well as the foliage beyond and the blue backdrop, are all common features of these portraits. However, it is the arresting directness and confidence of the young man's gaze and attitude that make this portrait so abnormally compelling. DE

38
Hans Holbein the Younger (*c.* 1497–1543)
'Hans of Antwerp', 1532
Oil on panel augmented with canvas, 63 x 48.4 cm
The Royal Collection / HM Queen Elizabeth II, RCIN 404443
PROVENANCE: Henry Vane; Charles I; Edward Bass and Dividend, Commonwealth Sale, 19 December 1651 (£30); recovered at the Restoration
SELECTED BIBLIOGRAPHY: Millar 1960, p. 69, no. 35 (Whitehall Palace, Chair Room); Salvini and Grohn 1971, no. 69; Millar 1972, p. 262, no. 108; Rowlands 1985, no. 36; Foister 2004, pp. 36–37

This portrait was formerly thought to represent Holbein's friend, a goldsmith called Hans of Antwerp, who witnessed his will, but it seems more likely to be a likeness of a stern-faced Hanseatic merchant, above all because the letter on the table in front of the sitter bears a merchant's mark, as well as the date 26 July 1532. One would expect a goldsmith to be shown with the tools of his trade, whereas this man is surrounded by such objects as a heap of coins, a quill pen, a metal key and a seal, all of which seem to confirm his association with the world of commerce. DE

39
Hans Holbein the Younger (*c.* 1497–1543)
Robert Cheseman, 1533
Oil on panel, 58.8 x 62.8 cm
Mauritshuis, The Hague, inv. 276
PROVENANCE: first recorded in the inventory of James II; William III, after 1688; Johan Willem Friso, Prince of Orange, 1702–11; thereafter by descent; transferred to the Mauritshuis in 1822
SELECTED BIBLIOGRAPHY: Rowlands 1985, no. 46; The Hague 2003B, no. 19; Buvelot 2004, no. 29; Foister 2004, pp. 232–33; London 2006, no. 36

Robert Cheseman, depicted here at the age of 48, was Falconer to Henry VIII. He appears a stern man with a sneering air. His aquiline nose bears a remarkable resemblance to the beak of the hooded bird of prey he proudly holds. Sometimes identified as part of Charles I's impressive assembly of Holbeins, the picture first appears in an inventory of the collection of James II. Charles I also owned a copy by Daniel Mytens after a lost original of James IV of Scotland with a falcon on his fist. NM/DST

40
Joos van Cleve (fl. 1505/08–1540/41)
Self-portrait, *c.* 1535–40
Oil on panel, 64.7 x 50.8 cm
The Royal Collection / HM Queen Elizabeth II, RCIN 405780

41
Joos van Cleve (fl. 1505/08–1540/41)
Katlijne van Mispelteeren (The Artist's Wife), *c.* 1535–40
Oil on panel, 64.7 x 50.3 cm
The Royal Collection / HM Queen Elizabeth II, RCIN 405779

PROVENANCE: David Tint; Charles I, 1636; Richard Wright, Commonwealth Sale, 21 May 1650 (£61 for both); recovered at the Restoration
SELECTED BIBLIOGRAPHY: Millar 1960, pp. 64–65, nos 13, 15 (Whitehall Palace, Chair Room); Millar 1972, p. 263, no. 120; Campbell 1985, nos 13–14; Hand 2004, nos 100A, 100B; Edinburgh 2007, nos 7–8; Edinburgh 2011, nos 15–16; London 2016B, nos 3–4

Van der Doort notes that the first of this pair is a self-portrait, writing that it was 'said to bee his owne Picture Done by – himselfe'. However, he attributed it to Joos van Cleve's son ('sotto' or 'foolish' Cleve). Between the portraits' two entries in the Chair Room at Whitehall Palace, Van der Doort records an 'ascension of our lady' on copper of a similarly modest size (attributed to Denys Calvaert); we can imagine this being hung thoughtfully above Joos and Katlijne, who act as oblivious worshippers. NM

42
Pieter Bruegel the Elder (*c.* 1525/30–1569)
Three Soldiers, 1568
Oil on panel, 20.3 x 17.8 cm
The Frick Collection, New York. Purchase, 1965, inv. 1965.1.163
PROVENANCE: Charles I; Thomas Greene, Commonwealth Sale, 1 February 1653 (£5); recovered at the Restoration; by descent until 1714; William van Huls; his sale, 1722; private collection, England, from *c.* 1900; Mr Marks, *c.* 1960; his sale, 1964; Edward Speelman, Agnew's and one other, 1964; acquired in 1965
SELECTED BIBLIOGRAPHY: Millar 1960, p. 69, no. 36 (Whitehall Palace, Chair Room, as Pieter Brueghel the Younger); Millar 1972, p. 259, no. 61; London 2016C, no. 8

Extremely unusually, this intimate panel, which is signed and dated 1568, is painted in monochrome, but Pieter Bruegel the Elder employed the same technique on at least two other occasions, for his *Christ and the Woman Taken in Adultery* (Courtauld Gallery, London) and his *Dormition of the Virgin* (Upton House, Warwickshire). Unlike the other two, the theme of this painting is secular: it depicts three soldiers in contemporary dress, one beating a large drum, one raising a flag and one playing the flute. Bruegel's flautist and drummer were freely adapted from two corresponding figures in Lucas van Leyden's engraving of the *Dance of St Mary Magdalene* of 1519. Van der Doort records the panel as a gift from Endymion Porter following a diplomatic visit to the Netherlands in 1634–35, but the 'CP' brand on the back of the panel suggests that the painting entered Charles I's collection earlier, when he was still Prince of Wales. At Whitehall Palace, it hung in the Chair Room in the company of other small northern pictures such as Dürer's *Burkhard of Speyer* (cat. 35). LC/DE

43
Hans Vredeman de Vries (1526–1609)
Christ in the House of Martha and Mary, 1566
Oil on panel, 79.4 x 109.2 cm
The Royal Collection / HM Queen Elizabeth II, RCIN 405475
PROVENANCE: Henry, Prince of Wales; Anne of Denmark; Charles I; recovered at the Restoration
SELECTED BIBLIOGRAPHY: Millar 1960, p. 52, no. 56 (Whitehall Palace, Long Gallery); Campbell 1985, no. 73; Strong 1986, p. 193; London 2007B, no. 13; London 2012, no. 51

Christ's impromptu arrival at the home of Mary and Martha elicits two different responses: Mary sits at his feet listening attentively while Martha – here shown through the doorway to the right – busies herself around the household. The biblical story allowed artists to draw attention to the struggle between spiritual and material concerns.

Having passed from Henry, Prince of Wales, to Anne of Denmark and on to Charles I, this picture was clearly well-liked by the Stuarts, probably because of its dramatic use of perspective. An understanding of perspective was a privilege of the educated elite, and there is evidence that the technique could confuse even the most learned of courtiers. De Vries was the master of this technique and wrote a famous book on the subject. The present picture had a clear impact on Inigo Jones's set designs for court masques, such as the set for Ben Jonson's *Masque of Augurs*, performed in 1622. NM

44
Hans Holbein the Younger (*c.* 1497–1543)
'Noli me tangere', 1526–28
Oil on panel, 76.7 x 95.8 cm
The Royal Collection / HM Queen Elizabeth II, RCIN 400001
PROVENANCE: probably Henrietta Maria at the Château de Colombes, 1669; Charles II, by 1680
SELECTED BIBLIOGRAPHY: Millar 1963, vol. 1, no. 32; Foister 2004, pp. 42–46; London 2006, no. 136; Barclay 2010, p. 2; Edinburgh 2011, no. 68; Griffey and Hibbard 2012, pp. 167–68; Griffey 2015, p. 287

This painting depicts the dramatic moment when Mary Magdalene discovers Christ's empty tomb. Holbein captures her confusion as she reaches towards a man she thinks is a gardener, who identifies himself as Christ by saying, 'Touch me not; for I am not yet ascended to my father' (John 20:17). Holbein's scene is one of great emotional intensity, with its striking central hand gestures and the astonishment and incredulity expressed on the Magdalene's face. Although probably painted during Holbein's first trip to England from 1526 to 1528, the picture seems to be first documented at Henrietta Maria's château at Colombes, where she died in 1669. The subject had strong resonance for Henrietta Maria, who appears to have identified with Mary Magdalene in her later years. EG

45
Titian (*c.* 1488/90–1576)
The Supper at Emmaus, *c.* 1534
Oil on canvas, 169 x 244 cm
Musée du Louvre, Paris, Department of Paintings, inv. 746
PROVENANCE: Count Nicola Maffei; thereafter by descent; Vincenzo I Gonzaga, Duke of Mantua, *c.* 1593; thereafter by descent; Charles I; Robert Houghton and Dividend, Commonwealth Sale, 23 October 1651 (£600); Everard Jabach, before 1656; Louis XIV of France, 1662; thereafter by descent; transferred to the Louvre in 1792
SELECTED BIBLIOGRAPHY: Millar 1960, p. 16, no. 9 (Whitehall Palace, First Privy Lodging Room); Wethey 1969–75, vol. 1, no. 143; Millar 1972, p. 206, no. 333; Paris 1993, pp. 567–69; Brown 1995, pp. 72–73; Rebecchini 1995; Bodart 1998; Rebecchini 2002, pp. 62–66; Boston 2009, pp. 148–50, 292–93

Between 1530 and 1534 Count Nicola Maffei negotiated the purchase of some land in the vicinity of Treviso on Titian's behalf. Although the purchase ultimately failed, it is almost certain that Maffei received the present work during these negotiations. The picture once prominently featured the Maffei coat of arms on the stool upon which the right-hand pilgrim sits, and the canvas is listed in a Maffei inventory of 1589. A few years later, in 1593, the Maffei family gave it, along with other paintings (including cat. 18), to Vincenzo I Gonzaga to thank him for his assistance in resolving a legal dispute. Presumably it was at this point that the Maffei coat of arms, which is still just visible, was painted over. The imperial eagle, partially covered by a column to the left, is included as a sign of Maffei's service to the Gonzaga family and his allegiance to the Holy Roman Emperor Charles V. The painting stayed in Mantua until it was purchased on behalf of Charles I in 1629–30. At the time of the sale of the King's collection in 1649, it was reported by the Spanish ambassador Alonso de Cárdenas to be valued at the hefty sum of £600, one of the highest prices attached to any of the King's pictures. GR

46
Titian (*c.* 1488/90–1576)
The Allocution of Alfonso d'Avalos to His Troops, 1540–41
Oil on canvas, 223 x 165 cm
Museo Nacional del Prado, Madrid, inv. P00417
PROVENANCE: Alfonso d'Avalos, Marquis del Vasto; Dukes of Mantua; Charles I; Edmund Harrison and Dividend, Commonwealth Sale, 23 October 1651 (£250); Philip IV, 1651; transferred to the Prado in 1817
SELECTED BIBLIOGRAPHY: Millar 1960, p. 15, no. 8 (Whitehall Palace, First Privy Lodging Room); Wethey 1969–75, vol. 2, no. 10; Millar 1972, p. 313, no. 243; Madrid 2002, no. 38; Madrid 2003, no. 20

The event illustrated in this canvas took place in 1537, when, as related by Paolo Giovio, the Spanish general Alfonso d'Avalos addressed his troops with such eloquence that he crushed a mutiny of his forces in Lombardy. Alfonso is represented on a raised podium and accompanied by his son Francesco Ferrante, whom he fearlessly left behind with his troops as a guarantee of his sincerity. He gesticulates theatrically with his right hand, and is shown holding a baton of command in his left one. A vast throng of soldiers listen with rapt attention to his every word, and their lances are shown stretching away into the far distance. DE

47
Titian (*c.* 1488/90–1576)
Conjugal Allegory ('The Allegory of Alfonso d'Avalos'), *c.* 1530–35
Oil on canvas, 121 x 107 cm
Musée du Louvre, Paris, Department of Paintings, inv. 754
PROVENANCE: Almonedo; Charles I; John Hutchinson, Commonwealth Sale, 24 May 1650 (£51); Everard Jabach, before 1660; Louis XIV, 1662; thereafter by descent; transferred to the Louvre in 1792
SELECTED BIBLIOGRAPHY: Millar 1960, p. 16, no. 10 (Whitehall Palace, First Privy Lodging Room); Wethey 1969–75, vol. 3, no. 1; Millar 1972, no. 13; Paris 1993, no. 164

The bearded man was formerly thought to be Alfonso d'Avalos, but is very different-looking (see cat. 46) and remains stubbornly unidentified. Nevertheless, the subject is surely a conjugal allegory, in which a married couple – he in the guise of Mars and wearing armour, she in that of Venus, with her right breast exposed – are accompanied by Cupid and his arrows, representing Charity, and two further figures representing Faith and Hope. The symbolic meaning of the crystal sphere held by the lady remains mysterious, but the work's underdrawing, which was separated from it during restoration and is also in the Louvre, reveals that its inclusion was an afterthought. DE

48
Lorenzo Costa (*c.* 1460–1535)
Virgin and Child, *c.* 1520–30
Oil on panel, 53.2 x 37.8 cm
Private collection
PROVENANCE: Dukes of Mantua; Charles I; Fernando Salamanca Livermore, 2nd Marquess of Salamanca; private collection
SELECTED BIBLIOGRAPHY: Millar 1960, p. 56, no. 80 (Whitehall Palace, Long Gallery, as Sodoma)

Lorenzo Costa was born in Ferrara and was subsequently active, above all as a painter of altarpieces, in Bologna from the 1480s, before working for Isabella d'Este on canvases for her *studiolo* in the Palazzo Ducale at Mantua, and succeeding Mantegna as court painter to the Gonzaga after the latter's death in 1506. This hitherto unpublished representation of the Virgin and Child in half-length against a dark background, which was believed to be by Sodoma when in Charles's collection, shows the Madonna looking affectionately down to her left towards her Son, who rests his head on his folded arms and looks as if he is about to fall asleep. The position of the Virgin's hands makes it tempting to suspect that Costa was inspired by Correggio's *Virgin and Child with an Angel* of the mid-1520s (Szépmüvészeti Múzeum, Budapest). DE

49
Circle of Raphael (1483–1520)
Virgin and Child with the Infant St John the Baptist ('The Bankes Madonna'), 1516–17
Oil on panel, 76 x 53.3 cm
Kingston Lacy, The Bankes Collection, National Trust, inv. NT 1257083
PROVENANCE: Dukes of Mantua; Charles I; Robert Houghton and Dividend, Commonwealth Sale, 23 October 1651 (£800); Philip IV; looted by French troops from the sacristy of the Escorial, 1807–13; William John Bankes, 1813; thereafter by descent; transferred to the National Trust in 1981
SELECTED BIBLIOGRAPHY: Millar 1960, p. 36, no. 9 (Whitehall Palace, Bedchamber); Millar 1972, p. 205, no. 326; Mantua 1989, pp. 271–72; Mantua 2002, vol. 1, no. 61; Meyer zur Capellen 2001–09, vol. 2, no. A6; Madrid 2012, no. 60

The present painting, which appeared in the Commonwealth Sale as the work of Raphael for the extremely high sum of £800, is now usually given to his associate Gianfrancesco Penni, although in the past it has also been attributed to Giulio Romano. The panel shows a meeting between the Christ Child, sitting on a capital, and his only slightly older cousin John the Baptist, who proffers his cross. Jesus seems minded to take it from him, while his mother appears to counsel restraint. In the tumbledown classical architecture beyond, the diminutive figure of Joseph is just visible in the darkness, holding up a candle. DE

50
Franciabigio (1484–1525)
Jacopo Cennini ('Il Fattore'), 1523
Oil on panel, 65.4 x 49.6 cm
The Royal Collection / HM Queen Elizabeth II, RCIN 405766
PROVENANCE: Jacopo Cennini; Charles I; recovered at the Restoration
SELECTED BIBLIOGRAPHY: Millar 1960, p. 40, no. 14 (Whitehall Palace, Little Room between the Breakfast Chamber and the Privy Gallery, as Andrea del Sarto); McKillop 1974, pp. 83–84, 166–67; Shearman 1983, no. 99

What must be this very portrait is listed in Giorgio Vasari's biography of Franciabigio, where it is described as having been painted 'for a countryman, the steward of Pierfrancesco de' Medici at the Palace of San Girolamo da Fiesole, which seems absolutely alive'. The individual in question, Jacopo Cennini, was a member of a well-known Florentine family, and he is shown looking out at us as if distracted from writing in his ledger. The appropriate attributes of a pruning hook, a billhook and a bunch of keys, and the inclusion of the Medici coat of arms of five red balls and a single blue one on a gold ground on the parapet in front of him serve to identify his lord. DE

51
Agnolo Bronzino (1503–1572)
Portrait of a Woman in Green, *c.* 1530–32
Oil on panel, 76.6 x 66.2 cm
The Royal Collection / HM Queen Elizabeth II, RCIN 405754
PROVENANCE: probably Dukes of Mantua; Charles I; Edward Bass and Dividend, Commonwealth Sale, 19 December 1651 (£100), as Andrea del Sarto; recovered at the Restoration
SELECTED BIBLIOGRAPHY: Millar 1960, p. 41, no. 20 (Whitehall Palace, Little Room between the Breakfast Chamber and the Privy Gallery, as Sebastiano del Piombo); Millar 1972, p. 265, no. 151; Shearman 1983, no. 55; Costamagna 1994, no. A62; Philadelphia 2004, no. 20; London 2007A, no. 7

The authorship of this arrestingly beautiful portrait, which was variously attributed to Sebastiano del Piombo and Andrea del Sarto when it belonged to Charles I, has been much debated. Increasingly, a consensus appears to be emerging that it – like the no less stunning *Portrait of a Woman in Red* in the Städelsches Kunstinstitut, Frankfurt – is an early work by Bronzino. If so, it could very possibly be, to quote Giorgio Vasari, the 'much praised painting' of the daughter of a Florentine customs official, Matteo Sofferoni, which he recorded as having been executed during Bronzino's stay in Pesaro, where the young artist lived from 1530 to 1532. DE

52
Correggio (1489–1534)
The Holy Family with St Jerome, *c.* 1519
Oil on panel, 68.9 x 56.6 cm
The Royal Collection / HM Queen Elizabeth II, RCIN 400029
PROVENANCE: Dukes of Mantua; Charles I; William Proctor, Commonwealth Sale, 3 November 1649 (£50); recovered at the Restoration
SELECTED BIBLIOGRAPHY: Millar 1972, p. 64, no. 67; Gould 1976, p. 285; Shearman 1983, no. 72; Ekserdjian 1997, pp. 172–73; London 2007A, no. 34; Parma 2008, no. II.27

This intimate half-length is constructed along a rising diagonal that proceeds from the aged and partially naked figure of St Jerome, in profile at bottom left, by way of the central Virgin and Child, before concluding with Joseph, shown holding a stick, his traditional attribute. St Jerome looks intently at the Infant Saviour, whom he has come to worship, and the Holy Family all look across at him, while the Christ Child extends his right hand in a gesture of blessing. The setting is a woody glade, and the only strong accents of colour are in the blue, red and yellow of the Virgin's costume. DE

53
Correggio (1489–1534)
St Catherine Reading, *c.* 1530–32
Oil on canvas, 64.5 x 52.2 cm
The Royal Collection / HM Queen Elizabeth II, RCIN 405768
PROVENANCE: first recorded in the collection of James II, 1688
SELECTED BIBLIOGRAPHY: Gould 1976, p. 210; Shearman 1983, no. 73; Ekserdjian 1997, pp. 172–73; London 2007A, no. 35; Parma 2008, no. III.35; Rome 2016B, no. 20

St Catherine is shown holding a palm branch and resting her arm on a broken wheel, both symbols of her martyrdom. She looks downwards and is represented reading a small devotional book. The mood and colour scheme are both deliberately restrained, and the only virtuoso passages are the sleeve of Catherine's white shift and the panache of her hair, the detail which Giorgio Vasari, in his biography of Correggio, singled out among all the many qualities of his art. DE

54
Dosso Dossi (*c.* 1490–*c.* 1541/42)
Virgin and Child with Saints, *c.* 1527–28
Oil on canvas, 169.7 x 172.7 cm
The Royal Collection / HM Queen Elizabeth II, RCIN 402853
PROVENANCE: Dukes of Mantua; Charles I; William Proctor, Commonwealth Sale, 7 November 1649 (£100); recovered at the Restoration
SELECTED BIBLIOGRAPHY: Millar 1960, p. 49, no. 42 (Whitehall Palace, Long Gallery); Gibbons 1968, no. 28; Millar 1972, p. 302, no. 65; Shearman 1983, no. 81; Ferrara 1998, no. 37; London 2007A, no. 32

Dosso represents the Virgin seated at the centre of the composition, wearing a splendid deep blue and gold damask robe. At her feet is the Christ Child, who has a cruciform halo, and – most unusually – is shown embracing a large cockerel. The identities of the three supplementary figures are less certain: the two men standing at the left margin may be St Peter and St Paul but have also been thought to be Joseph and an apostle, while the older woman to the right may well be Mary's mother, St Anne. Beyond her, Dosso has painted a luminous visionary landscape and a cloud of cherubim at top right. DE

55
Workshop of Giulio Romano (*c.* 1499–1546)
Sacrifice of a Goat to Jupiter, *c.* 1536–39
Oil on panel, 123 x 66.2 cm
The Royal Collection / HM Queen Elizabeth II, RCIN 406166
PROVENANCE: Dukes of Mantua; Charles I; Ralph Grynder and Dividend, Commonwealth Sale, 23 October 1651 (£100 for eleven panels); recovered at the Restoration
SELECTED BIBLIOGRAPHY: Millar 1960, p. 18, no. 7 (Whitehall Palace, Second Privy Lodging Room); Millar 1972, p. 270, no. 220; Shearman 1983, no. 119; Mantua 1989, pp. 400–05; London 2007A, no. 39.iii

This panel originally formed part of the decoration of a room in the Palazzo Ducale in Mantua known as the Gabinetto dei Cesari, where it was one of a number of panels contributed by the workshop of Giulio Romano between 1536 and 1539. They accompanied a series of eleven canvases of Roman emperors by Titian, also in the collection of Charles I. These were widely regarded as ranking among the Venetian master's supreme achievements, but were subsequently destroyed in a fire in Spain in 1734. The fact that Giulio was directly involved in the planning of the present work is proved by the existence of an autograph preparatory drawing for the figure group (National Gallery of Art, Washington, D.C.). DE

56
Polidoro da Caravaggio (*c.* 1499–1543)
Psyche Abandoned, *c.* 1527–28
Oil on panel, 87.5 x 161.5 cm
The Royal Collection / HM Queen Elizabeth II, RCIN 402919
PROVENANCE: William Frizell for Charles I, 1638; Jerome Lanier, Commonwealth Sale, 14 May 1650 (£42); recovered at the Restoration
SELECTED BIBLIOGRAPHY: Millar 1960, p. 43, no. 6 (Whitehall Palace, Long Gallery); Marabottini 1969, vol. 1, pp. 56–62, 254–57; Millar 1972, p. 303, no. 84; Shearman 1983, no. 198; de Castris 2001, pp. 268–77; London 2007A, no. 5.i

This painting forms part of a series depicting scenes from Apuleius' mythological story of Cupid and Psyche. The sequence may have been produced for an interior decorative scheme; its sketchlike quality and loose execution suggest that it was intended to be viewed from a distance. Described by Van der Doort as 'done in fresco', the panel is reminiscent of Polidoro's celebrated palace façades in Rome, the majority of which are now lost. The *Cupid and Psyche* series was acquired by Charles in 1638 from William Frizell, previously Postmaster to the King. The three narrative panels (the present work included) hung in the Long Gallery at Whitehall Palace, while six smaller, decorative scenes were displayed in the Privy Lodging Rooms, alongside important works by Titian and Correggio. LC

57
Jacopo Tintoretto (1518–1594)
Esther before Ahasuerus, *c.* 1546–47
Oil on canvas, 207.7 x 275.5 cm
The Royal Collection / HM Queen Elizabeth II, RCIN 407247
PROVENANCE: Dukes of Mantua; Charles I; Smith (unidentified), Commonwealth Sale, 18 June 1650 (£120); recovered at the Restoration
SELECTED BIBLIOGRAPHY: Millar 1960, p. 226, no. 10 (St James's Palace, Gallery); Millar 1972, p. 273, no. 275; Pallucchini and Rossi 1974–82, vol. 1, no. 129; Shearman 1983, no. 255; London 2007A, no. 75

Titian dominated the Venetian artistic scene of the sixteenth century, and his younger contemporary Tintoretto reacted to his influence by consciously striving to create a different style of painting. Already in this relatively early work, Tintoretto is thrillingly untroubled by the long shadow cast by Titian. It represents the Old Testament subject of Queen Esther fainting in the presence of her husband Ahasuerus. A vital aspect of her story is the fact that she is secretly Jewish and that her people are threatened by the machinations of Haman, the King's chief minister, who ultimately meets a bad end on the gallows. The way in which the spotlight falls dramatically upon Esther, who stands out from the crowd of figures behind her, and the palpable anxiety of Ahasuerus as he descends from the raised dais that denotes his supreme power, are both brilliantly managed. DE

58
Jacopo Bassano (*c.* 1510–1592)
The Adoration of the Shepherds, *c.* 1546
Oil on canvas, 139.1 x 218.5 cm
The Royal Collection / HM Queen Elizabeth II, RCIN 405772
PROVENANCE: Charles I; Emanuel De Critz and Dividend, Commonwealth Sale (£35); recovered at the Restoration
SELECTED BIBLIOGRAPHY: Millar 1972, p. 218, no. 20; Shearman 1983, no. 16; Bassano del Grappa 1992, no. 17; London 2007A, no. 33

Jacopo Bassano was one of the most distinctive painters active in the region of Venice in the sixteenth century, and was the founder of a whole family tradition, which was particularly celebrated for its evocations of peasant and pastoral life. Charles I's profound admiration of his art is underlined by the fact that he owned no fewer than 24 paintings by Jacopo and his workshop, of which the present example is without question one of the finest. Jacopo depicts the arrival of three rustic shepherds at the classical ruins in which the Nativity was customarily represented in Italian Renaissance art. The kneeling shepherd offers up a trussed lamb, an allusion to St John the Baptist's reference to Christ as the Lamb of God. DE

59
Jacopo Bassano (*c.* 1510–1592)
The Journey of Jacob, *c.* 1561
Oil on canvas, 129.4 x 184.2 cm
The Royal Collection / HM Queen Elizabeth II, RCIN 402928
PROVENANCE: Charles I; Henry Willett, Commonwealth Sale, 7 May 1650 (£50); recovered at the Restoration
SELECTED BIBLIOGRAPHY: Millar 1960, p. 10, no. 11 (Whitehall Palace, Adam and Eve Stairs); Millar 1972, p. 70, no. 27; Shearman 1983, no. 19; Bassano del Grappa 1992, no. 17; Ballarin 1996, vol. 2, p. 45; London 2007A, no. 73

Jacopo Bassano was unusually fond of representing scenes from the Old Testament that allowed him to portray men and beasts in expansive landscape settings. Here he chose the story recounted in Genesis of Jacob's return journey to his father in the land of Canaan in the company of his two wives, Rachel and Leah, who were the daughters of his master, Laban. By comparison with his earlier *Adoration of the Shepherds* (cat. 58), the treatment of the brushwork of this coarsely woven canvas is notably more free, and the overall tonality is significantly more muted, albeit with occasional bold accents of yellow, pink and green. DE

60
Palma Giovane (1548–1628)
The Triumph of David, *c.* 1590–95
Oil on canvas, 207 x 337 cm
Museo Nacional del Prado, Madrid, inv. P00271
PROVENANCE: Charles I; Edmund Harrison and Dividend, Commonwealth Sale, 23 October 1651 (£100); Philip IV; transferred to the Prado in 1817
SELECTED BIBLIOGRAPHY: Millar 1960, p. 228, no. 51 (St James's Palace, Gallery); Millar 1972, p. 272, no. 254; Mason Rinaldi 1984, no. 137; Madrid 2002, no. 44

Palma Giovane was entrusted with the responsibility of completing Titian's final painting, the *Pietà* (Gallerie dell'Accademia, Venice), and also left a memorable description of the aged artist's way of painting. He was the most prominent painter active in Venice after the deaths of Titian, Tintoretto and Veronese, and the present work – together with its pendant (cat. 61) – are among his most energetic productions. It represents the boy David, clutching the bloodied and severed head of Goliath, and returning to the city of Jerusalem in triumph. Behind him is the crowned figure of King Saul on horseback with various soldiers and a small bounding spaniel, while he is greeted by a group of women making music and brandishing a palm branch to celebrate his victory over the champion of the Philistines. DE

61
Palma Giovane (1548–1628)
The Conversion of St Paul, *c.* 1590–95
Oil on canvas, 207 x 337 cm
Museo Nacional del Prado, Madrid, inv. P00272
PROVENANCE: Charles I; Edmund Harrison and Dividend, Commonwealth Sale, 23 October 1651 (£100); Philip IV; transferred to the Prado in 1817
SELECTED BIBLIOGRAPHY: Millar 1960, p. 228, no. 52 (St James's Palace, Gallery); Millar 1972, p. 272, no. 253; Mason Rinaldi 1984, no. 138; Madrid 2002, no. 45

This monumental canvas and its pendant (cat. 60) represent two very different scenes of triumph. Unlike David's, which is altogether more muted, Paul's fall from his white charger, in which his collapsed body represents the still centre of an exploding maelstrom of fleeing bodies, could hardly be portrayed more dramatically. In the Acts of the Apostles, Paul is blinded by the light from heaven (Acts 9:3–9), and the artist has gone to great pains to render its radiant brightness, and to contrast it with the surrounding darkness. The figure at bottom right appears to have been derived from an invention of Cornelis van Haarlem, found in a painting of two followers of Cadmus devoured by a dragon of 1588 (National Gallery, London), which was engraved by Hendrick Goltzius that same year. DE

62
Gerrit van Honthorst (1592–1656)
Charles I, 1628
Oil on canvas, 76.2 x 64.1 cm
National Portrait Gallery, London, inv. NPG 4444
PROVENANCE: Ulysse Marsalli; acquired in 1965
SELECTED BIBLIOGRAPHY: Millar 1954, p. 39, no. 15; Judson and Ekkart 1999, no. 415; London 2007B, no. 31

Painted between April and December 1628, when Honthorst was in London at the King's invitation, this relaxed portrait presents Charles as a well-dressed scholar momentarily diverted from his reading. The portrait is closely related to Honthorst's grandiose mythological group portrait *Apollo and Diana* (Hampton Court Palace), commissioned by Buckingham, which shows the Duke as Mercury presenting the Liberal Arts to the King and Queen as Apollo and Diana, surrounded by the Muses. A year before, the King had acquired the Gonzaga collection; it is no coincidence that these images of informal scholarship and Olympian patronage were painted so soon afterwards. NM/DST

63
Daniel Mytens (*c.* 1590–1647)
Charles I, 1628
Oil on canvas, 219.4 x 139.1 cm
The Royal Collection / HM Queen Elizabeth II, RCIN 404448
PROVENANCE: Princess Elizabeth, Queen of Bohemia, or Prince Rupert; William, 1st Earl of Craven; Cornelia, Countess of Craven; bequeathed to Her Majesty The Queen in 1961
SELECTED BIBLIOGRAPHY: Millar 1963, vol. 1, no. 118; ter Kuile 1969, no. 25; London 1999B, no. 1; London 2009, no. 12; London 2013, pp. 96, 115, 155

Daniel Mytens was Charles I's first court painter and his works were prominently located at Whitehall Palace: his full-length portraits of courtiers and royalty dominated the Bear Gallery, and his self-portrait (cat. 7) kept company with Rubens (cat. 4) and Van Dyck in the Little Room between the Breakfast Chamber and the Privy Gallery.

According to the inscription, the present portrait was painted 'from the life' in 1628 and represents the best that was to be had before Van Dyck settled in London four years later. The pose may be a little stiff, but there is real brilliance in the painting of the sheen of the fabric, the glint of the sword hilt and the crumpled leather of the boot. This portrait was given to the King's sister, Elizabeth of Bohemia. NM/DST

64
Anthony van Dyck (1599–1641)
Charles I and Henrietta Maria Holding a Laurel Wreath, 1632
Oil on canvas, 104 x 176 cm
Archbishopric of Olomouc, inv. KE 2372, O 406
PROVENANCE: Charles I; possibly John Jackson and Dividend, Commonwealth Sale, 23 October 1651 (£60); possibly Diego Duarte; Franz and Bernhard Albert von Imstenraedt; Karl von Liechtenstein-Kastelkorn, Bishop of Olomouc; thereafter by descent
SELECTED BIBLIOGRAPHY: Millar 1972, p. 317, no. 354; Brown 1982, pp. 180–81; Togner et al. 1999, no. 91; Barnes et al. 2004, no. IV.46; London 2009, no. 18; New York 2016, no. 68

On display in the Drawing Room at Somerset House, the Queen's residence, this double portrait replaced a similar composition by Daniel Mytens (Royal Collection). The King appears to be bringing the fruits of his labours – a victor's laurel wreath – and offering them as a tribute due to his wife. In return she proffers a sprig of olive, symbolic of peace. The fact that he looks at her with such a respectful gaze while she looks out at the viewer – a reversal of the conventions in contemporary portraits of husband and wife – creates a unique aura of chivalrous deference and nuptial harmony. Peace and union were central themes in Stuart culture, appearing in poetry, painting and court masques. DST

65
Anthony van Dyck (1599–1641)
Charles I and Henrietta Maria with Prince Charles and Princess Mary, 1632
Oil on panel, 19.7 x 23.5 cm
The Royal Collection / HM Queen Elizabeth II, RCIN 408584

PROVENANCE: Robert Edward King, 1st Viscount Lorton, or Robert King, 2nd Viscount Lorton; private collection, Austria; acquired in 2016

In this rapidly painted preparatory oil sketch for the *Greate Peece* (cat. 66), Van Dyck explored the arrangement of the sitters in his monumental portrait of the royal family. The sketch differs from the final composition in a number of details, including the dresses, but the most notable change is the position of the future Charles II. Shown here between his parents, glancing affectionately at his sister, the prince is eventually placed next to the royal regalia on the left, his gaze redirected towards the viewer. His place is taken by a couple of Italian greyhounds, adding a playful element to the grandeur of the final composition. PR

66
Anthony van Dyck (1599–1641)
Charles I and Henrietta Maria with Prince Charles and Princess Mary ('The Greate Peece'), 1632
Oil on canvas, 303.8 x 256.5 cm
The Royal Collection / HM Queen Elizabeth II, RCIN 405353
PROVENANCE: Charles I; Emanuel De Critz and Dividend, Commonwealth Sale, 23 October 1651 (£150); recovered at the Restoration
SELECTED BIBLIOGRAPHY: Hookham Carpenter 1844, p. 71; Millar 1960, p. 42, no. 1 (Whitehall Palace, Long Gallery); Millar 1963, vol. 1, no. 150; Millar 1972, p. 306, no. 132; London 1982, no. 7; Howarth 1997, pp. 85–89; Gordenker 2001, pp. 36–38; Barnes et al. 2004, no. IV.45; London 2009, no. 17

This monumental family portrait, first referred to as the 'greate peece' in a 1632 warrant issuing payment to Van Dyck, shows Charles I and Henrietta Maria with Prince Charles (born in 1630) and Princess Mary (born in 1631). The view of Westminster Hall in the background alludes to the King's power over Parliament and country. Commissioned by the King immediately after Van Dyck's arrival in London, the picture hung on the vista of the Long Gallery at Whitehall Palace, where it would have represented a modern response to Holbein's so-called *Whitehall Mural*, now lost, showing Henry VIII and Jane Seymour with Henry's parents Henry VII and Elizabeth of York. PR

67
Anthony van Dyck (1599–1641)
Charles I in Robes of State, 1636
Oil on canvas, 248 x 153.6 cm
The Royal Collection / HM Queen Elizabeth II, RCIN 404398
PROVENANCE: Charles I; William Webb, Commonwealth Sale, 29 October 1649 (£60, with a pendant of Henrietta Maria); recovered at the Restoration
SELECTED BIBLIOGRAPHY: Millar 1963, vol. 1, no. 145; Millar 1972, p. 318, no. 312; Barnes et al. 2004, no. IV.53; Griffey 2015, pp. 121–22

This magnificent portrait was first recorded in the Cross Gallery, Somerset House, as part of a display of European royalty. It was accompanied by a matching portrait of the Queen (subsequently lost), and both were much copied as diplomatic gifts. King and Queen wear coronation robes and stand before columns and cloth of gold, a formula that subsequently became known as the 'State Portrait'. At the same time, Van Dyck's portrait is surprisingly informal: the King's pose has an easy grace and Van Dyck's brushwork is loose and suggestive. DST

68
Anthony van Dyck (1599–1641)
Henrietta Maria with Sir Jeffrey Hudson, 1633
Oil on canvas, 219.1 x 134.8 cm
National Gallery of Art, Washington, Samuel H. Kress Collection, inv. 1952.5.39
PROVENANCE: Richard Newport, 2nd Earl of Bradford; Charles Coote, 7th Earl of Mountrath; Joseph Damer, 1st Earl of Dorchester; Henry Dawson-Damer, 3rd Earl of Portarlington; Thomas Baring, 1st Earl of Northbrook, 1881; Francis Baring, 2nd Earl of Northbrook; William Randolph Hearst; M. Knoedler & Co., New York; Samuel H. Kress, 1952
SELECTED BIBLIOGRAPHY: Eisler 1977, no. K1911; Washington 1990, no. 67; Wheelock 1995, pp. 84–89; Gordenker 2001, pp. 35–36; Wheelock 2001; Griffey 2003, p. 45; Barnes et al. 2004, no. IV.119; Griffey 2015, p. 118; New York 2016, no. 72

Van Dyck's majestic portrait depicts the Queen, accompanied by her servant, Jeffrey Hudson. Even though the Queen seems to have largely eschewed the pursuit in real life, both are dressed magnificently for the hunt. The portrait showcases her style and serenity alongside her lively dwarf and pet monkey. While serenity was considered an essential virtue for queens and often led to rather stiff portrayals of royal women, Van Dyck's masterful characterisation imparts Henrietta Maria with a quiet vivaciousness and elegance that are mirrored in the delicate, bristling handling of her dress, her playful companions, the gentle curves of the curtain and the wispy foliage of the orange tree in the background. EG

69
Anthony van Dyck (1599–1641)
George Villiers, 2nd Duke of Buckingham, and Francis Villiers, 1635
Oil on canvas, 137.2 x 127.7 cm
The Royal Collection / HM Queen Elizabeth II, RCIN 404401
PROVENANCE: Charles I; Clement Kynnersley, Commonwealth Sale, 22 March 1650 (£50); recovered at the Restoration
SELECTED BIBLIOGRAPHY: Millar 1960, p. 226, no. 7 (St James's Palace, Long Gallery); Millar 1963, vol. 1, no. 153; Millar 1972, p. 269, no. 202; Barnes et al. 2004, no. IV.34; London 2009, no. 33

George and Francis Villiers, sons of the Duke of Buckingham, the elder born in 1628, the year of his father's assassination, and the younger the following year, were 'bred up by the King' with his own, slightly younger children. They were also painted in the same way: the present work and the *Three Eldest Children of Charles I* (Royal Collection) are both dated 1635 and have often been treated as natural companions. Part of the appeal of the pairing is the affecting contrast between the happy childishness of the royal children and the solemn gravity of the two orphans, then still only six and seven years old. A preparatory drawing for the painting (British Museum, London) reveals that Van Dyck was uncertain about the position of Francis's feet, and tried a number of different placements before settling on the subtly hesitant stance seen here. NM/DST

70
Anthony van Dyck (1599–1641)
The Five Eldest Children of Charles I, 1637
Oil on canvas, 163.2 x 198.8 cm
The Royal Collection / HM Queen Elizabeth II, RCIN 404405
PROVENANCE: Charles I; William Geere, Commonwealth Sale, 14 May 1650 (£120); recovered at the Restoration
SELECTED BIBLIOGRAPHY: Millar 1960, p. 35, no. 1 (Whitehall Palace, Breakfast Chamber); Millar 1963, vol. 1, no. 152; Millar 1972, p. 206, no. 338; Brown 1982, pp. 183–85; Barnes et al. 2004, no. IV.62; London 2004, no. 155

This group portrait hung in the King's Breakfast Chamber; the only other painting in the room was Giulio Romano's monstrous *Mermaid Feeding Her Young* (Royal Collection), which hung as an over-door. The pairing of these disparate images was clearly intended as a joke: a nod to Aesop's fable of the eagle and the owl, which hangs on the fact that every creature considers its offspring to be perfectly beautiful, however ugly to the impartial eye. In a study for this painting (Royal Collection), the future Charles II props his elbow upon a cushion; in the finished work the cushion's place is taken by a giant and ungainly Lyme Mastiff, a now-extinct breed of fighting dog, which appears similarly monstrous and comic in this context. DST

71
William Dobson (1611–1646)
Charles II, when Prince of Wales, with a Page, c. 1642
Oil on canvas, 153.6 x 129.8 cm
National Galleries of Scotland. Purchased 1935, inv. PG 1244
PROVENANCE: Grinling Gibbons; Thomas Walker, 1722; Stephen Skinner; Eliab Harvey; Campbell Munro; acquired in 1935
SELECTED BIBLIOGRAPHY: London 1983A, no. 9

William Dobson, the King's painter after Van Dyck's death in 1641 and much inspired by his illustrious predecessor, established a wartime studio at Oxford, the Royalist headquarters for part of the

1640s. The future Charles II is shown here at the age of twelve, his cheeks having not yet shed their youthful plumpness, with an attendant apparently of a similar age holding his helmet. In the distance rages the Battle of Edgehill (1642), at which the young Prince of Wales was present. In the bottom-left corner lies Medusa's severed serpent-haired head – a symbol of rebellion – among captured Parliamentarian standards. According to the Roman poet Lucan, Athena affixed the gorgon's head to her *aegis* and used it to bring an end to civil war among the gods. NM/DST

72
Anthony van Dyck (1599–1641)
Charles I on Horseback with M. de St Antoine, 1633
Oil on canvas, 370 x 270 cm
The Royal Collection / HM Queen Elizabeth II, RCIN 405322
PROVENANCE: Charles I; Hugh Pope, Commonwealth Sale, 22 December 1652 (£150); recovered at the Restoration
SELECTED BIBLIOGRAPHY: Millar 1960, p. 226, no. 1 (St James's Palace, Gallery); Millar 1963, vol. 1, no. 143; Millar 1972, pp. 273–74, no. 279; Brown 1982, pp. 166–68; Raatschen 2001; Barnes et al. 2004, no. IV.47; Wilks 2005, pp. 157, 159, 164; London 2009, no. 21

This monumental equestrian portrait was designed to hang on the vista of the Gallery at St James's Palace, creating the illusion that the space opened out onto the landscape beyond, with the King entering the space through a triumphal arch. The King is placed fractionally off-centre, turning very slightly away from the viewer. Other elements in the composition also contrast with the flatness of the arch: the slight shying of the horse, the asymmetry of the swathes of drapery, and the contrast between the coat of arms to the left and the striding and admiring equerry M. de St Antoine to the right.

The composition is based on Rubens's *Duke of Lerma* of 1603 (Museo Nacional del Prado, Madrid), which Charles would have seen in the gallery of Philip IV's Casa Real at Valladolid. Preparatory studies (British Museum, London; Staaliche Museen, Berlin) show Van Dyck refining this original, with more tilt to the head and balletic counterpoise to the body. DST

73
Anthony van Dyck (1599–1641)
Charles I on Horseback, *c.* 1635–36
Oil on canvas, 96 x 86.3 cm
The Royal Collection / HM Queen Elizabeth II, RCIN 400571
PROVENANCE: Charles I; John Boulton, Commonwealth Sale, 22 November 1649 (£46); recovered at the Restoration
SELECTED BIBLIOGRAPHY: Millar 1960, p. 62, no. 2 (Whitehall Palace, Chair Room); Millar 1963, vol. 1, no. 144; Martin 1970, p. 44; Millar 1972, pp. 205–06, no. 332; London 1999B, no. 6; Barnes et al. 2004, no. IV.52

Van der Doort recorded this 'first model' for Van Dyck's equestrian portrait (cat. 74) in the Chair Room at Whitehall Palace, surrounded by some of the King's Stuart ancestors and many Northern Renaissance pictures. A number of alterations (such as those on the King's right arm and around his head) and differences between this and the final version (in the helmet held by the attendant, for example) confirm that this is a working model. Considering that Van Dyck, when left to his own devices, worked out ideas through summary monochrome oil sketches (such as cat. 65), we can assume that this complete anticipation of the final work was created for the benefit of the King rather than the artist. It suggests that both were thinking of the work – the second of Van Dyck's equestrian portraits of the King – not so much as a new composition but as an entirely new way of integrating figure and landscape. NM/DST

74
Anthony van Dyck (1599–1641)
Charles I on Horseback, *c.* 1637–38
Oil on canvas, 367 x 292.1 cm
The National Gallery, London. Bought 1885, inv. NG1172
PROVENANCE: Charles I; Balthasar Gerbier, Commonwealth Sale, 21 June 1650 (£200); Maximilian II Emanuel, Elector of Bavaria; looted by Emperor Joseph I from Munich; John Churchill, 1st Duke of Marlborough; thereafter by descent; acquired in 1885
SELECTED BIBLIOGRAPHY: Martin 1970, no. 1172; Millar 1972, p. 316, no. 283; Strong 1972; Brown 1982, pp. 168–69; Egerton 1998, pp. 77–79; Barnes et al. 2004, no. IV.51

Charles I must have approved the model (cat. 73) before Van Dyck undertook this portrait, the largest and most ambitious of his works for the King. At the Commonwealth Sale, when royal portraits might have been available at a discount, the model sold for a respectable £46 and the finished work for £200, a record price for Van Dyck. The epic character of Van Dyck's earlier equestrian portrait of the King (cat. 72) has not disappeared, but it is here expressed in natural forms: in the giant scale of the elm and in the extent of the distance measured out in sunlit grass terraces.

The tree in the background is closely related to a landscape study which survives from Van Dyck's English period (British Museum, London). Van Dyck had studied the English landscape as well as the paintings of Titian and was inspired by the imagery of court masques, such as Walter Montagu's pastoral *Shepherd's Paradise* of 1633. These influences come together to produce this moody and atmospheric image of Charles as the Prince of Arcadia. DST

75
Anthony van Dyck (1599–1641)
Charles I, *c.* 1632–36
Black chalk on paper, 47.9 x 36.5 cm
Rijksmuseum, Amsterdam. Purchased with the support of the Vereniging Rembrandt, inv. RP-T-1887-A-1162
PROVENANCE: probably Gerard ter Borch the Younger; Theodorus Zebinden; his sale, 1886; Frederik Muller; acquired in 1887
SELECTED BIBLIOGRAPHY: Antwerp 1949, no. 105; Kettering 1988, vol. 2, no. FC 21; New York 1991, no. 69; Paris 2008B, no. II; New York 2016, no. 69

Van Dyck often made quick sketches for his portraits, exploring the main elements of their composition, including the sitter's pose and the setting. He usually painted the face directly from life, however, which makes this large study, the artist's only portrait drawing of Charles I, something of an anomaly. The King is shown wearing a broad-brimmed hat, reminiscent of the one worn by Rubens in his self-portrait (cat. 4), thus representing a fascinating link between the latter work and Van Dyck's *Charles I in the Hunting Field* (cat. 76), in which the King wears a similar hat. The drawing was probably acquired by the artist Gerard ter Borch the Younger on his sojourn in London in 1635–36, when he visited his uncle, the engraver Robert van Voerst (see cat. 134), a close collaborator of Van Dyck. PR

76
Anthony van Dyck (1599–1641)
Charles I in the Hunting Field, *c.* 1636
Oil on canvas, 266 x 207 cm
Musée du Louvre, Paris, Department of Paintings, inv. 1236
PROVENANCE: Charles I; Jeanne Baptiste d'Albert de Luynes, Comtesse de Verrue; Léon de Madaillan de Lesparre, Marquis de Lassay; Guy Armand de Gramont, Comte de Guiche, 1769; his sale, 1771; Jeanne Bécu, Comtesse du Barry; Louis XV, 1775; transferred to the Louvre in 1797
SELECTED BIBLIOGRAPHY: Hookham Carpenter 1844, p. 67; Held 1958; Brussels 1965, no. 68; Moffitt 1983; Smuts 1987, pp. 172–77; Johns 1988; Howarth 1997, pp. 132–36; Barnes et al. 2004, no. IV.50; Lens 2013, no. 58

Painted in around 1636, between his two equestrian portraits of the King (cats 72, 74), this is Van Dyck's most personal and arguably most accomplished portrait of Charles I. In allusion to earlier portraits of the King's brother, Henry, Prince of Wales, by Robert Peake (fig. 31) and his mother, Anne of Denmark, by Paul van Somer (Royal Collection), Charles I is shown in the hunting field. He wears the decorations of the Order of the Garter, the riband as well as the garter, tied just below his left knee.

The portrait is listed as 'Le Roi à la ciasse' in a memorandum to the King written by the artist in 1638. We do not know where it was displayed, but it is tempting to suppose that it replaced Van Somer's portrait of Queen Anne, when the latter was moved to the Bear Gallery at Whitehall. Van Dyck's portrait does not appear in the Commonwealth Sale inventory, and it is possible that it was one of the pictures Henrietta Maria took with her when she went into exile in 1644. PR

77
Anthony van Dyck (1599–1641)
Italian Sketchbook, 1621–27
19.9 x 15.2 cm
The British Museum, London.
Accepted by HM Government in lieu of Inheritance Tax and allocated to the British Museum, 1957, inv. 1957,1214.207
PROVENANCE: Peter Lely; Hugh Howard; William Cavendish, 2nd Duke of Devonshire; Samuel William Reynolds; George Agar-Ellis, 1st Baron Dover; Henry George Agar-Ellis, 4th Viscount Clifden; his sale, 1893; Desprez; Charles Fairfax Murray; Herbert Cook; Spencer Cavendish, 8th Duke of Devonshire; acquired in 1957
SELECTED BIBLIOGRAPHY: Adriani 1940; Brown 1982, pp. 61–99; Brown 1987; Jaffé 2001; Jaffé 2002, nos 986–1132; London 2012, no. 5; New York 2016, pp. 16–17

Van Dyck kept this sketchbook as an *aide-mémoire* during his sojourn in Italy between 1621 and 1627. On some 120 folios, many covered on both sides, he recorded the paintings he saw in Genoa, Venice, Rome, Florence, Palermo and elsewhere, and listed their owners and locations. The sketchbook was rebound in the late nineteenth century.

Although Van Dyck included some works by contemporary artists, such as Guercino and Annibale Carracci, he showed considerably more interest in sixteenth-century artists, most importantly Titian. One of the works he saw in Venice and recorded in his sketchbook, Titian's *Venus and Music* (fig. 27), was later acquired by Charles I and displayed with other works by Titian (cats 45–47) in the First Privy Lodging Room at Whitehall Palace. On the sketchbook's facing page, Van Dyck recorded a figure closely related to the figure of Andromeda in Titian's *Perseus and Andromeda* (The Wallace Collection, London), a painting the artist was eventually to acquire for his own collection. PR

78
Anthony van Dyck (1599–1641)
Cupid and Psyche, 1639–40
Oil on canvas, 200.2 x 192.6 cm
The Royal Collection / HM Queen Elizabeth II, RCIN 405571
PROVENANCE: Charles I; Robert Houghton, Commonwealth Sale, 8 October 1651 (£110); Peter Lely; recovered at the Restoration
SELECTED BIBLIOGRAPHY: Hookham Carpenter 1844, p. 68; Millar 1960, p. 43, no. 10 (Whitehall Palace, Long Gallery); Millar 1963, vol. 1, no. 166; London 1968, no. 15; London 1972, no. 109; Millar 1972, p. 217, no. 1; London 1982, no. 58; Washington 1990, no. 85; Antwerp 1999, no. 100; Barnes et al. 2004, no. IV.3; London 2009, no. 29

During his time in England, Van Dyck worked largely as a portraitist, both for the royal household and the English aristocracy. *Cupid and Psyche* is his only mythological painting to survive from this period. The story is told in the *Metamorphoses* of Apuleius (also known as *The Golden Ass*): Psyche, sent to the underworld by Venus to bring back a small dose of Proserpine's beauty, yields to the temptation of opening the box that contains it and is sent into a deep sleep as punishment. Cupid eventually comes to the rescue and awakens her from her slumber. The composition clearly shows Van Dyck's admiration of Titian (see pp. 150–55).

The picture may have originally been commissioned for the Queen's House at Greenwich as part of a series devoted to the story of Cupid and Psyche, and it may possibly be identified as the 'pièce pour la maison à Green Witz' mentioned by Van Dyck in 1638. The series was never completed, however, and the unframed canvas was eventually displayed in the Long Gallery at Whitehall Palace. PR

79
Anthony van Dyck (1599–1641)
Margaret Lemon, *c.* 1638
Oil on canvas, 93.3 x 77.8 cm
The Royal Collection / HM Queen Elizabeth II, RCIN 402531
PROVENANCE: Charles I; Jan Baptist Gaspars, Commonwealth Sale, 22 March 1650 (£23); recovered at the Restoration
SELECTED BIBLIOGRAPHY: Millar 1963, vol. 1, no. 157; Millar 1972, p. 265, no. 153; Gordenker 2001, p. 47; Barnes et al. 2004, no. IV.157

Van Dyck modelled this portrait of his mistress, Margaret Lemon, on Titian's *Woman with a Fur Coat* (fig. 13), which Charles had acquired on his visit to Madrid in 1623 and which was on display in the First Privy Lodging Room at Whitehall Palace with other works by Titian (cats 45–47). The pose of her right arm, covering herself, is also reminiscent of the so-called *Crouching Venus* (cat. 24). In early 1640 Van Dyck married Mary Ruthven, the teenage daughter of a Scottish nobleman and maid of honour to Henrietta Maria. PR

80
Anthony van Dyck (1599–1641)
Self-portrait, *c.* 1640
Oil on canvas, 56 x 46 cm
National Portrait Gallery, London, inv. NPG 6987
PROVENANCE: possibly Peter Lely; his sale, 1682; Francis Newport, later 1st Earl of Bradford; Richard Graham; his sale, 1712; Francis Child; Robert Child; Sarah Anne, Countess of Westmorland; George Child Villiers, 5th Earl of Jersey; acquired in 2014
SELECTED BIBLIOGRAPHY: London 1982, no. 65; Barnes et al. 2004, no. IV.5; London 2009, no. 67; MacLeod 2014

This is Van Dyck's last known self-portrait, showing the artist shortly before his premature death in 1641. The pose is reminiscent of his earliest known self-portrait (Akademie der bildenden Künste, Vienna), as well as Titian's *Man with a Blue Sleeve* (National Gallery, London), which was for sale at the time and had been brought to the artist's attention. The sunflower adorning the elaborate seventeenth-century frame calls to mind *Self-portrait with a Sunflower* (cat. 5). Another self-portrait by Van Dyck, also in an oval carved frame, was documented in the Little Room between the Breakfast Chamber and the Privy Gallery at Whitehall Palace. PR

81
Anthony van Dyck (1599–1641)
Charles I and the Knights of the Garter in Procession, *c.* 1639–40
Oil on panel, 29.2 x 130.8 cm
Ashmolean Museum, Oxford.
Accepted by HM Government in lieu of Inheritance Tax from the estate of the 10th Duke of Rutland and allocated to the Ashmolean Museum, 2002, inv. A1247
PROVENANCE: Charles I; Margaret Wagstaff, Commonwealth Sale, 16 July 1650 (£5); recovered at the Restoration; Peter Lely; his sale, 1682; Robert Henley, by 1758; his son's sale, 1787; Charles Manners, 4th Duke of Rutland; thereafter by descent; acquired in 2002
SELECTED BIBLIOGRAPHY: Hookham Carpenter 1844, p. 68; Millar 1960, p. 158, no. 10 (Whitehall Palace, Store); Millar 1972, p. 151, no. 2; Barnes et al. 2004, no. IV.59; Turner 2012, fig. 8

This long, narrow oil sketch is arguably the most ambitious of Van Dyck's paintings *en grisaille*. The design was intended for a series of tapestries in celebration of the Order of the Garter, which was never completed. Listed in Van Dyck's *Mémoire* to the King of 1638, the present panel shows the annual procession of the Order, with the King at the rear beneath a canopy. The imaginary setting of a grandiose Palladian-style arcade echoes Inigo Jones's Banqueting House, for which the tapestries were intended. Such a project would have appealed to Charles, whose father had provided the necessary grants to establish the tapestry manufactory at Mortlake. PR

82
Peter Paul Rubens (1577–1640)
The Apotheosis of James I and Other Studies, *c.* 1628–30
Oil on panel, 94.7 x 63 cm
Tate, London. Purchased with assistance from the National Heritage Memorial Fund, Tate Members, the Art Fund in memory of Sir Oliver Millar (with a contribution from the Wolfson Foundation), Viscount and Viscountess

Hampden and Family, Monument Trust, Manny and Brigitta Davidson and the Family, and other donors, 2008, inv. T12919
PROVENANCE: Thomas Hampden-Trevor, by 1799; thereafter by descent; on loan to the National Gallery, London, from 1985; acquired in 2008
SELECTED BIBLIOGRAPHY: Millar 1956; Held 1980, vol. 1, no. 133; Martin 2005, vol. 1, no. 1

The Banqueting House, designed by Inigo Jones in 1619, was the ceremonial centre of Whitehall Palace. Before 1623, Rubens was approached to create canvases for the nine openings in its ceiling. The present oil sketch is for the central canvas, showing James I being crowned by Peace-bearing Victory. To either side, James's virtues triumph over opposing vices, and processions of children, putti and animals demonstrate the happiness of his reign. Several elements of the composition are upside-down, following the different viewpoints within the Banqueting House. The sketch may have been the basis for the discussions between Rubens and Charles's advisors about the ceiling decoration that took place during the artist's stay in London in 1629–30. The finished canvases were installed in late 1636 and early 1637, and are still *in situ* (fig. 37). PR

83
Peter Paul Rubens (1577–1640)
Landscape with St George and the Dragon, 1630–35
Oil on canvas, 152.5 x 226.9 cm
The Royal Collection / HM Queen Elizabeth II, RCIN 405356
PROVENANCE: Endymion Porter; Charles I, 1634–35; William Latham and Dividend, Commonwealth Sale, 23 October 1651 (£150); private collection, Spanish Netherlands; Armand Jean de Vignerot du Plessis, 2nd Duke of Richelieu, by 1677; Louis, Duke of Orléans; thereafter by descent; William Morland; acquired by George IV in 1814
SELECTED BIBLIOGRAPHY: Croft-Murray 1947; Millar 1960, p. 171, no. 1 (Whitehall Palace, Store); Burchard and d'Hulst 1963, vol. 1, no. 146; Millar 1972, p. 137, no. 5; Adler 1982, no. 35; Merle du Bourg 2004, pp. 131–34, 252–53; White 2007, no. 63

This picture is closely linked with Rubens's sojourn in England, and news about it was current in London before the artist's return to Antwerp in May 1630. Rubens did not present it to the King, however, but continued to work on it once home in Flanders. It was not acquired by Charles I until 1634–35. St George is shown handing the princess her girdle, with which she will lead the defeated dragon back to the city. The features of St George strongly resemble those of Charles, and the landscape can be identified as a view of the Thames looking south, with Lambeth Palace to the left. PR

84
Orazio Gentileschi (1563–1639)
Lot and His Daughters, 1628
Oil on canvas, 226 x 282 cm
Museo de Bellas Artes de Bilbao, inv. 69/101
PROVENANCE: Henrietta Maria; William Latham and Dividend, Commonwealth Sale, 23 October 1651 (£80); Luis Méndez de Haro y Guzmán, 6th Marqués of Carpio; thereafter by descent; Duke of Alba, until after 1911; Luis de Ardanaz; acquired in 1924
SELECTED BIBLIOGRAPHY: Millar 1960, p. 194, no. 1 (Greenwich Palace, Queen's Withdrawing Chamber); Millar 1972, p. 137, no. 2; Bissell 1981, no. 61; London 1999A, no. 7; Rome 2001, no. 46; Wood 2001, pp. 112, 120–22; Rome 2016A, no. 96

On a visit to England in mid-1628, the German biographer Joachim von Sandrart saw this large canvas in progress in Gentileschi's studio at York House, residence of the painter's patron, the Duke of Buckingham. A year later the late Duke's agent, Balthasar Gerbier, valued the painting at the considerable sum of £100. It was ultimately acquired by Henrietta Maria and installed in the Queen's House at Greenwich in the late 1630s, with a ceiling ensemble and two other large paintings by Gentileschi (cats 85–86).

It shows the elderly Lot and his two daughters, who, having fled the city of Sodom, destroyed by God as punishment for the sins of its inhabitants, found refuge in the mountains. The sisters realise that, as the sole survivors, their only hope of descendants now lies with their father, and they ply him with wine and commit incest with him as he sleeps (Genesis 19:30–35). Gentileschi had depicted this theme on several occasions earlier in his career (J. Paul Getty Museum, Los Angeles; Gemäldegalerie, Berlin; National Gallery of Canada, Ottawa). Here, his treatment differs, with full-length figures draped in luscious textiles and a broader setting that recalls the grotto in his *Penitent Magdalene* of 1621–23 (Kunsthistorisches Museum, Vienna), an earlier gift to the Duke of Buckingham. KS

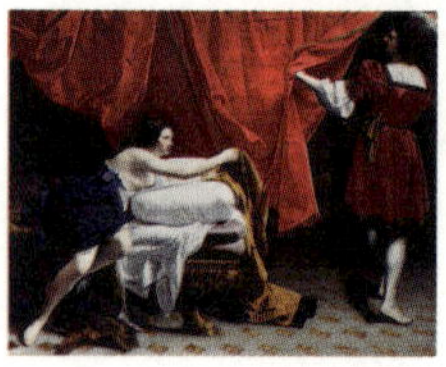

85
Orazio Gentileschi (1563–1639)
Joseph and Potiphar's Wife, c. 1630–32
Oil on canvas, 206 x 261.9 cm
The Royal Collection / HM Queen Elizabeth II, RCIN 405477
PROVENANCE: Henrietta Maria; George Wilson, Commonwealth Sale (£50); recovered at the Restoration; Henrietta Maria at the Château de Colombes, 1661; Charles II
SELECTED BIBLIOGRAPHY: Millar 1972, p. 137, no. 9; Bissell 1981, no. 64; Levey 1991, no. 501; London 1999A, no. 10; Wood 2001, pp. 120–22; London 2007A, no. 105

This episode from the life of Joseph is recounted in the Old Testament: when he was a slave in Egypt in the service of Potiphar, Captain of the Pharaoh's guard, Joseph resisted the advances of his master's wife. In his flight, Joseph left behind his cloak, which she later used as evidence to accuse him and seek vengeance. Gentileschi's painting is a compilation of sumptuous textures and textiles, whose polished rendering almost overpowers the figures and the narrative. The composition, however, is highly theatrical, with the drapery acting as backdrop and the viewer thrust up close to the strongly lit scene. Although paid for by the King, *Joseph and Potiphar's Wife* was probably commissioned for the Queen's House at Greenwich. KS

86
Orazio Gentileschi (1563–1639)
The Finding of Moses, c. 1630–33
Oil on canvas, 257 x 301 cm
Private collection. Courtesy of Pyms Gallery, London, inv. L951
PROVENANCE: Henrietta Maria; William Latham and Dividend, Commonwealth Sale, 23 October 1651 (£80); Emanuel De Critz; Philip Sidney, Viscount Lisle; recovered at the Restoration; Henrietta Maria at the Château de Colombes, 1661; her daughter Henrietta Anne; Philippe, Duke of Orléans; Orléans sale, 1798; Frederick Howard, 5th Earl of Carlisle; acquired in 1995
SELECTED BIBLIOGRAPHY: Millar 1972, p. 137, no. 1; Bissell 1981, no. 66; London 1999A, no. 8; Rome 2001, no. 48; Wood 2001, pp. 120–22

According to the Old Testament, Moses' mother placed her infant son in a basket and hid him in the reeds along the banks of the Nile, to evade the Pharaoh's order that all Israelite boys be killed (Exodus 2:1–4). Gentileschi shows the baby's discovery by the Pharaoh's daughter, clad in yellow at the centre of the composition, and her attendants who had come to the river to bathe. Completed by 1633, the painting was installed at the end of the decade in the Queen's House at Greenwich where it held a prominent place, hanging in the Great Hall alongside a ceiling painting and other large-scale Old Testament scenes by Gentileschi (cats 84–85). In the summer of 1633 and with the blessing of his British royal patrons, the painter sent a second version of the composition to Philip IV of Spain, whose spouse was Henrietta Maria's sister. The painting may have carried a dynastic message, celebrating the birth of the future Charles II in 1630. Certainly, the green hills in the background are more reminiscent of the Thames at Greenwich than of the banks of the Nile. KS

87
Orazio Gentileschi (1563–1639)
Head of a Woman, c. 1630–35
Oil on panel, 42 x 37 cm
Private collection
PROVENANCE: Charles I; Robert Houghton and Dividend, Commonwealth Sale, 16 January 1652 (£4); Colin Agnew, by 1930; Harry Eustace Marsland Benn, 1951–81; Thomas Agnew and Sons Ltd, by 1988; Martha McGeary Snider and Bryn Mawr, 1989; acquired in 2017
SELECTED BIBLIOGRAPHY: Millar 1960, p. 38, no. 7 (Whitehall Palace, Little Room between the Breakfast Chamber and the Privy Gallery); Millar 1972, p. 266, no. 158; Bissell 1981, no. 68; Nicolson 1990, vol. 1, pp. 66, 116; London 1999A, p. 22; Rome 2001, no. 50; Wood 2001, p. 114

This arresting depiction of an unknown woman is a fragment of a half-length figure, described by Van der Doort as having 'her left breast naked her right breast covered with a part of her Smock'. The unusual lighting from the right results in a dramatic play of light and shade. Gentileschi was best known in England for his large-scale paintings for the Queen's House at Greenwich (cats 84–86). According to Van der Doort, however, the present work was bought from the artist by Charles I and hung alongside self-portraits by Van Dyck, Rubens (cat. 4) and Mytens (cat. 7). LC

88
Artemisia Gentileschi (1593–1652/53)
Allegory of Painting, *c.* 1638–39
Oil on canvas, 98.6 x 75.2 cm
The Royal Collection / HM Queen Elizabeth II, RCIN 405551
PROVENANCE: Charles I; John Jackson and Dividend, Commonwealth Sale, 28 October 1651 (£10); recovered at the Restoration
SELECTED BIBLIOGRAPHY: Millar 1972, p. 191, no. 97; Garrard 1989, pp. 85–88, 337–70; Levey 1991, no. 499; Bissell 1999, no. 42; Rome 2001, no. 81; Mann 2005; London 2007A, no. 106; Terzaghi 2014, pp. 31–32; London 2016B, no. 101

After a career spent in Rome, Florence, Venice and Naples, Artemisia Gentileschi joined her father, Orazio, and her three brothers in London in around 1638–39. Charles I and Henrietta Maria already owned at least three of her paintings by that date and she found steady employment in England. Although the present work does not appear in Van der Doort's inventory, it was probably painted for the King and was described a decade later in the inventories of the Commonwealth Sale as a personification of 'Pintura A Painteinge: by Arthemesia'. She holds a brush and palette and wears a gold chain from which hangs a mask, following the recommendations of Cesare Ripa's *Iconologia*.

Some scholars have identified the painting as a self-portrait, noting the similarity between the dark-haired personification described by Ripa and known portraits of the artist. Representing herself in the guise of the allegorical figure of Painting would have been a cunning way for Gentileschi to distinguish herself from her male colleagues, to use her gender as an advantage and to reinforce the elevated status of artists in general. However, undermining this interpretation is the discrepancy in age between the youthful female personification and the artist, who would have been 46 years old when the work was painted. In addition, the painting is not described as a self-portrait in the 1649 Commonwealth Sale inventory, where a known self-portrait by Artemisia is valued at double the price. KS

89
Cristofano Allori (1577–1621)
Judith with the Head of Holofernes, 1613
Oil on canvas, 120.4 x 100.3 cm
The Royal Collection / HM Queen Elizabeth II, RCIN 404989
PROVENANCE: Dukes of Mantua; Charles I; possibly George Greene and Dividend, Commonwealth Sale, 23 October 1651 (£60); recovered at the Restoration
SELECTED BIBLIOGRAPHY: Millar 1960, p. 226, no. 9 (St James's Palace, Gallery); Millar 1972, p. 270, no. 227 (as Bronzino); Shearman 1979; Shearman 1983, no. 2; Florence 1984, pp. 78–81; London 1988, no. 6; London 1991, no. 23; London 2005, no. 7; London 2007A, no. 93; London 2016B, no. 98

The story of Judith and Holofernes (Judith 13:6–10) was a popular subject for artists in the seventeenth century. Cristofano Allori painted several versions of the dramatic scene, but this painting is the only one bearing an inscription. According to the biographer Filippo Baldinucci, the work results from the artist's traumatic love affair with a woman known as 'La Mazzafirra'. Baldinucci suggests that Allori depicts Judith as his lover, the servant as her mother, and Holofernes' severed head as a tormented self-portrait. The painting was probably acquired by Charles I in 1628 as part of the Gonzaga collection and was hung in the company of important works by Tintoretto and Van Dyck, among others. LC

90
Guido Reni (1575–1642) and workshop
The Toilet of Venus, *c.* 1620–25
Oil on canvas, 281.9 x 205.7 cm
The National Gallery, London. Presented by William IV, 1836, inv. NG90
PROVENANCE: Ferdinando Gonzaga, Duke of Mantua; Charles I; Edmund Harrison and Dividend, Commonwealth Sale, 23 October 1651 (£200); Alonso de Cárdenas for Luis Méndez de Haro y Guzmán, 6th Marqués of Carpio; Gaspar de Haro y Guzmán, 7th Marqués of Carpio; Pedro Rodríguez, 1692; Francesco De Mari, by 1694; his son, Ippolito De Mari, until at least 1715; John Law; George I, 1723; thereafter by descent; presented to the nation by William IV in 1836
SELECTED BIBLIOGRAPHY: Millar 1972, p. 316, no. 285; Burke 1984, vol. 1, pp. 118, 310, vol. 2, pp. 167, 170, 172, 183; Pepper 1984, no. 83; Loomie 1989, pp. 261, 265; Burke and Cherry 1997, no. 7; Furlotti 2000, pp. 188–93; de Frutos Sastre 2009, pp. 164, n. 460; Cropper and Pericolo forthcoming

With the bulk purchase of the Gonzaga collection in 1627–28, Charles I acquired a number of masterpieces by his favourite contemporary Italian artist, Guido Reni. Alongside the four *Labours of Hercules* (Musée du Louvre, Paris) was a painting described as Venus being dressed by the Three Graces. Embodying charm, beauty and mirth, the daughters of Jupiter tend to the goddess by lacing her sandals and adorning her with a gold tiara and bracelet. A mischievous red-haired Cupid holds up a pearl earring, while a putto at the back, a late addition, adjusts a vase of flowers. The subject of Venus at her toilet was an acceptable way to represent a languid female nude and it may have been chosen by Reni himself to showcase his mastery in rendering soft flesh, lustrous drapery and scintillating jewels. Nevertheless, the painting took him much longer to complete than he had expected and he delayed sending it to his patron, the Duke of Mantua, for over a year in order to fine-tune the composition and the figures.

Reni's reputation in England in the mid-seventeenth century is substantiated by the high value placed on this work by the commissioners of the Commonwealth Sale. Several seventeenth- and eighteenth-century copies of the painting are known, which has previously made it difficult to trace the present work back to Charles's collection. New research by Cropper and Pericolo has now substantiated the provenance. The painting's quality, most notably in the rendering of the figure of Venus herself, and the numerous changes in the composition point to Reni's authorship with the help of assistants, on whom the busy painter frequently relied. KS

91
Mortlake Workshop after Raphael (1483–1520), borders designed by Francis Cleyn (*c.* 1582–1658)
The Miraculous Draught of Fishes, *c.* 1636–37
Wool, silk and gilt-metal-wrapped thread, 530 x 580 cm
Mobilier national, Paris, inv. GMTT 16/4

92
Mortlake Workshop after Raphael (1483–1520), borders designed by Francis Cleyn (*c.* 1582–1658)
The Death of Ananias, *c.* 1630–31
Wool, silk and gilt-metal-wrapped thread, 530 x 700 cm
Mobilier national, Paris, inv. GMTT 16/6

93
Mortlake Workshop after Raphael (1483–1520), borders designed by Francis Cleyn (*c.* 1582–1658)
The Blinding of Elymas, *c.* 1631–36
Wool, silk and gilt-metal-wrapped thread, 538 x 713 cm
Mobilier national, Paris, inv. GMTT 16/3

94
Mortlake Workshop after Raphael (1483–1520), borders designed by Francis Cleyn (*c.* 1582–1658)
The Sacrifice at Lystra, *c.* 1639–40
Wool, silk and gilt-metal-wrapped thread, 535 x 720 cm
Mobilier national, Paris, inv. GMTT 16/5

PROVENANCE: Charles I; Abel Servien, by 1649; Cardinal Mazarin, 1659; by descent to the Duke of Mazarin; Louis XIV of France, 1665; Louis XVI;

transferred to the Garde-Meuble des Consuls in 1800 (later called Mobilier national)
SELECTED BIBLIOGRAPHY: Thomson 1914, pp. 72–73, 129; Shearman 1972, pp. 145–47; Thomson 1973, pp. 283–84, 294–95; Paris 1983, nos 1–6; Hefford 2007, pp. 175–79, 184–89; Vittet 2007, pp. 185–86; Denis 2009; Vittet and Brejon de Lavergnée 2010, no. 34

The Miraculous Draught of Fishes, probably the best known of Raphael's designs for the *Acts of the Apostles* and the first in the series (fig. 44), shows Christ in the boat of the poor fishermen Simon Peter and Andrew, who were to be chosen as the first Apostles. After a fruitless night fishing in the Sea of Galilee, Christ asked them to cast their nets once more, and they brought in a miraculous catch. Peter recognised Christ as a holy man and fell on his knees before him, but Jesus told him, 'Fear not: from henceforth thou shalt catch men' (Luke 5:10). Andrew is shown with his arms spread wide, while James and John, sons of Zebedee, haul in another net on the boat behind. Cleyn's new borders include putti holding giant fish, and attributes of the Apostles, including the Keys of St Peter and the cords that bound Andrew to his cross. The Greek and Hebrew names of Christ and Yahweh appear on the side borders, while in the four corners cartouches imitating gilt-bronze plaques show miracles performed by Christ.

The Death of Ananias tells the story of a wealthy man who, having pledged to sell land and donate the proceeds to the Church, kept back a portion of his wealth. Peter questioned him, saying, 'Thou hast not lied unto men, but unto God', and Ananias 'fell down, and gave up the ghost' (Acts 5:4–5). In Raphael's design for this tapestry (fig. 45), Peter and the Apostles are seen grouped on a central dais while townsfolk react in shock as Ananias falls backwards. On the far left his wife Sapphira counts her money; she too held back part of her wealth and was to be similarly struck down a few hours later, an event depicted by Francis Cleyn in a new scene designed for the Mortlake *Acts* (fig. 50). Surrounding the arms of Charles I at the top centre, Cleyn's border for the *Death of Ananias* includes putti with attributes of the cardinal and theological virtues (though Charity is absent) and, in the lower corners, life-size female figures of Falsehood and Divine Truth. One of the first two *Acts* to be woven at Mortlake, this tapestry bears the monograms of Sir Francis Crane, the workshop's first owner and director, and the chief weaver Philip de Maecht, as well as a white shield with a cross of St George, which appears on every tapestry in the set.

The Blinding of Elymas depicts the Roman Proconsul Sergius Paulus who summoned Paul and Barnabas to preach; however, a sorcerer named Elymas sought to prevent his conversion to Christianity. Paul spoke to Elymas, saying that he was perverting the right way of the Lord: 'and now, behold, the hand of the Lord is upon thee, and thou shalt be blind, not seeing the sun for a season' (Acts 13:11). This was the first of Paul's miracles in his mission to preach to the Gentiles. The Proconsul, in his toga and laurel wreath, sits on a raised platform that bears an inscription describing his conversion through Paul's preaching, while Elymas wears the soft cap of a barbarian. Cleyn's borders take up the central theme of Raphael's cartoon (fig. 46), with life-size figures on the left and right of Paul and Elymas. The small imitation gilt-bronze plaques contain scenes from the life of Christ, including his early preaching, while putti at the lower corners hold the tablet of Moses (left) and the book of the Evangelists (right), juxtaposing the Old and New Laws. This tapestry also bears the monograms of Crane and de Maecht.

The Sacrifice at Lystra shows the apostles Paul and Barnabas who, having healed a lame man in the city, were proclaimed as gods by its inhabitants. As the people prepared to sacrifice an ox, the apostles rent their clothes, protesting that they were mere mortals and that 'ye should turn from these vanities unto the living God' (Acts 14:15). Raphael's design (fig. 47) refers to antique examples, notably a celebrated relief of *Marcus Aurelius Sacrificing Before the Temple of Jupiter* (Musei Capitolini, Rome); details such as the statue of Mercury and the triangular altar all demonstrate an archaeological approach to recreating the scene. The borders, with the arms of Charles I at the top centre, include putti at the lower corners conducting a Pagan and a Christian sacrifice, and a series of eight reliefs with stories from the life of Moses and of Christ. In the centre of the lower border, as on every tapestry in the set, is a cartouche with a Latin inscription describing the scene, and the abbreviated letters *CAR:[OLO] RE:[GE] REG:[NANTE] MORTL:[AKE]* (in the reign of Charles, Mortlake). Both this tapestry and the *Miraculous Draught of Fishes* bear the monogram of Sir James Palmer, who took over as director at Mortlake in 1636. HW

95
Quinten Massys (1465/66–1530)
Desiderius Erasmus, 1517
Oil on panel, 50.5 x 45.2 cm
The Royal Collection / HM Queen Elizabeth II, RCIN 405759
PROVENANCE: Thomas More; Vincenzo II Gonzaga, Duke of Mantua, 1627; Charles I, 1628; recovered at the Restoration

96
Quinten Massys (1465/66–1530)
Pieter Gillis, 1517
Oil on panel, 74.5 x 53.4 cm
Longford Castle Collection
PROVENANCE: Thomas More; Vincenzo II Gonzaga, Duke of Mantua, 1627; Charles I, 1628; Thomas Rawlinson and Richard Mead; Jacob Bouverie, 1st Viscount Folkestone; thereafter by descent

SELECTED BIBLIOGRAPHY: Millar 1960, p. 79, no. 18 (Whitehall Palace, Cabinet); Campbell et al. 1978; Silver 1984, no. 58; Campbell 1985, no. 54; Edinburgh 2007, no. 5; London 2008, no. 42; Edinburgh 2011, no. 6; Leuven 2016, no. 13A

Judging from the early Netherlandish paintings that Charles I set out to acquire, he seems to have been particularly interested in sixteenth-century portraits. Like some of the most interesting early Netherlandish paintings in Charles I's collection, this pair of outstanding portraits came into his ownership by chance with the Gonzaga purchase.

The Dutch theologian and humanist Desiderius Erasmus, the scholar and town clerk of Antwerp Pieter Gillis, and the English Lord Chancellor and martyr, Sir Thomas More, were all friends. In 1517 Erasmus and Gillis, both living in Antwerp, decided to commission their portraits from Quinten Massys to send to More in London. Originally the same size, the completed portraits were probably hinged together like a diptych with the sitters appearing to share the same space.

Erasmus is shown as if he were St Jerome translating the Bible in his study; prominent behind him is his new edition of St Jerome. The lines of text imitating his own hand (painted to resemble the reed pen he preferred) are the opening of his *Paraphrase of the* [St Paul's] *Epistle to the Romans*. Like Erasmus, Gillis is soberly dressed. He pauses in thought, gazing at Erasmus and presumably thinking about More, having just read the letter he holds from his friend in London. Here too, the writing is a convincing imitation of More's own hand; indeed, More asked Gillis to return his letter to him so that it could be 'put up beside the picture, it will make it seem more wonderful than ever'. LW

97
Jan Gossaert (Jean Gossart) (*c.* 1478–1532)
Portrait of a Man Holding a Glove, *c.* 1530–32
Oil on panel, 24.3 x 16.8 cm
The National Gallery, London. Wynn Ellis Bequest, 1876, inv. NG946
PROVENANCE: Dukes of Mantua; Charles I; recovered at the Restoration; William III; United Provinces, by 1700–02; Palace of Het Loo, Apeldoorn, until at least 1757; William Wells; Charles Scarisbrick; Wynn Ellis; bequeathed to the National Gallery in 1876
SELECTED BIBLIOGRAPHY: Millar 1960, p. 90, no. 73; Von der Osten 1961, p. 472; Friedländer 1967–76, vol. 8, no. 70; Davies 1968, p. 61; London 1975, no. 15; Campbell 1985, pp. 51–56; The Hague 1988, pp. 107–09; New York 2010, no. 60; Campbell 2014, vol. 1, pp. 320–25

Charles I had four paintings by the Antwerp painter Jan Gossaert. In addition to the present work, he had inherited the small *Children of Christian II of Denmark* recorded in Henry VIII's collection, he was to acquire the large *Adam and Eve* (cat. 34) in 1636, and a portrait of an elderly man was recorded in the Commonwealth Sale. The present portrait, still unattributed in Van der Doort's inventory, was attributed to Holbein during the reign of James II. Typical of Gossaert is the portrait's vitality and the meticulous rendering of its different textures. Velvet contrasts with fur and even the individual hairs of the sitter's beard are depicted. The small panel was skilfully and speedily painted, with the fur worked wet-in-wet as if both sitter and artist were short of time. The sitter has not been identified, but the style of his clothes and the cut of his beard suggest a date of around 1530. LW

98
Hans Holbein the Younger (*c.* 1497–1543)
William Reskimer, *c.* 1532–34
Black and coloured chalks, pen and brown ink and metalpoint on pale pink prepared paper, 29 x 21 cm
The Royal Collection / HM Queen Elizabeth II, RCIN 912237

PROVENANCE: Henry VIII; Edward VI, 1547; Henry FitzAlan, 12th Earl of Arundel; Lord John Lumley, 1580; Henry, Prince of Wales, 1609; Charles I, when Prince of Wales, 1612; Philip Herbert, 4th Earl of Pembroke, 1627–28; Thomas Howard, 14th Earl of Arundel; Charles II, by 1675

99
Hans Holbein the Younger
(*c.* 1497–1543)
William Reskimer, *c.* 1532–34
Oil on panel, 46 x 33.5 cm
The Royal Collection / HM Queen Elizabeth II, RCIN 404422
PROVENANCE: William Reskimer; possibly his daughter, Anne Reskimer; Sir Jonathan Trelawny; Sir Robert Killigrew; given to Charles I; recovered at the Restoration

SELECTED BIBLIOGRAPHY: Millar 1963, vol. 1, no. 31; London 1978, nos 28–29; Parker 1983, no. 31; Rowlands 1985, no. 39; Houston 1987, no. 19; Edinburgh 1993, no. 16; Klinger and Höttler 1998, no. 42; The Hague 2003B, nos 14–15; Foister 2004, pp. 58–59; London 2006, no. 34; Edinburgh 2011, nos 73–74

The Cornishman William Reskimer was almost continuously at court from 1526, when he was appointed Page of the Chamber to Henry VIII. It was a descendant of William, Sir Robert Killigrew, who presented the painted portrait to Charles I. The King would never have seen the drawing and finished portrait side by side in his new Cabinet Room because in 1627–28 he had given away Holbein's album of drawings to Philip Herbert, 4th Earl of Pembroke, in exchange for Raphael's small panel painting of *St George and the Dragon* (fig. 53).

The painting closely follows the drawing. Holbein probably traced the principal contours of the drawing onto the panel with a stylus or metalpoint using a carbon-covered intermediary sheet. The rather awkward hands must have been traced from a separate study and reworked with free-hand underdrawing. The brilliant single white lines of the ties of Reskimer's shirt dramatise the painted portrait compared to the drawing. LW

100
Hans Holbein the Younger
(*c.* 1497–1543)
Sir John More, *c.* 1526–27
Black and coloured chalks on paper, 35.1 x 27.3 cm
The Royal Collection / HM Queen Elizabeth II, RCIN 912224

101
Hans Holbein the Younger
(*c.* 1497–1543)
Anne Cresacre, *c.* 1526–27
Black and coloured chalks on paper, 37.2 x 26.6 cm
The Royal Collection / HM Queen Elizabeth II, RCIN 912270

102
Hans Holbein the Younger
(*c.* 1497–1543)
John More, *c.* 1526–27
Black and coloured chalks on paper, 38.1 x 28.1 cm
The Royal Collection / HM Queen Elizabeth II, RCIN 912226

PROVENANCE: Henry VIII; Edward VI, 1547; Henry FitzAlan, 12th Earl of Arundel; Lord John Lumley, 1580; Henry, Prince of Wales, 1609; Charles I, when Prince of Wales, 1612; Philip Herbert, 4th Earl of Pembroke, 1627–28; Thomas Howard, 14th Earl of Arundel; Charles II, by 1675
SELECTED BIBLIOGRAPHY: London 1977, nos 9, 178, 179; London 1978, nos 3, 7, 8; Parker 1983, nos 1, 6, 7; Houston 1987, nos 1, 4, 6; Edinburgh 1993, nos 1, 4, 5; Foister 2004, pp. 58–59; Basel 2006, no. 122; London 2006, nos 25–27; London 2017, no. 30

In 1526 Holbein arrived in England with a letter of recommendation from Erasmus, addressed to the great humanist, philosopher and statesman Sir Thomas More. Holbein was invited to stay at More's Chelsea home, where he undertook his first important commission, a large group portrait of the More family, perhaps to commemorate his host's fiftieth birthday, for which these three portrait drawings are studies. The original painting was probably destroyed in 1752 in a fire at Kroměříž Castle in the Czech Republic but a pen-and-ink design, sent as a gift to Erasmus and now in the Kunstmuseum Basel, and copies by Rowland Lockey from the end of the sixteenth century (among them, one at the National Portrait Gallery, London) record the composition. Eight of the eighty-five portrait drawings in the album of Holbein's drawings in Charles's possession until the late 1620s depict members of the More family.

The first of the present drawings shows the father of Sir Thomas, the lawyer Sir John More. The soft, slack skin of the seventy-six-year-old contrasts with Holbein's dynamic strokes outlining the fur collar of his gown, which is transformed in the final painting into judge's robes.

Anne Cresacre was a ward of Sir Thomas who grew up and was educated in the More family. In 1527 she was betrothed to Sir Thomas's son John and two years later they were married. Holbein has recorded her young, thoughtful face enclosed by a double-band headdress with remarkable economy, combining subtle shading and a single, modulated outline. Anne's importance to the household is indicated by her position in the Basel drawing between Sir Thomas and Sir John, facing her future husband. She was seated for this portrait drawing, as is indicated by the shape of a chair at the left edge.

John More was Sir Thomas's fourth child and only son. In the final composition, he stands immediately on his father's right, respectfully bare-headed unlike in the drawing. His book shows the serious, scholarly and devout atmosphere of the More household. The sensitivity of Holbein's treatment of John's face contrasts with the vigorous use of chalk for his clothing, the free hatching suggesting the reflective surface of the satin of his slashed sleeves, and his hand and book boldly outlined with abrupt strokes. LW

103
Hans Holbein the Younger
(*c.* 1497–1543)
Charles Brandon, 1541
Watercolour on vellum laid on card, diameter 5.5 cm
The Royal Collection / HM Queen Elizabeth II, RCIN 422295

104
Hans Holbein the Younger
(*c.* 1497–1543)
Henry Brandon, *c.* 1541
Watercolour on vellum laid on card, diameter 5.6 cm
The Royal Collection / HM Queen Elizabeth II, RCIN 422294

PROVENANCE: Henry Fanshawe; Charles I; recovered at the Restoration
SELECTED BIBLIOGRAPHY: Vertue 1929–51, vol. 1, pp. 73–74, and vol. 4, p. 67; Millar 1960, p. 119, nos 64–65 (Whitehall Palace, Cabinet); London 1983B, nos 34–35; Strong 1983, nos 12–13; Rowlands 1985, nos M10–11; London 1997, nos 3–4; Reynolds 1999, nos 7–8; London 2006, nos 119–20; Edinburgh 2011, nos 84–85

Charles and Henry Brandon were the sons of Charles Brandon, 1st Duke of Suffolk, and his fourth wife, Katherine Willoughby. Their father had previously been married to Henry VIII's sister, Princess Mary, and the boys enjoyed a quasi-royal status at court, receiving their early education with Edward VI, then Prince of Wales. As scholarly prodigies at Cambridge, they were widely mourned when they died from the sweating sickness within half an hour of each other in 1551. Charles I kept these miniatures, given to him as a young man, at the heart of his Cabinet Room at Whitehall Palace. VR

105
Adam Elsheimer (1578–1610)
after Albrecht Dürer (1471–1528)
Witch Riding Backwards on a Goat, *c.* 1596–98
Oil on copper, 13.6 x 9.9 cm
The Royal Collection / HM Queen Elizabeth II, RCIN 404717
PROVENANCE: Arthur Hopton; Charles I; John Baptist Gaspars, Commonwealth Sale, 22 March 1650 (£5); recovered at the Restoration
SELECTED BIBLIOGRAPHY: Millar 1960, p. 77, no. 5 (Whitehall Palace, Cabinet); Millar 1972, p. 256, no. 6; Andrews 1977, no. 1; Frankfurt 2006, no. 1

This beguiling piece, after an engraving by Albrecht Dürer, is an early work by Adam Elsheimer dating from before he went to Italy. The witch would not have seemed a fantastic subject for Charles; in fact, his father James I had produced a detailed philosophical treatise entitled *Daemonologie* (1597) about the necromancy he believed to be rife in his kingdom. An admirer of Shakespeare from his youth, Charles might also have remembered Macbeth's weird sisters' 'Double, double, toil and trouble' on encountering this work. NM

106
Paul Bril (*c.* 1554–1626)
Landscape with Goatherds, *c.* 1620
Oil on copper, 11.3 x 14.3 cm
The Royal Collection / HM Queen Elizabeth II, RCIN 403033
PROVENANCE: Charles I; Henry Woodson, Commonwealth Sale, 24 May 1650 (£20); recovered at the Restoration
SELECTED BIBLIOGRAPHY: Millar 1960, p. 91, no. 79 (Whitehall Palace, Cabinet); Millar 1972, p. 256, no. 7; Edinburgh 2007, no. 17; White 2007, no. 5

In his treatise on the art of miniatures, Edward Norgate gives advice on recession from his 'old friend' Paul Bril, which he said 'will make a landscape *Caminare*, that is move or walk away, and that is by placing Darke against Light, and light against Darke'. Such a technique is clear in the present work. Bril's delicate style evidently appealed as the picture hung in the Cabinet. Small-scale pastoral scenes of this nature were much sought after by the King and appear throughout his collection, particularly in his Bedchamber at Whitehall Palace. NM

107
Rembrandt van Rijn (1606–1669)
Portrait of an Old Woman ('The Artist's Mother'), *c.* 1627–29
Oil on panel, 61.3 x 47.4 cm
The Royal Collection / HM Queen Elizabeth II, RCIN 405000
PROVENANCE: Robert Kerr, later 1st Earl of Ancram, before 1633; Charles I; Edward Bass and Dividend, Commonwealth Sale, 19 December 1651 (£4); recovered at the Restoration
SELECTED BIBLIOGRAPHY: Millar 1960, p. 60, no. 101 (Whitehall Palace, Long Gallery); London 1964, no. 56; Bauch 1966, no. 251; Gerson 1968, no. 37; Bredius and Gerson 1969, no. 70; Millar 1972, p. 265, no. 156; Bruyn et al. 1982, no. A32; White 1982, no. 158; Bruyn et al. 1986, pp. 839–40 (as probably Lievens); New York 1995, vol. 2, pp. 10–11 (as Lievens); Edinburgh 2004B, pp. 133–35

At the outset of his career, Rembrandt often used his mother as a model. Although it calls to mind some of his early etchings of her, this picture is probably not a conventional portrait, but a genre painting in portrait format known as a 'tronie' (meaning 'face'). Robert Kerr presented it to Charles I, with two works then also attributed to Rembrandt: an early self-portrait (Walker Art Gallery, Liverpool) and another painting, now lost, probably by Jan Lievens. By 1639 all three were on display in the Long Gallery at Whitehall Palace. Rembrandt and Lievens worked closely together during their early careers in Leiden, and the authorship of many pictures from this time, including the present work, is often difficult to discern. LC/PR

108
Orazio Samacchini (1532–1577)
The Risen Christ, after 1564
Oil on panel, 38.1 x 24.8 cm
Cobbe Collection, Hatchlands Park, inv. CC548
PROVENANCE: Dukes of Mantua; Charles I; Emanuel De Critz and Dividend, Commonwealth Sale, 18 November 1651 (£5); recovered at the Restoration; Alicia Raynal (*née* Kent); Alfred Kent, 1886; Mrs Borlase; sale in London (as Correggio), 1921; Moore; Miss de Costobadie; sale in London (as Correggio), 1958; sale in London, 1981; acquired in 2005
SELECTED BIBLIOGRAPHY: Millar 1960, p. 89, no. 68 (Whitehall Palace, Cabinet); Millar 1972, p. 259, no. 63

The Bolognese artist Orazio Samacchini was active in his native Emilia-Romagna but also worked in Rome. In 1563 he participated in the decoration of the Vatican's Apostolic Palace, notably working with the brothers Federico and Taddeo Zuccaro on the Sala Regia. The date of the present painting is not known, though compositionally it displays a knowledge of art from central Italy. Christ's pose and the swirling red drapery that surrounds him recall Michelangelo's dynamic series of drawings of the same subject, particularly that at the British Museum, London, while the *pentimento* of an earlier 'true' cross evokes Michelangelo's sculpture of the *Risen Christ* at Santa Maria sopra Minerva in Rome. A variant of this painting, also at Hatchlands Park, shows Christ holding the larger cross and wearing a white loincloth. The alterations made to the present work suggest that it is the later version. Charles I acquired the painting as part of the Gonzaga purchase in 1628. LC

109
Lucas Vorsterman (1595–1675)
after Annibale Carracci (1560–1609)
The Agony in the Garden, 1627
Engraving, 39.5 x 30 cm
The British Museum, London. Bequeathed by Clayton Mordaunt Cracherode, 1799, inv. U,1.120
PROVENANCE: Clayton Mordaunt Cracherode; acquired in 1799
SELECTED BIBLIOGRAPHY: Hollstein et al. 1949–2010, vol. 43, no. 26.1; Hind 1952–64, vol. 3, no. 200.13; Millar 1960, p. 148, no. 1 (Whitehall Palace, Cabinet, plate); Hymans 1972, no. 27; Millar 1972, p. 246, no. 351 (plate); Levey 1991, p. 72; London 1998, no. 31

This engraving was commissioned by Charles I after a small painting by Annibale Carracci (cat. 110) that hung in the Queen's House at Greenwich. It is invaluable in recording details now lost in Carracci's painting, such as the cross at the feet of the angel and the sleeping apostles in the shadows. The copper plate for the print, despite its functional purpose, is curiously recorded by Van der Doort as framed and on display in the Cabinet Room at Whitehall. Following Charles's death, the plate was valued at £20 but retained by the Commonwealth. Lucas Vorsterman, who had worked for Rubens in Antwerp, came to England in 1623 and was employed by the King and his circle. It was in England that he met Van Dyck, with whom he was later to work as an engraver on a series of portraits, known as the *Iconographie*, depicting distinguished figures of the time. LC

110
Annibale Carracci (1560–1609)
The Agony in the Garden, *c.* 1596–97
Oil on panel, 39.1 x 30.3 cm
The Royal Collection / HM Queen Elizabeth II, RCIN 402990
PROVENANCE: Henrietta Maria; William Webb, Commonwealth Sale, 25 October 1649 (£40); recovered at the Restoration
SELECTED BIBLIOGRAPHY: Posner 1971, vol. 2, no. 95; Millar 1972, p. 63, no. 51; Cooney and Malafarina 1976, no. 89; Levey 1991, no. 434

Annibale Carracci was born in Bologna and moved to Rome in 1595 to work for the distinguished Farnese family. This small panel, probably painted shortly after his arrival there, depicts Christ and an angel in the Garden of Gethsemane. Imbued with grace and sentimentality, Carracci's style is here reminiscent of earlier Emilian artists such as Correggio. Although the painting is significantly damaged, areas such as Christ's hands beautifully demonstrate Carracci's delicate technique. The picture belonged to Henrietta Maria 'at Grenwich in the little roome hanged with hreene damask towards the water side'. The King owned a painting of the same subject, attributed to one of the Carracci, which hung in the Chair Room at Whitehall Palace. LC

111
Peter Oliver (1589–1647)
after Titian (*c.* 1488/90–1576)
Conjugal Allegory ('The Allegory of Alfonso d'Avalos'), 1629
Watercolour and bodycolour with gold paint on vellum, 12.2 x 12.5 cm
The Royal Collection / HM Queen Elizabeth II, RCIN 452459
PROVENANCE: Charles I; John Hutchinson, Commonwealth Sale, 24 May 1650 (£51); recovered at the Restoration
SELECTED BIBLIOGRAPHY: Oppé 1950, no. 461; Millar 1960, p. 104, no. 4 (Whitehall Palace, Cabinet); Millar 1972, p. 256, no. 13

Titian's original (cat. 47), on which this miniature is based, was long believed to represent Charles V's general Alfonso d'Avalos, Marquis del Guasto, with his wife, Mary of Aragon, in an allegorical scene of marital happiness, but this interpretation is no longer supported. Two further miniature copies survive, by David des Granges (Ham House, Surrey) and Richard Gibson (Welbeck Abbey, Nottinghamshire), taken from the original, which hung in the First Privy Lodging Room at Whitehall Palace, and two full-scale oil copies on canvas remain in the Royal Collection. Like other miniatures copied from old-master paintings by Oliver (including cat. 114), this fetched the very large sum of £50 in the Commonwealth Sale. The sum was consistent with the value of original works by some of the most sought-after names such as Correggio. VR

112
Attributed to Isaac Oliver (*c.* 1565–1617)
after Hans Holbein the Younger
(*c.* 1497–1543)
The Dance of Death: The Prince, *c.* 1610–15
Watercolour with gold paint on paper, 6.3 x 5.3 cm
The Royal Collection / HM Queen Elizabeth II, RCIN 452454
PROVENANCE: Charles I
SELECTED BIBLIOGRAPHY: Oppé 1950, no. 458; Millar 1960, p. 121, no. 75 (Whitehall Palace, Cabinet); Finsten 1981, pp. 146–47

This unusual limning by Isaac Oliver is a life-size copy after a woodcut by Holbein from his 1538 series the *Dance of Death*. The message of the image – that Death reaches out to all alike – is admirably well-expressed in Van der Doort's description: 'Don by ould Isack Oliver after Holben … a little peece where death with a greene Garland about his head streatching both his Armes to apprehend a Pilate in the habbitt of one of the spirituall Prince Ellectors of Germany'. The miniature is mounted on a small, bevelled wooden panel branded with Charles I's cipher. VR

113
Peter Oliver (1589–1647)
after Correggio (1489–1534)
Venus and Cupid with a Satyr, 1633
Watercolour and bodycolour on vellum, 20.6 x 14.1 cm
The Royal Collection / HM Queen Elizabeth II, RCIN 452457
PROVENANCE: Charles I; George Greene and Dividend, Commonwealth Sale, 23 October 1651 (£80); Henry George Bohn; his sale, London, 1885; acquired by Queen Victoria
SELECTED BIBLIOGRAPHY: Oppé 1950, no. 463; Millar 1960, p. 104, no. 7 (Whitehall Palace, Cabinet); Millar 1972, p. 256, no. 15; London 2002, no. 54

114
Peter Oliver (1589–1647)
after Correggio (1489–1534)
Venus with Mercury and Cupid ('The School of Love'), 1634
Watercolour and bodycolour on vellum, 19.1 x 12.2 cm
The Royal Collection / HM Queen Elizabeth II, RCIN 452458
PROVENANCE: Charles I; John Embree, Commonwealth Sale, 21 May 1650 (£50); Henry George Bohn; his sale, London, 1885; acquired by Queen Victoria
SELECTED BIBLIOGRAPHY: Oppé 1950, no. 462; Millar 1960, p. 104, no. 8 (Whitehall Palace, Cabinet Room); Millar 1972, p. 256, no. 12

Correggio's *Venus and Cupid with a Satyr* (fig. 20) and its pair, *Venus with Mercury and Cupid ('The School of Love')* (cat. 18), on which these limnings are based, had both entered Charles I's collection from the Gonzaga collection in Mantua and hung at Whitehall Palace. When Van der Doort recorded the miniature of *Venus and Cupid with a Satyr* in the Cabinet Room, the original hung nearby in the Third Privy Lodging Room. In the inscriptions he added to both limnings, Peter Oliver refers to himself as 'imitatus', emphasising his role as copyist. However, his copies vie with the originals in their extraordinary, rich softness and powerful sensuality. The depth of the *School of Love* is enhanced by the three-dimensional gilt border which surrounds it. VR

115
Francesco Fanelli (1577–after 1641)
St George and the Dragon, *c.* 1635–40
Bronze, height 19.2 cm
Victoria and Albert Museum, London. Given by W. L. Hildburgh, inv. A.5-1953

116
Francesco Fanelli (1577–after 1641)
Cupid on Horseback, *c.* 1635–40
Bronze, height 14.9 cm
Victoria and Albert Museum, London. Given by W. L. Hildburgh, inv. A.37-1952

PROVENANCE: W. L. Hildburgh; presented in 1953
SELECTED BIBLIOGRAPHY: Pope-Hennessy 1953; Millar 1960, p. 94, no. 17, and p. 95, no. 28 (Whitehall Palace, Cabinet); Millar 1972, p. 273, nos 269–70; Radcliffe and Thornton 1978; Howarth 1989, pp. 92–103; New York 2004, pp. 31–53, 325–27; Radcliffe and Penny 2004, nos 53–54; Warren 2016, vol. 1, no. 100

Although only two of the small sculptures in the window embrasures of Charles I's Cabinet Room are specifically given by Van der Doort to 'ffrancesco ffanello, the one-eyed Italian', on the basis of their descriptions several others have now been identified as the work of the Florentine sculptor. Exactly when Fanelli moved from Genoa to England is unclear, but it was probably in 1631, since he is first recorded working for the King the following year. According to George Vertue, Fanelli's sculptures were 'much esteemed in K. Charles I time – and afterwards'. They were new in Britain and collected with great enthusiasm. Their dynamic movement contrasts with earlier works by Giambologna that Fanelli would have known in Florence and seen in the King's collection.

Both present sculptures are recorded by Van der Doort and in the Commonwealth Sale inventory, although Van der Doort describes *Cupid on Horseback* as having 'another Cupid running by'. They are difficult to identify today not only because Fanelli produced several of the same design, but also because he cast parts of his groups separately and then assembled them. This means a second Cupid, now lost, could have been affixed to *Cupid on Horseback*. The composition of the saint and dragon is different to that by Raphael in his painting (fig. 53), but it must have given great pleasure to the King to have the painting and the sculpture of St George and the dragon together in the Cabinet Room, so neatly complementing one another. LW

117
Peter Oliver (1589–1647)
after Raphael (1483–1520)
St George and the Dragon, 1628
Bodycolour and gold paint on vellum, 22 x 16.5 cm
The Royal Collection / HM Queen Elizabeth II, RCIN 452455
PROVENANCE: Charles I; probably sold in the Commonwealth Sale; Hamilton Palace Sale, 1882; acquired by Queen Victoria
SELECTED BIBLIOGRAPHY: Oppé 1950, no. 464; Millar 1960, p. 103, no. 2 (Whitehall Palace, Cabinet)

This miniature and Raphael's original (fig. 53) were displayed in close proximity to each other in Charles I's Cabinet Room at Whitehall Palace. Van der Doort described the miniature as 'dated 1628'. If this date is correct, this limning is one of the earliest examples by Peter Oliver. Only a year earlier, Raphael's painting was still in the possession of the Earl of Pembroke, and the copy is likely to have been commissioned when Raphael's painting came into the King's possession. VR

118
Nicholas Hilliard (1547–1619) after Hans Holbein the Younger (*c.* 1497–1543)
Henry VII, *c.* 1600
Watercolour and bodycolour on vellum laid on card, diameter 3.4 cm
The Royal Collection / HM Queen Elizabeth II, RCIN 420012

119
Nicholas Hilliard (1547–1619) after Hans Holbein the Younger (*c.* 1497–1543)
Henry VIII, *c.* 1600
Watercolour and bodycolour on vellum laid on card, diameter 3.2 cm
The Royal Collection / HM Queen Elizabeth II, RCIN 420013

120
Nicholas Hilliard (1547–1619) after Hans Holbein the Younger (*c.* 1497–1543)
Jane Seymour, *c.* 1600
Watercolour and bodycolour on vellum laid on card, diameter 3.2 cm
The Royal Collection / HM Queen Elizabeth II, RCIN 420014

121
Nicholas Hilliard (1547–1619) after Hans Holbein the Younger (*c.* 1497–1543)
Edward VI, *c.* 1600
Watercolour and bodycolour on vellum laid on card, diameter 3.3 cm
The Royal Collection / HM Queen Elizabeth II, RCIN 420015

PROVENANCE: Laurence Hilliard; Charles I, 1625–30; recovered at the Restoration
SELECTED BIBLIOGRAPHY: Vertue 1929–51, vol. 1, pp. 73–74, and vol. 4, p. 67; Millar 1960, p. 116, nos 50–53 (Whitehall Palace, Cabinet); London 1983B, nos 105–08; Strong 1983, p. 113; London 1997, nos 11–14; Reynolds 1999, nos 31–34

When these four miniatures were presented to Charles I by Nicholas Hilliard's son, Laurence, they were set in an elaborate gold and enamel locket, the so-called Bosworth Jewel. Hilliard drew on his goldsmith's training to produce both jewel and miniatures to celebrate the Battle of Bosworth (1485), an event that came to represent the Tudor dynasty's enduring success, as well as marking its inception. The Bosworth Jewel featured an enamelled scene from the battle on the lid, and red and white Tudor roses on the reverse. It was sold during the Commonwealth and, by the time that the miniatures were returned to the Royal Collection during the reign of Charles II, the jewel had been lost. VR

122
Isaac Oliver (*c.* 1565–1617)
Henry, Prince of Wales, *c.* 1610
Watercolour on vellum laid on card, 13.2 x 10 cm
The Royal Collection / HM Queen Elizabeth II, RCIN 420058
PROVENANCE: probably Henry, Prince of Wales; Charles I; recovered at the Restoration
SELECTED BIBLIOGRAPHY: Millar 1960, p. 107, no. 17; London 1972, no. 179; Edmond 1983, pp. 152–55; Strong 1983, pp. 171–73; Strong 1986, p. 119; London 1997, no. 17; Reynolds 1999, no. 54; London 2012, no. 32; London 2013, pp. 226–27

Officially appointed as 'Painter' to Henry, Prince of Wales, in 1608, Isaac Oliver fashioned the young Henry's image as a warrior prince. Here, Henry wears contemporary armour and is seen in front of a military encampment. Oliver was perhaps inspired by Henry's starring role as Meliadus, the reviver of chivalry, in a masque on Twelfth Night in 1610. Oliver's mastery of spatial recession is evident in the composition of the curtain and the scene behind; he confidently plays with notions of space by placing the Garter in front of the gold border surrounding the miniature so that it seems to occupy the viewer's space. VR

123
Nicholas Hilliard (1547–1619)
Henry, Prince of Wales, 1607
Watercolour and bodycolour on vellum laid on card, 6.1 x 5.1 cm
The Royal Collection / HM Queen Elizabeth II, RCIN 420642
PROVENANCE: Charles I; recovered at the Restoration
SELECTED BIBLIOGRAPHY: Reynolds 1954, no. C.I; Millar 1960, p. 108, no. 20 (Whitehall Palace, Cabinet); Auerbach 1961, no. 158; London 1972, no. 178; Murdoch et al. 1981, p. 61; London 1983B, no. 245; Strong 1983, p. 140; Strong 1986, p. 118; Reynolds 1999, no. 35; Hearn 2005, pp. 84–85; London 2012, no. 31; London 2013, pp. 226–28

This miniature shows Henry, Prince of Wales, wearing a lavishly decorated French suit of armour that survives at Windsor Castle. The armour was modish and expensive, but Hilliard's technique remained entrenched in the sixteenth century and could not do it – nor his brilliant young subject – justice. Indeed, Henry preferred the work of Hilliard's cosmopolitan young pupil, Isaac Oliver. Van der Doort's handwritten label locating this miniature within the Cabinet Room at Whitehall Palace remains on the reverse, although it is now indistinct. VR

124
Nicholas Hilliard (1547–1619)
James I, *c.* 1609–15
Watercolour on vellum laid on card, 4.6 x 3.8 cm
The Royal Collection / HM Queen Elizabeth II, RCIN 420039
PROVENANCE: first recorded in the collection of Charles I; recovered at the Restoration
SELECTED BIBLIOGRAPHY: Vertue 1929–51, vol. 4, p. 67; Reynolds 1954, no. A8; Millar 1960, p. 113, no. 44 (Whitehall Palace, Cabinet); Auerbach 1961, pp. 157–58; Reynolds 1999, no. 28; London 2012, no. 54

On his accession, James I renewed the appointment of Nicholas Hilliard as Court Limner. Hilliard's portrait miniatures of the King fall into three broad types: this example shows the King in middle age and is almost certainly the miniature described by Van der Doort in Charles I's Cabinet Room at Whitehall Palace as 'king James of famous memory Picture wthout a hatt in a bone lac'd falling band in a Lavender Cloth suite', although there is a discrepancy in the measurements given. Van der Doort also notes that it was 'Don by old Hilliard Bought by yor Matie'. VR

125
Isaac Oliver (*c.* 1565–1617)
Anne of Denmark, *c.* 1611–12
Watercolour on vellum laid on card, 5.3 x 4.2 cm
The Royal Collection / HM Queen Elizabeth II, RCIN 420041
PROVENANCE: first recorded in the collection of Charles I; recovered at the Restoration
SELECTED BIBLIOGRAPHY: Millar 1960, p. 111, no. 36 (Whitehall Palace, Cabinet); London 1968, no. 93; Cardiff 1998, no. 3; Reynolds 1999, no. 53; London 2013, pp. 71, 163

Anne of Denmark appointed Isaac Oliver as Queen's Limner in 1605, preferring his more up-to-date and cosmopolitan style to that of his master, Nicholas Hilliard. Charles I may have inherited this miniature directly from his mother and, by 1639, it hung in the Cabinet Room at Whitehall Palace in a frame of eight miniatures of his forebears. The inscription on the reverse refers to this arrangement. Van der Doort described the miniature as showing the Queen 'in a blwe habbitt adorned wth pearles and a picture Box at her left breast'. The 'picture Box' worn by the Queen is a type of contemporary jewel in which miniatures like this one would typically have been set. VR

126
Isaac Oliver (*c.* 1565–1617)
Princess Elizabeth, *c.* 1610
Watercolour on vellum laid on card, 4.9 x 4.1 cm
The Royal Collection / HM Queen Elizabeth II, RCIN 420031
PROVENANCE: first recorded in the collection of Charles I; recovered at the Restoration
SELECTED BIBLIOGRAPHY: Reynolds 1954, p. 25; Millar 1960, p. 117, no. 54 (Whitehall Palace, Cabinet); Auerbach 1961, no. 254; London 1972, no. 181; London 1983B, no. 262; London 1997, no. 18; Reynolds 1999, no. 59; London 2013, p. 162

Charles I's sister, Princess Elizabeth, is portrayed here aged about fourteen. Her marriage three years later to the ill-fated Elector Palatine, Frederick V of Bohemia, put her at the heart of the European conflict that became known as the Thirty Years' War. This exceptional miniature, painted directly from life, was in the possession of Charles I at Whitehall Palace, confirmed by Van der Doort's vivid description of the sitter 'adorne'd at her head wth some single Elengtine Roases wth Jewlls and Pearls and a neck lace wth .3. Jewells about her neck'. VR

127
Isaac Oliver (*c.* 1565–1617)
Charles I, when Duke of York, *c.* 1611–16
Watercolour on vellum laid on card, 5.4 x 4.1 cm
The Royal Collection / HM Queen Elizabeth II, RCIN 420048
PROVENANCE: first recorded in the collection of Charles I; recovered at the Restoration
SELECTED BIBLIOGRAPHY: Millar 1960, p. 112, no. 38 (Whitehall Palace, Cabinet); London 1972, no. 180; London 1999B, no. 10; Reynolds 1999, no. 58

The inscription on the reverse of this miniature indicates that it was housed in the Cabinet Room at Whitehall Palace in a frame of miniatures of Charles I's immediate family. The frame contained a number of portrait miniatures: Charles's grandmother, Mary, Queen of Scots; her first husband, François, Dauphin of France; Charles's great-grandmother, Lady Margaret Douglas; James I; Anne of Denmark (cat. 125); and Henry, Prince of Wales. Two spaces were left empty for two further portraits of Charles I's ancestors. This portrait presents the young Charles wearing an elaborate gilt armour with the ribbon of the Order of the Garter, in a similar manner to Oliver's earlier miniatures of Henry, Prince of Wales (cat. 122). Oliver's eloquent characterisation illuminates Charles's reticence in comparison to the confidence of his older brother. VR

128
Peter Oliver (1589–1647)
Charles I, when Prince of Wales, *c.* 1620
Watercolour on vellum laid on card, 5.1 x 3.9 cm
The Royal Collection / HM Queen Elizabeth II, RCIN 420049
PROVENANCE: possibly acquired by William Hawley for Charles II
SELECTED BIBLIOGRAPHY: Murdoch et al. 1981, p. 94; London 1999B, no. 11; Reynolds 1999, no. 66

After Isaac Oliver's death in 1617, his eldest son Peter took over his role as Court Limner, producing portraits of Charles, Prince of Wales, his sister, Elizabeth of Bohemia, and her husband Frederick V. This is the earliest of Peter Oliver's miniatures of Charles, and is clearly indebted to his father's portrait of the same subject (cat. 127). Father and son both used the same compositional format and adopted the same technique of floating the red lake pigment onto the vellum. Despite these similarities, the increased maturity of the Prince and the differences in the armour indicate that the miniature derived from a separate sitting and was not merely a studio repetition. VR

129
John Hoskins (*c.* 1590–1665)
Henrietta Maria, *c.* 1632
Watercolour on vellum, 9.2 x 7.9 cm
The Royal Collection / HM Queen Elizabeth II, RCIN 420891
PROVENANCE: Charles I; Dowager Countess of Gosford; her sale, London, 1925; E. M. W. O. de la Hey; R. M. O. de la Hey; his sale, London, 1968; acquired by Her Majesty The Queen
SELECTED BIBLIOGRAPHY: Millar 1960, p. 106, no. 12 (Whitehall Palace, Cabinet); London 1972, no. 196; London 1997, no. 28; Reynolds 1999, no. 81; London 2013, pp. 275–76

John Hoskins was the leading miniature painter at Charles I's court until he was superseded by his nephew Samuel Cooper in around 1641. This is his finest surviving work and demonstrates how far the portrait miniature had moved away from Hilliard's idiom during the 1620s and early 1630s under the influence of Van Dyck. Indeed, a number of other miniatures of Henrietta Maria painted by Hoskins derive directly from portraits by Van Dyck. This, however, was 'Don by the life' according to Van der Doort. Her dramatic star-spangled gown is similar to the one designed by Inigo Jones for the Queen's performance as Divine Beauty in *Tempe Restor'd* for Twelfth Night in 1632. A comparison with Jones's design shows that Hoskins has retained the main body of the gown, with its spectacular textures, but has added a lace collar and partlet, in accordance with more conventional court dress. The soft modelling of the face and intricate handling of the clothing and jewellery, especially the astonishing virtuoso textures of the unusual headdress, mark the miniature out as Hoskins's masterpiece. EG/VR

130
Pierre Regnier (*c.* 1577–1640)
Medal Commemorating the Marriage of Charles I and Henrietta Maria, *c.* 1625
Silver, cast and chased, diameter 2.3 cm (obverse and reverse)
The Royal Collection / HM Queen Elizabeth II, RCIN 443087

131
Nicolas Briot (1579–1646)
Medal Commemorating the Coronation of Charles I, 1626
Gold, struck, diameter 3 cm (obverse and reverse)
The Royal Collection / HM Queen Elizabeth II, RCIN 443108

132
Nicolas Briot (1579–1646)
Medal Commemorating the Scottish Coronation of Charles I, 1633
Gold, struck, diameter 2.8 cm (obverse and reverse)
The Royal Collection / HM Queen Elizabeth II, RCIN 443093

133
Nicolas Briot (1579–1646)
Medal Commemorating the Return of Charles I to London after His Coronation in Scotland, 1633 (obverse and reverse)
Gold, struck, diameter 4.3 cm
The Royal Collection / HM Queen Elizabeth II, RCIN 443109

PROVENANCE: first recorded in the collection of Her Majesty The Queen
SELECTED BIBLIOGRAPHY: Hawkins, Franks and Grueber 1885, nos MI i, 238/1, 243/10, 265/60, 266/62; Millar 1960, p. 130, no. 13, p. 137, no. 1 (Whitehall Palace, Cabinet); Wollaston 1981, nos 2–3; London 1987, no. 7; Peacock 1999, p. 193; Barber 2006, pp. 23–26; Eimer 2010, nos 105A, 106, 123–24; Dykes 2016

Medals both antique and contemporary formed a key part of Charles I's art collection. In this he took after his elder brother, Henry, who had been an ambitious numismatist, spending more on coins than on pictures. Henry hired Van der Doort, a specialist in this field, to take care of his collection, some of which Charles was to inherit. At the time of Van der Doort's inventory, medals appear in the Cabinet Room at Whitehall Palace, recorded alongside some of Charles's most precious paintings and miniatures and with equal punctiliousness; indeed, the time and effort given to cataloguing these medals is testament to their importance for the King. After the King's execution, we lose trace of his numismatic collection, and it is difficult to identify any specific examples that survive today. The four examples shown here were acquired during later reigns.

Charles was the first British monarch regularly to commission medals to commemorate public events in the vein of a Roman emperor. Next to the court masques, medals provide us with compelling evidence of the Caroline court's predilection for mythology. For instance, cat. 130, struck to commemorate the King's marriage to Henrietta Maria, shows busts of the royal couple, face to face, while on its reverse a cupid walks beneath celestial rays scattering roses and lilies. Much like Van Dyck's equestrian portraits (cats 72, 74), cat. 133 shows Charles on horseback, its reverse showing the sun shining over a tranquil bank of the Thames. Struck in 1633 to commemorate Charles's return from his Scottish coronation, the King's version of this medal was clearly so cherished that it is listed in the inventory as 'much worne in the Kings pockett', as is a version of cat. 132, the medal commemorating the coronation itself. NM

134
Robert van Voerst (1597–1635/36) after Anthony van Dyck (1599–1641)
Charles I and Henrietta Maria Holding a Laurel Wreath, 1634
Engraving, 42.2 x 57.1 cm
The Royal Collection / HM Queen Elizabeth II, RCIN 601870
PROVENANCE: possibly George III, *c.* 1810
SELECTED BIBLIOGRAPHY: Hollstein et al. 1949–2010, vol. 41, p. 241, no. 3; Millar 1960, p. 176, no. 27 (Whitehall Palace, The Queen's Little Dressing Room); London 1998, no. 42; New York 2016, no. 67

This print, the most extravagant ever made by Robert van Voerst, copies Van Dyck's double portrait of Charles I and Henrietta Maria (cat. 64) 'by royal privilege'. It is recorded by Van der Doort as having been given to the Queen by Charles I. The large quantity of copies in the King's collection made after this image of tranquil union attests to its iconographic importance for the King and his circle. The Latin inscription asks what shoot will issue from this son of 'James the Great' (James I) and daughter of 'Henry the Great' (Henri IV of France). By the time the print was made, the couple already had two sons and a daughter. NM

135
Roman
Claudius, AD 43–45
Sardonyx, 20.5 x 16 cm
The Royal Collection / HM Queen Elizabeth II, RCIN 65238

PROVENANCE: probably Abraham Gorlaeus of Delft; Henry, Prince of Wales, 1609; Charles I, when Prince of Wales, 1612; recovered at the Restoration
SELECTED BIBLIOGRAPHY: Millar 1960, p. 128, no. 1 (Whitehall Palace, Cabinet); Piacenti and Boardman 2008, no. 1

This important antique cameo of the Emperor Claudius formed part of the collection of agates and cameos which Charles I kept in his Cabinet Room at Whitehall Palace. Van der Doort suggested that Charles may have inherited it from his older brother. In that event, it is likely to have come from the celebrated cabinet of Abraham Gorlaeus of Delft, which was purchased on Prince Henry's behalf in 1609. The cameo remained at St James's Palace during the Interregnum, perhaps because it was considered unsuitable for sale due to its poor condition. It had been damaged in about 1613–15, when, according to Van der Doort, it was 'Crackt and broken' by Lady Somerset, the wife of James I's favourite, Robert Carr. VR

136
Pietro Tacca (1577–1640)
Pacing Horse, 1600
Bronze, height 27.3 cm
The Royal Collection / HM Queen Elizabeth II, RCIN 35467
PROVENANCE: Cosimo II, Grand Duke of Tuscany; Henry, Prince of Wales, 1612; Charles I, when Prince of Wales, 1612; Remigius van Leemput, Commonwealth Sale, 26 March 1650 (£3 10s); recovered at the Restoration
SELECTED BIBLIOGRAPHY: Millar 1960, p. 92, no. 4 (Whitehall Palace, Cabinet); Millar 1972, p. 272, no. 259; Watson and Avery 1973; Edinburgh 1978, no. 152; London 2012, no. 53

This bronze is reputed to be part of the gift of fifteen statuettes from Giambologna's workshop presented in 1612 to Henry, Prince of Wales, by Cosimo II, Grand Duke of Tuscany. It would have made a perfect present for the aspiring knight-gallant, then only eighteen years old. A riderless equestrian statuette in the same pose as Giambologna's statue of Cosimo I in Piazza della Signoria, Florence, it clearly captivated both the young princes: Van der Doort notes that it was one of the statues the twelve-year-old Charles was given when he visited the sickbed of his ailing brother Henry at Richmond. Charles was later to receive, as a gift, Giambologna's *Samson Slaying a Philistine* (fig. 14), the only monumental marble sculpture by the artist ever to have left Florence, which he promptly handed over to the Duke of Buckingham. NM

137
Hubert Le Sueur (*c.* 1580–1658)
Charles I on Horseback, *c.* 1630–33
Bronze, height 33 cm
Ickworth, The Bristol Collection. Acquired through the National Land Fund and transferred to the National Trust in 1956, inv. NT 850841
PROVENANCE: Charles I; John Jackson and Dividend, Commonwealth Sale, 23 October 1651 (£10); probably Frederick Augustus Hervey, 4th Earl of Bristol; transferred to the National Trust in 1956
SELECTED BIBLIOGRAPHY: Millar 1960, p. 95, no. 24 (Whitehall Palace, Cabinet); Millar 1972, p. 273, no. 272; Avery 1979; Avery 1982, no. 15; Evelyn 2000, p. 152

The French sculptor Hubert Le Sueur established himself in Paris, working for Louis XIII. In 1625, the year Charles I married Henrietta Maria, the French King's sister, Le Sueur relocated to the Stuart court. In keeping with the European tradition of grand equestrian monuments, Le Sueur made a larger-than-life statue of the King on horseback, dated 1633 (Trafalgar Square, London). The present statuette, which differs slightly from the larger version, notably in the horse's pose and Charles's armour, was displayed in the Cabinet at Whitehall Palace, alongside a portrait bust of Charles I by Le Sueur and equestrian statuettes by the Italian sculptors Pietro Tacca (cat. 136) and Francesco Fanelli (cats 115–16). LC

138
Speculum Romanae Magnificentiae, 1519–75
50 x 35 cm (album)
The British Library, London, inv. C.77.i.11
PROVENANCE: William Cecil, 2nd Earl of Exeter; Charles I; George II; presented to the British Museum, 1757; transferred to the British Library in 1973
SELECTED BIBLIOGRAPHY: Hülsen 1921; Millar 1960, p. 126, no. 50 (Whitehall Palace, Cabinet); Foot 1984, p. 96

In the 1540s the French publisher Antonio Lafreri started printing and distributing engravings of Rome's major monuments and antiquities. Bespoke compilations of these prints were bound and purchased by travellers and collectors. In the mid-1570s, he produced a frontispiece with the title *Speculum Romanae Magnificentiae* or 'Mirror of Roman Magnificence'. The present version was given to Charles I by William Cecil, 2nd Earl of Exeter. Embossed into the cover is the emblem of the entwined Tudor rose and Scottish thistle, suggesting that this volume was bound following Charles's Scottish coronation in 1633. The 135 plates include maps of Rome and many of the city's famed ancient and modern sites – including an antique view of the Piazza del Campidoglio illustrated here – and would have functioned as a valuable visual record for the King, who never visited the city. LC

139
Busts and Statues at Whitehall Gardens ('The Whitehall Album'), *c.* 1628–29
(first two series of drawings)
44.4 x 28.3 cm (album)
The Royal Collection / HM Queen Elizabeth II, RCIN 970148
PROVENANCE: Charles I; Sir John Stanley; recovered after 1744
SELECTED BIBLIOGRAPHY: Scott-Elliot 1959; London 1981, pp. 229–30; Rausa 2002; Anderson 2015, pp. 138–40

This album contains three series of drawings that were collated at a later date. The first two series – one including 157 images of male and female busts outlined in pen and brown ink, the other featuring 64 statues in red chalk – reproduce antiquities formerly in the Gonzaga collection, including the *Crouching Venus* (cat. 24). Sending drawings of antiquities available for sale to prospective collectors was a well-established practice during the seventeenth century, and it may have been Daniel Nijs who commissioned these two sets of drawings for Charles I while negotiating the purchase of the Gonzaga antiquities on his behalf. The drawings were possibly made in Mantua before the sculptures were boxed and shipped to Murano on the first leg of their journey to England; the accompanying inscriptions provide information about the subjects and, in some cases, the dimensions of the pieces. The album had been temporarily in the custody of Lord Stanley, secretary to the Lord Chamberlain's office, and was returned to the Royal Collection by his descendants in the eighteenth century. BF

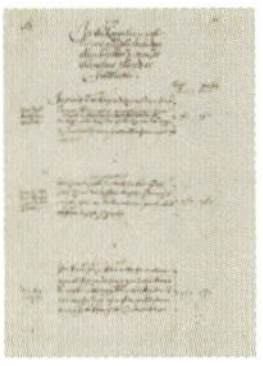

140
Abraham van der Doort (*c.* 1575–1640)
Catalogue of the Collections of Charles I, 1639
31.8 x 21 cm (album)
The Bodleian Libraries, University of Oxford, inv. MS Ashmole 1514
PROVENANCE: Elias Ashmole; presented to the University of Oxford, 1683; Ashmolean Museum, Oxford; transferred to the Bodleian Library in 1833
SELECTED BIBLIOGRAPHY: Vertue 1757; Black 1845, no. 1514; Millar 1960

This is the working draft for the inventory of the collection of Charles I, compiled by Abraham van der Doort, Surveyor of the King's Pictures. Probably never intended for the King's own use, it served as the basis for three extant fair copies (The Royal Collection; British Museum, London; Bodleian Library, Oxford). It was written by a scribe but contains numerous annotations in the hand of Van der Doort, who probably kept this volume with him until his death in 1640. An invaluable document, the catalogue provides attributions, descriptions and measurements of the works on display and in store at Whitehall Palace in 1639.

Curiously, Van der Doort often added references to the direction of the light in each composition, an obsession that may go back to discussions with Francis Cleyn about his borders for the Mortlake tapestries of Raphael's *Acts of the Apostles* (cats 91–94). Devised for tapestries in the Sistine Chapel in the Vatican, half of Raphael's cartoons are unconventionally lit from the right, a detail that seems to have caught the attention of both the King and his Surveyor. PR

ENDNOTES

'THE GREATEST AMATEUR OF PAINTINGS AMONG THE PRINCES OF THE WORLD'
Per Rumberg and Desmond Shawe-Taylor (pp. 17–25)

1 For a detailed account of the ceiling decoration of Banqueting House, see Martin 2005.
2 Rubens in a letter of 10 January 1625 to his friend Palamède Fabri de Valavez; Rooses and Ruelens 1886–1909, vol. 3, p. 320.
3 Millar 1972, p. 43.
4 See in particular Griffey 2015.
5 See Bolland 2011 for a summary of the Tudor Renaissance.
6 That 'Italian' had come to mean 'in the classical tradition' and therefore 'universal' is implied by the title of Vincenzo Scamozzi's 1615 treatise, *L'Idea dell'Architettura Universale*. See also Howell 1650, p. 42 ('Italy hath beene alwayes accounted the Nurse of Policy, Learning, Musique, Architecture, and Limning, with other perfections, which she disperseth to the rest of Europe').
7 For an account of Colbert and state control of the arts, including a very comprehensive bibliography, see Burchard 2017, pp. 110–53.
8 Angelicoussis 2004; Howarth 1985, pp. 77–96.
9 Hart 2011 has Jones making comparisons with antique examples in the architect's annotated copy of Andrea Palladio's *I Quattro Libri dell'Architettura* (the copy survives in the library of Worcester College, Oxford).
10 For a comprehensive and erudite account of the collecting of Italian paintings in Britain until Charles I's reign (including the Venetian *Prometheus* collected by Henry, Prince of Wales), see Goldring 2016. John Donne's Titian came into the collection of Charles I and is recorded in Millar 1960, p. 89, no. 71; Charles I is described as loving Venetian painting already in 1622, see Millar 1977, p. 29.
11 Norman and Eaves 2016, no. 10, pp. 175–91.
12 The extent of Charles's involvement with the Mortlake tapestry works can be seen in his command to Sir Francis Crane on departing for Madrid in 1623 to 'keep the fire goinge' despite the financial difficulties which beset the manufactory, quoted in Thomson 1973, p. 281.
13 Lightbown 1989, p. 67.
14 Vertue 1929–51, vol. 1, p. 156 and Walpole 1762–71, vol. 1, pp. 149–50.
15 For a critical edition of the surviving manuscripts of Van der Doort's inventory, see Millar 1960.
16 We are indebted to Simon Thurley for this reconstruction. See also Thurley 1999.
17 Millar 1960, pp. 41–61.
18 Millar 1960, pp. 23–24.
19 Millar 1960, pp. 14–16.
20 Millar 1960, pp. 16–22.
21 Millar 1960, pp. 34–36.
22 Millar 1960, pp. 37–41.
23 Millar 1960, pp. 62–73 (Chair Room) and pp. 76–157 (Cabinet Room).
24 Millar 1960, pp. 62–75.
25 Millar 1960, p. 62, no. 2 and p. 91, no. 77.
26 Charles I and his court 'so exquisitely understand it [painting]', cited in Lightbown 1969, p. 420.
27 For the Carraccis' influence on early seventeenth-century artistic debates in Rome, see Mahon 1971, pp. 193–203.
28 Howarth 1985, pp. 38–52, particularly pp. 40–41.
29 For a clear display of preference for the artists Leonardo, Raphael and Correggio (in that order), see Arundel's letter to Petty published in Hervey 1921, pp. 394–95.
30 Annibale Carracci's annotations (*postille*) of Vasari, which demonstrate an affection for Venetian painting, are discussed in Robertson 2008, pp. 54–67.
31 For anti-Caravaggio sentiment, see Mahon 1971, pp. 176–203.
32 Millar 1972, p. 305, no. 113 (fig. 4), p. 305, no. 112 (fig. 20) and p. 271 (figs 18–19).
33 The three most highly valued Titians were the *Pardo Venus* (fig. 15), the *Entombment of Christ* (Musée du Louvre, Paris), and the *Supper at Emmaus* (cat. 45). See Millar 1972, p. 310, no. 184 and p. 206, nos 333–34.
34 Millar 1972, p. 268, no. 192 (fig. 52), p. 72, no. 57 (Giulio Romano's *Nativity* at the Louvre), and p. 298, no. 8 (Andrea del Sarto's *Virgin and Child* at the Prado).
35 Millar 1972, p. 263, no. 112; p. 273, no. 275; p. 272, nos 253–54.
36 Millar 1972, p. 316, no. 285, and p. 272, no. 256.
37 Millar 1972, p. 63, no. 51 and Millar 1960, p. 148, no. 1.
38 Millar 1972, p. 186, unnumbered.
39 Millar 1972, p. 266, no. 166.
40 Millar 1972, p. 259, no. 51; p. 193, no. 120; p. 204, no. 304.
41 Millar 1972, p. 256, nos 12, 13, 15; see also p. 258, no. 40.
42 Millar 1972, p. 206, no. 340.
43 An unidentified 'Peece' by Rubens sold for £150 (Millar 1972, p. 70, no. 25).
44 Millar 1972, p. 273, no. 279; p. 316, no. 283.
45 The arrangement of paintings in these rooms seems to be inspired by the so-called 'Vaulted Rooms' in the Alcazar, Madrid, hung with Titian's *poesie*, which Charles must have seen during his visit of 1623 and which are described in the 1626 diaries of Cassiano del Pozzo; see Wethey 1969–75, vol. 3, pp. 80–82.
46 Millar 1960, pp. 103–05, nos 2–10.
47 Reynolds 1769.
48 Antwerp 2004, pp. 328–33 for a printed list of Rubens's collection with supposed 'prickings' made on behalf of Charles I.
49 On the history of their display, see Shearman 1972, pp. 147–64.

CONNOISSEURSHIP AT THE CAROLINE COURT
Jeremy Wood (pp. 30–35)

1 Sharpe 1987, pp. 233–34, 242–43.
2 For agents, see Peck 2005, pp. 171–79; Cools, Keblusek and Noldus 2006.
3 Smuts 2004, p. 106.
4 Van der Stighelen 1994, pp. 24–25, 36–39.
5 Hookham Carpenter 1844, p. 29.
6 Barnes et al. 2004, p. 9.
7 Kathman 2004, pp. 31–32.
8 Millar 1963, vol. 1, p. 111, no. 197.
9 For example, Aslet 1999, p. 73. My thanks to Gordon Higgott for discussing this point.
10 Hibbard 2008, p. 125.
11 Hervey 1921, p. 393. Spelling modernised.
12 Springell 1963, p. 230. Spelling modernised.
13 Wood 2000; see also Johnson 1997.
14 See Bertolotti 1880, pp. 77–78.
15 Published by Lightbown 1969. The best interpretation, with full translations, is Dalivalle 2011, pp. 125–30.
16 For the identifications, see Lunn 1972. The confusion survives in Barnes et al. 2004, p. 9.
17 Wood 1990.
18 Lightbown 1969, p. 420 ('quante trufferie'); Dalivalle 2011, p. 128.
19 'Poichè ne escano dalle scuole di valentissimi maestri ben spesso anche delli asini'; Lightbown 1969, p. 420; Dalivalle 2011, p. 127.
20 For his career, see Millar 1960, pp. xiii–xvii.
21 Anderson 2015, p. 178.
22 For Duarte's appointment, see National Archives, SO 3/11 (February 1634/35). In addition, de Paepe 2010, pp. 173–74.
23 Sharpe 1987, p. 244.
24 White 1982, pp. 9–11, nos 5–7.
25 Millar 1960, p. 161; Gordon et al. 2015, p. 91.
26 Peck 2005, pp. 42–68.
27 John Chamberlain to Sir Dudley Carleton, 12 July 1623, in Birch 1848, vol. 2, p. 410.
28 Philip 1957.
29 See Muller 1989, p. 78, with further references.
30 Peck 2005, pp. 121–42.
31 Wilks 1989.
32 Sainsbury 1859, p. 301.
33 Antwerp 2004, pp. 266–67, no. 64.
34 Anderson 2015, p. 92.
35 Shakeshaft 1986.
36 Hibbard 2008, p. 123.
37 Avery 1982, pp. 148–51, 178, no. 17; Griswold et al. 2014, pp. 61, 62, 65.
38 Wittkower 1948.
39 Green 1857, p. 30 (wrongly dated 1631); Griffey 2015, p. 24 (dated 1636).
40 Friedman 1995, p. 369.
41 Smuts 1996, p. 102.
42 For his career, see Spezzaferro 1984.
43 Sainsbury 1859, pp. 354–55 (wrongly dated *c.* 1614).
44 Shakeshaft 1981, p. 550.
45 Millar 1960, p. 36.
46 Wood 2001, pp. 103–11, 119–23.

CHARLES I'S VISIT TO MADRID
Guido Rebecchini (pp. 50–53)

1 On the relationship between Titian and the Habsburg courts, see Mancini 1998.
2 For the acquisitions in Spain, Brotton 2006A is fundamental (see p. 17 for the purchase of the two Titian paintings).
3 Edinburgh 2004A, pp. 188–89, no. 69; London 2014, pp. 194, 263, no. 43.
4 Avery 1993, p. 75; Warren 2006, 137–38.

'RARE AND UNIQUE IN THIS WORLD': MANTEGNA'S 'TRIUMPH' AND THE GONZAGA COLLECTION

Barbara Furlotti and Guido Rebecchini (pp. 54–59)

1 Wood 2010, vol. 1, pp. 80–90, no. 104.
2 Among other pictures, Rubens produced at this time a monumental *Adoration of the Holy Trinity* representing the Gonzaga family (Palazzo Ducale, Mantua), which in turn may have served as a model for his portrait of the young Vincenzo II Gonzaga (cat. 12).
3 Isabella Stewart Gardner Museum, Boston, inv. P21e10.
4 Elam 2008.
5 Lapenta and Morselli 2006, pp. 224–50.
6 See Agosti 2005, pp. 274–75, 435–40.
7 Chambers, Martineau and Signorini 1992; Agosti 2005, pp. 199–200, 228–29, 274–75.
8 Vasari 1996, vol. 1, p. 561.
9 Vasari 1996, vol. 1, p. 561.
10 Elam 2008, pp. 370–72; Hope 2006.
11 Chambers 2010.
12 For a detailed analysis of the literary sources, see Martindale 1979; Charles Hope in London 1992, pp. 357–62; Tosetti Grandi 2008.
13 Campbell 2004.
14 In general, for the sale of the Gonzaga collection to Charles I, see Sainsbury 1859, pp. 320–40; Luzio 1913, pp. 63–86, 137–67; Morselli 2000, pp. 146–58; Whitaker 2002; Anderson 2015, pp. 115–43.
15 Luzio 1913, p. 137.
16 Morselli 2000, pp. 57–59, 151.
17 This series, executed in 1536–40 for a Camerino in the Palazzo Ducale is now known through a series of engravings by Aegidius Sadeler. It was sent to England along with the rest of the Gonzaga collection and after the Commonwealth Sale was acquired by the Spanish Crown. It perished by fire in the Royal Alcázar of Madrid in 1734. See Bodart 1998, pp. 150–61.
18 Every step of this sale can be followed through the archival material published by Luzio 1913 and, more recently, Anderson 2015.
19 Whitaker 2002, pp. 241–42.
20 Anderson 2015, p. 145.
21 For Nijs's bankruptcy following Charles I's delayed payments, see Anderson 2015, pp. 144–63.
22 Whitaker 2002, p. 247.
23 Millar 1972, p. 186.
24 Mantegna's paintings arrived in England badly damaged. A thorough restoration, amounting effectively to a very extensive repainting, was undertaken by the French painter Louis Laguerre at the end of the seventeenth century and was paid for in 1701–02. In the nineteenth century, new attempts to consolidate the pictorial surface and recover Mantegna's painting ultimately failed and the canvases were subsequently conserved in the early 1930s, when non-removable alterations were made, and again in 1962. Since then, only light treatments have been undertaken to preserve the integrity of the canvases. See Martindale 1979, pp. 105–18; Elam 2008, p. 374, note 4.
25 On the looting of the Palazzo Ducale, see Morselli 2000, pp. 158–73.

CHARLES I AND THE NORTHERN RENAISSANCE

David Ekserdjian (pp. 82–87)

1 Campbell 1985, pp. xxxv–xl, xxxix.
2 Haskell 1989, especially p. 207.
3 Haskell 2013, p. 56.
4 Lightbown 1989, especially p. 55.
5 London 1993.
6 Thompson and Campbell 1974.
7 Campbell 1985 lists twenty-two paintings currently in the Royal Collection which belonged to Charles I. Of these, seven are religious (nos 5, 7, 10, 33, 45, 65, 71), and there are single examples of mythological (no. 35), genre (no. 1) and landscape (no. 41) paintings.
8 Campbell 1985, no. 71, plates 85–88, no. 10, plate 10.
9 Campbell 1985, p. xxxvii and fig. 19; Pächt 1989, pp. 83–84, plate 7.
10 London 2006, no. 136; Foister 2004, pp. 42–45, figs 40–41.
11 Campbell 1985, no. 33, plate 39; New York 2010, no. 2 (entry by Lorne Campbell).
12 New York 2010, pp. 120–22, no. 3 (entry by Maryan W. Ainsworth).
13 Campbell 1985, no. 34; New York 2010, pp. 272–73, no. 51, and pp. 294–96, no. 60 (entries by Lorne Campbell).
14 Campbell 1985, nos 13–14, plates 16–17, for Joos van Cleve, pp. 86–89, no. 54, plate 66, and fig. 18.
15 Bruyn and Millar 1962.
16 Haskell 1989, p. 217, plates 42–43.
17 Campbell 1985, p. xxxix.
18 MacGregor 1989, plate 51.
19 Haskell 1989, p. 221.
20 Haskell 1989, p. 217.
21 Friedländer and Rosenberg 1978, plates 43–44, 112–14, 191–99, 356–57, for *Adam and Eve*, plates 147–49, 189, 312, 314, 423, for *Portrait of Martin Luther*, and plates 6–7, for *Dr Johannes and Anna Cuspinian.*
22 Haskell 1989, p. 216, plates 35–36.
23 Haskell 1989, p. 216, and plate 32 for the Raphael (reproduced in reverse).
24 Edinburgh 1993, especially pp. 20–23, for the drawings, and Meyer zur Capellen 2001–09, vol. 1, pp. 195–200, no. 21, for the painting.
25 See Howarth 1985 and Malibu 1995 for more general considerations of Arundel's collecting.
26 Foister 2004, pp. 130–37, figs 133–35.
27 See Foister 2004, pp. 267–69, for the inventory, p. 251, fig. 254, pp. 201–02, fig. 203, and p. 207, fig. 207, for the portraits, and The Hague 2003A, pp. 94–97, no. XVII, for Born.
28 Haskell 2013, p. 179, fig. 171.
29 Foister 2004, p. 37, fig. 35, and p. 58, figs 59–60, and The Hague 2003A, pp. 88–91, nos XIV–XV, for Reskimer.
30 Haskell 1989, p. 217.
31 Anzelewsky 1991, vol. 1, pp. 150–56, nos 48–49, and vol. 2, plates 53–56, where the National Gallery painting is accepted as autograph.
32 Campbell 1985, p. xxxvi.
33 Frick 1968, p. 13.

CHARLES I AND THE ITALIAN RENAISSANCE

David Ekserdjian (pp. 100–05)

1 Haskell 1989, p. 203.
2 See Haskell 2013, pp. 1–76, for a very full account of art collectors and art collections on the eve of the Civil War.
3 Haskell 2013, p. 21.
4 See pp. 50–53.
5 See Rubin 1995; Vasari 1996.
6 See Martindale 1979 for the *Triumph*.
7 Haskell 2013, p. 45.
8 Zöllner 2007, pp. 194, 198, and 248, no. XXX.
9 Haskell 2013, p. 47.
10 'El cupido per cosa moderna non ha pari'. See Hirst 2011, pp. 27–29; MacGregor 1989, p. 77, fig. 30, for an anonymous drawing that illustrates the piece.
11 Haskell 2013, pp. 52–53.
12 Shearman 1972, p. 146.
13 Shearman 1972, pp. 145–47.
14 Meyer zur Capellen 2001–09, vol. 1, pp. 195–200, no. 21.
15 Madrid 2012, pp. 200–07, no. 50.
16 Brotton 2006B, pp. 293–94.
17 Madrid 2012, pp. 200–07, no. 50.
18 Madrid 2012, pp. 230–32, no. 60.
19 Spagnolo 2005, for an exemplary consideration of the earlier period.
20 Ekserdjian 1997, pp. 274–79, figs 283–84.
21 Ekserdjian 1997, pp. 268–74, figs 278, 280.
22 Ekserdjian 1997, pp. 68–70, fig. 65.
23 Ekserdjian 1997, pp. 68–70, fig. 66; Shearman 1983, pp. 78–79, no. 72, and plate 67.
24 Ekserdjian 1997, pp. 172–73, fig. 193; Shearman 1983, pp. 78–79, no. 73, and plate 68.
25 Shearman 1983, pp. 104–06, no. 99, and plate 87, pp. 205–06, no. 213, and plate 183, and pp. 59–61, no. 55, and plate 50.
26 Vasari 1996, vol. 1, p. 923.
27 Shearman 1983, pp. 221–22, no. 235, and plate 197.
28 Shearman 1983, pp. 21–23, no. 16, and plate 13.

THE 'ACT AND POWER OF A FACE': VAN DYCK'S ROYAL PORTRAITS

Desmond Shawe-Taylor (pp. 126–31)

1 Waller 1730, pp. 32–33.
2 The hang is recorded in the Commonwealth Sale, see Millar 1972, pp. 318–21.
3 Millar 1972, pp. 318–19, nos 310, 314, 320, 323, 331–32.
4 Millar 1972, pp. 318–19, nos 326–27.
5 Millar 1960, pp. 2–7, nos 4, 8, 16–18, 28–33.
6 Millar 1960, pp. 2–7, nos 5–7, 10, 16–17, 19, 21, 23; Millar 1963, vol. 1, pp. 16–17, describes the old-fashioned character of this hang and concludes that we can overlook Charles I's desire 'to keep alive the old patterns that had pleased his forebears'.
7 The Bear Gallery, described by Van der Doort, contained one Titian (cat. 16) and five Van Dycks (including cat. 13), see Millar 1960, pp. 2–7, nos 3, 12, 24–25, 34–35; the Cross Gallery, described in the Commonwealth Inventories, contained one Titian and eight Van Dycks (including cat. 67), see Millar 1972, pp. 318–19, nos 308–09, 311–13, 316–17, 319, 335.
8 For Velázquez's portrait of Charles I, see cat. 15, for Bernini's bust, see cat. 2; Rubens's self-portrait was valued in the Commonwealth Sale at a mere £16 and Rembrandt's at £5 (Millar 1972, p. 264, no. 128, and p. 272, no. 250).
9 Puget de la Serre 1639, p. 44; de Piles 1699, p. 269; Piper 1968, p. 18.
10 Jonson 1892, p. 49; see also Sir Philip Sidney, who defined poetry as 'a speaking Picture – with this end, to teach and delight' (Sidney 2003, p. 505), a definition which in turn depends upon Horace (see *Ars Poetica*, ll. 333–34).
11 Sidney 2003, pp. 508–09.
12 Sidney 2003, p. 503.
13 Sidney 2003, p. 504.
14 Sanderson 1658, p. 19, see also Gordenker 2001, pp. 51–66, for the best account of this concept and the way Van Dyck's handling of dress expresses it.
15 Enthusiasts for the spirit of poetry, like Sir Philip Sidney, tend to make light of the letter of her laws, knowing that their readers will be familiar with all the rhetorical devices, carefully described by Gabriel Harvey and grammarians of his ilk.
16 Van Dyck wrote to congratulate the author upon receiving a copy of Junius's work.
17 Bellori describes the King's visits to Van Dyck's studio on the authority of Sir Kenelm Digby, his principal source for Van Dyck's English years (Bellori 2005, p. 218); the Office of Works records a payment in 1634–35 for a landing-stage and stairs so that

the King could visit the painter's studio from the royal barge (see Edmond 1980, p. 125).

18 For Van Dyck's historical and mythological portraits of Buckingham and his wife, see Barnes et al. 2004, nos I.157, 158; for portraits commissioned by Kenelm Digby, all with some emblematic element, see Barnes et al. 2004, nos VI.93–99. The fact that Digby was Bellori's source of information, combined with his own predilections, makes for a disproportionately long discussion of emblematic portraits in Bellori's life of Van Dyck.

19 White 2015, no. 74.

20 Hookham Carpenter 1844, p. 24.

21 Millar 1963, vol. 1, p. 86, no. 119 and fig. 12.

22 For an account of this episode, including an X-radiograph of Mytens's double portrait, see the entry on the Hoskins copy in London 2009, no. 18; the copy is listed in the Cabinet Room at Whitehall Palace (Millar 1960, p. 106, no. 15); Horace Walpole reports that Mytens felt jealousy towards Van Dyck, but provides no specific evidence (Walpole 1762–71, vol. 1, p. 167).

23 Van der Doort describing the Hoskins miniature (see below, note 24), which also specifies that the original hangs over the chimney in Denmark (now Somerset) House. Bellori mentions that a 'myrtle branch' is held between the two figures (Bellori 2005, p. 218).

24 These laurels do not necessarily imply military triumphs: the poet Thomas Carew refers to the 'bloodless Trophies' brought home by Charles I's 'strong vertues' (see Parry 1981, p. 211).

25 Barnes et al. 2004, nos IV.60–61; Millar 1972, p. 306, no. 133.

26 Millar 1963, vol. 1, p. 99, no. 152; Millar 1960, p. 35, no. 1.

27 Millar 1960, p. 36, no. 8; White 2015, no. 75.

28 For the portrait of Henri IV, see Millar 1960, p. 195, no. 7; Millar 1963, vol. 1, p. 18.

29 Millar 1960, p. 226, no. 1; see also Wilks 2005, p. 157.

30 For instance, a set of Mortlake tapestries depicting the *Twelve Months*, commissioned by Charles I in 1623 when Prince of Wales, are between 3.9 and 4 metres high.

31 Inigo Jones's annotated copy of *I quattro libri dell'architettura di Andrea Palladio* (1601) is in the library of Worcester College, Oxford. Jones used the composite order in a Roman atrium setting designed for Aurelian Townshend's 1632 masque *Albion's Triumph*, in which the King played Albanactus, a Romano-British Emperor; the design is at Chatsworth and reproduced in Orgel and Strong 1973, vol. 2, no. 191; see also Peacock 2006A, p. 55.

32 Bellori 2005, pp. 217–18.

33 London 1982, p. 21; Hookham Carpenter 1844, p. 71; Millar 1960, p. 174, no. 14.

34 Millar 1960, pp. 226–27, nos 19–20, 23–26, 28–35.

35 Wilks 2005, pp. 156–69, explores many of these themes and relates them to the previous occupant of St James's Palace, Henry, Prince of Wales.

36 Millar 1960, p. 180, no. 6.

37 Millar 1960, p. 62, no. 2.

38 Roy Strong suggested that it would similarly have completed the vista at the end of the gallery (Strong 1972, p. 22, fig. 6).

39 Bellori 2005, p. 218.

40 Peacock 1999, p. 193; Millar 1960, p. 137, no. 1.

41 This list of works, basically an invoice with many of the prices marked down (in this case from £100 to £200), was published by Hookham Carpenter 1844, p. 67; Barnes et al. 2004, no. IV.50 (entry by Oliver Millar).

42 See also Millar 1960, p. 5, nos 20, 21; the Salviati, which cannot be traced, was 2 ft 4 in. by 4 ft 8 in. and depicted three life-sized angels flying in the clouds holding palm branches and garlands of flowers; Millar noted the relationship of sizes (Barnes et al. 2004, p. 468).

43 The Royal Collection version of this composition is an adaptation of fig. 31; see Millar 1963, vol. 1, p. 79, no. 100.

44 Millar 1963, vol. 1, no. 120.

45 Held 1958, p. 145; Turbeville 1908, p. 134.

46 William Shakespeare, *Antony and Cleopatra*, Act V, Scene II, lines 287–88.

VAN DYCK, TITIAN AND CHARLES I

Per Rumberg (pp. 150–55)

I would like to thank Jeremy Wood for his invaluable comments.

1 See Fraschetti 1900, p. 110.

2 See Vickers 1978; Raatschen 1996; London 1998, no. 43.

3 Millar 1960, p. 20, no. 18.

4 See Brown 1987.

5 See Howarth 1985; Brown 1982, pp. 52–60.

6 For Van Dyck and Titian, see Brown 1982, pp. 61–99.

7 Adriani 1940; Jaffé 2002, pp. 70–71.

8 See Jaffé 2001.

9 See Millar 1960, p. 15, no. 2, and p. 16, no. 5; Wethey 1969–75, vol. 1, no. 132, and vol. 3, no. 50; cat. 165, fols 19, 111; Adriani 1940, nos 19, 111; see also Jaffé 2002, nos 1022, 1112.

10 First described as the 'greate peece' in a warrant of 8 August 1632 to issue payment of £100 to Van Dyck for 'One greate peece of or royall selfe, Consort and children'. See Hookham Carpenter 1844, p. 71, app. VI.

11 See also an eighteenth-century watercolour by George Vertue (Royal Collection).

12 Wethey 1969–75, vol. 2, no. 72. Van Dyck included Palazzo Farnese in the list of places he visited in Rome. Adriani 1940, no. 120; see also Jaffé 2002, no. 1128.

13 Wethey 1969–75, vol. 2, no. 76.

14 Adriani 1940, no. 108, verso; see also Jaffé 2002, no. 1107. On the previous page of his sketchbook (fol. 107, verso), Van Dyck recorded Raphael's famous portrait of Pope Leo X (Galleria degli Uffizi, Florence).

15 Wethey 1969–75, vol. 1, no. 55.

16 Adriani 1940, nos 3, 9; see also Jaffé 2002, nos 991, 1002.

17 Jaffé 2002, no. 991. Adriani did not include a reproduction of fol. 3, which may be the reason it has thus far been largely overlooked, see Adriani 1940, no. 3.

18 Adriani 1940, no. 9; see also Jaffé 2002, no. 1002.

19 Titian had first painted a barrel vault, which is still partly visible beneath the final paint layer. Some scholars have argued, unconvincingly, that the columns were added at a later stage, see for example Rosand 1971.

20 Barnes et al. 2004, no. IV.184.

21 Adriani 1940, no. 27; see also Jaffé 2002, no. 1034.

22 Van Dyck may have seen the version now at the Cleveland Museum of Art (attributed to Titian and workshop), which was then in Genoa. Wethey 1969–75, vol. 1, no. 5.

23 In another portrait of Charles I (Private collection), Van Dyck copied the pose of Otho from Titian's lost series of Roman emperors, then in the collection of Charles I. See Barnes et al. 2004, no. IV.56. Otho's pose is recorded in prints by Aegidius Sadeler and Robert van Voerst. See Wood 1990, p. 680.

24 Wethey 1969–75, vol. 1, no. 133.

25 Although Van Dyck did not record the composition in his sketchbook, he is known to have visited that great Venetian church: 'S. Giovanni e Paolo'. Adriani 1940, no. 120; see also Jaffé 2002, no. 1128.

26 Wethey 1969–75, vol. 3, no. 14.

27 'P. di Aldibrandino'. Adriani 1940, no. 120; see also Jaffé 2002, no. 1128.

28 For Van Dyck's 'Cabinet de Titien', see Wood 1990.

29 Wethey 1969–75, vol. 2, no. 110, and vol. 3, no. 30.

RUBENS, PAINTER AND DIPLOMAT

Gregory Martin (pp. 156–61)

1 For a full discussion, see Sharpe 1992, pp. 66–68, also for the eventual peace of Madrid (1631); for the basic account of Rubens's role, see Gachard 1877; for the documents, see Rooses and Ruelens 1886–1909, vol. 5, pp. 1–292; for annotated translations into English of Rubens's letters, see Magurn 1955, pp. 299–353.

2 Martin 2005, vol. 1, pp. 23–30.

3 Rooses and Ruelens 1886–1909, vol. 4, pp. 83–84.

4 Patterson 1997, pp. 293–338, for the point of view of Charles's father, James I.

5 Sainsbury 1859, pp. 68–70; Rooses and Ruelens 1886–1909, vol. 4, pp. 47–49.

6 Rooses and Ruelens 1886–1909, vol. 5, pp. 37–39; the patent is dated 6 May.

7 Rooses and Ruelens 1886–1909, vol. 5, p. 47.

8 Loomie 1987, p. 62.

9 Rooses and Ruelens 1886–1909, vol. 5, pp. 74–77; Magurn 1955, pp. 299–302.

10 Magurn 1955, p. 352.

11 Magurn 1955, p. 77.

12 Patterson 1997, pp. 357–62; Martin 2005, vol. 1, pp. 152–55, under no. 3.

13 See the entry in the Oxford Dictionary of National Biography.

14 See the entry in the Oxford Dictionary of National Biography.

15 Martin 2005, vol. 1, pp. 52–89.

16 Magurn 1955, p. 320.

17 Wood 2010, vol. 1, nos 114–15, vol. 2, figs 41, 46.

18 Wheelock 2005, p. 166, under *Daniel in the Lions' Den*.

19 White 2007, no. 64.

20 Magurn 1955, p. 292.

21 Wood 2010, vol. 1, no. 141, vol. 2, fig. 129, and vol. 1, no. App. Titian 9.

22 Martin 2011, pp. 93–96.

23 Wheelock 2005, pp. 196–205.

24 Martin 1970, pp. 116–25, no. 46; Roy 1999.

25 Millar 1960, pp. 2, 4.

26 McGrath forthcoming, in which she describes the two maidens as 'one bearing riches, the other dancing…'

27 See New York 2005, no. 87, for the drawing of the head of George as Hymenaeus, with references to the other studies.

28 White 2007, no. 63.

29 Rooses and Ruelens 1886–1909, vol. 5, pp. 287–88; White 2007, p. 218.

30 Magurn 1955, pp. 343–44.

31 Magurn 1955, p. 321.

32 Magurn 1955, p. 320.

33 Loomie 1987, p. 81.

34 Rooses and Ruelens 1886–1909, vol. 5, pp. 347–48.

HENRIETTA MARIA, CHARLES I AND THE ITALIAN BAROQUE

Karen Serres (pp. 172–79)

1 Letter from Panzani to Cardinal Barberini, 11 July 1635, quoted in Wittkower 1948, p. 50, and Madocks Lister 2000, p. 158. The pronouncement was nuanced:

Panzani remarks that the King is interested in paintings as long as they are good, but Old Masters will be preferred because of their rarity. Correspondence between papal envoys and Cardinal Barberini is held in the Biblioteca Apostolica Vaticana (Barb. Lat. 8633–41) but later transcripts exist in England: for Panzani, 1634–37, see National Archives, P.R.O.31/9/17 and P.R.O.31/10/10; for George Conn, from 1637, see British Library, Add. MS 15390.

2 Haskell 1989; Levey 1991, p. xiv; London 2007A, pp. 17–28; Wood 2001, p. 123; Haskell 2013.

3 Wittkower 1948, p. 51. See also MacGregor 1996, p. 147.

4 Prynne 1645, p. 147, quoted in MacGregor 1996, p. 154, and Madocks Lister 2000, p. 152. See also Hibbard 1983. Making use of the dispatches between envoys and the pontifical court, Albion 1935 and Madocks Lister 2000 provide the most thorough account of the gifts presented to the King and his courtiers. See also Panzani 1793.

5 For the fullest account, see Lightbown 1981.

6 See Avery 1982; Howarth 1998; Avery 2002.

7 British Library, Add. MS 15390, p. 237 and pp. 359–61.

8 Vertue 1929–51, vol. 2, pp. 50, 57; Raatschen 1996; Marsden 1999. It has also been suggested that the engraving represents a bust by François Dieussart, see Vickers 1978. See also Griffiths 1988, no. 43.

9 British Library, Add. MS 15390, p. 450 and pp. 482–84.

10 Madocks 1984, p. 546.

11 Letter from Balthasar Gerbier to Edward Norgate, 25 January 1640, quoted in Sainsbury 1859, p. 214. This was undoubtedly a way for Gerbier to disparage the ceilings commissioned from Gentileschi and Reni in, respectively, the Great Hall and the Bedchamber of the Queen's House, and to ensure either of the 'Dutchmen' Peter Paul Rubens or Jacob Jordaens was awarded the commission for the Cabinet.

12 Madocks 1984, p. 547.

13 Félibien 1725, vol. 4, p. 206.

14 Indeed, a number of proposed fragments have recently emerged, see Rome 2002. See also Montanari 2004 and *Two Fauns in a Bacchic Dance*, attributed to Reni and sold at Sotheby's, New York, 6 June 2012, lot 20, now with Moretti Fine Art.

15 Walpole 1762–71, vol. 2, pp. 51–52, who also cites invitations to the French painter Simon Vouet (recently returned from Rome) and Carlo Maratta (the latter from the Duke of Buckingham). The biographer of Angelo Caroselli mentioned several (untraced) commissions directly from the King of England to the Roman painter (see Passeri 1934, p. 190).

16 Haskell 1959, p. 49. For attitudes to the Italian Baroque in other courts, see for example Laurain-Portemer 1975.

17 Thurley 2002.

18 London 1999A; Finaldi and Wood 2001; Terzaghi 2017.

19 Millar 1960, pp. 46, 177, 194; Millar 1972, pp. 65, 186, 191, 312, 315, 316.

20 For Henrietta Maria as patron, see Hibbard 1991; Griffey 2008; Hibbard 2009; Griffey 2015.

21 Griffey and Hibbard 2012, pp. 167–69.

22 Bertolotti 1880, pp. 77–78. See also Bracken and Hill 2012, p. 188.

23 Philip 1957.

24 Arundel only converted to the Church of England in 1616, upon joining the Privy Council; see Hervey 1921, pp. 112–19. For other Catholic collectors and agents at court, see Chaney 2000.

25 Howarth 2002, p. 77.

26 Letter from Arundel to Sir Dudley Carleton, 20 July 1621, quoted in Sainsbury 1859, p. 292, and Hervey 1921, p. 196. The painting was *Aeneas Fleeing from Troy*, a recent gift from Carleton to Arundel.

27 'Un Pittore Fiorentino, che è qua assai bravo', quoted in Wittkower 1948, p. 50, no. 8.

28 The painters suggested were Cortona, Domenichino, Lanfranco, Poussin, Reni, Albani, Guercino, Spagnoletto (Ribera) and Carracci (Finaldi, in London 1999A, p. 19, suggests this may be Caracciolo); see Madocks Lister 2000, p. 158.

29 See for example, Shakeshaft 1986; Pitacco 2007; Bracken and Hill 2012.

30 Betcherman 1970, p. 252.

31 Davies 1907; Jervis 1997; McEvansoneya 2003. Honthorst stayed in London from April to December 1628, probably at the Duke of Buckingham's behest, painting *Apollo and Diana*, a thinly veiled allegorical painting of the royal couple and the Duke (Royal Collection).

32 Shakeshaft 1986, p. 115.

33 Puget de la Serre 1639, not paginated.

34 Millar 1960, p. 228. For the possible influence of Prince Henry's collection on the arrangement of St James's Palace, see Wilks 2005.

35 Letter from Cesare Alessandro Scaglia to Carlo Emanuele of Savoy, 1 November 1625, quoted in Osborne 2007, p. 33.

36 Shakeshaft 1986, p. 126, letter no. 31. In a later letter (no. 63), Feilding expressed hesitation about offering 'modern peeces' to the King.

37 Letter from Panzani to Cardinal Barberini, 11 July 1635, cited in Wittkower 1948, p. 50.

38 Smuts 1981.

CHARLES I AND RAPHAEL'S 'ACTS OF THE APOSTLES'

Helen Wyld (pp. 190–97)

1 Howard 2012.

2 Wyld and Hodge forthcoming; Campbell 2007A.

3 Smuts 1996; Campbell 2007B.

4 Letter of *c.* 1623 from Charles I to Francis Crane, quoted in Thomson 1973, p. 281.

5 The cost per ell of the first piece, probably the *Death of Ananias*, is given in a warrant to Crane of January 1630 (see National Archives, inv. E 403/2566, fol. 54v). Six tapestries from the first weaving made for Charles I survive in the Mobilier national in Paris and a seventh, *Paul Preaching at Athens*, was lost in Warsaw in 1945; the total cost can be established from the dimensions of the surviving tapestries. The Mobilier national also owns one tapestry from a second, even richer weaving, of which the only other piece is today in the Royal Collection. Weavings 'of the second sort' with smaller borders and no metal thread were made for the Earl of Pembroke and the Earl of Holland and survive in the Mobilier national, the Palazzo Ducale, Mantua and at Boughton House, Northamptonshire. See Vittet and Brejon de Lavergnée 2010, pp. 92–98; Hefford 2007, pp. 187–88.

6 Puget de la Serre 1639, quoted in Palme 1957, p. 28.

7 For the iconography and context of Raphael's *Acts*, see Shearman 1972; Fermor 1996; New York 2002, pp. 187–203; London 2010.

8 Shearman 1972, pp. 38, 42, and note 50, p. 8.

9 New York 2002, pp. 190–93.

10 Palme 1957, pp. 7–39.

11 Thomas P. Campbell, in New York 2007, pp. 17–27.

12 Thomson 1914, p. 68.

13 For full details of the founding of Mortlake, see Anderson 1894; Thomson 1914; Thomson 1973; Hefford 2007.

14 Hefford 1990A.

15 Siple 1939; Thomson 1973, pp. 282–83, 289; Hefford 1999; Hefford 2006. A coarse set of grotesques woven with the arms of the Earl of Portland, of which one panel survives at Ham House, Richmond, also shows a clear French influence and must be a very early Mortlake weaving; see Wyld 2013.

16 Fuller 1662, p. 201.

17 National Archives, E 404/153; see also Campbell 1987, p. 82 and Myson 1955. Hefford argues for a date of 1625 rather than 1626 (Hefford 2007, p. 183, note 30). The 'Love and Folly' drawings reappeared in the recently rediscovered Southampton album; see Howarth 2011, pp. 440–45.

18 For a weaving of Hero and Leander, see National Trust Collections, inv. 348324.3 (Cotehele, Cornwall).

19 Mulherron and Wyld 2011; Mulherron and Wyld 2012.

20 Hefford 1990B.

21 Mulherron 2012; Wyld 2016.

22 *St George and the Dragon* is in a private collection, see Campbell 1987, p. 28. For Van Dyck's Garter Procession, see Brown 2005.

23 See above, note 17. Other entries on the bill for mural paintings at Somerset House specify that he had assistants.

24 In July 1628 a warrant was sent to the Keeper of the Standing Wardrobe at the Tower of London to deliver to Crane 'A peece of Hangings of ye story of Acts of ye Ap[ost]les … Ananias or any other peece which hee shall desire'. Quoted in Hefford 2007, p. 177.

25 See New York 2002, pp. 196–99.

26 Fermor and Derbyshire 1998, p. 250; Millar 1960, pp. 76, 171–72, 179. Hefford suggests that Raphael's original cartoons may have been used on the looms when two or more editions were being woven concurrently (Hefford 2007, p. 189).

27 The narrow panel of *Paul in Prison* had been designed to fill a space next to the choir stall in the Sistine Chapel, and was not rewoven as it was of limited use in any other context; Shearman suggests it was destroyed soon after the papal edition was made (Shearman 1972, pp. 145–47).

28 Howarth 1994, p. 156.

29 Suggested in Hefford 2007, p. 176.

30 Hefford 2007, p. 177.

31 Howarth 2011, pp. 449–55. Cleyn made one further intervention into the main scenes of the Acts, designing a figure for the strip of architecture on the right-hand side of the *Conversion of the Proconsul*, which is not included in Raphael's cartoon but which replaces a similar strip in the sixteenth-century weavings. See Hefford 2007, p. 176.

32 Campbell 2007A, pp. 272–74.

33 Smuts 1987, pp. 218–43; Sharpe 1992, pp. 275–308.

34 'les plus somptueuses peut-être de toute l'histoire de la tapisserie'. Vittet and Brejon de Lavergnée 2010, p. 93; Denis 2009, p. 18. I am very grateful to Ross Anderson for obtaining a copy of Denis's article for me.

35 Smuts 1987, pp. 234–36.

36 Adamson 1994.

37 Charles's *editio princeps* does not appear in the Commonwealth inventories. They may be the 'certaine hangings wch have Superstitiouse & idolatrose pictures in them', sold to provide for troops quartered in the Banqueting House in 1647; Palme 1957, p. 270.

A 'MORE SOLITARY PLACE': CHARLES I'S CABINET
Vanessa Remington and Lucy Whitaker (pp. 206–11)

1 Junius 1638, vol. 1, p. 59, cited in Novikova 2003, p. 332, note 73. The Dutch humanist Franciscus Junius was appointed librarian to Thomas Howard, Earl of Arundel.
2 Millar 1960, p. 76.
3 Millar 1960, pp. 76–156.
4 Thurley 1999, p. 93. Colvin 1976, vol. 4, part 2, pp. 341–42.
5 Millar 1960, p. 91, no. 77. See Martin 2005, vol. 1, nos 2, 4e; White 2007, p. 11.
6 Millar 1960, pp. 62–75.
7 Wilks 1988, pp. 189–200. Prince Henry had cabinet rooms at St James's, Richmond and Whitehall Palaces.
8 Bathoe 1757, pp. 164–65.
9 Millar 1960, pp. xiii–xiv.
10 Millar 1960, p. xiv.
11 Millar 1960, pp. xv–xvii.
12 Cox and Norman 1930, pp. 36–39; Colvin 1976, vol. 5, pp. 286–99; Thurley 1999, pp. 127–33.
13 Bodleian MS, Ashmole 1514.
14 Windsor MS, RCIN 1047433.
15 Millar 1960, p. 76.
16 Millar 1960, p. 77, no. 4 (Royal Collection).
17 Millar 1960, p. 78, no. 13 (Royal Collection).
18 Millar 1960, p. 90, no. 73.
19 Millar 1960, p. 77, no. 5 (Royal Collection).
20 Cited in Chaney 2003, p. 62.
21 Millar 1960, p. 81, no. 27, p. 89, no. 71, p. 79, no. 14.
22 The exceptions are Millar 1960, p. 153, nos 22–25.
23 Millar 1960, p. 125, no. 42; see Roberts 1989, p. 120.
24 Millar 1960, p. 126, no. 49.
25 Millar 1960, p. 124, no. 36 (Royal Collection).
26 Howarth 1989, p. 101; Lightbown 1989, pp. 234–40; Millar 1960 p. 97, no. 3.
27 Millar 1960, p. 97, nos 35–36.
28 Five of the ten limnings grouped together in the Cabinet Room were returned to the Royal Collection after the Restoration.
29 Millar 1960, p. 102.
30 Gerbier 1648, p. 161.
31 Lightbown 1989, p. 57; Walpole 1762–71, vol. 2, p. 136.
32 Rowell 1996; Rowell 2013, pp. 14–31.
33 Hutchinson 1973, p. 207.

BIBLIOGRAPHY

ADAMSON 1994
J. S. A. Adamson, 'Chivalry and Political Culture in Caroline England', in Kevin Sharpe and Peter Lake (eds), *Culture and Politics in Early Stuart England*, Basingstoke, 1994, pp. 161–98

ADLER 1982
Wolfgang Adler, *Corpus Rubenianum Ludwig Burchard: XVIII (1). Landscapes*, London and Turnhout, 1982

ADRIANI 1940
Gert Adriani, *Anton van Dyck: Italienisches Skizzenbuch*, Vienna, 1940

AGOSTI 2005
Giovanni Agosti, *Su Mantegna*, vol. 1, Milan, 2005

ALBION 1935
Gordon Albion, 'Appendix 1: Rome, Charles I and Art', in *Charles I and the Court of Rome: A Study in Seventeenth-century Diplomacy*, Leuven, 1935, pp. 393–401

ANDERSON 1894
John Eustace Anderson, *A Short Account of the Tapestry Works at Mortlake*, Richmond, 1894

ANDERSON 2015
Christina Anderson, *The Flemish Merchant of Venice: Daniel Nijs and the Sale of the Gonzaga Art Collection*, New Haven and London, 2015

ANDREWS 1977
Keith Andrews, *Adam Elsheimer: Paintings, Drawings, Prints*, Oxford, 1977

ANGELICOUSSIS 2003
Elizabeth Angelicoussis, 'The Stuart Legacy: Ancient Busts at Hampton Court Palace', *Mitteilungen des Deutschen Archäologischen Instituts Römische Abteilung*, 110, 2003, pp. 57–84

ANGELICOUSSIS 2004
Elizabeth Angelicoussis, 'The Collection of Classical Sculptures of the Earl of Arundel, "Father of Vertu in England"', *Journal of the History of Collections*, 16, 2004, pp. 143–59

ANTWERP 1949
Frank van den Wijngaert (ed.), *Van Dyck Tentoonstelling*, exh. cat., Koninklijk Museum voor Schone Kunsten, Antwerp, 1949

ANTWERP 1999
Christopher Brown, Hans Vlieghe et al. (eds), *Van Dyck*, exh. cat., Koninklijk Museum voor Schone Kunsten, Antwerp; Royal Academy of Arts, London, 1999

ANTWERP 2004
Kristin Lohse Belkin and Fiona Healy (eds), *A House of Art: Rubens as Collector*, exh. cat., Rubenshuis, Antwerp, 2004

ANZELEWSKY 1991
Fedja Anzelewsky, *Albrecht Dürer: Das malerische Werk*, 2 vols, Berlin, 1991

ASLET 1999
Clive Aslet, *The Story of Greenwich*, London, 1999

AUERBACH 1961
Erna Auerbach, *Nicholas Hilliard*, London, 1961

AUWERS 2013
Michael Auwers, 'The Gift of Rubens: Rethinking the Concept of Gift-giving in Early Modern Diplomacy', *European History Quarterly*, 43, 2013, pp. 421–41

AVERY 1979
Charles Avery, 'Hubert Le Sueur's Portraits of King Charles I in Bronze, at Stourhead, Ickworth and Elsewhere', *National Trust Studies*, 147, 1979, pp. 128–47; reprinted in Avery 1981, pp. 189–204

AVERY 1981
Charles Avery (ed.), *Studies in European Sculpture*, London, 1981

AVERY 1982
Charles Avery, 'Hubert Le Sueur, the "Unworthy Praxiteles" of King Charles I', *The Walpole Society*, 48, 1980–82, pp. 135–209

AVERY 1993
Charles Avery, *Giambologna: The Complete Sculpture*, London, 1993

AVERY 2002
Charles Avery, '"Sculpture Gone Wild": Bernini and the English', in Chantal Grell and Milovan Stanic (eds), *Le Bernin et l'Europe: Du baroque triomphant à l'âge romantique*, Paris, 2002, pp. 160–78

AVERY 2006
Charles Avery, 'The Collector Earl and His Modern Marbles: Thomas Howard and François Dieussart', *Apollo*, 163, 2006, pp. 46–53

AZNAR 1964
José Camón Aznar, *Velázquez*, 2 vols, Madrid, 1964

BALLARIN 1996
Alessandro Ballarin, *Jacopo Bassano*, 3 vols, Cittadella, 1996

BARBER 2006
Peter Barber, 'London in Miniature: Medallic Panoramas of London, 1633–1795', *London Topographical Record*, 29, 2006, pp. 22–42

BARCLAY 2010
Andrew Barclay, 'The Inventories of the English Royal Collection, temp. James II', *Journal of the History of Collections*, 22, 2010, pp. 1–13

BARNES ET AL. 2004
Susan J. Barnes et al. (eds), *Van Dyck: A Complete Catalogue of the Paintings*, New Haven and London, 2004

BASEL 2006
Christian Müller et al. (eds), *Hans Holbein the Younger: The Years in Basel, 1515–32*, exh. cat., Kunstmuseum Basel, 2006

BASSANO DEL GRAPPA 1992
Beverly Louise Brown and Paola Marini (eds), *Jacopo Bassano*, exh. cat., Museo Civico, Bassano del Grappa; Kimbell Art Museum, Fort Worth, Texas, 1992–93

BATHOE 1757
William Bathoe, *A Catalogue and Description of King Charles the First's Capital Collection of Pictures, Limnings, Statues, Bronzes, Medals and Other Curiosities*, London, 1757

BAUCH 1966
Kurt Bauch, *Rembrandt*, Berlin, 1966

BELLORI 2005
Giovanni P. Bellori, *The Lives of the Modern Painters, Sculptors and Architects*, A. S. Wohl (trans.), Cambridge, 2005

BERTOLOTTI 1880
Antonio Bertolotti, 'Esportazione di Oggetti di Belle Arti da Roma per l'Inghilterra', in Fabio Gori (ed.), *Archivio storico, artistico, archeologico e letterario della città e provincia di Roma*, vol. 4, Spoleto, 1880, pp. 74–90

BETCHERMAN 1970
Lita-Rose Betcherman, 'The York House Collection and Its Keeper', *Apollo*, 92, 1970, pp. 250–59

BINYON 1898-1907
Laurence Binyon, *Catalogue of Drawings by British Artists and Artists of Foreign Origin Working in Great Britain, Preserved in the Department of Prints and Drawings in the British*

Museum, 4 vols, London, 1898–1907

BIRCH 1848
Thomas Birch, *The Court and Times of James the First, Illustrated by Authentic and Confidential Letters from Various Public and Private Collections*, 2 vols, London, 1848

BISSELL 1981
R. Ward Bissell, *Orazio Gentileschi and the Poetic Tradition in Caravaggesque Painting*, University Park, PA, 1981

BISSELL 1999
R. Ward Bissell, *Artemisia Gentileschi and the Authority of Art: Critical Reading and Catalogue Raisonné*, University Park, PA, 1999

BLACK 1845
William H. Black, *A Descriptive, Analytical and Critical Catalogue of the Manuscripts Bequeathed unto the University of Oxford by Elias Ashmole*, Oxford, 1845

BOBER AND RUBINSTEIN 2010
Phyllis Pray Bober and Ruth Rubinstein, *Renaissance Artists and Antique Sculpture: A Handbook of Sources*, second edition, London, 2010

BODART 1998
Diane H. Bodart, *Tiziano e Federico II Gonzaga: Storia di un rapporto di committenza*, Rome, 1998

BODART 2011
Diane H. Bodart, *Pouvoirs du portrait sous les Habsbourg d'Espagne*, Paris, 2011

BOLLAND 2011
Charlotte Bolland, 'Italian Material Culture at the Tudor Court', PhD thesis, Queen Mary University of London, 2011

BOSTON 2009
Frederick Ilchman (ed.), *Titian, Tintoretto, Veronese: Rivals in Renaissance Venice*, exh. cat., Museum of Fine Arts, Boston; Musée du Louvre, Paris, 2009–10

BRACKEN AND HILL 2012
Susan Bracken and Robert Hill, 'Sir Isaac Wake, Venice and Art Collecting in Early Stuart England: A New Document', *Journal of the History of Collections*, 24, 2012, pp. 183–98

BREDIUS AND GERSON 1969
Abraham Bredius, *Rembrandt: The Complete Edition of the Paintings*, Horst Gerson (ed.), London, 1969

BROTTON 2006A
Jerry Brotton, 'Buying the Renaissance: Prince Charles's Art Purchases in Madrid, 1623', in Alexander Samson (ed.), *The Spanish Match: Prince Charles's Journey to Madrid, 1623*, Aldershot and Burlington, VT, 2006, pp. 9–26

BROTTON 2006B
Jerry Brotton, *The Sale of the Late King's Goods: Charles I and His Art Collection*, London, 2006

BROWN 1982
Christopher Brown, *Van Dyck*, London, 1982

BROWN 1986
Jonathan Brown, *Velázquez: Painter and Courtier*, New Haven and London, 1986

BROWN 1987
Christopher Brown, 'Van Dyck and Titian', in Görel Cavalli-Björkman (ed.), *Bacchanals by Titian and Rubens*, Stockholm, 1987, pp. 153–60

BROWN 1995
Jonathan Brown, *Kings and Connoisseurs: Collecting Art in Seventeenth-century Europe*, Princeton, NJ, 1995

BROWN 2005
Christopher Brown, '"A Record and Memorial of His Talents for Posterity": Anthony van Dyck's Sketch of the Garter Procession', in Marieke van den Doel (ed.), *The Learned Eye: Regarding Art, Theory and the Artist's Reputation*, Amsterdam, 2005, pp. 132–39

BRUSSELS 1965
Philippe Roberts-Jones (ed.), *Le siècle de Rubens*, exh. cat., Musées Royaux des Beaux-Arts de Belgique, Brussels, 1965

BRUYN AND MILLAR 1962
Josua Bruyn and Oliver Millar, 'Notes on the Royal Collection: The "Dutch Gift" to Charles I', *Burlington Magazine*, 104, 1962, pp. 291–94

BRUYN ET AL. 1982
Josua Bruyn et al., *A Corpus of Rembrandt Paintings*, vol. 1, The Hague, Boston and London, 1982

BRUYN ET AL. 1986
Josua Bruyn et al., *A Corpus of Rembrandt Paintings*, vol. 2, Dordrecht, Boston and Lancaster, 1986

BURCHARD AND D'HULST 1963
Ludwig Burchard and Roger-A. d'Hulst, *Rubens Drawings*, 2 vols, Brussels, 1963

BURCHARD 2017
Wolf Burchard, *The Sovereign Artist*, London, 2017

BURKE 1984
Marcus B. Burke, 'Private Collections of Italian Art in Seventeenth-century Spain', PhD thesis, 2 vols, New York University, 1984

BURKE AND CHERRY 1997
Marcus B. Burke and Peter Cherry, *Collections of Paintings in Madrid, 1601–1755*, vol. 1, Los Angeles, 1997

BÜTTNER 2002
Nils Büttner, '"… is said to follow the light of the sun": Van Dycks Selbstbildnis mit der Sonnenblume', *Zeitschrift für Kunstgeschichte*, 65, 2002, pp. 24–42

BÜTTNER FORTHCOMING
Nils Büttner, *Corpus Rubenianum Ludwig Buchard: XII. Allegories and Subjects from Literature*, London and Turnhout, forthcoming

BUVELOT 2004
Quentin Buvelot (ed.), *Portraits in the Mauritshuis, 1430–1790*, The Hague, 2004

CAMPBELL ET AL. 1978
Lorne Campbell et al., 'Quentin Matsys, Desiderius Erasmus, Pieter Gillis and Thomas More', *Burlington Magazine*, 120, 1978, pp. 716–25

CAMPBELL 1985
Lorne Campbell, *The Early Flemish Pictures in the Collection of Her Majesty The Queen*, Cambridge, 1985

CAMPBELL 1987
Thomas P. Campbell, *A Consideration of the Career and Work of Francis Clein*, MA thesis, Courtauld Institute of Art, University of London, 1987

CAMPBELL 2004
Stephen J. Campbell, 'Mantegna's Triumph: The Cultural Politics of Imitation "all'antica" at the Court of Mantua, 1490–1530', in Stephen J. Campbell and Evelyn S. Welch (eds), *Artists at Court: Image-making and Identity, 1300–1550*, Boston, 2004, pp. 91–105

CAMPBELL 2007A
Thomas P. Campbell, *Henry VIII and the Art of Majesty: Tapestries at the Tudor Court*, New Haven and London, 2007

CAMPBELL 2007B
Thomas P. Campbell, 'Collectors and Connoisseurs: The Status and Perception of Tapestry, 1600–60', in New York 2007, pp. 325–39

CAMPBELL 2014
Lorne Campbell, *National Gallery Catalogues: The Sixteenth-century Netherlandish Paintings with French Paintings before 1600*, 2 vols, London, 2014

CARDIFF 1998
Mark Evans (ed.), *Princes as Patrons: The Art Collections of the Princes of Wales from the Renaissance to the Present Day*, exh. cat., National Museum of Wales, Cardiff, 1998

CHAMBERS, MARTINEAU AND SIGNORINI 1992
David S. Chambers, Jane Martineau and Rodolfo Signorini, 'Mantegna and the Men of Letters', in London 1992, pp. 8–30

CHAMBERS 2010
David S. Chambers, 'Il marchese Federico I Gonzaga e il "Trionfo di Giulio Cesare" di Andrea Mantegna', in Sara Tammaccaro, Rodolfo Signorini and Viviana Rebonato (eds), *Andrea Mantegna, l'impronta del genio*, vol. 2, Florence, 2010, pp. 507–20

CHANEY 2000
Edward Chaney, 'Pilgrims to Pictures: Art, English Catholics and the Evolution of the Grand Tour', in *The Evolution of the Grand Tour: Anglo-Italian Cultural Relations since the Renaissance*, London and Portland, OR, 2000, pp. 203–14

CHANEY 2003
Edward Chaney (ed.), *The Evolution of English Collecting: Receptions of Italian Art in the Tudor and Stuart Periods*, New Haven and London, 2003

CHECA 2008
Fernando Checa, *Velzáquez: The Complete Paintings*, Antwerp, 2008

CHRISTIANSEN 1992
Keith Christiansen, 'The Studiolo of Isabella d'Este and Late Themes', in London 1992, pp. 418–26

COLVIN 1976
Howard M. Colvin (ed.), *The History of the King's Works, 1660–1782*, vols 4–5, London, 1976

COOLS, KEBLUSEK AND NOLDUS 2006
Hans Cools, Marika Keblusek and Badeloch Noldus (eds), *Your Humble Servant: Agents in Early Modern Europe*, Hilversum, 2006

COONEY AND MALAFARINA 1976
Patrick J. Cooney and Gianfranco Malafarina (eds), *L'opera completa di Annibale Carracci*, Milan, 1976

CORNS 1999
Thomas N. Corns (ed.), *The Royal Image: Representations of Charles I*, Cambridge, 1999

COSTAMAGNA 1994
Philippe Costamagna, *Pontormo: L'opera completa*, Milan, 1994

COX AND NORMAN 1930
Montagu H. Cox and Philip Norman (eds), *Survey of London*, vol. 13, part 2, *The Parish of St Margaret's, Westminster, Neighbourhood of Whitehall*, vol. 2, London, 1930

CRAWFORD LUBER 2005
Katherine Crawford Luber, *Albrecht Dürer and the Venetian Renaissance*, Cambridge, 2005

CROFT-MURRAY 1947
Edward Croft-Murray, 'The Landscape Background in Rubens's "St George and the Dragon"', *Burlington Magazine*, 89, 1947, pp. 89–91

CROFT-MURRAY AND HULTON 1960
Edward Croft-Murray and Paul Hulton, *Catalogue of British Drawings in the British Museum, XVI and XVII Centuries*, vol. 1, London, 1960

CROPPER AND PERICOLO FORTHCOMING
Elizabeth Cropper and Lorenzo Pericolo (eds), *Malvasia's Felsina pittrice: Lives of the Bolognese Painters. 9: Life of Guido Reni*, London and Turnhout, forthcoming

DALIVALLE 2011
Margaret Dalivalle, '"Borrowed Comlinesse": Copying from Pictures in Seventeenth-century England', PhD thesis, University of Oxford, 2011

DALLAS 2012
Javier Portús et al. (eds), *Diego Velázquez: The Early Court Portraits*, exh. cat., Meadows Museum, Dallas, 2012–13

DAVIES 1907
Randall Davies, 'An Inventory of the Duke of Buckingham's Pictures, etc., at York House in 1635', *Burlington Magazine*, 10, 1906–07, pp. 376–82

DAVIES 1968
Martin Davies, *National Gallery Catalogues: The Early Netherlandish School*, third edition, London, 1968

DE CASTRIS 2001
Pierluigi Leone de Castris, *Polidoro da Caravaggio: L'opera completa*, Naples, 2001

DE FRUTOS SASTRE 2009
Leticia M. de Frutos Sastre, *El Templo de la Fama: Alegoría del Marqués del Carpio*, Madrid, 2009

DE PAEPE 2010
Timothy de Paepe, 'Diego Duarte II: A Converso's Experience in Seventeenth-century Antwerp', *Jewish History*, 24, 2010, pp. 169–93

DE PILES 1699
Roger de Piles, *Abregé de la vie des peintres, avec des reflexions sur leurs ouvrages*, Paris, 1699

DENIS 2009
Isabelle Denis, 'Symboles et allegories dans les bordures de la tenture des "Actes des Apôtres" de Charles Ier d'Angleterre', in François Michaud-Fréjaville (ed.), *Tapisseries et Broderies: Relectures des mythes antiques et iconographie chrétienne*, *Art Sacré*, 27, 2009, pp. 15–27

DÍAZ PADRÓN 2012
Matías Díaz Padrón, *Van Dyck en España*, 2 vols, Madrid, 2012

DYKES 2016
D. W. Dykes, 'A Forgotten Jacobethan Coin Collector', *British Numismatic Journal*, 86, 2016, pp. 215–31

EDINBURGH 1978
Charles Avery and Anthony Radcliffe (eds), *Giambologna: Sculptor to the Medici*, exh. cat., Royal Scottish Museum, Edinburgh; Victoria and Albert Museum, London; Kunsthistorisches Museum, Vienna, 1978–79

EDINBURGH 1993
Jane Roberts (ed.), *Holbein and the Court of Henry VIII: Drawings and Miniatures from the Royal Library, Windsor Castle*, exh. cat., Scottish National Gallery, Edinburgh; Fitzwilliam Museum, Cambridge; National Portrait Gallery, London, 1993–94

EDINBURGH 2004A
Peter Humfrey et al. (eds), *The Age of Titian: Venetian Renaissance Art from Scottish Collections*, exh. cat., Royal Scottish Academy, Edinburgh, 2004

EDINBURGH 2004B
Christopher Lloyd (ed.), *Enchanting the Eye: Dutch Paintings of the Golden Age*, exh. cat., The Queen's Gallery, Palace of Holyroodhouse, Edinburgh; The Queen's Gallery, Buckingham Palace, London, 2004–05

EDINBURGH 2007
Desmond Shawe-Taylor and Jennifer Scott (eds), *Bruegel to Rubens: Masters of Flemish Painting*, exh. cat., The Queen's Gallery, Palace of Holyroodhouse, Edinburgh; Koninklijke Museum voor Schone Kunsten, Brussels; The Queen's Gallery, Buckingham Palace, London, 2007–09

EDINBURGH 2011
Kate Heard and Lucy Whitaker (eds), *The Northern Renaissance: Dürer to Holbein*, exh. cat., The Queen's Gallery, Palace of Holyroodhouse, Edinburgh; The Queen's Gallery, Buckingham Palace, London, 2011–13

EDMOND 1980
Mary Edmond, 'Limners and Picturemakers', *The Walpole Society*, 47, 1978–80, pp. 60–242

EDMOND 1983
Mary Edmond, *Hilliard and Oliver: The Lives and Works of Two Great Miniaturists*, London, 1983

EGERTON 1998
Judy Egerton, *National Gallery Catalogues: The British Paintings*, London, 1998

EIMER 2010
Christopher Eimer, *British Commemorative Medals and Their Values*, London, 2010

EISLER 1977
Colin Eisler, *Paintings from the Samuel H. Kress Collection: European Schools Excluding Italian*, Oxford, 1977

EKSERDJIAN 1997
David Ekserdjian, *Correggio*, New Haven and London, 1997

ELAM 2008
Caroline Elam, 'I Trionfi di Mantegna: Forma e vita', in Paris 2008A, pp. 367–75

EVELYN 2000
Peta Evelyn, 'The Equestrian Bronzes of Hubert Le Sueur', in Sabine Eiche (ed.), *Giambologna tra Firenze e l'Europa*, Florence, 2000, pp. 141–56

FÉLIBIEN 1725
André Félibien, *Entretiens sur les vies et sur les ouvrages des plus excellens peintres, anciens et modernes*, 6 vols, second edition, Paris, 1725

FERINO-PAGDEN AND BEYER 2005
Sylvia Ferino-Pagden and Andreas Beyer (eds), *Tizian versus Seisenegger: Die Portraits Karls V. mit Hund*, Turnhout, 2005

FERMOR 1996
Sharon Fermor, *The Raphael Tapestry Cartoons: Narrative, Decoration and Design*, London, 1996

FERMOR AND DERBYSHIRE 1998
Sharon Fermor and Alan Derbyshire, 'The Raphael Tapestry Cartoons Re-examined', *Burlington Magazine*, 140, 1998, pp. 236–50

FERRARA 1998
Peter Humfrey and Mauro Lucco (eds), *Dosso Dossi: Court Painter in Renaissance Ferrara*, exh. cat., Pinacoteca Nazionale, Ferrara; Metropolitan Museum of Art, New York; J. Paul Getty Museum, Los Angeles, 1998–99

FILIPCZAK 1987
Zirka Zaremba Filipczak, *Picturing Art in Antwerp, 1550–1700*, Princeton, NJ, 1987

FINALDI AND WOOD 2001
Gabriele Finaldi and Jeremy Wood, 'Orazio Gentileschi at the Court of Charles I', in Rome 2001, pp. 223–31

FINSTEN 1981
Jill Finsten, *Isaac Oliver: Art at the Courts of Elizabeth I and James I*, New York and London, 1981

FITTSCHEN 1982
Klaus Fittschen, *Die Bildnistypen der Faustina minor und die Fecunditas Augustae*, Göttingen, 1982

FLORENCE 1984
Miles L. Chappell (ed.), *Cristofano Allori: 1577–1621*, exh. cat., Palazzo Pitti, Florence, 1984

FOISTER 2004
Susan Foister, *Holbein and England*, New Haven and London, 2004

FOOT 1984
Mirjam M. Foot, 'Some Bindings for Charles I', in G. A. M. Janssens and F. G. A. M. Aarts (eds), *Studies in Seventeenth-century English Literature, History and Bibliography: Festschrift for Professor T. A. Birrell on the Occasion of His Sixtieth Birthday*, Amsterdam, 1984, pp. 95–106

FRANKFURT 2006
Rüdiger Klessmann (ed.), *Adam Elsheimer*, exh. cat., Städelsches Kunstinstitut, Frankfurt am Main; Scottish National Gallery, Edinburgh; Dulwich Picture Gallery, London, 2006

FRANKFURT 2013
Jochen Sander (ed.), *Albrecht Dürer: His Art in Context*, exh. cat., Städel Museum, Frankfurt am Main, 2013–14

FRASCHETTI 1900
Stanislao Fraschetti, *Il Bernini: La sua vita, la sua opera, il suo tempo*, Milan, 1900

FRICK 1968
Paintings in the Frick Collection: American, British, Dutch, Flemish and German, vol. 1, New York, 1968

FRIEDLÄNDER 1967–76
Max J. Friedländer, *Early Netherlandish Painting*, Heinz Norden (trans.), 14 vols, Leiden and Brussels, 1967–76

FRIEDLÄNDER AND ROSENBERG 1978
Max J. Friedländer and Jakob Rosenberg, *The Paintings of Lucas Cranach*, Secaucus, NJ, 1978

FRIEDMAN 1995
Alice T. Friedman, 'Constructing an Identity in Prose, Plaster and Paint: Lady Anne Clifford as Writer and Patron of the Arts', in Lucy Gent (ed.), *Albion's Classicism: The Visual Arts in Britain, 1550–1660*, New Haven and London, 1995, pp. 359–76

FULLER 1662
Thomas Fuller, *The History of the Worthies of England*, London, 1662

FURLOTTI 2000
Barbara Furlotti, *Le collezioni Gonzaga: Il carteggio tra Bologna, Parma, Piacenza e Mantova, 1563–1634*, Cinisello Balsamo, 2000

FURLOTTI AND MORSELLI 2003
Barbara Furlotti and Raffaella Morselli, *Le collezioni Gonzaga: Il carteggio tra Roma e Mantova, 1587–1612*, Cinisello Balsamo, 2003

GACHARD 1877
Louis Prosper Gachard, *Histoire politique et diplomatique de Pierre-Paul Rubens*, Brussels, 1877

GALLAGHER 2010
Michael Gallagher, 'Velázquez's "Philip IV" in the Metropolitan Museum', *Metropolitan Museum Journal*, 45, 2010, pp. 187–98

GARRARD 1989
Mary Garrard, *Artemisia Gentileschi: The Image of the Female Hero in Italian Baroque Art*, Princeton, NJ, 1989

GERBIER 1648
Balthasar Gerbier, *The Interpreter of the Academie for Forrain Languages and All Noble Sciences and Exercises*, London, 1648

GERSON 1968
Horst Gerson, *Rembrandt Paintings*, Amsterdam, 1968

GIBBONS 1968
Felton Gibbons, *Dosso and Battista Dossi: Court Painters at Ferrara*, Princeton, NJ, 1968

GOLDRING 2016
Elizabeth Goldring, 'Patronage and Art Collecting in Shakespeare's England', in R. Malcolm Smuts (ed.), *The Oxford Handbook of the Age of Shakespeare*, Oxford, 2016

GORDENKER 2001
Emilie E. S. Gordenker, *Anthony van Dyck and the Representation of Dress in Seventeenth-century Portraiture*, Turnhout, 2001

GORDON ET AL. 2015
Dillian Gordon et al., *The Wilton Diptych*, London, 2015

GOULD 1976
Cecil Gould, *The Paintings of Correggio*, London, 1976

GREEN 1857
Mary Anne Everett Green (ed.), *Letters of Queen Henrietta Maria, Including Her Private Correspondence with Charles the First ...*, London, 1857

GREENWICH 2004
Peter C. Sutton and Marjorie E. Wieseman (eds), *Drawn by the Brush: Oil Sketches by Peter Paul Rubens*, exh. cat., Bruce Museum of Arts and Science, Greenwich, CT; Berkeley Art Museum and Pacific Film Archive; Cincinnati Art Museum, 2004–05

GRIFFEY 2003
Erin Griffey, 'Multum in Parvo: Portraits of Jeffrey Hudson, Court Dwarf to Henrietta Maria', *British Art Journal*, 4, 2003, pp. 39–53

GRIFFEY 2008
Erin Griffey (ed.), *Henrietta Maria: Piety, Politics and Patronage*, Aldershot, 2008

GRIFFEY AND HIBBARD 2012
Erin Griffey and Caroline Hibbard, 'Henrietta Maria's Inventory at Colombes: Courtly Magnificence and Hidden Politics', *Journal of the History of Collections*, 24, 2012, pp. 159–81

GRIFFEY 2015
Erin Griffey, *On Display: Henrietta Maria and the Materials of Magnificence at the Stuart Court*, New Haven and London, 2015

GRISWOLD ET AL. 2014
John Griswold et al., 'Casts After the Antique by Hubert Le Sueur', in David Bourgarit et al. (eds), *French Bronze Sculpture: Materials and Techniques, Sixteenth to Eighteenth Centuries*, London, 2014, pp. 56–75

THE HAGUE 1988
Rieke van Leeuwen et al. (eds), *Paintings from England: William III and the Royal Collections*, exh. cat., Mauritshuis, The Hague, 1988–89

THE HAGUE 2003A
Stephanie Buck and Jochen Sander (eds), *Hans Holbein the Younger: Painter at the Court of Henry VIII*, exh. cat., Mauritshuis, The Hague, 2003

THE HAGUE 2003B
Ariane van Suchtelen et al. (eds), *Hans Holbein the Younger: Portraitist of the Renaissance*, exh. cat., Mauritshuis, The Hague, 2003

HAND 2004
John O. Hand, *Joos van Cleve: The Complete Paintings*, New Haven and London, 2004

HARRIS 1968
Enriqueta Harris, 'Velázquez and Charles I: Antique Busts and Modern Paintings from Spain for the Royal Collection', *Journal of the Warburg and Courtauld Institutes*, 30, 1967, pp. 414–20; reprinted in *Estudios completos sobre Velázquez*, Madrid, 2006, pp. 85–96

HARRIS 1982
Enriqueta Harris, *Velázquez*, Oxford, 1982

HART 2011
Vaughan Hart, *Inigo Jones: The Architect of Kings*, New Haven and London, 2011

HASKELL 1959
Francis Haskell, 'The Market for Italian Art in the Seventeenth Century', *Past & Present*, 15, 1959, pp. 48–59

HASKELL AND PENNY 1981
Francis Haskell and Nicholas Penny, *Taste and the Antique: The Lure of Classical Sculpture, 1500–1900*, New Haven, 1981

HASKELL 1989
Francis Haskell, 'Charles I's Collection of Pictures', in MacGregor 1989, pp. 203–31

HASKELL 2013
Francis Haskell, *The King's Pictures: The Formation and Dispersal of the Collections of Charles I and His Courtiers*, Karen Serres (ed.), New Haven and London, 2013

HAWKINS, FRANKS AND GRUEBER 1885
Edward Hawkins, Augustus W. Franks and Herbert A. Grueber, *Medallic Illustrations of the History of Great Britain and Ireland to the Death of George II*, London, 1885

HEARN 2005
Karen Hearn, *Nicholas Hilliard*, London, 2005

HEFFORD 1990A
Wendy Hefford, 'Prince Behind the Scenes: The Founding of the Mortlake Manufactory', *Country Life*, 4, 1990, p. 132

HEFFORD 1990B
Wendy Hefford, 'Cleyn's Noble Horses', *National Art Collections Fund Review*, 87, 1990, pp. 97–102

HEFFORD 1999
Wendy Hefford, 'The

Duke of Buckingham's Mortlake Tapestries of 1623', *Bulletin du Centre International d'Etudes des Textiles Anciens*, 76, 1999, pp. 90–103

HEFFORD 2006
Wendy Hefford, 'I "Mesi" di Mortlake, una serie di arazzi inglesi a Genova', in Piero Boccardo and Clario Di Fabio (eds), *Genova e l'Europa atlantica: Opere, artisti, committenti, collezionisti. Inghilterra, Fiandre, Portogallo*, Milan, 2006, pp. 167–81

HEFFORD 2007
Wendy Hefford, 'The Mortlake Manufactory, 1619–49', in New York 2007, pp. 171–201

HEINEN 2011
Ulrich Heinen, 'Rubens's Pictorial Peacekeeping Force: Negotiating Through "Visual Speech Acts"', in Udo J. Hebel and Christoph Wagner (eds), *Pictorial Cultures and Political Iconographies*, Berlin, 2011, pp. 33–62

HELD 1958
Julius S. Held, '"Le Roi à la Ciasse"', *The Art Bulletin*, 40, 1958, pp. 139–49

HELD 1976
Julius S. Held, 'Rubens's Sketch of Buckingham Rediscovered', *Burlington Magazine*, 118, 1976, pp. 547–51

HELD 1980
Julius S. Held, *The Oil Sketches of Peter Paul Rubens: A Critical Catalogue*, 2 vols, Princeton, NJ, 1980

HERVEY 1921
Mary F. S. Hervey, *The Life, Correspondence and Collections of Thomas Howard, Earl of Arundel*, Cambridge, 1921

HIBBARD 1983
Caroline M. Hibbard, *Charles I and the Popish Plot*, Chapel Hill, 1983

HIBBARD 1991
Caroline M. Hibbard, 'The Role of a Queen Consort: The Household and Court of Henrietta Maria, 1625–42', in Ronald G. Asch and Adolf M. Birke (eds), *Princes, Patronage and the Nobility: The Court at the Beginning of the Modern Age, c. 1450–1650*, London, Oxford and New York, 1991, pp. 393–414

HIBBARD 2008
Caroline M. Hibbard, '"By Our Direction and For Our Use": The Queen's Patronage of Artists and Artisans Seen Through Her Household Accounts', in Griffey 2008, pp. 115–37

HIBBARD 2009
Caroline M. Hibbard, 'The Somerset House Chapel and the Topography of London Catholicism', in Marcello Fantoni, George Gorse and R. Malcolm Smuts (eds), *The Politics of Space: European Courts, c. 1500–1750*, Rome, 2009, pp. 317–38

HIND 1952-64
Arthur M. Hind, *Engraving in England in the Sixteenth and Seventeenth Centuries*, 3 vols, Cambridge, 1952–64

HIRST 2011
Michael Hirst, *Michelangelo: The Achievement of Fame, 1475–1534*, New Haven and London, 2011

HOLLSTEIN ET AL. 1949-2010
Friedrich W. Hollstein et al., *Dutch and Flemish Etchings, Engravings and Woodcuts, 1450–1700*, 72 vols, Amsterdam, 1949–2010

HOOKHAM CARPENTER 1844
William Hookham Carpenter, *Pictorial Notices Consisting of a Memoir of Sir Anthony van Dyck with a Descriptive Catalogue of the Etchings Executed by Him ...*, London, 1844

HOPE 1992
Charles Hope, 'The Triumphs of Caesar', in London 1992, pp. 350–56

HOPE 2005
Charles Hope, 'Titian and Some Portraits of Charles V', in Ferino-Pagden and Beyer 2005, pp. 89–97

HOPE 2006
Charles Hope, 'I Trionfi di Cesare di Andrea Mantegna', in Rodolfo Signorini (ed.), *A casa di Andrea Mantegna: Cultura artistica a Mantova nel Quattrocentro*, Cinisello Balsamo, 2006, pp. 287–97

HOUSTON 1987
Jane Roberts (ed.), *Drawings by Holbein from the Court of Henry VIII: 50 Drawings from the Collection of Her Majesty Queen Elizabeth II, Windsor Castle*, exh. cat., Museum of Fine Arts, Houston, 1987

HOWARD 2012
Peter Howard, *Creating Magnificence in Renaissance Florence*, Toronto, 2012

HOWARTH 1985
David Howarth, *Lord Arundel and His Circle*, New Haven and London, 1985

HOWARTH 1989
David Howarth, 'Charles I, Sculpture and Sculptors', in MacGregor 1989, pp. 73–113

HOWARTH 1994
David Howarth, 'William Trumbull and Art Collecting in Jacobean England', *British Library Journal*, 20, 1994, pp. 140–62

HOWARTH 1997
David Howarth, *Images of Rule: Art and Politics in the English Renaissance, 1485–1659*, London, 1997

HOWARTH 1998
David Howarth, 'Bernini and Britain', in Aidan Weston-Lewis (ed.), *Effigies and Ecstasies: Roman Baroque Sculpture and Design in the Age of Bernini*, exh. cat., National Gallery of Scotland, Edinburgh, 1998, pp. 29–36

HOWARTH 2002
David Howarth, 'The Arundel Collection: Collecting and Patronage in England in the Reigns of Philip III and Philip IV', in Madrid 2002, pp. 69–86

HOWARTH 2011
David Howarth, 'The Southampton Album: A Newly Discovered Collection of Drawings by Francis Cleyn the Elder and His Associates', *Master Drawings*, 49, 2011, pp. 435–78

HOWELL 1650
James Howell, *Instructions for Forreine Travel*, second edition, London, 1650

HUEMER 1977
Frances Huemer, *Corpus Rubenianum Ludwig Buchard: XIX (1). Portraits Painted in Foreign Countries*, London and Turnhout, 1977

HÜLSEN 1921
Christian Hülsen, *Das Speculum Romanae Magnifientiae des Antonio Lafreri*, Munich, 1921

HUTCHINSON 1973
Lucy Hutchinson, *Memoirs of the Life of Colonel Hutchinson*, J. Sutherland (ed.), London, 1973

HYMANS 1972
Henri Hymans, *Lucas Vorsterman et son œuvre gravé: Catalogue raisonné de l'œuvre de Lucas Emile Vorsterman*, G. W. Hissink (ed.), Brussels, 1972

JAFFÉ 2001
David Jaffé, 'New Thoughts on Van Dyck's Italian Sketchbook', *Burlington Magazine*, 143, 2001, pp. 614–24

JAFFÉ 2002
Michael Jaffé, *The Devonshire Collection of Northern European Drawings*, vol. 1, Turin, 2002

JERVIS 1997
Simon Jervis, 'Furniture for the First Duke of Buckingham', *Furniture History*, 33, 1997, pp. 48–74

JOHNS 1988
Christopher M. S. Johns, 'Politics, Nationalism and Friendship in Van Dyck's "Le Roi à la ciasse"', *Zeitschrift für Kunstgeschichte*, 51, pp. 243–61

JOHNSON 1997
Anthony W. Johnson (ed.), *Three Volumes Annotated by Inigo Jones: Vasari's Lives (1568), Plutarch's Moralia (1614), Plato's Republic (1554)*, Turku, 1997

JONSON 1892
Ben Jonson, *Timber or Discoveries Made upon Men and Matter*, Felix Schelling (ed.), Boston, 1892

JUDSON AND EKKART 1999
J. Richard Judson and Rudolf E. O. Ekkart, *Gerrit van Honthorst*, Doornspijk, 1999

JUNIUS 1638
Franciscus Junius, *The Painting of the Ancients*, London, 1638; reprinted in Keith Aldrich, Philipp Fehl and Raina Fehl (eds), *The Literature of Classical Art*, Berkeley, CA, 1991

KATHMAN 2004
David Kathman, 'Grocers, Goldsmiths and Drapers: Freemen and Apprentices in the Elizabethan Theatre', *Shakespeare Quarterly*, 55, 2004, pp. 1–49

KETTERING 1988
Alison McNeil Kettering, *Drawings from the Ter Borch Studio Estate*, 2 vols, The Hague, 1988

KLINGER AND HÖTTLER 1998
D. M. Klinger and Antje Höttler, *Die Malerbrüder Ambrosius und Hans d. J. Holbein: Werkverzeichnis, Gemälde und Miniaturen*, Nuremberg, 1998

KRISTELLER 1901
Paul Kristeller, *Andrea Mantegna*, Berlin and Leipzig, 1901

LAPENTA AND MORSELLI 2006
Stefania Lapenta and Raffaella Morselli, *Le collezioni Gonzaga: La quadreria nell'elenco dei beni del 1626–27*, Milan, 2006

LARSEN 1988
Erik Larsen, *The Paintings of Anthony van Dyck*, 2 vols, Freren, 1988

LAURAIN-PORTEMER 1975
Madeleine Laurain-Portemer, 'Mazarin, militant de l'art baroque au temps de Richelieu (1634–42)', *Bulletin de la Société de l'Histoire de l'Art Français*, 1975, pp. 65–100

LENS 2013
Blaise Ducos (ed.), *L'Europe de Rubens*, exh. cat., Musée du Louvre, Lens, 2013

LEUVEN 2016
Jan van der Stock (ed.), *In Search of Utopia: Art and Science in the Era of Thomas More*, exh. cat., M-Museum Leuven, 2016–17

LEVEY 1991
Michael Levey, *The Later Italian Pictures in the Collection of Her Majesty The Queen*, second edition, Cambridge, 1991

LIGHTBOWN 1969
Ronald Lightbown, 'Van Dyck and the Purchase of Paintings for the English Court', *Burlington Magazine*, 111, 1969, pp. 418–21

LIGHTBOWN 1981
Ronald Lightbown, 'Bernini's Busts of English Patrons', in Moshe Barasch, Lucy Freeman Sandler and Patrician Egan (eds), *Art, the Ape of Nature: Studies in Honor of H. W. Janson*, New York, 1981, pp. 439–76

LIGHTBOWN 1986
Ronald Lightbown, *Mantegna*, Oxford, 1986

LIGHTBOWN 1989
Ronald Lightbown, 'Charles I and the Tradition of European Princely Collecting', in MacGregor 1989, pp. 53–72

LONDON 1964
A. G. H. Bachrach et al. (eds), *The Orange and the Rose: Holland and Britain in the Age of Observation, 1600–1750*, exh. cat., Victoria and Albert Museum, London, 1964

LONDON 1968
Oliver Millar (ed.), *Van Dyck, Wenceslaus Hollar and Miniature-painters at the Court of the Early Stuarts*, exh. cat., The Queen's Gallery, Buckingham Palace, London, 1968

LONDON 1972
Oliver Millar (ed.), *The Age of Charles I: Painting in England, 1620–49*, exh. cat., Tate Gallery, London, 1972

LONDON 1975
The Rival of Nature: Renaissance Painting in Its Context, exh. cat., National Gallery, London, 1975

LONDON 1977
'The King's Good Servant': Sir Thomas More, exh. cat., National Portrait Gallery, London, 1977–78

LONDON 1978
Holbein and the Court of Henry VIII, exh. cat., The Queen's Gallery, Buckingham Palace, London, 1978–79

LONDON 1981
David S. Chambers and Jane Martineau (eds), *Splendours of the Gonzaga*, exh. cat., Victoria and Albert Museum, London, 1981

LONDON 1982
Oliver Millar (ed.), *Van Dyck in England*, exh. cat., National Portrait Gallery, London, 1982–83

LONDON 1983A
Malcolm Rogers (ed.), *William Dobson*, exh. cat., National Portrait Gallery, London, 1983

LONDON 1983B
Roy Strong (ed.), *Artists of the Tudor Court: The Portrait Miniature Rediscovered, 1520–1620*, exh. cat., Victoria and Albert Museum, London, 1983

LONDON 1987
Malcolm Warner (ed.), *The Image of London: Views by Travellers and Emigrés, 1550–1920*, exh. cat., Barbican Art Gallery, London, 1987

LONDON 1988
Treasures from the Royal Collection, exh. cat., The Queen's Gallery, Buckingham Palace, London, 1988–89

LONDON 1991
Christopher Lloyd (ed.), *The Queen's Pictures: Royal Collectors Through the Centuries*, exh. cat., National Gallery, London, 1991–92

LONDON 1992
Jane Martineau, Suzanne Boorsch et al. (eds), *Andrea Mantegna*, exh. cat., Royal Academy of Arts, London; Metropolitan Museum of Art, New York, 1992

LONDON 1993
Dillian Gordon (ed.), *Making and Meaning: The Wilton Diptych*, exh. cat., National Gallery, London, 1993

LONDON 1997
Christopher Lloyd and Vanessa Remington (eds), *Masterpieces in Little: Portrait Miniatures from the Collection of Her Majesty Queen Elizabeth II*, exh. cat., The Queen's Gallery, Buckingham Palace, London, 1997

LONDON 1998
Antony Griffiths (ed.), *The Print in Stuart Britain, 1603–89*, exh. cat., British Museum, London, 1998

LONDON 1999A
Gabriele Finaldi (ed.), *Orazio Gentileschi at the Court of Charles I*, exh. cat., National Gallery, London; Museo de Bellas Artes, Bilbao; Museo Nacional del Prado, Madrid, 1999

LONDON 1999B
Jane Roberts and Jonathan Marsden (eds), *The King's Head: Charles I, King and Martyr*, exh. cat., The Queen's Gallery, Buckingham Palace, London, 1999

LONDON 2000
Kim Sloan (ed.), *A Noble Art: Amateur Artists and Drawing Masters, c. 1600–1800*, exh. cat., British Museum, London, 2000

LONDON 2002
Jane Roberts (ed.), *Royal Treasures: A Golden Jubilee Celebration*, exh. cat., The Queen's Gallery, Buckingham Palace, London, 2002

LONDON 2004
Jane Roberts and Christopher Lloyd (eds), *George III and Queen Charlotte: Patronage, Collecting and Court Taste*, exh. cat., The Queen's Gallery, Buckingham Palace, London, 2004

LONDON 2005
Anthony Bond and Joanna Woodall (eds), *Self-portrait: Renaissance to Contemporary*, exh. cat., National Portrait Gallery, London; Art Gallery of New South Wales, Sydney, 2005–06

LONDON 2006
Susan Foister (ed.), *Holbein in England*, exh. cat., Tate Britain, London, 2006–07

LONDON 2007A
Martin Clayton and Lucy Whitaker (eds), *The Art of Italy in the Royal Collection: Renaissance and Baroque*, exh. cat., The Queen's Gallery, Buckingham Palace, London, 2007–08

LONDON 2007B
Rudolf Ekkart and Quentin Buvelot (eds), *Dutch Portraits: The Age of Rembrandt and Frans Hals*, exh. cat., National Gallery, London; Mauritshuis, The Hague, 2007–08

LONDON 2008
Lorne Campbell et al. (eds), *Renaissance Faces: Van Eyck to Titian*, exh. cat., National Gallery, London, 2008–09

LONDON 2009
Karen Hearn (ed.), *Van Dyck and Britain*, exh. cat., Tate Britain, London, 2009

LONDON 2010
Mark Evans, Clare Browne and Arnold Nesselrath (eds), *Raphael: Cartoons and Tapestries for the Sistine Chapel*, exh. cat., Victoria and Albert Museum, London, 2010

LONDON 2012
Catherine MacLeod et al. (eds), *The Lost Prince: The Life and Death of Henry Stuart*, exh. cat., National Portrait Gallery, London, 2012–13

LONDON 2013
Anna Reynolds (ed.), *In Fine Style: The Art of Tudor and Stuart Fashion*, exh. cat., The Queen's Gallery, Buckingham Palace, London, 2013

LONDON 2014
Xavier F. Salomon (ed.), *Veronese: Magnificence in Renaissance Venice*, exh. cat., National Gallery, London, 2014

LONDON 2015
Ian Jenkins (ed.), *Defining Beauty: The Body in Ancient Greek Art*, exh. cat., The British Museum, London, 2015

LONDON 2016A
Simone Facchinetti and Arturo Galansino (eds), *In the Age of Giorgione*, exh. cat., Royal Academy of Arts, London, 2016

LONDON 2016B
Martin Clayton, Lucy Peter and Anna Reynolds (eds), *Portrait of the Artist*, exh. cat., The Queen's Gallery, Buckingham Palace, London, 2016–17

LONDON 2016C
Karen Serres (ed.), *Bruegel in Black and White: Three Grisailles Reunited*, exh. cat., Courtauld Gallery, London, 2016

LONDON 2017
Tarnya Cooper (ed.), *The Encounter: Drawings from Leonardo to Rembrandt*, exh. cat., National Portrait Gallery, London, 2017

LOOMIE 1987
Albert J. Loomie (ed.), *Ceremonies of Charles I: The Note Books of John Finet, 1628–41*, New York, 1987

LOOMIE 1989
Albert J. Loomie, 'New Light on the Spanish Ambassador's Purchases from Charles I's Collection, 1649–53', *Journal of the Warburg and Courtauld Institutes*, 52, 1989, pp. 257–67

LÓPEZ-REY 1996
José López-Rey, *Velázquez*, 2 vols, Cologne, 1996; first published 1979

LOS ANGELES 2008
Andrea Bacchi, Catherine Hess and Jennifer Montagu (eds), *Bernini and the Birth of Baroque Portrait Sculpture*, exh. cat., J. Paul Getty Museum, Los Angeles; National Gallery of Canada, Ottowa, 2008–09

LUNN 1972
Dom Maurus Lunn, 'Van Dyck and the Purchase of Paintings', *Burlington Magazine*, 114, 1972, p. 334

LUZIO 1913
Alessandro Luzio, *La Galleria dei Gonzaga venduta all'Inghilterra nel 1627–28*, Milan, 1913

MCEVANSONEYA 2003
Philip McEvansoneya, 'Italian Paintings in the Buckingham Collection', in Chaney 2003, pp. 315–36

MACGREGOR 1989
Arthur MacGregor (ed.), *The Late King's Goods: Collections, Possessions and Patronage of Charles I in the Light of the Commonwealth Sale Inventories*, London and Oxford, 1989

MACGREGOR 1996
Arthur MacGregor, 'King Charles I: A Renaissance Collector?', *Seventeenth Century*, 11, 1996, pp. 141–60

MCGRATH FORTHCOMING
Elizabeth McGrath, 'Diplomacy and Political Engagement in Rubens's Allegories of War and Peace', in Francesco Solinas (ed.), *Les arts de la paix dans une Europe en guerre, 1450–1945*, forthcoming

MCKILLOP 1974
Susan Regan McKillop, *Franciabigio*, Berkeley, CA, 1974

MACLEOD 2014
Catherine MacLeod, *Van Dyck: The Last Self-portrait*, London, 2014

MADOCKS 1984
Susan Madocks, '"Trop de beautez découvertes": New Light on Guido Reni's Late "Bacchus and Ariadne"', *Burlington Magazine*, 126, 1984, pp. 544–47

MADOCKS LISTER 2000
Susan Madocks Lister, '"Trumperies Brought from Rome": Barberini Gifts to the Stuart Court in 1635', in Elizabeth Cropper (ed.), *The Diplomacy of Art: Artistic Creation and Politics in Seicento Italy*, Milan, 2000, pp. 151–76

MADRID 1999
Jonathan Brown (ed.), *Velázquez, Rubens y Van Dyck. Pintores cortesanos del siglo XVII*, exh. cat., Museo Nacional del Prado, Madrid, 1999

MADRID 2002
Jonathan Brown and John H. Elliott (eds), *The Sale of the Century: Artistic Relations Between Spain and Great Britain, 1604–55*, exh. cat., Museo Nacional del Prado, Madrid, 2002

MADRID 2003
Miguel Falomir Faus (ed.), *Tiziano*, exh. cat., Museo Nacional del Prado, Madrid, 2003

MADRID 2005
William B. Jordan (ed.), *Juan van der Hamen y León and the Court of Madrid*, exh. cat., Palacio Real, Madrid; Meadows Museum, Dallas, 2005–06

MADRID 2008
Miguel Falomir Faus (ed.), *El retrato del Renacimiento*, exh. cat., Museo Nacional del Prado, Madrid, 2008

MADRID 2012
Tom Henry and Paul Joannides (eds), *Late Raphael*, exh. cat., Museo Nacional del Prado, Madrid; Musée du Louvre, Paris, 2012–13

MAGURN 1955
Ruth Saunders Magurn (ed.), *The Letters of Peter Paul Rubens*, Cambridge, MA, 1955

MAHON 1971
Denis Mahon, *Studies in Seicento Art and Theory*, Westport, 1971

MALIBU 1995
David Jaffé and Denise Allen (eds), *The Earl and Countess of Arundel: Renaissance Collectors*, exh. cat., J. Paul Getty Museum, Malibu, 1995

MANCINI 1998
Matteo Mancini, *Tiziano e le corti d'Asburgo nei documenti degli archivi spagnoli*, Venice, 1998

MANN 2005
Judith W. Mann, 'The Myth of Artemisia as Chameleon: A New Look at the "London Allegory of Painting"', in Judith W. Mann (ed.), *Artemisia Gentileschi: Taking Stock*, Turnhout, 2005, pp. 51–77

MANTUA 1989
Ernst Gombrich et al. (eds), *Giulio Romano*, exh. cat., Palazzo Te and Palazzo Ducale, Mantua, 1989

MANTUA 2002
Raffaella Morselli (ed.), *Gonzaga: La celeste galeria*, exh. cat., 2 vols, Palazzo Te and Palazzo Ducale, Mantua, 2002

MARABOTTINI 1969
Alessandro Marabottini, *Polidoro da Caravaggio*, 2 vols, Rome, 1969

MARSDEN 1999
Jonathan Marsden, 'Portrait Busts', in London 1999B, pp. 36–41

MARTIN 1970
Gregory Martin, *National Gallery Catalogues: The Flemish School, c. 1600–c. 1900*, London, 1970

MARTIN 2005
Gregory Martin, *Corpus Rubenianum Ludwig Burchard: XV. The Ceiling Decoration of the Banqueting Hall*, 2 vols, London and Turnhout, 2005

MARTIN 2011
Gregory Martin, *Rubens in London: Art and Diplomacy*, London and Turnhout, 2011

MARTINDALE 1979
Andrew Martindale, *The 'Triumphs of Caesar' by Andrea Mantegna in the Collection of Her Majesty The Queen at Hampton Court*, London, 1979

MASON RINALDI 1984
Stefania Mason Rinaldi, *Palma il Giovane: L'opera completa*, Milan, 1984

MEIJ 2001
A. F. Meij (ed.), *Rubens, Jordaens, Van Dyck and Their Circle: Flemish Master Drawings from the Museum Boijmans Van Beuningen*, Rotterdam, 2001

MERLE DU BOURG 2004
Alexis Merle du Bourg, *Rubens au Grand Siècle: Sa réception en France, 1640–1715*, Rennes, 2004

MEYER ZUR CAPELLEN 2001–09
Jürg Meyer zur Capellen, *Raphael: The Paintings*, 3 vols, Landshut, 2001–09

MILLAR 1954
Oliver Millar, 'Charles I, Honthorst, and Van Dyck', *Burlington Magazine*, 96, 1954, pp. 36–42

MILLAR 1956
Oliver Millar, 'The Whitehall Ceiling', *Burlington Magazine*, 98, 1956, pp. 258–66

MILLAR 1960
Oliver Millar (ed.), *Abraham van der Doort's Catalogue of the Collections of Charles I, The Walpole Society*, 37, Glasgow, 1960

MILLAR 1963
Oliver Millar (ed.), *The Tudor, Stuart and Early Georgian Pictures in the Collection of Her Majesty The Queen*, 2 vols, London, 1963

MILLAR 1972
Oliver Millar (ed.), *The Inventories and Valuations of the King's Goods, 1649–51, The Walpole Society*, 43, Glasgow, 1972

MILLAR 1977
Oliver Millar, *The Queen's Pictures*, New York, 1977

MOFFITT 1983
John F. Moffitt, '"Le Roi a la ciasse"? Kings, Christian Knights and Van Dyck's Singular "Dismounted Equestrian Portrait" of Charles I', *Artibus et Historiae*, 7, 1983, pp. 19–99

MONTANARI 2004
Tomaso Montanari, 'Francesco Barberini, l'"Arianna" di Guido Reni e altri doni per la corona d'Inghilterra: L'ultimo atto', in Maria Grazia Bernardini (ed.), *Studi sul Barocco romano: Scritti in onore di Maurizio Fagiolo dell'Arco*, Milan, 2004, pp. 77–88

MORSELLI 2000
Raffaella Morselli, *Le collezioni Gonzaga: L'elenco dei beni del 1626–27*, Cinisello Balsamo, 2000

MULHERRON AND WYLD 2011
Jamie Mulherron and

Helen Wyld, 'Mortlake's Big Swim', *Apollo: National Trust Historic Houses and Collections Annual*, 175, 2011, pp. 20–29

MULHERRON 2012
Jamie Mulherron, 'A Mortlake Tapestry after Titian: The Importance of "The Supper at Emmaus" at Hardwick', *National Trust Arts, Buildings and Collections Bulletin*, 2012, pp. 11–12

MULHERRON AND WYLD 2012
Jamie Mulherron and Helen Wyld, 'Mortlake's Banquet of the Senses', *Apollo*, 2012, pp. 122–28

MULLER 1989
Jeffrey M. Muller, *Rubens: The Artist as Collector*, Princeton, NJ, 1989

MURDOCH ET AL. 1981
John Murdoch et al., *The English Miniature*, New Haven and London, 1981

MYSON 1955
William Myson, 'Notes on British Painting from Archives: II', *Burlington Magazine*, 97, 1955, p. 120

NEW HAVEN 1994
Richard T. Godfrey (ed.), *Wenceslaus Hollar: A Bohemian Artist in England*, exh. cat., Yale Center for British Art, New Haven, 1994

NEW YORK 1991
Christopher Brown (ed.), *The Drawings of Anthony van Dyck*, exh. cat., Pierpont Morgan Library, New York; Kimbell Art Museum, Fort Worth, Texas, 1991

NEW YORK 1995
Hubert von Sonnenburg et al. (eds), *Rembrandt/Not Rembrandt in the Metropolitan Museum of Art: Aspects of Connoisseurship*, 2 vols, exh. cat., Metropolitan Museum of Art, New York, 1995–96

NEW YORK 2002
Thomas P. Campbell (ed.), *Tapestry in the Renaissance: Art and Magnificence*, exh. cat., Metropolitan Museum of Art, New York, 2002

NEW YORK 2004
Manfred Leithe-Jasper and Patricia Wengraf (eds), *European Bronzes from the Quentin Collection*, exh. cat., The Frick Collection, New York, 2004–05

NEW YORK 2005
Anne-Marie Logan and Michiel C. Plomp (eds), *Peter Paul Rubens: The Drawings*, exh. cat., Metropolitan Museum of Art, New York, 2005

NEW YORK 2007
Thomas P. Campbell (ed.), *Tapestry in the Baroque: Threads of Splendor*, exh. cat., Metropolitan Museum of Art, New York; Museo Nacional del Prado, Madrid, 2007–08

NEW YORK 2010
Maryan W. Ainsworth (ed.), *Man, Myth and Sensual Pleasures: Jan Gossaert's Renaissance*, exh. cat., Metropolitan Museum of Art, New York; National Gallery, London, 2010–11

NEW YORK 2016
Stijn Alsteens and Adam Eaker (eds), *Van Dyck: The Anatomy of Portraiture*, exh. cat., The Frick Collection, New York, 2016

NICOLSON 1990
Benedict Nicolson, *Caravaggism in Europe*, 3 vols, Turin, 1990; first published 1979

NORMAN AND EAVES 2016
A. V. B. Norman and Ian Eaves, *Arms and Armour in the Collection of Her Majesty The Queen*, London, 2016

NOVIKOVA 2003
Anastasia Novikova, 'Virtuosity and Declensions of Virtue: Thomas Arundel and Aletheia Talbot Seen by Virtue of a Portrait Pair by Daniel Mytens and a Treatise by Franciscus Junius', *Nederlands Kunsthistorisch Jaarboek*, 54, 2003, pp. 309–33

OPPÉ 1950
A. P. Oppé, *English Drawings: Stuart and Georgian Periods in the Collection of His Majesty The King at Windsor Castle*, London, 1950

ORGEL AND STRONG 1973
Stephen Orgel and Roy Strong, *Inigo Jones: The Theatre of the Stuart Court*, 2 vols, London, 1973

ORSO 1993
Steven N. Orso, *Velázquez, Los Borrachos and Painting at the Court of Philip IV*, Cambridge, 1993

OSBORNE 2007
Toby Osborne, 'Van Dyck, Alessandro Scaglia and the Caroline Court: Friendship, Collecting and Diplomacy in the Early Seventeenth Century', *The Seventeenth Century*, 22, 2007, pp. 24–41

PÄCHT 1989
Otto Pächt, *Van Eyck: Die Begründer der altniederländischen Malerei*, Munich, 1989

PALLUCCHINI AND ROSSI 1974–82
Rodolfo Pallucchini and Paola Rossi (eds), *Jacopo Tintoretto: L'opera completa*, 3 vols, Milan, 1974–82

PALME 1957
Per Palme, *Triumph of Peace: A Study of the Whitehall Banqueting House*, London, 1957

PANZANI 1793
Gregorio Panzani, *The Memoirs of Gregorio Panzani, Giving an Account of His Agency in England in the Years 1634–36*, Joseph Berington (ed.), Birmingham, 1793

PARIS 1983
Sylvie Béguin, Françoise Viatte and André Chastel (eds), *Raphael dans les Collections Françaises*, exh. cat., Grand Palais, Paris, 1983–84

PARIS 1993
Gilles Fage (ed.), *Le Siècle de Titien: L'âge d'or de la peinture à Venise*, exh. cat., Grand Palais, Paris, 1993

PARIS 2008A
Giovanni Agosti and Dominique Thiébaut (eds), *Mantegna*, exh. cat., Musée du Louvre, Paris, 2008–09

PARIS 2008B
Alexis Merle du Bourg (ed.), *Antoon van Dyck: Portraits*, exh. cat., Musée Jacquemart-André, Paris, 2008–09

PARKER 1983
Karl T. Parker, *The Drawings of Hans Holbein in the Collection of Her Majesty The Queen*, Susan Foister (ed.), London and New York, 1983

PARMA 2008
Lucia Fornari Schianchi (ed.), *Correggio*, exh. cat., Galleria Nazionale, Camera di San Paolo, Cattedrale, San Giovanni Evangelista, Parma, 2008–09

PARRY 1981
Graham Parry, *The Golden Age Restor'd: The Culture of the Stuart Court, 1603–42*, Manchester, 1981

PASSERI 1934
Giovanni Battista Passeri, *Die Künstlerbiographien von Giovanni Battista Passeri*, Jacob Hess (ed.), Leipzig, 1934; first published as *Vite de' pittori, scultori ed architetti che hanno lavorato in Roma morti dal 1641 al 1673*, 1772

PATTERSON 1997
William B. Patterson, *King James VI and I and the Reunion of Christendom*, Cambridge, 1997

PEACOCK 1999
John Peacock, 'The Visual Image of Charles I', in Corns 1999, pp. 176–239

PEACOCK 2006A
John Peacock, 'The Image of Charles I as a Roman Emperor', in Ian Atherton and Julie Sanders (eds), *The 1630s: Interdisciplinary Essays on Culture and Politics in the Caroline Era*, Manchester and New York, 2006, pp. 50–73

PEACOCK 2006B
John Peacock, *The Look of Van Dyck: The Self-portrait with a Sunflower and the Vision of the Painter*, Aldershot, 2006

PECK 2005
Linda Levy Peck, *Consuming Splendour: Society and Culture in Seventeenth-century England*, Cambridge, 2005

PENNINGTON 2002
Richard Pennington, *A Descriptive Catalogue of the Etched Work of Wenceslaus Hollar*, Cambridge, 2002; first published 1982

PEPPER 1984
D. Stephen Pepper, *Guido Reni: A Complete Catalogue of His Works with an Introductory Text*, Oxford, 1984

PHILADELPHIA 2004
Carl Brandon Strehlke and Elizabeth Cropper (eds), *Pontormo, Bronzino, and the Medici: The Transformation of the Renaissance Portrait in Florence*, exh. cat., Philadelphia Museum of Art, 2004–05

PHILIP 1957
I. G. Philip, 'Balthasar Gerbier and the Duke of Buckingham's Pictures', *Burlington Magazine*, 99, 1957, pp. 155–56

PIACENTI AND BOARDMAN 2008
Kirsten Aschengreen Piacenti and John Boardman, *Ancient and Modern Gems and Jewels in the Collection of Her Majesty The Queen*, London, 2008

PIPER 1968
David Piper, *Van Dyck*, Milan, 1968

PITACCO 2007
Francesca Pitacco, 'Dal secolo d'oro ai secoli d'oro: I collezionisti stranieri e i loro agenti', in Linda Borean and Stefania Mason (eds), *Il collezionismo d'arte a Venezia: Il Seicento*, Venice, 2007, pp. 103–23

POPE-HENNESSY 1953
John Pope-Hennessy, 'Some Bronze Statuettes by Francesco Fanelli', *Burlington Magazine*, 95, 1953, pp. 156–62; reprinted in Pope-Hennessy 1968, pp. 172–98

POPE-HENNESSY 1968
John Pope-Hennessy, *Essays on Italian Sculpture*, London, 1968

POSNER 1971
Donald Posner, *Annibale Carracci: A Study in the Reform of Italian Painting around 1590*, 2 vols, London, 1971

PRYNNE 1645
William Prynne, *Hidden Works of Darkenes Brought to Publike Light ...*, London, 1645

PUGET DE LA SERRE 1639
Jean Puget de la Serre, *Histoire de l'entrée de la Reine Mère du Roy Très-Chrestien dans la Grande Bretagne*, London, 1639; reprinted, London, 1775

RAATSCHEN 1996
Gudrun Raatschen, 'Plaster Casts of Bernini's Bust of Charles I', *Burlington Magazine*, 138, 1996, pp. 813–16

RAATSCHEN 2001
Gudrun Raatschen, 'Van Dyck's Charles I on Horseback with M. de St Antoine', in Vlieghe 2001, pp. 139–50

RADCLIFFE AND THORNTON 1978
Anthony Radcliffe and Peter Thornton, 'John Evelyn's Cabinet', *Connoisseur*, 197, 1978, pp. 254–62

RADCLIFFE AND PENNY 2004
Anthony Radcliffe and Nicholas Penny, *Art of the Renaissance Bronze, 1500–1650: The Robert H. Smith Collection*, London, 2004

RAUSA 2002
Federico Rausa, 'Li disegni delle statue et busti sono rotolate drento le stampe. L'arredo di sculture antiche delle residenze dei Gonzaga nei disegni seicenteschi della Royal Library a Windsor Castle', in Mantua 2002, vol. 2, pp. 67–91

REBECCHINI 1995
Guido Rebecchini, 'Tiziano e Mantova: "La Cena in Emmaus" per Nicola Maffei', *Venezia Cinquecento*, 10, 1995, pp. 41–68

REBECCHINI 2002
Guido Rebecchini, *Private Collectors in Mantua, 1500–1630*, Rome, 2002

REYNOLDS 1769
Joshua Reynolds, *A Discourse Delivered at the Opening of the Royal Academy*, London, 1769

REYNOLDS 1954
Graham Reynolds, 'Portraits by Nicholas Hilliard and His Assistants of King James I and His Family', *The Walpole Society*, 34, 1952–54, pp. 14–26

REYNOLDS 1999
Graham Reynolds, *The Sixteenth- and Seventeenth-century Miniatures in the Collection of Her Majesty The Queen*, London, 1999

ROBERTS 1989
Jane Roberts, 'The Limnings, Drawings and Prints in Charles I's Collection', in MacGregor 1989, pp. 115–29

ROBERTSON 2008
Clare Robertson, *The Invention of Annibale Carracci*, Milan, 2008

ROME 2001
Keith Christiansen and Judith W. Mann (eds), *Orazio and Artemisia Gentileschi*, exh. cat., Museo del Palazzo di Venezia, Rome; Metropolitan Museum of Art, New York; Saint Louis Art Museum, 2001–02

ROME 2002
Sergio Guarino (ed.), *L'Arianna di Guido Reni*, exh. cat., Musei Capitolini, Rome; Pinacoteca Nazionale, Bologna, 2002–03

ROME 2007
Kristina Herrmann Fiore (ed.), *Dürer e l'Italia*, exh. cat., Scuderie del Quirinale, Rome, 2007

ROME 2008
Anna Coliva (ed.), *Correggio e l'antico*, exh. cat., Galleria Borghese, Rome, 2008

ROME 2016A
Francesca Baldassari (ed.), *Artemisia Gentileschi e il suo tempo*, exh. cat., Palazzo Braschi, Museo di Roma, Rome, 2016–17

ROME 2016B
David Ekserdjian (ed.),

Correggio and Parmigianino: Art in Parma During the Sixteenth Century, exh. cat., Scuderie del Quirinale, Rome, 2016

ROOSES AND RUELENS 1886–1909
Max Rooses and Charles Ruelens (eds), *Correspondance de Rubens et documents épistolaires concernant sa vie et ses œuvres*, 5 vols, Antwerp, 1886–1909

ROSAND 1971
David Rosand, 'Titian in the Frari', *The Art Bulletin*, 53, 1971, pp. 196–213

ROWELL 1996
Christopher Rowell, 'A Seventeenth-century "Cabinet" Restored: The Green Closet at Ham House', *Apollo*, 143, 1996, pp. 18–23

ROWELL 2013
Christopher Rowell (ed.), *Ham House: 400 Years of Collecting and Patronage*, New Haven and London, 2013

ROWLANDS 1985
John Rowlands, *Holbein: The Paintings of Hans Holbein the Younger*, London, 1985

ROY 1999
Ashok Roy, 'Rubens's Peace and War', *National Gallery Technical Bulletin*, 20, 1999, pp. 89–95

RUBIN 1995
Patricia Rubin, *Giorgio Vasari: Art and History*, New Haven and London, 1995

SAINSBURY 1859
William N. Sainsbury (ed.), *Original Unpublished Papers Illustrative of the Life of Sir Peter Paul Rubens as an Artist and a Diplomatist ...*, London, 1859

SALVINI AND GROHN 1971
Roberto Salvini and Hans Werner Grohn, *L'opera pittorica completa di Holbein il Giovane*, Milan, 1971

SANDERSON 1658
William Sanderson, *Graphice, or the Use of the Pen and Pencil, or The Most Excellent Art of Painting*, London, 1658

SCARPELLINI 1984
Pietro Scarpellini, *Perugino*, Milan, 1984

SCOTT-ELLIOT 1959
A. H. Scott-Elliot, 'The Statues from Mantua in the Collection of King Charles I', *Burlington Magazine*, 101, 1959, pp. 218–27

SHAKESHAFT 1981
Paul Shakeshaft, 'Elsheimer and G. B. Crescenzi', *Burlington Magazine*, 123, 1981, pp. 550–51

SHAKESHAFT 1986
Paul Shakeshaft, '"To Much Bewiched with Thoes Intysing Things": The Letters of James, 3rd Marquis of Hamilton, and Basil, Viscount Feilding, Concerning Collecting in Venice, 1635–39', *Burlington Magazine*, 128, 1986, pp. 114–32

SHARPE 1987
Kevin Sharpe, 'The Image of Virtue: The Court and Household of Charles I, 1625–42', in David Starkey (ed.), *The English Court from the Wars of the Roses to the Civil War*, London and New York, 1987, pp. 226–60

SHARPE 1992
Kevin Sharpe, *The Personal Rule of Charles I*, New Haven and London, 1992

SHEARMAN 1972
John Shearman, *Raphael's Cartoons in the Collection of Her Majesty The Queen and the Tapestries for the Sistine Chapel*, London, 1972

SHEARMAN 1979
John Shearman, 'Cristofano Allori's "Judith"', *Burlington Magazine*, 121, 1979, pp. 2–10

SHEARMAN 1983
John Shearman, *The Early Italian Pictures in the Collection of Her Majesty The Queen*, Cambridge, 1983

SIDNEY 2003
Philip Sidney, 'The Defence of Poesy', in Michael Payne and John Hunter (eds), *Renaissance Literature: An Anthology*, Malden and Oxford, 2003, pp. 501–27

SILVER 1984
Larry Silver, *The Paintings of Quinten Massys with Catalogue Raisonné*, Oxford, 1984

SIPLE 1939
Ella S. Siple, 'A Flemish Set of Venus and Vulcan Tapestries: Their Influence on English Tapestry Design', *Burlington Magazine*, 74, 1939, pp. 268–79

SMUTS 1981
R. Malcolm Smuts, 'The Political Failure of Stuart Cultural Patronage', in Guy Fitch Lytle and Stephen Orgel (eds), *Patronage in the Renaissance*, Princeton, NJ, 1981, pp. 165–87

SMUTS 1987
R. Malcolm Smuts, *Court Culture and the Origins of a Royalist Tradition in Early Stuart England*, Philadelphia, 1987

SMUTS 1996
R. Malcolm Smuts, 'Art and the Material Culture of Majesty in Early Stuart England', in R. Malcolm Smuts (ed.), *The Stuart Court and Europe: Essays in Politics and Political Culture*, Cambridge, 1996, pp. 86–112

SMUTS 2004
R. Malcolm Smuts, 'The Structure of the Court and the Roles of the Artist and Poet under Charles I', *The Court Historian*, 9, 2004, pp. 103–17

SPAGNOLO 2005
Maddalena Spagnolo, *Correggio: Geografia e storia della fortuna, 1528–1657*, Cinisello Balsamo, 2005

SPEZZAFERRO 1984
Luigi Spezzaferro, 'Giovanni Battista Crescenzi', *Dizionario Biografico degli Italiani*, 30, 1984

SPRINGELL 1963
Francis C. Springell, *Connoisseur and Diplomat: The Earl of Arundel's Embassy to Germany in 1636 as Recounted in William Crowne's Diary, the Earl's Letters and Other Contemporary Sources with a Catalogue of the Topographical Drawings Made on the Journey by Wenceslaus Hollar*, London, 1963

SPRINZELS 1938
Franz Sprinzels, *Hollar: Handzeichnungen*, Vienna, 1938

STRONG 1972
Roy Strong, *Van Dyck: Charles I on Horseback*, London, 1972

STRONG 1983
Roy Strong, *The English Renaissance Miniature*, London, 1983

STRONG 1986
Roy Strong, *Henry, Prince of Wales, and England's Lost Renaissance*, London, 1986

TER KUILE 1969
Onno ter Kuile, 'Daniel Mijtens, "His Majesties Picture-Drawer"', *Nederlands Kunsthistorisch Jaarboek*, 20, 1969, pp. 1–106

TERZAGHI 2014
Maria Cristina Terzaghi, 'Notes on Artemisia in London', in Giuseppe Porzio and Maria Cristina Terzaghi, *Artemisia Gentileschi*, Paris, 2014, pp. 31–45

TERZAGHI 2017
Maria Cristina Terzaghi, *Orazio and Artemisia Gentileschi: Between Paris and London*, Milan, 2017

THOMPSON AND CAMPBELL 1974
Colin Thompson and Lorne Campbell, *Hugo van der Goes and the Trinity Panels in Edinburgh*, Edinburgh, 1974

THOMSON 1914
William G. Thomson, *Tapestry Weaving in England from the Earliest Times to the End of the Eighteenth Century*, London, 1914

THOMSON 1973
William G. Thomson, *A History of Tapestry from the Earliest Times until the Present Day*, third edition, Wakefield, 1973

THURLEY 1999
Simon Thurley, *Whitehall Palace: An Architectural History of the Royal Apartments, 1240–1698*, New Haven and London, 1999

THURLEY 2002
Simon Thurley, 'The Stuart Kings, Oliver Cromwell and the Chapel Royal, 1618–85', *Architectural History*, 45, 2002, pp. 238–74

TOGNER ET AL. 1999
Milan Togner et al., *Kroměříž Picture Gallery: Catalogue of the Painting Collection in the Archbishop's Palace in Kroměříž*, Klará Smithová (trans.), Kroměříž, 1999

TOSETTI GRANDI 2008
Paola Tosetti Grandi, *I Trionfi di Cesare di Andrea Mantegna: Fonti umanistiche e cultura antiquaria alla corte dei Gonzaga*, Mantua, 2008

TURBEVILLE 1908
George Turbeville, *Turbeville's Book of Hunting, 1576*, Oxford and New York, 1908

TURNER 2012
Simon Turner, 'Van Dyck and Tapestry in England', *Tate Papers*, 17, 2012

VAN DER STIGHELEN 1994
Katlijne Van der Stighelen, 'Young Anthony: Archival Discoveries Relating to Van Dyck's Early Career', in Susan J. Barnes and Arthur K. Wheelock (eds), *Studies in the History of Art, 46: Van Dyck 350*, Washington, D.C., 1994, pp. 17–46

VASARI 1996
Giorgio Vasari, *Lives of the Painters, Sculptors and Architects*, David Ekserdjian (ed.), Gaston du C. de Vere (trans.), 2 vols, New York, 1996

VENICE 1999
Bernard Aikema, Beverly Louise Brown and Giovanna Nepi Sciré (eds), *Renaissance Venice and the North: Crosscurrents in the Time of Bellini, Dürer and Titian*, exh. cat., Palazzo Grassi, Venice, 1999

VERONA 2014
Paola Marini and Bernard Aikema (eds), *Paolo Veronese: L'illusione della realtà*, exh. cat., Palazzo della Gran Guardia, Verona, 2014

VERTUE 1757
George Vertue (ed.), *A Catalogue and Description of King Charles I's Capital Collection of Pictures, Limnings, Statues, Bronzes, Medals and Other Curiosities*, London, 1757

VERTUE 1929–51
George Vertue, 'Vertue Note Books, Volumes 1–6', *The Walpole Society*, 18, 20, 22, 24, 26, 29, 30, 1929–51

VEY 1962
Horst Vey, *Die Zeichnungen Anton van Dycks*, 2 vols, Brussels, 1962

VICENZA 2008
Guido Beltramini and Howard Burns (eds), *Palladio*, exh. cat., Palazzo Barbaran da Porto, Vicenza; Royal Academy of Arts, London, 2008–09

VICKERS 1978
Michael Vickers, 'Rupert of the Rhine: A New Portrait by Dieussart and Bernini's Charles I', *Apollo*, 107, 1978, pp. 161–69

VITTET 2007
Jean Vittet, 'Les tapisseries de la Couronne à l'epoque de Louis XIV. Du nouveau sur les achats effectués sous Colbert', *Versalia: revue de la Société des amis de Versailles*, 10, 2007, pp. 182–201

VITTET AND BREJON DE LAVERGNÉE 2010
Jean Vittet and Arnauld Brejon de Lavergnée, *La collection de tapisseries de Louis XIV*, Dijon, 2010

VLIEGHE 1987
Hans Vlieghe, *Corpus Rubenianum Ludwig Burchard: XIX (2). Portraits of Identified Sitters Painted in Antwerp*, London and Turnhout, 1987

VLIEGHE 2001
Hans Vlieghe (ed.), *Van Dyck 1599–1999: Conjectures and Refutations*, Turnhout, 2001

VON DER OSTEN 1961
Gert von der Osten, 'Studien zu Jan Gossaert', in Millard Meiss (ed.), *De Artibus Opuscula XL: Essays in Honor of Erwin Panofsky*, vol. 1, pp. 454–75, vol. 2, pp. 154–60, New York, 1961

WALLER 1730
The Works of Edmund Waller, Esq: In Verse and Prose, Elijah Fenton (ed.), London, 1730

WALPOLE 1762–71
Horace Walpole, *Anecdotes of Painting in England*, 4 vols, London, 1762–71

WARREN 2006
Jeremy Warren, '"A little ould man called John Bollognia … not inferior much to Michell Angelo": Giambologna in Inghilterra e in America', in Beatrice Paolozzi Strozzi and Dimitrios Zikos (eds), *Giambologna: Gli dei, gli eroi*, exh. cat., Museo Nazionale del Bargello, Florence, 2006, pp. 126–41

WARREN 2016
Jeremy Warren, *The Wallace Collection: Catalogue of Italian Sculpture*, 2 vols, London, 2016

WASHINGTON 1988
William R. Rearick (ed.), *The Art of Paolo Veronese*, exh. cat., National Gallery of Art, Washington, D.C., 1988

WASHINGTON 1990
Arthur K. Wheelock et al. (eds), *Anthony van Dyck*, exh. cat., National Gallery of Art, Washington, D.C., 1990–91

WATSON AND AVERY 1973
Katherine Watson and Charles Avery, 'Medici and Stuart: A Grand Ducal Gift of "Giovanni Bologna" Bronzes for Henry Prince of Wales (1612)', *Burlington Magazine*, 115, 1973, pp. 493–507

WETHEY 1969–75
Harold E. Wethey, *The Paintings of Titian*, 3 vols, London, 1969–75

WHEELOCK 1995
Arthur K. Wheelock, *The Collections of the*

National Gallery of Art: Flemish Paintings of the Seventeenth Century, Washington, D.C., 1995

WHEELOCK 2001
Arthur K. Wheelock, 'The Queen, the Dwarf and the Court: Van Dyck and the Ideals of the English Monarchy', in Vlieghe 2001, pp. 151–66

WHEELOCK 2005
Arthur K. Wheelock, *The Collections of the National Gallery of Art: Flemish Paintings of the Seventeenth Century*, Washington, D.C., 2005

WHINNEY 1966
Margaret Whinney, *Sculpture in Britain, 1530–1830*, London and New Haven, 1966

WHITAKER 2002
Lucy Whitaker, 'L'accoglienza della collezione Gonzaga in Inghilterra', in Mantua 2002, vol. 2, pp. 233–49

WHITE 1982
Christopher White, *The Dutch Pictures in the Collection of Her Majesty The Queen*, Cambridge, 1982

WHITE 1995
Christopher White, *Anthony van Dyck: Thomas Howard, the Earl of Arundel*, Los Angeles, 1995

WHITE 2007
Christopher White, *The Later Flemish Pictures in the Collection of Her Majesty The Queen*, London, 2007

WHITE 2015
Christopher White, *The Dutch Pictures in the Collection of Her Majesty The Queen*, London, 2015

WILKS 1988
Timothy Wilks, 'The Court Culture of Henry, Prince of Wales, 1603–13', PhD thesis, University of Oxford, 1988

WILKS 1989
Timothy Wilks, 'The Picture Collection of Robert Carr, Earl of Somerset, Reconsidered', *Journal of the History of Collections*, 1, 1989, pp. 167–77

WILKS 2005
Timothy Wilks, '"Paying attention to the adorning of a most beautiful gallery": The Picture Gallery at St James's Palace, 1609–49', *The Court Historian*, 10, 2005, pp. 149–72

WITTKOWER 1948
Rudolf Wittkower, 'Inigo Jones – "Puritanissimo Fiero"', *Burlington Magazine*, 90, 1948, pp. 50–51

WOLLASTON 1981
Henry Wollaston, *The Commemorative Collectors Guide to British Official Medals for Coronations and Jubilees*, Nottingham, 1981

WOOD 1990
Jeremy Wood, 'Van Dyck's "Cabinet de Titien": The Contents and Dispersal of His Collection', *Burlington Magazine*, 132, 1990, pp. 680–95

WOOD 2000
Jeremy Wood, 'Taste and Connoisseurship at the Court of Charles I: Inigo Jones and the Work of Giulio Romano', in Eveline Cruickshanks (ed.), *The Stuart Courts*, Stroud, 2000, pp. 118–40

WOOD 2001
Jeremy Wood, 'Orazio Gentileschi and Some Netherlandish Artists in London: The Patronage of the Duke of Buckingham, Charles I, and Henrietta Maria', *Simiolus: Netherlands Quarterly for the History of Art*, 28, 2000–01, pp. 103–28

WOOD 2010
Jeremy Wood, *Corpus Rubenianum Ludwig Burchard: XXVI (2.2). Copies and Adaptations from Renaissance and Later Artists. Italian Masters II. Titian and North Italian Art*, 2 vols, London and Turnhout, 2010

WYLD 2013
Helen Wyld, 'Seventeenth-century Tapestries at Ham House', in Rowell 2013, pp. 178–93

WYLD 2016
Helen Wyld, 'Seventeenth-century Tapestries at Hardwick: Sources and Iconography', in David Adshead and David A. H. B. Taylor (eds), *Hardwick Hall: A Great Old Castle of Romance*, New Haven and London, 2016, pp. 208–21

WYLD AND HODGE FORTHCOMING
Helen Wyld and Arkady Hodge, *The Scottish Royal Tapestry Collection in the Sixteenth Century*, research report for Historic Environment Scotland, forthcoming

ZAMPA AND OTTINO DELLA CHIESA 1968
Giorgio Zampa and Angela Ottino della Chiesa, *L'opera completa di Dürer*, Milan, 1968

ZÖLLNER 2007
Frank Zöllner, *Leonardo da Vinci: The Complete Paintings and Drawings*, Cologne, 2007

LENDERS TO THE EXHIBITION

Her Majesty The Queen

AMSTERDAM
Rijksmuseum

Archbishopric of Olomouc

BILBAO
Museo de Bellas Artes

The Trustees of the Chatsworth Settlement

Cobbe Collection, Hatchlands Park

DALLAS
Meadows Museum

FORT WORTH, TEXAS
Kimbell Art Museum

THE HAGUE
Mauritshuis

Ickworth, The Bristol Collection

Kingston Lacy, The Bankes Collection

LONDON
The British Library
British Museum
The National Gallery
National Portrait Gallery
Tate
Victoria and Albert Museum

Longford Castle Collection

LOS ANGELES
The J. Paul Getty Museum

MADRID
Museo Nacional del Prado

The National Trust

NEW YORK
The Frick Collection

The Duke of Norfolk

OXFORD
The Ashmolean Museum
The Bodleian Libraries

PARIS
Mobilier national
Musée du Louvre

Saltram, The Morley Collection

Scottish National Galleries

WASHINGTON
National Gallery of Art

and others who wish to remain anonymous

PHOTOGRAPHIC ACKNOWLEDGEMENTS

All works of art are reproduced by kind permission of the owners. Every attempt has been made to trace the photographers of works reproduced. Specific acknowledgements are as follows:

Amsterdam, © Rijksmuseum, Amsterdam: cat. 75

Antwerp, Royal Museum of Fine Arts © www.lukasweb.be – Art in Flanders vzw. Photo Hugo Maertens: fig. 34

Bilbao, © Bilboko Arte Ederren Museoa / Museo de Bellas Artes de Bilbao: cat. 84

By kind permission of the Duke of Buccleuch and Queensberry KBE: fig. 50

Chatsworth, © Devonshire Collection, Chatsworth. Reproduced by permission of Chatsworth Settlement Trustees: cat. 6

© Christopher Chard LSWPP: cat. 48

© Cobbe Collection, Hatchlands Park: cat. 108

Cologne, © Rheinisches Bildarchiv Köln: fig. 55

Dallas, © Meadows Museum, SMU, Dallas. Algur H. Meadows Collection, MM.67.23. Photograph by Michael Bodycomb: cat. 15

Edinburgh, © Photography Antonia Reeve. © National Galleries of Scotland: cats 17, 71

Florence, © Photo Scala, 2017: figs 30, 35, 36, 49 (courtesy of the Ministero Beni e Att. Culturali e del Turismo); fig. 22 (bpk, Berlin / Staatliche Kunstsammlungen Dresden / Hans-Peter Klut); fig. 6 (Image copyright The Metropolitan Museum of Art / Art Resource)

Fort Worth, © Kimbell Art Museum, Fort Worth, Texas: cat. 11

The Hague, © Mauritshuis, The Hague: cat. 39

Kroměříž, © Archbishopric of Olomouc – Kroměříž Archdiocesan Museum. Photography: Zdeněk Sodoma: cat. 64

London, © Bridgeman Images: fig. 7 (© Devonshire Collection, Chatsworth / Reproduced by permission of Chatsworth Settlement Trustees); cats 2 (© His Grace The Duke of Norfolk. Arundel Castle); 5 (Private collection)

London, © British Library Board (C.77.i.11 pp. 114–15): cat. 138

London, © The Trustees of the British Museum: figs 5, 12, 17, 41; cats 1, 77, 109

London, © HRP Images. Photo Peter Dazeley: fig. 37

London, © The National Gallery, London: figs 16; 21 (bought with a special grant and contributions from Samuel Courtauld, Viscount Rothermere, C. T. Stoop and the National Art Collections Fund, 1929); cats 14, 18, 74; 86 (on loan from a private collection); 90 (presented by William IV, 1836); 97

London, © National Maritime Museum, Greenwich: fig. 40

London, © National Portrait Gallery, London: cats 62, 80

London, Private collection, courtesy of The Weiss Gallery: fig. 9

London, © Tate, London 2018: cat. 82

London, © Victoria and Albert Museum, London; fig. 14; cats 115–16

London, City of Westminster Archives, Photo Hugh McDermott: fig. 3

Los Angeles, © Digital image courtesy of the Getty's Open Content Program: cat. 10

Madrid, © Museo Nacional del Prado: figs 4, 11, 25, 27–29, 32, 54; cats 13, 16, 46, 60–61

© National Trust Images: cats 12 (© Rob Matheson); 49 (© Federico Pérez)

New York, © The Frick Collection: cat. 42

New York, The Metropolitan Museum of Art, CC0 1.0 Universal license: fig. 31

Oxford, © Ashmolean Museum, University of Oxford: cat. 81

Oxford, © The Bodleian, University of Oxford: cat. 140

Paris, © Collection du Mobilier national: cats 91 (Photography: Lawrence Perquis); 92–94 (Photography: Philippe Sébert)

Paris, Photo © RMN-Grand Palais (Musée du Louvre): figs 15 (© Michel Urtado); 18, 19 (© Hervé Lewandowski); 20 (©Franck Raux); 42 (© René-Gabriel Ojéda); 43 (© Franck Raux); 52 (© Tony Querrec); cats 45, 47 (© Stéphane Maréchalle); 76 (© Christian Jean)

© Private collection: cat. 8

Royal Collection Trust / © Her Majesty Queen Elizabeth II 2018: figs 8, 39, 44-47, 51; cats 3, 4, 7, 9, 19–33; 34 (photographer: The National Gallery); 35–38, 40, 41, 43, 44, 50-59, 63, 65-67, 69, 70, 72, 73, 78, 79, 83, 85, 88, 89, 95, 98-107, 110-114, 117-136, 139

© Roy Fox Fine Art Photography: cat. 137

Salisbury, © Longford Castle Collection: cat. 96

Southampton University, Special Collections: fig. 48

© Courtesy Sotheby's: cat. 87

St Petersburg, © The State Hermitage Museum, Photo Vladimir Terebenin: fig. 1

Vienna, © KHM-Museumsverband: figs 10, 13, 33

Warsaw, © National Museum, from the collection of the Potocki family in Krzeszowice and Krakow: fig. 26

Washington, © Courtesy National Gallery of Art, Washington: figs 38, 53; cat. 68

Winterthur, Oskar Reinhart Collection 'Am Römerholz': figs 23–24

INDEX

Page numbers in bold type indicate catalogue plates; those in italic type indicate essay illustrations.

Adventure (ship) 158
Aertgen van Leyden 33
St Jerome 85
Aesop 243
Agucchi, Giovanni Battista
Treatise on Painting 24
Albani, Francesco 175, 176
Alciati (Andrea Alciato) 195
Alexander VI, Pope 102, 150, *152*
Alexander the Great 235
Allori, Cristofano
Judith with the Head of Holofernes **186**, 247
Andrea del Sarto 103, 240
Andreani, Andrea
The Triumph of Caesar 54, 56, *56*, 59
Anglo-Flemish School
Portrait of a Gentleman, probably Nicholas Lanier 31, *32*, 34
Anne, Princess (daughter of Charles I) 131
Anne of Denmark 22, 26, 131, 155, 175, 210, **227**, 239, 244, 252, 253
Antinous (Roman) 34, **68**, 236
Antoninus Pius, Emperor 236
Antwerp 34, 54, 59, 155, 156, 158, 248
Apelles 129, 235
Aphrodite ('The Crouching Venus') (Roman) 59, **69**, 237, 245, 254
Appian 55, 237
Apuleius 241
Metamorphoses 245
Aristotle 190
Arundel, Aletheia Howard, Countess of 26, 33–34, 56, 150
Arundel, Thomas Howard, 14th Earl of 25, 26, 211
and Charles I's collection 30, 32, 34
employs Hollar 233
in Mantua 56
personal collection 17, 18, 32, 33–34, 50, 82, 86–87, 100, 150, 160, 176, 179
portrait of 30, **46**, 234
Augustus, Emperor 236
Avalos, Alfonso d', Marquis del Guasto 50, 104, **108–09**, **222**, 240, 250–51
Avalos, Francesco Ferrante d' 240

Baglione, Giovanni
Madonna and Child 176
St Francis 176
Baldinucci, Filippo 247
Banqueting House *see* Whitehall Palace
Barberini, Cardinal Francesco 27, 35, 172, 174, 175, 176
Baroque art 82, 172–79
Basel 87
Bassano, Jacopo 25, 50, 176, 179
The Adoration of the Shepherds 105, **120**, 241–42
The Journey of Jacob **121**, 242
Bassano family 105
Belcamp, Jan van 30
A View of Greenwich with Charles I and Henrietta Maria among a Group of Courtiers 30, *31*
Bellini, Giovanni 238
Bellori, Giovanni Pietro
Lives of the Modern Painters, Sculptors and Architects 24, 129, 131
Bergh, Hendrik van den 22, **61**, 235
Bernini, Gianlorenzo 27, 126, 150, 151, 172, 174, 179, 233, 234
Biondo, Flavio
De Roma triumphante 55, 237
Blackfriars 30, 34
Bologna 105, 235, 240
Bolognini, Giovanni Battista
Bacchus and His Companions Finding Ariadne Abandoned on the Island of Naxos *174*
Borgia, Cesare 102, 237
Borgianni, Orazio 176
Born, Derich 86, **91**, 238
Bosworth, Battle of (1485) 252
Bosworth Jewel 252
Bourbon dynasty 18
Bracciolini, Poggio 238
Brandon, Charles **217**, 249
Brandon, Henry **217**, 249
Bril, Paul
Landscape with Goatherds 34, **218**, 250
Briot, Nicholas
Medal Commemorating the Coronation of Charles I **228**, 253
Medal Commemorating the Return of Charles I to London after His Coronation in Scotland 131, **228**, 253
Medal Commemorating the Scottish Coronation of Charles I **228**, 253
Britto, Giovanni 105
bronzes 18, 34, 35, 206, 210, 224, 230–31, 251, 254
Bronzino, Agnolo
Portrait of a Woman in Green 103–04, **113**, 240
Portrait of a Woman in Red 240
Bruegel, Pieter the Elder 24
Christ and the Woman Taken in Adultery 239
Dormition of the Virgin 239
Three Soldiers 87, **95**, 239
Brueghel, Pieter the Younger
Massacre of the Innocents 83
Brussels 18, 34, 156, 158, 190, 191, 192, 193
Buckingham, George Villiers, 1st Duke of 17, 33, 211, 242, 254
assassination 26, 35, 158, 172, 175
and Gentileschi 246
military career 26, 156–58
personal collection 34, 50, 51, 100, 159, 176, 179, 192
portraits of 47, 128–29, 131, 160, 234
and Rubens 34, 158
tries to buy *Mona Lisa* 102
York House 159, 160, 175
Buckingham, George Villiers, 2nd Duke of 140, 243
Bunel, Jacob 126
Burkhard of Speyer 24, 87, **89**, 238, 239
Bust of a Young Man (Roman) **68**, 236

Caesar, Julius **79**, 237–38
Calvaert, Denys 239
Calvinism 196
cameos 229, 253–54
Caracciolo, Battistello 176
Caravaggio, Michelangelo Merisi da 22, 24, 34, 104, 176, 179
The Death of the Virgin 22, 54, 176–78, *177*
Madonna of Loreto 179
Cárdenas, Alonso de 102, 239
Carleton, Sir Dudley 34, 35, 160
Carracci, Annibale 176, 245
The Agony in the Garden 24, **221**, 250
Carracci family 24, 25, 176
Catholic Church 172, 176, 190, 194–96
Charles I, King
agents and connoisseurs 30–33, 34, 56
and Baroque art 82, 172–79
busts and statues of 27, 38, 150, 172, 174, 179, 210, 231, 233, 234, 254
Cabinet Room 206–11
coronation 26, 27, 228, 253
cosmopolitanism 17–18
execution 17, 27, 102
limning ability 211
in Madrid 50–51, 53, 100
marriage 17, 26, 172, 175, 228, 253
and the Mortlake tapestries 190–97
portraits of 7, 22, **39**, 126, 128–31, **132–38**, **143–47**, 150–51, **166**, 179, **227**, **228**, 233, 242–43, 244–45, 246, 252–54
proposed marriage to Infanta 17, 50
Charles II, King 27, 83, 129, 136–37, **142**, 176, 242–44
Charles V, Emperor 22, 50, 53, **65**, 129, *130*, 131, 235, 239
Cherubini, Laerzio 176, 179
Cheseman, Robert **93**, 238–39
Christian II, King of Denmark 84
Christian IV, King of Denmark 35
Christine, Duchess of Savoy 128
Church of England 194–96
Cicero 156
Civil War (1642–48) 27, 197
Claudius (Roman cameo) **229**, 253–54
Cleve, Joos van 20
Katlijne van Mispelteeren (The Artist's Wife) 84, **94**, 239
Self-portrait 84, **94**, 239
Cleyn, Francis 35, 192–93, 195, *195*, 247–48, 255
The Death of Sapphira 193–94, *197*
Study of a Boy Leading a Blind Man *195*
Clifford, Lady Anne 35
Codner, David 31–32
Colbert, Jean-Baptiste 18
Coloma, Don Carlos 158
Colombes, Château de 22, 27, 175–76, 239
Commonwealth Sale 17, 22, 24–25, 27, 59, 176, 179, 207, 211, 244, 247, 248, 251
Conn, George 35
Cooper, Samuel 253
Cornelis van Haarlem 242
Correggio 24, 25, 102–03, 211, 251
Allegory of Vice 56, *57*, 102–03
Allegory of Virtue 56, *57*, 102–03
The Holy Family with the Infant St John the Baptist 103
The Holy Family with St Jerome 103, **114**, 241
St Catherine Reading 103, **114**, 241
Venus and Cupid with a Satyr 20, 56, *58*, 103, 223, 236, 251
Venus with Mercury and Cupid ('The School of Love') 20, 56, **67**, 103, 223, 236, 251
Virgin and Child with an Angel 240
Cortona, Pietro da 176
Cosimo II, Grand Duke of Tuscany 254
Costa, Lorenzo
Virgin and Child **110**, 240
Cottington, Sir Francis 158
Council of State 102
Cranach, Lucas the Elder 87
Adam and Eve 85
Anna Cuspinian 85, *85*
Johannes Cuspinian 85, *85*
Portrait of Martin Luther 85
Crane, Sir Francis 26, 190, 192, 248
Cresacre, Anne **217**, 249
Crescenzi, Giovanni Battista 35
Cromwell, Oliver 27
Cuspinian, Anna 85, *85*
Cuspinian, Johannes 85, *85*

Danvers, Henry, 1st Earl of Derby 233
della Nave, Bartolomeo 34
Denmark House *see* Somerset House
des Granges, David 251
Dieussart, François 174
Charles I **38**, 150, 233
Digby, Sir Kenelm 128
Dobson, William
Abraham van der Doort *18*
Charles II, when Prince of Wales, with a Page **142**, 243–44
Domenichino 176
Dondi, Ludovico 54
Donne, John 85
Dossi, Dosso 54
Virgin and Child with Saints **115**, 241
Douglas, Lady Margaret 253
Dover 158
drawings 209–10, 254
Duarte, Diego II 32
Dunkirk 158
Duquesnoy, François 210
Dürer, Albrecht 20, 24, 82–83, 87, 211, 235
Adam and Eve 238
Burkhard of Speyer 24, 87, **89**, 238, 239
Feast of the Rose Garlands 238
Four Books of Human Proportion 238
Self-portrait *86*, 87, 238
Temptation of the Idler 238
Witch Riding Backwards on a Goat 209, **218**, 249–50
'Dutch Gift' 84–85

Edgehill, Battle of (1642) 244
Edward VI, King 151, **226**, 249, 252
Eighty Years' War (1568–1648) 156
Elizabeth I, Queen 26, 126
Elizabeth of Bohemia 26, **227**, 242, 252
Elizabeth of York 151, 243
Elle, Ferdinand 126
Elsheimer, Adam 24
Witch Riding Backwards on a Goat 209, **218**, 249–50
emblem books 210
Emmanuel Philibert, Duke of Savoy 211
Erasmus, Desiderius 84, 85, 87, **212**, 238, 248, 249
Escorial, Madrid 18, 50
Este, Alfonso d', Duke of Ferrara 155
Este, Isabella d' 102, 103, 236, 237, 238, 240
Este, Leonello d', Duke of Ferrara 238
Eyck, Jan van
Virgin and Child with St Michael, St Catherine and a Donor 83, *84*

Fanelli, Francesco 174, 210, 254
Cupid on Horseback **224**, 251
St George and the Dragon **224**, 251
Farnese, Alessandro 151, *153*
Farnese, Ottavio 151, *153*
Farnese family 250
Faustina the Younger (Roman) **68**, 236
Feilding, Basil, 2nd Earl of Denbigh 34, 179
Ferdinand of Habsburg 235
Ferrara 155, 238
Fetti, Domenico 176
Five Senses (tapestry) 192
Florence 24, 103–04, 254
Fontainebleau 34
Fontebuoni, Anastasio
Madonna and Child 176
Franciabigio
Jacopo Cennini ('Il Fattore') 103–04, **112**, 240
François I, King of France 18, 34, 190–91
François II, King of France 253
Frederick V, Prince Palatine of the Rhine 26, 252, 253
Frizell, William 241
Froben, Johannes 87, **90**, 238
Fuller, Isaac 192

Gabinetto dei Cesari 129, 241
Gage, George 158
Geertgen tot Sint Jans
Burning of the Bones of St John the Baptist 84–85
Lamentation 84–85
Genoa 150, 190, 193
Gentileschi, Artemisia 175
Allegory of Painting **185**, 247
Gentileschi, Orazio 17, 22, 24, 26, 27, 34, 35, *35*, *173*, 175, 176, 210
Apollo and the Muses 175
The Finding of Moses 175–76, 179, **182–83**, 246
Head of a Woman **184**, 246–47
Joseph and Potiphar's Wife 175, 176, **181**, 246
Lot and His Daughters 175, 179, **180**, 246
Peace and the Arts 175
Penitent Magdalene 246
Gerbier, Balthasar 34, 158, 159, 160, 161, 174, 176, 211, 235, 246

- Giambologna 210, 251, 254
  - *Samson Slaying a Philistine* 51, *51*, 254
- Gibson, Richard 211, 251
- Gillis, Pieter 84, **213**, 248
- Giorgione 24
- Giovio, Paolo 240
- Giulio Romano 54, 129, 234
  - *Mermaid Feeding Her Young* 243
  - *Sacrifice of a Goat to Jupiter* **116**, 241
- Giustiniani, Marchese Vincenzo 176
- Goes, Hugo van der
  - *Trinity Altarpiece* 82–83
- Goltzius, Hendrick 242
- Gonzaga, Cardinal Ercole 190–91
- Gonzaga, Marchese Federico 55, 103
- Gonzaga, Ferdinando, Duke of Mantua 26, 56
- Gonzaga, Marchese Francesco II 55, 237–38
- Gonzaga, Vincenzo I, Duke of Mantua 52, 54, 179, 235, 237, 239
- Gonzaga, Vincenzo II, Duke of Mantua 26, 56, 60, 160, 234–35
- Gonzaga collection 17, 26, 27, 31, 32, 34, 54–59, 83, 100, 102, 103, 160, 179, 235, 236, 237, 242, 247, 248, 252, 255
- Gonzaga-Nevers, Duke Carlo I 56–57
- Gorlaeus, Abraham 254
- Gossaert, Jan (Jean Gossart, Mabuse)
  - *Adam and Eve* 7, 24, 84, 85, **88**, 238, 249
  - *Children of Christian II of Denmark* 248
  - *Portrait of a Man Holding a Glove* 84, 207–09, **214**, 248
- Grammatica, Antiveduto 176
- Greenwich *22*
  - Queen's House 22, 27, 173, 174–75, 179, 245, 246, 247, 251
  - Greenwich Palace 35
  - Royal Armoury 18
- Gregory XV, Pope 26
- Guarino da Verona 238
- Guercino 175, 176, 245
- Guzmán, Don Gaspar de (Count-Duke of Olivares) 33, 158

- Habsburg dynasty 50, 53
- Hadrian, Emperor 236
- The Hague 34
- Hals, Frans 126
- Ham House 211
- Hamilton, James, 1st Duke of 34, 85, 176, 179, 211
- Hampton Court 22, 27, 59, 84, 131
- 'Hans of Antwerp' 87, **92**, 238
- Hanseatic League 238
- Harington, Sir John *129*
- Henri IV, King of France 17, 26, 128, 129, 172, 192, 253
- Henrietta Maria, Queen
  - collection 17, 35, 83, 174–76, 179, 239, 245, 246, 251
  - commissions bust of Charles I 233
  - in exile 22, 27
  - gifts to 35
  - marriage 17, 26, 172, 175, 228, 254
  - portraits of *23*, 45, 128, 131, **134–37**, **139**, 150–51, **227**, **228**, 234, 242–43, 253
  - Queen's House, Greenwich 22, *173*, 174–75, 179
  - Somerset House 22, 175, 206
- Henry, Prince of Wales (brother of Charles I) 17, 100
  - armour 18
  - collection 32, 206, 210, 239, 253–54
  - death 26, 32, 50
  - Oatlands Palace 22
  - portraits of 129, *129*, 131, 155, **226**, **227**, 244, 252, 254
  - at St James's Palace 22
- Henry VII, King 151, **226**, 243, 251–52
- Henry VIII, King 17, 22, 82, 126, 151, 190, 193, 194, **226**, 238, 243, 248, 251–52
- Hilliard, Laurence 252
- Hilliard, Nicholas 254
  - *Edward VI* **226**, 252
  - *Henry, Prince of Wales* **227**, 252
  - *Henry VII* **226**, 251–52
  - *Henry VIII* **226**, 251–52
  - *James I* **227**, 252
  - *Jane Seymour* **226**, 252
- Holbein, Hans the Younger 24, 25, 82–83
  - drawings 85–86, 102, 209, 248, 249
  - *Anne Cresacre* **217**, 249
  - *Charles Brandon* **217**, 249
  - *Christina of Denmark* 86
  - *The Dance of Death: The Prince* **222**, 251
  - *Derich Born* 86, **91**, 238
  - *Edward VI* **226**, 252
  - *Family of Sir Thomas More* 86
  - *'Hans of Antwerp'* 87, **92**, 238
  - *Henry VII* **226**, 251–52
  - *Henry VIII* **226**, 251–52
  - *Henry Brandon* **217**, 249
  - *Jane Seymour* **226**, 252
  - *Johannes Froben* 87, **90**, 238
  - *John More* **217**, 249
  - *'Noli me tangere'* 83, **97**, 239
  - *Portrait of Erasmus* 85
  - *Robert Cheseman* **93**, 238–39
  - *Sir John More* **216**, 249
  - *Triumph of Poverty* 86
  - *Triumph of Riches* 86
  - *Whitehall Mural* 17, 20, 151, 243
  - *William Reskimer* 87, **214–15**, 248–49
- Hollar, Wenceslaus 233
  - *Greenwich* 22, *22*
  - *Whitehall Palace* 20, **36–37**, 233
- Holy Roman Empire 156
- Honthorst, Gerrit van 24, 26, 126, 128–29, 176
  - *Apollo and Diana* 24, 128, 242
  - *Charles I* 128, **132**, 242
- *Horses* (tapestry) 192
- Hoskins, John 128, 211
  - *Henrietta Maria* **227**, 253
- Houses of Parliament 150
- Hudson, Sir Jeffrey 34, 131, **139**, 243
- Huguenots 156
- Hutchinson, Colonel John 211

- Isabella Clara Eugenia, Archduchess 156
- Isle of Wight 27
- Italian Renaissance 100–05

- James I, King 18, 22, 33, 53, 126, 128, 255
  - Banqueting House ceiling 17, 20, *157*, 158–59, 167, 246
  - *Daemonologie* 250
  - death 26
  - Mortlake tapestries 26, 192
  - portrait of **227**, 252
- James II, King 27, 103, 239
- James III, King of Scots 82
- James IV, King of Scotland 82, 239
- James V, King of Scotland 190
- Jerome, St 241
  - *Paraphrase of the Epistle to the Romans* 248
- Jones, Inigo 18, 35, 194
  - Banqueting House 20, 26, 158, 159, 191, 233, 245
  - Cabinet, Whitehall Palace 206
  - court masques 25, *25*, 30, 239, 253
  - influence of 24, 30, 31, 176
  - portrait of **42**, 233–34
  - Queen's Chapel, Somerset House 27
  - Queen's House, Greenwich 22, 175
- Jonson, Ben 30, 127
  - *Masque of Augurs* 239
- Jordaens, Jacob 175
- Josephus 237
- Junius, Franciscus
  - *De pictura veterum* 128

- Kerr, Robert 250
- Key, Adriaen Thomasz. 87
- Key, Willem 87
- Killigrew, Sir Robert 249
- 'Kint, David' 84
- Knyff, Leonard
  - *Bird's Eye View of Whitehall Palace* 20

- La Rochelle, Battle of (1627) 26
- El Labrador 207
- Lambeth Palace 246
- Lanfranco, Giovanni 176
- Lanier, Nicholas 25, 31, 32, 34, 56, 176
- Laud, William, Archbishop 194, 196
- Law, Don Gregorio 31–32
- Le Sueur, Hubert 26, 27, 34, 35, 129, 174, 210
  - *Charles I on Horseback* **231**, 254
- Leemput, Remigius van 151
- Lely, Peter 237
- Lemon, Margaret **164**, 245
- Leo X, Pope 190–91
- Leonardo da Vinci 18, 24, 82, 102, 211
  - *Mona Lisa* 102
  - *St John the Baptist* 20, 85, 102, **208**, 209
- Lerma, Duke of 51
- Liancourt, Duc de 85
- Lievens, Jan 250
- limnings 24, 210–11, 250–53
- *Livia Drusilla* (Roman) **68**, 236
- Livy 55, 237
- Lockey, Rowland 249
- Lombardy 240
- Lotto, Lorenzo
  - *Portrait of a Goldsmith in Three Positions* 150, *151*, 233
- Louis XIII, King of France 17, 254
- Louis XIV, King of France 18
- *Love and Folly* (tapestry) 192
- Lucan 244
- Lucas van Leyden
  - *Dance of St Mary Magdalene* 239
  - *St Jerome* 85

- Mabuse *see* Gossaert, Jan
- Madrid 17, 18, 26, 34, 50–53, 100, 158
- Maecht, Philip de 192, 248
- Maffei, Count Nicola 103, 236, 239
- Malpizzi, Bernardino 54
- Maltravers, Lord 31, 32
- Mander, Karel van
  - *Schilder-boeck* 24
- Manfredi, Bartolomeo 176, 179
  - *Biblical Scene* 176
  - *David* 176
- Mantegna, Andrea 100, 236, 240
  - *Death of the Virgin* 20, 209, *210*
  - *The Triumph of Caesar* 22, 24, 27, 54–59, *56*, 71–79, 82, 100, 237–38
- Mantua 52, 54–57, 59, 100, 103, 238, 240, 241
- Mantua, Dukes of 17
- *Marcus Aurelius* (Roman) **68**, 236
- *Marcus Aurelius Sacrificing Before the Temple of Jupiter* (Roman) 248
- Margaret of Denmark, Queen of Scots 82
- Maria Anna, Infanta of Spain 17, 26, 50
- Marie de' Medici 17, 26, 34, 59, 126, 155, 172, 175
- Marlowe, Christopher 192
- Marston Moor, Battle of (1644) 27
- Mary, Princess (daughter of Charles I) **136–37**, 242–43
- Mary, Princess (sister of Henry VIII) 249
- Mary, Queen of Scots 253
- Mary of Aragon 251
- Massys, Quinten 87
  - *Desiderius Erasmus* 84, **212**, 248
  - *Pieter Gillis* 84, **213**, 248
  - *St Jerome* 24
- Matthew, Tobie 158
- Mead, Joseph 161
- medals 131, 206, 210, 228, 253
- Medici, Lorenzo di Pierfrancesco de' 102
- Medici, Pierfrancesco di Lorenzo de' 104, 240
- Medici family 102, 193
- Mennes, John 158
- Michelangelo 24, 59, 82, 100, 102, 190
  - *Doni Tondo* 102
  - *Risen Christ* 250
  - *Sleeping Cupid* 59, 102
- Miereveld, Michiel Jansz. van 126
- Milton, John
  - *Paradise Lost* 7, 238
- miniatures 25, 210–11, 226–27, 251–53
- Mispelteeren, Katlijne van 84, 94, 239
- Montagu, Walter
  - *Shepherd's Paradise* 244
- *Months* (tapestry) 192
- Mor, Antonis 87
- More, Sir John (father of Sir Thomas) **216**, 249
- More, John (son of Sir Thomas) **217**, 249
- More, Sir Thomas 86, 248, 249
- Mortlake tapestries 18, 26, 35, 190–97, 210, 245, 254
  - *The Blinding of Elymas* **202**, 247–48
  - *The Death of Ananias* **200–01**, 247–48
  - *The Death of Sapphira* 193–94, *197*
  - *The Miraculous Draught of Fishes* **198–99**, 247–48
  - *The Sacrifice at Lystra* **203**, 247–48
- Murano 56, 57, 59, 254
- Murray, Sir William 211
- Mytens, Daniel 24, 26, 27, 35, 126, 128, 131, 239
  - *Charles I* 126, **133**, 242
  - *Self-portrait* 34, **43**, 234, 243, 247

- Naples 30
- Naseby, Battle of (1645) 27
- New Exchange 33
- New Model Army 27
- Nijs, Daniel 32–33, 34, 56–59, 236, 237, 254
- Nonsuch Palace 22
- Norfolk, 4th Duke of 33
- Norgate, Edward
  - *Miniatura or the Arte of Limning* 210–11, 250
- Northern Renaissance art 82–87
- Nuremberg 87

- Oatlands Palace 22, 160
- Office of Works 30
- Old St Paul's Cathedral 194
- Oliver, Isaac 24, 211
  - *Anne of Denmark* **227**, 252
  - *Charles I, when Duke of York* **227**, 252–53
  - *The Dance of Death: The Prince* **222**, 251
  - *Henry, Prince of Wales* **226**, 252
  - *Princess Elizabeth* **227**, 252
- Oliver, Peter 24, 211
  - *Charles I, when Prince of Wales* **227**, 253
  - *Conjugal Allegory ('The Allegory of Alfonso d'Avalos')* **222**, 250–51
  - *St George and the Dragon* **225**, 251
  - *Venus and Cupid with a Satyr* **223**, 251
  - *Venus with Mercury and Cupid ('The School of Love')* **223**, 251
- Order of the Garter 161, 192, 196, 210, 234, 244, 245
- Ovid 192, 235

- Painter-Stainers' Company 175
- Palatinate 156, 158
- Palma Giovane 24
  - *The Conversion of St Paul* 105, **123**, 242
  - *The Triumph of David* 105, **122**, 242
- Palma Vecchio 24
  - *Virgin and Child with St Catherine of Alexandria and St John the Baptist* 207, *207*
- Palmer, Sir James 33, 211, 248
- Pantoja della Cruz, Juan 126
- Panzani, Gregorio 27, 172, 175, 176
- Paris 18, 22, 176, 192
- Parliamentarians 27
- Parmigianino 24, 211
- Particelli d'Émery, Michel 174–75
- Paul III, Pope 151, *153*, 155
- Peacham, Henry 211
- Peake, Robert
  - *Henry, Prince of Wales, with Sir John Harington in the Hunting Field* 129, *129*, 131, 155, 244
- Pembroke, Philip Herbert, 4th Earl of 85–86, 155, 194, 249, 251
- Penni, Gianfrancesco 240
  - *Holy Family with St John the Baptist and St Catherine* *101*, 102
- Pepys, Samuel 158
- Peretti, Cardinal Alessandro 237
- Pesaro 240
- Pesaro, Jacopo 150, 151–52, *152*
- Petty, Reverend William 32
- Philip II, King of Spain 18, 50, 53, 235
- Philip III, King of Spain 26
- Philip IV, King of Spain 17, 22, 26, 35, 50, 51, **64**, 102, 155, 156, 235, 244, 246
- Piles, Roger de 126–27
- Piper, David 127
- *Playing Boys* (tapestry) 192
- Pliny 237
  - *Natural History* 233
- Plutarch 55, 127, 237
- Polidoro da Caravaggio 179
  - *Psyche Abandoned* **117**, 241
- Pontius, Paulus 233, 235
- Porter, Endymion 30, 33, *33*, **44**, 234, 239
- Pourbus, Frans II 126

Poussin, Nicolas 176
Prague Castle 206
Praxiteles 59
Primaticcio, Francesco 34
Provoost, Jan 83
Prynne, William 172–73
Puget de la Serre, Jean 179
Puligo, Domenico 103
Puritans 194

The Queen of Sheba (tapestry) 192
Queen's House, Greenwich 22, 27, 173, 174–75, 179, 245, 246, 247, 250
Quellinus, Erasmus II 54

Raphael 24, 25, 82, 102, 179, 211
The Acts of the Apostles 17, 25, 26, 59, 102, 190–97, 191, 193, 247–48, 254
The Blinding of Elymas 192, *194*, 202, 247–48
The Conversion of Saul 193
The Death of Ananias 192, *193*, 194, 196, 200–01, 247–48
Madonna 32
The Miraculous Draught of Fishes *191*, **198–99**, 247–48
Paul in Prison 193
The Sacrifice at Lystra 193, *195*, 196, 203, 247–48
St George and the Dragon 20, 85–86, 102, 155, 209, *209*, 225, 249, 251
The Stoning of Stephen 193
Virgin and Child with St Anne and the Infant St John the Baptist ('La Perla') 20, *21*, 102
Raphael, Circle of
Virgin and Child with the Infant St John the Baptist ('The Bankes Madonna') 102, 111, 240
Regnier, Pierre
Medal Commemorating the Marriage of Charles I and Henrietta Maria **228**, 253
Rembrandt van Rijn 126
Old Woman ('The Artist's Mother') **219**, 250
Reni, Guido 24, 175, 176, 179
Bacchus and His Companions Finding Ariadne Abandoned on the Island of Naxos 172, 174–75, *174*
The Four Seasons 176, 179
The Labours of Hercules 22, 179, 247
Nessus Abducting Deianeira 178
St Sebastian 179
The Toilet of Venus 22, 56, **187**, 247
Reskimer, William 87, **214–15**, 248–49
Reynolds, Sir Joshua 25
Riario, Cardinal Raffaele 102
Ribera, Jusepe de 176
Richard II Presented to the Virgin and Child by His Patron St John the Baptist and St Edward and St Edmund ('The Wilton Diptych') 33, 82, *83*
Richelieu, Cardinal 59
Ripa, Cesare 195
Iconologia 247
Roman Empire 238
cameos **229**, 253–54
Rome 24, 31, 34, 84, 105, 150, 151, 155, 172, 176
Rosso Fiorentino
Challenge of the Peirides 35
'Royal Academy of Fine Art' 7, 18
Royalists 27
Rubens, Peter Paul 24, 34, 126, 158, 172, 237
Banqueting House ceiling 17, 27, 34, 35, *157*, 158–60, 175, 196, 206, 245–46
death 27
diplomatic career 27, 156–58, 161, 235
knighthood 27
Titian's influence 52
and Van Dyck 150
Adoration of the Trinity 235
Apotheosis of the Duke of Buckingham 175
The Apotheosis of James I and Other Studies 158–59, **167**, 245–46
Daniel in the Lions' Den 22, *159*, 160
Diana and Her Nymphs Spied upon by Satyrs 160, *160*
Duke of Lerma 244
George Villiers, 1st Duke of Buckingham, on Horseback **47**, 129, 131, 160, 234
Landscape with St George and the Dragon 27, 161, **168–69**, 246
Minerva Protects Pax from Mars ('Peace and War') 22, 24, 27, 52, **62–63**, 161, 235
A Roman Triumph 54, 55, 59
Self-portrait 34, 40, 126, 160, 233, 234, 242, 244, 247
Vincenzo II Gonzaga **60**, 160, 234–35
Rudolf II, Emperor 206
Ruthven, Mary 27, 245
St Antoine, M. de 131, **143**, 244
St George and the Dragon (tapestry) 192
St James's Palace 22, 129, 131, 159, 179, 206, 244
Salvetti, Amerigo 193
Salviati 131
Samacchini, Orazio
The Risen Christ **220**, 250
San Bartolomeo, Venice 238
Sanderson, William 128
Graphice 209
Sandrart, Joachim von 246
Savoldo, Girolamo
Virgin Adoring the Christ Child with Two Donors 104–05
Scaglia, Cesare Alessandro 179
sculpture 25, 34, 210, 251
Sebastiano del Piombo 240
Seisenegger, Jakob 235
Seymour, Jane 151, **226**, 243, 252
Shakespeare, William 26, 131, 250
Sidney, Sir Philip 128
Sistine Chapel, Vatican 190, 254
Snyders, Frans
Diana and Her Nymphs Spied upon by Satyrs *160*
Sofferoni, Matteo 240
Somer, Paul van 22, 126, 131, 155, 244
Somerset, Lady Frances 254
Somerset, Robert Carr, Earl of 34, 254
Somerset House 22, 35, 128, 206
Cross Gallery 126, 243
Drawing Room 242
Queen's Chapel 27, 175, 179
Spenser, Edmund 128
Stalbemt, Adriaen van
A View of Greenwich with Charles I and Henrietta Maria among a Group of Courtiers 30, *31*
Stanley, Lord 254
Steelyard, London 238
Steenwyck, Hendrick van
The Liberation of St Peter *32*
The Story of Hero and Leander (tapestry) 192
The Story of Venus and Vulcan (tapestry) 192
Stuart dynasty 17, 18, 53, 194, 196
Suetonius 55, 237

Tacca, Pietro
Pacing Horse **230**, 254
Tasso, Torquato 128
ter Borch, Gerard the Younger 244
Thames, River 34, 161, 233, 246, 253
Thirty Years' War (1618–48) 156, 235, 252
Tieghem, Jan van
The Sacrifice at Lystra 196
Tintoretto, Jacopo 24, 50, 235
The Abduction of Helen 105, *105*
Esther before Ahasuerus 105, **118–19**, 241
Muses 105
Titian 17, 18, 20, 22, 24, 30, 211, 242
Charles I's admiration for 100, 104–105, 150
as court painter 53
influence of 51–52, 126, 129
Van Dyck admires 32, 52, 150–55, 244, 245
Adoration of the Magi 155
The Allocution of Alfonso d'Avalos to His Troops 104, **108**, 240
Assumption of the Virgin 151
Bacchus and Ariadne 155
Charles V with a Dog 22, 50, **65**, 235
Conjugal Allegory ('The Allegory of Alfonso d'Avalos') 50, 104, **109**, 240
Diana and Callisto 192
Ecce Homo 50, 160, 176
Eleven Caesars 56, 129, 241
Charles V on Horseback 50, *130*, 131
Jacopo Pesaro Being Presented by Pope Alexander VI to St Peter 150, 151–52, *152*
Jupiter and Antiope ('Pardo Venus') 50, *52–53*, 155
Madonna 85
Man with a Blue Sleeve 245
Perseus and Andromeda 155, 245
Pesaro Madonna 151–52, *154*, 155
Pietà 242
Pope Paul III with Alessandro and Ottavio Farnese 151, *153*, 155
Portrait of Giulio Romano 234
St Margaret Triumphing over the Devil 179
St Peter Martyr 155
The Supper at Emmaus 104, **106–07**, 192, 239
Vendramin Family 155
Venus and Music *103*, 104, 150, 155, 245
Woman with a Fur Coat 50, *51*, 245
Tudor dynasty 17, 252
Turquet de Mayerne, Theodore 160
Twelve Years' Truce 156

Urban VIII, Pope 26, 35, 172, 234

Valladolid 244
Valturio, Roberto
De re militari 237
Van der Doort, Abraham 24, 26, 239, 247
Catalogue of the Collections of Charles I 18–20, 25, 27, 83, 85, 87, 129, 131, 161, 206–09, 249, 251, 252, 253, 254
commissions miniatures 211
death 27
gifts to Charles I 238
portrait of *18*
and Prince Henry's collection 206, 253
as Surveyor of the King's Pictures 32, 206
Van Dyck, Anthony 24, 172, 175
admiration for Titian 32, 52, 150–55, 244, 245
and Charles I's collection 32
as court painter 17, 27, 30, 35, 53, 150
death 155
knighthood 27, 233
portraits 24, 126–31
Charles I (black chalk) **146**, 244
Charles I and Henrietta Maria Holding a Laurel Wreath 128, **134–35**, 228, 242, 253
Charles I and Henrietta Maria with Prince Charles and Princess Mary ('The Greate Peece') 20, 27, **136–37**, 150–51, 152–55, 243
Charles I and the Knights of the Garter in Procession **166**, 245
Charles I in Robes of State 126, 128, **138**, 242–43
Charles I on Horseback (*c.* 1635–36) 20, **144**, 244
Charles I on Horseback (*c.* 1637–38) 22, 50, 131, **145**, 179, 244
Charles I on Horseback with M. de St Antoine 22, 131, **143**, 244
Charles I in the Hunting Field 7, 22, 131, **147**, 155, 244
Charles I in Three Positions 27, **39**, 150, 174, 233
Cupid and Psyche 20, 155, **163**, 175, 245
Endymion Porter **44**, 234
The Five Eldest Children of Charles I 128–29, 131, **141**, 243
George Villiers, 2nd Duke of Buckingham, and Francis Villiers **140**, 243
Hendrik van den Bergh 22, **61**, 235
Henrietta Maria (*c.* 1636) *23*
Henrietta Maria (1638) **45**, 234
Henrietta Maria with Sir Jeffrey Hudson 131, **139**, 243
Iconographie 234, 235, 250
Inigo Jones **42**, 233–34
Italian Sketchbook 150, **162**, 245
Margaret Lemon **164**, 245
Nicholas Lanier 31, *32*
Orazio Gentileschi *35*
Rinaldo and Armida 22, 128, 234
Self-portrait **165**, 245
Self-portrait with Endymion Porter 33, *33*
Self-portrait with a Sunflower **41**, 233, 245
Thomas Howard, 14th Earl of Arundel **46**, 234
The Three Eldest Children of Charles I *127*, 128
Vasari, Giorgio 104, 235, 240, 241
Lives of the Most Excellent Painters, Sculptors and Architects 24, 31, 54–55, 100, 102
Vatican 250, 254
Vauxhall 18
Vecellio, Francesco
Lucretia 207
Velázquez, Diego 51–52, 53, 126
Philip IV **64**, 235
Venice 25, 34, 50, 51–52, 100, 150, 151–52, 172, 176, 192
Veronese, Paolo 17, 235
David 105
The Finding of Moses *104*, 105
Hermes with Herse and Aglauros 235
Judith 105
Mars, Venus and Cupid 51, **66**, 235
Perseus and Andromeda 235
Rape of Europa 235
Venus and Adonis 235
Vertue, George 18, 251
Vianen, Paulus van
Jupiter and Io 210, *211*
Villiers, Francis **140**, 243
Vittet, Jean 195
Voerst, Robert van 234, 244
Charles I and Henrietta Maria Holding a Laurel Wreath 128, **228**, 253
Vorsterman, Lucas 24
The Agony in the Garden **221**, 250
Vries, Hans Vredeman de
Christ in the House of Martha and Mary **96**, 239

Wake, Sir Isaac 56
Waller, Edmund 128
To Van Dyck 126
Walpole, Horace 211
Westminster Hall 150
Weston, Richard, Lord 129, 158
White Mountain, Battle of the (1620) 156
The Whitehall Album 59, 236, 237, 254
Whitehall Palace 18–22, *19*, *20*, 36–37, 233
Banqueting House 17, 20, 22, 27, 34, 35, 131, 156, 158, 191–92, 196, 233, 245–46
Bear Gallery 22, 126, 131, 242, 244
Breakfast Chamber 20, 128, 243
Cabinet Room 20, 22, 25, 206–11, 249, 250, 251, 252, 253, 254
Chair Room 20, 22, 131, 206–07, 244, 250
fire 17, 20, 26, 150, 151, 159, 174, 233
King's Bedchamber 20, 128–29, 206
Little Room between the Breakfast Chamber and the Privy Gallery 20, 242, 251
Long Gallery 20, 150, 243, 245, 250
Privy Gallery 20
Privy Lodging Rooms 20, 25, 30, 33, 150, 206, 233, 245, 251
Willoughby, Katherine 249
The Wilton Diptych 33, 82, *83*
Wimbledon Manor 22
Wotton, Sir Henry 192

York House, London 159, 160, 161, 175, 234, 246

Zuccaro, Federico 250
Zuccaro, Taddeo 250

SUPPORTERS OF THE ROYAL ACADEMY

MAJOR BENEFACTORS

The Trustees of the Royal Academy Development Trust would like to thank all those who have been exceedingly generous over a number of years in support of the galleries, the exhibitions, the conservation of the Collections, the Library, the Royal Academy Schools, the education programme and capital redevelopments projects.

The 29th May 1961 Charitable Trust
Aldama Foundation
Lord and Lady Aldington
Joan and Robin Alvarez
The Band Trust
Barclays Bank
B A T Industries PLC
Sir David and Lady Bell
Big Lottery Fund (formerly New Opportunities Fund)
The Blavatnik Family Foundation
Aryeh and Elana Bourkoff
John Frye Bourne
William Brake Charitable Trust
British Telecom
Consuelo and Anthony Brooke
Sir Francis and The Hon. Lady Brooke
Brooke Brown Barzun
Mr and Mrs John Burns
Mr Raymond M Burton CBE
The Cadogan Charity
Jeanne and William Callanan
Carew Pole Charitable Trust
The CHEAR Foundation
Adrian Cheng
Sir Trevor Chinn CVO and Lady Chinn
The John S Cohen Foundation
Mr Jeremy Coller
John and Gail Coombe
The Lord Davies of Abersoch CBE
The Roger De Haan Charitable Trust
Lady Alison Deighton
Sir Harry and Lady Djanogly
The Dorfman Foundation
Clore Duffield Foundation
The Dulverton Trust
Dunard Fund
The John Ellerman Foundation
Mr Richard Elman
The Eranda Foundation
Ernst and Young
John and Fausta Eskenazi
The Lord Farringdon Charitable Trust
Mr and Mrs Stephen Fitzgerald
The Fidelity UK Foundation
The Foyle Foundation
Friends of the Royal Academy
Jacqueline and Michael Gee
J Paul Getty Jnr Charitable Trust
Mr Mark Getty
Zak and Candida Gertler OBE
Mr Thomas Gibson
GlaxoSmithKline PLC
Diane and Guilford Glazer
The late Sir Ronald Grierson
Sir Nicholas Grimshaw CBE PPRA
Mr and Mrs Jim Grover
The Golden Bottle Trust
Mr and Mrs Jack Goldhill
Maurice and Laurence Goldman
Horace W Goldsmith Foundation
Nicholas and Judith Goodison
HRH Princess Marie-Chantal of Greece
The Alexis and Anne-Marie Habib Foundation
Mr and Mrs Charles Hale
Robin Hambro
Harold Hyam Wingate Foundation
Mr and Mrs Jocelin Harris
The Philip and Pauline Harris Charitable Trust
The Charles Hayward Foundation
Heritage Lottery Fund
Hermes GB
Mr Julian Heslop
Mr Damien Hirst
Holbeck Charitable Trust
Mr and Mrs Jeremy Hosking
The Idlewild Trust
The Inchape Foundation
Lord and Lady Jacobs
The J P Jacobs Charitable Trust
Mrs Gabrielle Jungels-Winkler
P Kahn
The Lillian Jean Kaplan Foundation
Daniel Katz Gallery
The Kirby Laing Foundation
The Kresge Foundation
The Kress Foundation
Jon and Barbara Landau
The Lankelly Foundation
The David Lean Foundation
The Lennox and Wyfold Foundation
Lord Leverhulme's Charitable Trust
Christian Levett and Mougins Museum of Classical Art
Lex Service PLC
The Linbury Trust
Sir Sydney Lipworth QC and Lady Lipworth
Miss Rosemary Lomax Simpson
Mr William Loschert
Mr and Mrs Mark Loveday
John Lyons Charity
Dr Lee MacCormick Edwards Charitable Foundation
Sir John Madejski OBE DL
Mr and Mrs Donald Main
Her Majesty's Government
The Manifold Trust
Mr Javad and Mrs Narmina Marandi
The J P Marland Charitable Trust
Marks and Spencer
Philip and Val Marsden
The Lord Mayor's Appeal
Ronald and Rita McAulay
McKinsey and Company Inc
Mrs Monika McLennan
Mead Family Foundation
The Paul Mellon Estate
The Mercers' Company
Mr and Mrs Robert Miller
The Monument Trust
The Henry Moore Foundation
The Moorgate Trust Fund
The late Mr Minoru Mori HON KBE and Mrs Mori
Robin Heller Moss
Outset Contemporary Art Fund
Simon and Midge Palley
The Peacock Trust
P F Charitable Trust
Olive Pettit
Mr and Mrs Maurice Pinto
The Edith and Ferdinand Porjes Charitable Trust
John Porter Charitable Trust
The Porter Foundation
Mrs Tineke Pugh
Rio Tinto PLC
Red Butterfly Foundation
Mr John A Roberts FRIBA
Sir Simon and Lady Robertson
Sir Simon and Victoria, Lady Robey OBE
The Ronson Foundation
Rothmans International PLC
The Rothschild Foundation
Mr Jonathan Ruffer
Dame Jillian Sackler DBE
Mr Wafic Rida Saïd
Mrs Jean Sainsbury
The Saison Foundation
The Basil Samuel Charitable Trust
Mrs Coral Samuel CBE
The Schroder Foundation
Mr Sean Scully RA
Mrs Louisa Service OBE JP
Mr and Mrs Jake Shafran
Mr Richard S Sharp
Miss Dasha Shenkman
William and Maureen Shenkman
The Archie Sherman Charitable Trust
The late Pauline Sitwell
Mr James C Slaughter
Mr Brian Smith
Sir Paul and Lady Smith
Oliver Stanley Charitable Trust
Hugh and Catherine Stevenson
The Swire Charitable Trust
Sir Hugh Sykes DL
The late Sir Anthony Tennant and Lady Tennant
The Terra Foundation for American Art
The Thompson Family Charitable Trust
Baron Lorne Thyssen-Bornemisza
Tomasso Brothers Fine Art
Ware and Edythe Travelstead
Mr and Mrs Julian Treger
The Trusthouse Charitable Foundation
The Douglas Turner Trust
Sir Siegmund Warburg's Voluntary Settlement
The Weldon UK Charitable Trust
The Welton Foundation
Sian and Matthew Westerman
The Weston family
Mr W Galen Weston and the Hon Mrs Hilary M Weston
The Garfield Weston Foundation
Mr Chris Wilkinson OBE RA
Mr Peter Williams
Manuela and Iwan Wirth
The Maurice Wohl Charitable Foundation
The Wolfson Foundation
The Lord Leonard and Lady Estelle Wolfson Foundation
Unilever PLC
and those who wish to remain anonymous

RA PATRONS

CHAIR
Robert Suss

PLATINUM
Celia and Edward Atkin CBE
Mr and Mrs Christopher Bake
Mrs Deborah Brice
Mr and Mrs Frank Destribats
Mr Jim Grover
Charles and Kaaren Hale
Mr Yan Huo
Mr Miles Morland
David and Sophie Shalit
Alex Beard and Emma Vernetti

GOLD
Richard Bram and Monika Machon
Sir Francis Brooke Bt
Ms Lisa Carrodus
Caroline Cole
Christopher and Alex Courage
Mr Robin Hambro
Mrs Elizabeth Hosking
Sir Sydney Lipworth QC and Lady Lipworth CBE
Mr Nicholas Maclean
Scott and Laura Malkin
Sir Keith and Lady Mills
Mrs Patricia Underwood Moynihan
Lousie Nathanson
Lady Rayne Lacey
Jean and Geoffrey Redman-Brown
The Lady Renwick of Clifton
Richard Sharp
Mr Kevin Sneader and Ms Amy Muntner
Jane Spack
David Stileman
Mr Robert John Yerbury

SILVER
Lady Agnew
Liz Airey
Ms Ruth Anderson
Miss H J C Anstruther
Mrs Jacqueline Appel
Mr Brian Balfour-Oatts
Mrs Jane Barker
Catherine Baxendale
Mrs Elissa Benchimol
Mrs J K M Bentley, Liveinart
Mrs Francelle Bradford
Eleanor E Brass
Mr and Mrs Richard Briggs OBE
Mrs Marcia Brocklebank
Mr and Mrs Zak Brown
Jeremy Brown
Mrs Charles Brown
Lord Browne of Madingley
Sir Andrew Cahn
Katie Cardona
Mr F A A Carnwath CBE
Sir Roger and Lady Carr
Mrs Ann Chapman-Daniel
Sir Trevor and Lady Chinn
Mr and Mrs George Coelho
Denise Cohen Charitable Trust
Sir Ronald and Lady Cohen
Ms Linda Cooper
Andrew M Coppel CBE and June V Coppel
Mark and Cathy Corbett
Mr and Mrs Ken Costa
Julian Darley and Helga Sands
Gwendoline, Countess of Dartmouth
Mr Daniel Davies
Peter and Andrea De Haan
The de Laszlo Foundation
Mr Alexander de Mont
Mrs Kate de Rothschild
Dr Anne Dornhorst
Mr and Mrs Jim Downing
Ms Noreen Doyle
Thomas A Doyle
Mrs Janet Dwek
Lord and Lady Egremont
Mrs Jocelyn Fox
Mrs Jill Garcia
Mrs Mina Gerowin Herrmann
Caroline and Alan Gillespie
Mr Mark Glatman
Mrs Margaret Guitar
Mr James Hambro
Sir John Hegarty and Miss Philippa Crane
Sir Michael and Lady Heller
Mrs Katrin Henkel
Lady Heseltine
Mrs Pat Heslop
Mary Hobart
Mr Philip Hudson
Mr and Mrs Jon Hunt
S Isern-Feliu
Mrs Caroline Jackson
Sir Martin and Lady Jacomb
Mrs Raymonde Jay
Mr Alistair D K Johnston CMG and Ms Christina M Nijman
Fiona Johnstone
Mrs Ghislaine Kane
Dr Elisabeth Kehoe
Princess Jeet Khemka
Mr D H Killick
Mr and Mrs James Kirkman
Mrs Aboudi Kosta
Mr and Mrs Herbert Kretzmer
Kathryn Langridge
Joan H Lavender
Mr George Lengvari and Mrs Inez Lengvari
Lady Lever of Manchester
Miss R Lomax-Simpson
The Hon Mrs Virginia Lovell
Mr and Mrs Henry Lumley
Catherine MacDougall
Gillian McIntosh
Sir John Mactaggart
Madeline and Donald Main
Mr Charles Martin
Mr and Mrs Richard C Martin
Andrew and Judith McKinna
The Anthony and Elizabeth Mellows Charitable Trust
Mr David Mirvish
Mr Daniel Mitchell
Ms Bona Montagu
Mr Eli Muraidekh
Dr Ann Naylor
HRH Princess Marie-Chantal of Greece
Tamara O'Hara
Mr Richard Orders
Mr Michael Palin
Mr and Mrs D J Peacock
David Pike
Mr and Mrs Anthony Pitt-Rivers
Mr Basil Postan
Mr Pinto Rai Dhir
John and Anne Raisman
Erica Roberts
Rothschild Foundation
Miss Elaine Rowley
Sir Paul and Lady Ruddock
Christina, Countess of Shaftesbury
Mr Robert N Shapiro
Mr Richard Simmons CBE
Alan and Marianna Simpson
Mr Stuart Southall
The Lady Henrietta St George
Anne Elizabeth Tasca
Lady Tennant
Nick Thexton
Anthony Thornton
Mr Anthony J Todd
Mrs Carolyn Townsend
Miss M L Ulfane
John and Carol Wates
Mrs Anja Weiss
The Duke and Duchess of Wellington
Anthony and Rachel Williams
Mrs Janet Winslow
Mrs Adriana Winters
Alex Zadah
David Zwirner

DONORS
Geoffrey Ainsworth and Jo Featherstone
Jean Cass MBE and Eric Cass MBE
Mr Charles Holloway
William Brake Charitable Trust
Jacqueline and Marc Leland
Mrs Cynthia Olson
John Pattisson
The Michael H Sacher Charitable Trust
H M Sassoon Charitable Trust
Jake and Hélène Marie Shafran
Mr Nicholas Stanley
and those who wish to remain anonymous

ARCHITECTURE PATRONS GROUP

CHAIR
Mr Roger Zogolovitch

GOLD
Mr Michael Stiff
Mr Peter Williams

SILVER
Jacqueline and Jonathan Gestetner
Anne Holmes-Drewry
Alex Lifschutz
Mr and Mrs Robin Lough
Sally Mackereth
Heike Munro
Mr Stephen Musgrave
Mr Bruce Roe
and those who wish to remain anonymous

BENJAMIN WEST GROUP PATRONS

CHAIR
Lady Barbara Judge CBE

PLATINUM
David Giampaolo
Gareth Hughes
Christian Levett

GOLD
Kate Collins
Ms Alessandra Morra
Mr Michael Webber

SILVER
Lady J Lloyd Adamson
Mr Dimitry Afanasiev
Mrs Spindrift Al Swaidi
Mr Andy Ash
Marco and Francesca Assetto
Mrs Leslie Bacon
Francesca Bellini Joseph
Jean and John Botts
Ms Pauline Cacucciolo
Mrs Sophie Cahu
Brian and Melinda Carroll
Mrs Caroline Cartellieri Karlsen
Damian and Anastasia Chunilal
Andrew and Stefanie Clarke
Mr and Mrs Paul Collins
Vanessa Colomar de Enserro
Mrs Cathy Dishner
Mr and Mrs Jeff Eldredge
Suzanne Ferlic Johnson
Mrs Stroma Finston
Ronald and Helen Freeman
Mr and Mrs Jan Hagemeier
Mr Christopher Harrison
Katie Jackson
Syrie Johnson
Lady Barbara Judge CBE
Miss Rebecca Kemsley
Mr Andrew Konopelski
Amy Le Coz
Mrs Stephanie Léouzon
Ms Ida Levine
Mr Guido Lombardo
Charles G Lubar
Mrs Victoria Mills
Neil Osborn and Holly Smith
Lady Purves
Mrs Janice Sacher
Mrs Deborah Scott
Ms Elena Shchukina
Mr James B Sherwood
Sir Hugh and Lady Sykes
Mr Ian Taylor
Frederick and Kathryn Uhde
Mr Craig D Weaver
Mrs Juliana Wheeler
Mr and Mrs John Winter
and those who wish to remain anonymous

CONTEMPORARY CIRCLE PATRONS GROUP

CHAIR
Susan Elliott

GOLD
Sara Alireza
Joan and Robin Alvarez
Tom and Diane Berger
Mr Jeremy Coller
Patrick and Benedicte de Nonneville
Jessica Lavooy
Simon and Sabi North
Mr and Mrs Simon Oliver
Yana and Stephen Peel
Robert and Simone Suss
Erica Wax
Manuela and Iwan Wirth

SILVER
Mrs Susie Allen-Huxley
Ghalia and Omar Al-Qattan
Mrs Charlotte Artus
Mr Timothy Attias
Constance and Boris Baroudel
Ms Martina Batovic
Mr David Baty
Jeffrey Boone
Viscountess Bridgeman
Simon Morris and Annalisa Burello
Ms Debra Burt
Mr Steven Chambers
Jenny Christensson
Mrs Caroline Cullinan
Helen and Colin David
Mrs Georgina David
Ms Miel de Botton
Belinda de Gaudemar
Mr Paul Doyle
Mrs Jennifer Duke
Rosemary Edgington
Mrs Samira El Hachioui
Susan Elliott
Mr Timothy Ellis
Mr Alexander Flint
Maria Almudena Garcia Cano
Mr Stephen Garrett
Dicle Evin Guntas
Mrs Cally Guy
Mrs Susan Hayden
Mrs Michele Hillgarth
Zane Jackson, Director of Three Point Enterprises
Mrs Cathy Jeffrey
Mr Gerald Kidd
Mrs Anna Kirrage
Mrs Serena Lambert
Mr Matthew Langton
Mrs Julie Lee
Florian and Henriette Lefort
Mr Jeff Lowe
Ms Kathryn Ludlow
Mr Michael Marx
Mary McNicholas
Dr Carolina Minio Paluello
Mrs Sophie Mirman
Victoria Miro
Mr James Nicholls
Mrs Tessa Nicholson
Mr and Mrs Jeremy Nicholson
Roderick and Maria Peacock
Mr Malcolm Poynton
Mrs Tineke Pugh
Mrs Catherine Rees
Mrs Yosmarvi Rivas Rangel
Miss Harriet Ruffer
Edwina Sassoon
Ms Polina Semernikova
Mr Eric Shen
Mrs Veronica Simmons
Jeffery C Sugarman and Alan D H Newham
Mr Matt Symonds
Mrs Arabella Tullo
Mr and Mrs Maurice Wolridge
Professor George Yip
Mr Mario Zonias
and those who wish to remain anonymous

INTERNATIONAL PATRONS GROUP

PLATINUM
Mrs Niloufar Bakhtiar-Bakhtiari